D1880038

Down Memory Lane
Reminiscences of a Bengali Revolutionary

DOWN MEMORY LANE

Reminiscences of a Bengali Revolutionary

P. K. Ray

GIAN PUBLISHING HOUSE
New Delhi-110002

GIAN PUBLISHING HOUSE
4-C Ansari Road
Daryaganj, New Delhi 110002

ISBN 81-212-0303-1

PRINTED IN INDIA

Published by Mrs. Gayatri Garg for Gian Publishing House, New Delhi 110002.

Laser Typeset by Shiva Shakti Laser Printing Works 4B Ansari Road Daryaganj, New Delhi-110002.

Printed at Goyal Offset Printers, Delhi.

To those who sacrificed their lives in the struggle for India's Freedom
From
TIPU SULTAN to MATANGINI HAJRA

CONTENTS

Introduction ix

CHAPTER

1. The Renaissance In India And Its Impact (Prior to 1912) 1
2. Political, Social And Cultural Life In Bengal (1912-1920) 22
3. Collegiate Life In A Crucial Decade - 1921-1930 59
4. Roaring Thirties And Their Fall (1930-1934) 92
5. Storm Recedes But A New One Looms Large (1935-1938) 158
6. Gathering of International Storm And Its Impact on India 179
7. My Second Incarceration(1940-45) 198
8. Dawn of Independence And Agony of Partition 240

Epilogue 292

Index 303

Introduction

Quietly flows the river Kangsavati, which emerges from the Chotanagpur plateau of eastern India and curves down through the westernmost district of Midnapore, Bengal, and joins about fifty miles down south with the mighty Rupnarain, before joining the Bay of Bengal. Being winter, the river was at its lowest level. On the far side the embankment was rather steep as the main stream passed by it while on the near (northern) side was a broad and long sandy beach which was crowded in summer by people who wanted to get a temporary relief from the scorching heat of the rocky and dusty town of Midnapore. Part of the beach was occupied by people having license from government to grow vegetables, to supply to the town.

Being winter, however, the beach was practically deserted especially as the sun was going down as a rolling and dancing crimson disc. It was casting a mild red glow over the sky, over the big 'Sris' trees, on the other bank of the river, and a dimmer shadow over the sandy beach itself. The whole atmosphere was serene and calm. But it was the most excitable occasion in the year 1925 for five young boys, still in their teens who assembled there and sat on the sandy beach in a small circle. Their hearts were beating fast, their eyes and ears were alert, lest there should be anybody else to find or hear them. Their minds were determined to trail a new path -- to embark on an adventure compared to their elders and to many boys of their age, that is, to strive for a Free India. Clasping the most sacred of Hindu religious book, *Bhagvad Gita* in folded hands, each of the five boys took this oath: ''Holding this sacred book I promise to spare no efforts and no sacrifices including my life for the attainment of the freedom of India.''

By the time all of them had taken the oath it grew dark. But as they dispersed they knew that it was just a beginning. A beginning of a new and unknown life -- a leap in the dark. None the less, life to them was not the same as before. It acquired a new sense of value and an inner illumination which made them feel different from others.

The boys were all class fellows - students of Class VI of Town School, Midnapore. They were, Anadinath Majumdar, Birendra Nath Manjhi, Haripada Bhowmik, Santosh Kumar Mishra and myself. All were good students and enjoyed good reputation among the teachers. All came from the middle class families.

Thus, five teenagers returned home that evening with a new vision and with a grim determination. But they had scarcely any idea how to proceed on the new path they have chosen for themselves. One thing they presumed: whatever it might be it would be hard and arduous. It would need immense courage, endurance, skill and sacrifice, even of their very lives.

At home I continued to think over the possibilities. How would we succeed against the most powerful and extensive British Empire where it was said the sun never set. Depression struck me.

The British acquired their domination over India, when the mighty Moghul Emperors had been fading one after another. Their provincial satraps, governors and administrators were struggling to carve out little principalities of their own. Hindu, Sikh and Moslem Nawabs, Maharajas, Chiefs and lords were struggling to regain their independence.

Thus, the British who entered India early in the century as a trading company in search of profitable commerce, took advantage of this situation, both at the centre and in the provinces. They turned one hostile group against another, as the Romans did nearly fifteen hundred years ago in their empire with the active and military assistance, they finally subjugated the great country, after the Battle of Plassey in 1757. They adopted 'divide and rule' policy. By giving autonomy to some of the loyal and less ambitious chiefs, on the one hand, and non-interference with the local customs and religious practices on the other, gradually they consolidated their hold and even extended the frontiers of their rule beyond the erstwhile borders of India.

Yet the people of India never accepted the British rule. There were periodic outbursts against it. Their greatest manifestation was what has been called by the British historians as the Sepoy Mutiny of 1857 or the revolt of certain sections of the Indian army under the British administration in India on religious grounds of being obligated to biting, by the Hindu and Moslem units of army, leathertips of the bullets supposedly made of cow and pig hides, given by the British rulers. But, as true historians have established, it was not a mere sepoy rebellion but a massive and joint effort by certain Hindu and Moslem provincial rulers and administrators to shake the very foundation of the British rule in India. But again this widespread uprising was eventually suppressed with the support of certain other powerful loyal sections of the Indian army itself.

The results of this failure, and the mass executions and persecutions of the people, Rajas, chiefs, commoners and soliders are all well chronicled today. The 'Mutiny' failed but it left its impression on the minds and hearts of the people inspiring them to follow the example of these people who sacrificed their lives for the sake of country.

When the British settled down in India and were busy exploiting its vast riches, accumulating wealth in the form of gold, gems, jewels and other precious metals, valuable objects of arts and crafts and rich raw materials at throw away prices to feed their thriving industries at home, came the Russo-Japanese war of 1905. An important power of Europe Russia was humiliated by a relatively unknown and small power in the far end of East Asia, Japan, and was forced to cede certain strategic territories to the latter.

This generated a widespread feeling of delight and new sense of self-respect and pride among the educated and intelligent Indians in their own national identity. Its basic ground had already been laid by the introduction of English language and system of modern education by the British rulers. Of course, primarily for their own benefit of a smooth administration through the creation of a group of English educated elite. But this had its other effects as well including the formation of a progressive mental attitude of the generally intelligent Indian youth. It created a great cultural ferment and helped in the emergence of thinkers, educationists and reformers like Ram Mohan Roy, Swami Vivekananda, Bankim Chandra Chattopadhyay, Swami Dayananda, M.G. Ranade, G.K. Gokhale and many others. This spread and developed throughout the second half of the 18th and the whole of the 19th century. It was thus called the Renaissance Movement which started in Bengal but soon spread over other parts of India.

The magnitude of this cultural movement spread so effectively particularly in Bengal that the British rulers sensed evil and divided Bengal. This hurt terribly the feeling of the Bengalees who had been culturally one for hundreds of years and with a highly developed language, literature, common customs in spite of its people being two different religious communities--Hindus and Moslems--almost in equal proportions at the time. It led to mass protests and demonstrations all over Bengal. The first Revolutionary Group under the pioneering leadership of Aurobindo Ghose came into being.

* * *

The memories of these were enough sources of inspiration to us. Added to these were some of the actual expressions of the spirit of the Revolutionary Group, like the Alipore Bomb Case and the Midnapore Bomb cases of 1907 and 1908, the martyrdom of Khudiram Bose, Satyen Bose, Kanai Dutta. Incidentally, the first two were from Midnapore. They were noble examples before the new class of educated and intelligent youth.

Then was the start of the Congress movement in 1885 ironically by a senior British Civil Servant in India, Allan Octavian Hume, to deal in a legal and constitutional way (of course within the parameters laid down by the British Rulers in London) the problem of constitutional "concessions" which were not contradictory to the British interests in India. One of its basic objectives was to channel the new consciousness and spirit of unrest amongst the growing intellectual class. After initial wavering both as to the objectives and the means to achieve those objectives and a rapid change of leadership, appeared on the scene a most dynamic and committed politician, Mohandas Karamchand Gandhi in the year 1915 from his long experience of non-violent fight against the white racist minority rule in South Africa.

World War I had already broken out by then. Gandhi true to his principle of non-violence and policy of pacifism offered to help the British Government in what he called "their hour of adversity". However, the Revolutionary Groups in India did not think this policy could melt the mind and heart of the British Rulers of India to grant "real freedom" to India. So they organized India-wide revolutionary uprising under the dynamic leadership of two outstanding leaders - Rashbehari Bose of North India, and Jatindra Nath Mukherjee in Bengal. The organization was made with great deal of skill, money and cooperation with many leading Indian residents abroad, particularly in the USA, Germany and South-East Asia, with even certain elements in the British Indian army, and with the representatives of the then German Government especially for the concealed importation of arms.

While arrangements were made to receive three ship-loads of arms in some central and south Indian ports, the plan was leaked and the British made widespread arrests. Rashbehari Bose escaped to Japan, and Jatindra Nath died with his two colleagues fighting with the British security forces. This was the first open battle by the Indian revolutionaries with the forces of the British in India, after 1857. This had since provided a great inspiration to the future Indian fighters for freedom of their country.

The War ended in 1918 with the British and Allied victory. The Indian Congress, then under Gandhi's leadership, wanted 'Swaraj' (concept was still very vague). But the British responded by passing a strict security legislation (Rowlatt Act) empowering the Government with stringent and arbitrary powers to detain people without trial. When the people of Punjab, assembled in 1919 to protest at Jalianwalla Bagh, they were fired mercilessly killing hundreds of men, women and children.

This cruel and premeditated massacre of unarmed people roused all over India an extreme bitterness amongst the people especially the educated and conscious elite. People all over India realized that the only course to force the British rulers to quit India would be to carry on a series of fight in whatever way possible and people judged it appropriate. Gandhi opted for the non-violent; the Revolutionaries for the violent means insofar as it was essential.

*　　　*　　　*

We the members of the group and especially I was at first hesitant but later we joined the revolutionary group.

This opened a new path for me and the first source of a wide contact with not only in the then Province of undivided Bengal, then a premier province of India with nearly 70 million people, but also, in course of time, with the rest of India. The events developed, step by step which brought me in close touch with diverse groups of revolutionaries and Congress leaders including some of the top leaders of Bengal and even some stalwarts of all India politics like Gandhi, Nehru, Kripalani and Rajendra Prasad. I recall also my close contacts with some of the young martyrs of Bengal to the cause of India's freedom - Dinesh Gupta, Prodyot Bhattacharjee, Braja Kishore Chakravarty, Ramakrishna Ray, Nirmal Jiban Ghose and others.

Then came a series of radical shift in my life, e.g. from B.E. College, Shibpur as a student to a murder case prisoner in Midnapore prison, often put under iron hand-cuffs and rope tied round the waist. Later, I was released for lack of evidence but was rearrested and kept in detention without trial under different jails of India as a 'detenu' first for eight years (1931 - 1938). However, I utilized my time in appearing for the B.A., LL.B. and M.A. examinations of the Calcutta University while under detention.

During a part of my long detention I was kept in village internment for some time which gave me a close insight into the social and economic conditions of our villages. With my release in 1938, after some serious thinking I joined the Forward Bloc established by Subhas Bose. But my stay outside was very short. Because after the commencement of World War II, I was again put behind the bars as a "Security Prisoner" for nearly six years (1940-1946). But, again, this time I tried to concentrate, as much as possible, under these circumstances to prepare a long paper on the "Agricultural Economy of Bengal", then a somewhat new subject, with the encouragement of the then Vice-Chancellor of the Calcutta University, Dr. Shyama Prasad Mookherjee. I submitted it for one of the most distinguished scholarship of the University - Premchand Roychand Research Scholarship or P.R.S. Within a year, when the War was nearing its end, the results of the submission was out and I was awarded the scholarship.

On being released for the second time, in September 1946, I joined Gandhi's Congress and was elected a member of the powerful representative body, the All India Congress Committee. And as member I had to go through all the high level meetings of the Committee then considering the new British Government proposals of independence with partition. Then when eventually and finally Independence came to a trisected and truncated India, I had been invited at the midnight of 14-15 August, 1947 to preside over the national flag hoisting ceremony on the Independence eve in my ancestral place, Contai--a momentous and a rare and much sought after event in the life of every Indian living at that time.

* * *

It was a momentous occasion but indeed the most tragic. Because the India we were born into, the India that we had dreamt of having ever since we attained political consciousness, the India that our forefathers had lived and worked for hundreds of years - that India was trifurcated. As a result of this millions of people were converted into undesirable aliens in their own respective ancestral lands and homes. Millions killed. Places of art, architecture, culture, temples, mosques and churches which they had worshipped in different parts of the country, fell into 'alien' lands. There was an unprecedented movement of refugees - indeed as I have said later, the *world's greatest tragedy* of the twentieth century, and *greatest holocaust.*

I had to pass through this nightmare as almost every other Indian of the time had to. However, in the freedom of the new India, as in the then West Pakistan and East Pakistan (now Bangladesh) all our respective attention was diverted to console the bereaved families, nurse the sick and wounded and settle millions of homeless refugees. But Congress and its top leaders like Gandhi, Nehru, Patel, Azad and many others, were able to control the situation and devoted themselves to set up a stable, peaceful, democratic and secular establishment.

I had then taken up the post of a Senior Lecturer in Economics in one of the Graduate Colleges of Calcutta and at the same time was appointed an honorary member of a Statutory Advisory Board set up to advise the Agricultural Ministry of the Government of West Bengal formed under the Chief Ministership of veteran Congress leader Dr. Prafulla Chandra Ghose.

However, in a year's time I was selected by the Calcutta University for a foreign scholarship under the celebrated post-graduate Ghose Travelling Fellowship and sent to the University of Oxford, England (1948) for advanced studies in Agricultural Economics, ironically, in a country against which I fought for nearly three decades to achieve the freedom of my country and the people. This needed great adjustment. But fortunately, there were several things which made my adjustment easier. First, of course, was that our struggle was not against the British people as such but against the British rule in India, as we in India have traditionally valued freedom for individual, freedom of thought and conscience and freedom of religion and customs, all through our past history.

Secondly, as a result of heavy loss of life and property in the War in most countries directly or indirectly connected with it, there was the largest degree of radicalization and liberalizing of feeling, and a new sense of the oneness of the world and the interdependence of its different parts and even equality of peoples and races.

Thirdly, when I reached Liverpool on 3rd October, 1948, my wife Santi was already there, doing a post-graduate course of Labour and Social Welfare in Birmingham University. Before independence she was also in prison in India for her supposed part in keeping touch with Subhas Chandra Bose in the Far East. In Birmingham one of her University assignments was to work among the old and the infirm, and the poor, mostly among the British working class. I spent two nights with her in the Birmingham Settlement on my way to Oxford. There I had been shocked at the dark and dingy conditions under which the poorer classes in Imperial Britain were living to remedy which the new Attlee Government then had brought the admirable Social Security and National Health Schemes.

Fourthly, at Oxford, the University circle including my future Supervisor, Professor Arthur W. Ashby, the Director of the Agricultural Economics Research Institute as well as my College (Lincoln) Rector Keith Murray gave a most pleasant welcome and provided great help to me during my two years stay in Oxford including a Carnegie grant.

Finally, the family with whom I was to stay, welcomed me and treated me nicely for the whole duration of my stay.

In Oxford, I had my first experience with common British people and that confirmed my earlier belief that however cruelly most of the British administrators in England and India behaved towards the Indian people during their two hundred years' rule, all the British people were really not a party to it. I doubt that even many of them hardly had any idea of the real situation in India and how their compatriots ruled over that country.

After I completed my Ph.D. I was offered a job of an Economic Research Officer in the Geneva office of the United Nations. That Organization, at that time, only recently established (1945) was very vital for achieving and maintaining peace in the world, help in the reconstruction of the War devastated countries and assisting the newly independent countries in their health, educational, economic and social development. All these provided me an immense scope of work at the global level and I accepted it. I have since worked at all the major offices of the U.N. - Geneva, Rome, New York and other places, and had during the twenty-five years of my service, the opportunity of visiting no less than thirty countries and coming into contact with hundreds of diverse people at top and even at the lowest level especially among the farmers on the field. This has naturally immensely helped widen my views. Especially it has convinced me of several things : (a) men are essentially same everywhere, leaving aside the various trappings; they can be cruel, and also very kind; they can be very selfish but also can be utterly selfless; the problems facing them are certainly different in different countries and environments but there are many common ones like poverty, illiteracy, ignorance, old age, sickness and accident. These and many others indeed call for close cooperation and joint work at national and international levels.

With the further phenomenal revolutionary advances in technology in post - World War II years, the world has been drawn much closer increasing mutual dependence. Most of the problems of mankind today have taken the world proportion. So we should all work together, live together in peace. At least we should try. The history of imperialism and colonialism has shown at least one thing -- that in the process of their exploitation of other countries the colonisers have been materially rich and affluent but spiritually, largely bankrupt; their society is infected with varieties of social evils, old and new.

* * *

Reverting to the subject matter of this book, I have lived through a multiple variety of events and conditions. Many of them are of epoch-making andof great historical significance. But history is not just facts but is largely moulded by the spirit of the historians behind it. I have tried to depict the key facts through which I was born, brought up, worked and, one may say, suffered for and enjoyed in the light of my own spirit and outlook. But I have tried to keep the facts straight without mincing words if I found defects and faults with some highly venerated people. I am against unquestioning hero worship. I believe, and history is full of examples of this, that even the greatest men may have some weaknesses. A true historian must point this out. That does not lower the stature of a truly great man, but rather makes him truly human.

But it is not a total history of the period I have covered but mainly the background and the actual conditions under which I spent a great part of my life.

I started this book very late in my life after a great deal of persuasion by the people at Midnapore in West Bengal, my birth place and first place of studies and work; by my surviving revolutionary and Congress colleagues ; by my other close friends who have had a glimpse of my past life, including Dr. Benoy Ranjan Sen, a former District Magistrate of Midnapore, later an Ambassador of free India to Italy and U.S.A., and a former internationally reputed Director General of FAO; and one of my close foreign friends, Frank Shefrin, who was an FAO colleague in Rome, and a high official of the Canadian Ministry of Agriculture. I hope in reading this book, if it is published, they will find their expectations fulfilled.

But I would apologise to many of my past colleagues that in naming people I have noted the names more as examples than as a full and comprehensive list. There have been many omissions which in no way signify my ignoring them or minimizing their contributions to the cause of India's freedom.

However, I would be failing in my sacred obligation if I did not mention here the names of two sisters-in-law, Preeti Sudha Nag and Rita Sirkar who since my wife's death in 1975, have helped me enormously in preparing the background of and in writing this book, in Rome and India respectively. I need also acknowledge very sincere and painstaking typing of the manuscript done by Sri Subir Kumar Roy and Sri Nirmalendu Das. My nephew Dr. S.K. Roy read the whole typed script while I have been away from India.

Finally by way of an explanation, this volume is a memoir-cum-history of the first part of my life, from 1912 to 1948 - the period of my birth, education, work and fight for freedom and long periods of detentions in the context of the historical events which happened during that period. If God ever gives me the time I hope to write another volume dealing with my experiences of the wider world, especially as an International Civil Servant, that is, a U.N. official or a citizen of the world.

With apology for a long introduction.

London. P.K. RAY

CHAPTER 1

THE RENAISSANCE IN INDIA AND ITS IMPACT (Prior to 1912)

Background

The twentieth century, which may be regarded by most of us as our century, proved to be very crucial from both the international and India's national political points of view.

Internationally, the start of the century marked the emergence of relatively much smaller nations of Europe as the dominant colonial powers, each ruling over vast overseas territories in Asia, Africa, Central and South America. There was an intense rivalry among them not only to consolidate their already acquired overseas possessions but also to appropriate more at the cost of others, and thereby to strengthen their respective positions. This applied even in the heart of Europe, particularly in its central and eastern parts, which created sources of great and almost perpetual conflicts amongst them. The Balkan Wars[1] (1912-1913) were the clearest examples and were a prelude to the much more extensive and devastating First Great (World) War of this century--of 1914-1918.

Britain was one of the leading and mighty powers of Europe and of the entire world spread over all the oceans. It was then said that the sun never set in the British Empire. And India was rightly regarded as the "Jewel" of that Empire. For, India was the main source of glory, power and prosperity that Britain achieved in the nineteenth and twentieth centuries. This has been historically established by eminent historians, economists and public leaders in both Britain[2] and India[3]. They had shown the heavy annual economic ''drain'' by the British rulers in India, out of India, and the resulting progressive impoverishment of its people.

India was in complete bondage, politically and economically, virtually since 1757 when the then Nawab of Bengal Sirajudaula's combined Hindu and Moslem forces were defeated by the wily Clive at the Battle of Plassey. And the British rule was consolidated in India since the assumption of direct rule by then Queen Victoria in 1857.

But India was a great and ancient country with a varied, colourful and romantic history spread at least over the past five thousand years. So its people never accepted foreign domination without protest and fight. The so-called ''Sepoy Mutiny'' or in reality the first War of Independence fought by both the Hindu and Moslem forces against the British rule in 1857 was a mighty expression of the combined desire of all the peoples of India to free them from foreign domination. After this failed, sporadic and local revolts continued in many parts of the country.

High Priests of Indian Renaissance

Even after the British consolidated and established their power over the vast country with its rich resources a more effective challenge came during the second half of the nineteenth century and continuing through the beginning of the twentieth by way of intellectual, spiritual and cultural ''Renaissance'' amongst the growing intelligentsia, spearheaded by great people like Raja Rammohan Roy (Burdwan, 1772-1833), Dwaraka Nath Tagore (Calcutta, 1794-1846), Henry Louis Vivian Derozio (Calcutta, 1809-1831)[4], Devendra Nath Tagore (Calcutta, 1817-1905), Iswar Chandra Vidyasagar (Midnapore, 1820-1891), Bankim Chandra Chatterjee (1838-1894), Keshab Chandra Sen (1838-1884), Woomesh Chandra Banerjee (1844-1906), Ananda Mohan Bose (Mymensingh, 1847-1906), Ramesh Chandra Dutta (Calcutta, 1848-1909), Surendra Nath Banerjee (Calcutta, 1848-1925), Rabindranath Tagore (Calcutta, 1861-1941), Swami Vivekananda (Calcutta, 1863-1902), Sri Aurobindo Ghose (1872-1950), and many others, all of Bengal; Dadabhai Naoroji (1825-1917), Mahadev Govind Ranade (1842-1901), Gopal Krishna Gokhale (1866-1915) and others in Maharashtra; Swami Dayananda Saraswati (Gujarat, 1824-1883), and many otehrs.[5]

Their various writings, speeches and many pioneering activities inspired many especially the young intellectuals, to the path of intense patriotism and created an indomitable urge for social and economic equality and justice and above all the need for freedom from foreign rule. This finally led to a convulsion in 1905, especially in the then undivided Bengal. It was, however, directly triggered by the Partition of Bengal,[6] promulgated by Lord Curzon, the then Viceroy of the British Royalty in India which drew a severe and unprecedented protest meetings and demonstrations from all over Bengal. Eminent leaders of the province took a leading part. They included Gooroodas Banerjee, Surendranath Banerjee, Rabindranath Tagore, Motilal Ghose, Ananda Mohan Bose, Ramesh Chandra Dutta, Bipin Chandra Pal, Aswini Kumar Dutta, Ambica Charan Majumdar and Krishna Kumar Mitra.

Bengal : Partition of 1905

The movement was further strengthened by a very important international event--the victory of a new East Asian country, Japan, over what was regarded then a major European power, Russia, in the Russo-Japanese War of 1905. Indeed the entire protest movement assumed such great magnitude and intensity especially all over Bengal that Curzon had to annul it by a special declaration in 1911. However, Bengal was punished by shifting India's capital in the following year from the then premier city of Calcutta to a new place near Delhi, which was called New Delhi.

But the first partition of Bengal left a permenent mark and impact not only among the people in Bengal but in the rest of India as well. It rekindled the spirit of nationalism, of defiance against the foreign rule, and prompted many to think in terms of more positive and aggressive actions. The launching of the "Swadeshi Movement" with a strong urge to boycott foreign (mainly British) goods and "buy Indian" goods was the first major step. Second, the adoption of the slogan "Bande Mataram" in glorification of the Motherland India, and symbolizing a deep spirit of devotion and dedication to free India from foreign bondage. Both these marked a groundswell of anti-British feeling which started in Bengal, soon spread to other parts of India, especially Punjab, Maharashtra and Madhya Pradesh.

But for the first time it led a split in the then Indian National Congress, already established in 1885, under the leadership of some of the most prominent personalities of the time, the first initiative having been taken by a retired British officer of the Indian Civil Service, Allan

Octavian Hume,[7] and as its president --Woomesh Chandra Banerjee. The main aim of the Congress was then to establish a closer contact with the rulers to bring about unity and good relations and thus to improve the political and economic status of the then subjugated Indian people. The partition, however, brought a disagreement between the supporters of this view and what was regarded as the more "Extremists" in the Congress who advocated more aggressive methods.[8]

Rise of "Extremism"--Role of Aurobindo

These extremist groups then specially flourished in Maharashtra, Bengal, Punjab and the then Central Provinces (presently Madhya Pradesh). In Bengal especially, extensive attempts were made to secretly organize small groups from the educated middle class youth with a view to undertaking activities that would lead eventually to a violent overthrow of the British rule in India. Midnapore was pioneer in such activities. Even before the partition of Bengal, just about the beginning of this century, a young history teacher in the Midnapore Collegiate School, Jnanendra Nath Bose[9] used to teach patriotic lessons to his students and secretly tried to organize a small group among them for selected violent activities against the then government. He was later joined by his own brother, young Satyen Bose, who was subsequently arrested in Calcutta in connection with the Alipore Bomb Case (1908) and was hanged for the murder inside the jail of an approver in the case. The third person to join this group was Hem Chandra Kanungo who later went to France to learn the technique of bomb making.

Jnanendra Bose and Satyen were nephews of then Headmaster, Collegiate School, Raj Narain Bose who was a well-known educationist, social reformer and above all a great patriot. Of the three, Jnan and Hem Chandra were rather middle aged and Satyen was an energetic young man. But all three worked vigorously amongst the youth of Midnapore to prepare them physically and mentally for armed action against the British rulers. In 1902 Aurobindo Ghose (a grandson of Raj Narain Bose and a nephew of Jnan and Satyen) came to Midnapore and got in touch with the trio and specially inducted them to revolutionary path. He was present in the formal inauguration of the first Midnapore Revolutionary Cell formed by the trio. So also was Sister Nivedita (formerly Miss Margaret Noble of Ireland), a close and devoted disciple of Swami Vivekananda. After the death of her great Master she gave up Ashram life and took up the cause of the revolutionaries in Bengal. The trio and especially Satyen, who was chiefly in charge of recruiting suitable students and young men, organized them into different groups. Apart from giving them lessons in different forms of exercises like wielding of staves, horseriding, etc. selected youth were trained in use of small firearms. The most notable among these boys was Khudiram Bose, the first martyr of Midnapore, and in fact of Bengal. He was hanged in 1908 by the British rulers for his attempt to assasssinate the then British Judge of Muzaffarpur, Kingsford, [10] who was earlier the Chief Presidency Magistrate, Calcutta. In addition, the group enlisted the sympathy and support of many eminent personalities of Midnapore including Raja Narendra Lal Khan of Narajol (father of Devendra Lal Khan who was later a great supporter of Subhas Chandra Bose), lawyer Upendra Nath Maity and others.

As is now well-known, Aurobindo as well as his brother Barin's activities were not restricted to Midnapore alone but extended to Calcutta. Aurobindo especially worked on two fronts: secretly amongst the revolutionary minded youth who were skeptical of the pacifist role of the then Indian National Congress dominated by moderate leaders, and publicly and openly amongst those, both inside and outside Congress, who believed in more aggressive actions including armed struggle.

However, Aurobindo's vision and interest was far wider than mere sporadic violent actions, as is proved by his actions in his subsequent life. Indeed, it has been most appropriately said of him that he was "a leading Bengal revolutionary later turned yogi".[11] Having come from a highly educated and completely anglicised family, he had all his education in England where he spent 13 years from 1879-92. He had great aptitude for classical studies, especially in language and literature, and he developed his faculty for an elegant prose writer. But he also developed an intense feeling for India's nationalism and "an extreme hostility to the British rulers in India". [12] In 1893 Aurobindo returned to India and joined the civil service of the then Baroda State. He later joined Baroda College as a Professor and later became its Vice-Principal.

While in England he had been influenced by the revolutionary movements in different countries of Europe, especially the French Revolution. He joined the Indian Students Majlis and frequently delivered "impassioned patriotic speeches". He returned to India as a "dedicated patriot''. While in Baroda he also established contact with the incipient revolutionary movement of the then Bombay Province, (now Maharashtra).

With this background when he came to settle in Bengal in 1906[13] he naturally tried to apply, on the one hand, his ideas of a secret and violent revolution against the British rule, and on the other, to influence the then public politics of the All India Congress from ''prayers, petitions and protests'' to active opposition through (a) boycott of British goods and manufactured products and (b) replacement by 'national' institutions of various British establishments, like schools, courts of law and other units of administration. He was first to have said : ''no control, and no cooperation.'' In these he had in fact anticipated many of the stands propounded by Gandhiji about a decade later. He gave full support to ''Swadeshi'', that is, an emphasis on India's attaining independence and self-sufficiency with regard to her basic needs throught her peoples' own labour and her own resources.

Aurobindo justified violent uprisings, citing the great Indian philosophical texts of the Bhagavad Gita, on spiritual grounds, for the uplift of humanity, for freeing people from political and economic slavery. But his idea was not a movement of only selected bands but of masses in general. His idea was that of a ''spiritual nationalism'' in the context of a ''humanistic internationalism''. While emphasising the need for complete freedom for the Indians to shape their own destiny, he envisioned the broader role that India was destined to play in world affairs and that India's national development must be cast in ''the enlightened ideal of human unity''.[14]

Aurobindo propagated these ideas first secretly through some writings in Baroda and then openly through two important nationalist journals in Bengal, 'Jugantar' and 'Bandemataram'. He thus propounded the first systematic political philosophy and action programmes for all those who had then been working towards freedom of India from the British rule. These were comprehensive enough to inspire both the revolutionaries in Bengal and in other provinces of India who were contemplating and working for violent resistance, as well as to those in the Congress and other similar 'open' organization who were thinking of non-cooperation and passive resistance. But he had absolutely no faith in prayers and petitions. He himself had worked both with the revolutionaries and Congress leaders and workers who were sympathetic to his views. And his writings were "heady wine to the young radicals of Bengal", to the revolutionaries as well as to those who were considered as 'extremists' or 'aggressive nationalists' working within the Congress. As he had established links with revolutionary groups in Midnapore and Calcutta, he also worked through the Congress to convert it to his views especially with regard to non-cooperation with the Government and the boycott of British goods. He had also established a good rapport with leaders and workers of like-minded views in other provinces, notably with the most dynamic and aggressive leader of Maharashtra Bal Gangadhar Tilak and Lala Lajpat Rai of the Punjab.

Aurobindo was only for 10 years in politics (1901-1910) but he had a tremendous impact on the mental make up as well as the practical programmes of all concerned.

Early Revolutionary Outbursts

Aurobindo's political philosophy, as well as clearly defined action programmes, to achieve real freedom for India from the foreign rule led to unprecedented happenings not only in Bengal but also in other parts of India in the first decade of this century. On the revolutionary front there were a series of notable outbursts as a result of coordinated actions by the Midnapore - Calcutta groups, namely, an attempt on the life of the then Lt. Governor of Bengal (Sir) Andrew Fraser, by planting a bomb under railway near Naraingarh in Midnapore district when his train was passing over the line in December 1907, by a mixed Calcutta-Midnapore group of revolutionaries led by Aurobindo's brother Barindra and Ullaskar Dutta, another well-known member of their group. However, the Government was then unable to find the real 'culprits' and instead arrested, tried and convicted several railway labourers in a fake case.

Soon after, in April 1908 a young boy revolutionary of Midnapore Khudiram Bose and another Prafulla Chaki of Calcutta threw a bomb on a horse-drawn luxury cab in Muzaffarpur (now in Bihar) with the objective of killing former Chief Presidency Magistrate of Calcutta (that time the District and Sessions Judge of Muzaffarpur). But two British women were killed. Khudiram and Prafulla were later arrested separately. The latter committed suicide by shooting himself. Khudiram was tried and hanged, thus becoming the first and then the youngest martyr of Midnapore and of Bengal. Khudiram was a favourite of Satyen Bose, and

Prafulla of Barindra. Amongst those who took the decision to send Khudiram and Prafulla to 'punish' Kingsford in Muzaffarpur was Aurobindo himself.

These two incidents created an unprecedented stir in the minds of the then rulers as well as the people in Bengal and ultimately throughout India. The rulers felt the two incidents were the results of deep-seated and widespread disaffection amongst larger sections of people. The Goverment got really worried, which was expressed soon through various measures of repression. On the other hand, the people and especially those who had little faith in the mild approach of the moderates among the Congress and other public bodies, felt themselves greatly elated at the most daring actions and the self-sacrificing spirit shown by the two youth born out of their intense love for the motherland. Indeed their action, as the later history of the freedom struggle in India has shown, had the most deep-seated and widespread impact. Even the moderate leaders could not but acknowledge their bravery. But partly due to their natural moderate temperament and partly to their apparent unpreparedness to face the consequences of more aggressive actions, they expressed their opposition.

Thus at the beginning of this century, developed a deep cleavage of views and conceptions of actions amongst those who opposed the British rule in India, both as to the final objective (whether complete independence or limited autonomy) and more so about the means to attain that goal i.e. as Aurobindo had said : "petitions, prayers and protests" or violent actions. Obviously the latter caught the greater imagination of the youth, especially in Bengal, but not the least in other provinces, especially in Maharashtra and Punjab, under the most able guidance and inspiration of Aurobindo (in Bengal), Tilak (in Maharashtra) and Lala Lajpat Rai (in Punjab). In Bengal particularly, under the direct and indirect inspiration of Aurobindo, fed by aggressive nationalistic writings like 'Anandamath' of Bankim Chandra Chattopadhyay and in the nationalist journals like *Sandhya* and *Jugantar* in Bengali language, edited by a fire brand nationalist Brahma Bandhav Upadhyay, and by the well-known brother of Swami Vivekananda, Dr. Bhupendra Nath Dutta respectively and *Bandemataram* in English edited by Aurobindo himself and the fiery Bipin Chandra Pal. Large scale initiatives were taken by a number of key persons to establish secret revolutionary groups like Jugantar in Calcutta and Anushilan Samiti in Dacca and others in many of the districts of Bengal. In Midnapore the lead taken by the trio--Jnan, Satyen and

Hemchandra-- was followed by an extensive organization which could be divided into three strata -- first, the core of the secret groups consisting of many dedicated youngmen; second, a wider group of silent associates and sympathizers among the elite intellectuals and businessmen, and, finally, a group of public leaders working mostly in the Congress as a public platform.

As the secret organizations spread, certain initial actions, mostly by way of training and testing the courage and tactics of the young revolutionaries, were undertaken in Calcutta, Dacca and Midnapore, such as, political robberies and manufacture and use of some bomb like devices to attain certain limited ends. It may be said that Khudiram himself was involved in a postal robbery in Midnapore, prior to his much bigger 'action' at Muzaffarpur. And a bomb was inserted in a book by the Calcutta group led by Aurobindo and Barindra, and sent by post to Kingsford, then Chief Presidency Magistrate of Calcutta. The "book" with the bomb was received by Kingsford but was not opened by him. It was later found following a statement by some of the arrested men in Manicktola (or Alipore) Bomb case. This bomb, along with the bomb that Khudiram and Prafulla later used at Muzaffarpur was of the same type and was considered to have been made in Calcutta in a small bomb factory started by Hemchandra (of Midnapore) after his return from France in January 1908. Some similar devices were later also found in Midnapore.

Government Reprisals : Alipore and Midnapore Bomb Cases

Alarmed at these developments, the Government made large-scale arrests first in Calcutta of leading revolutionaries like Aurobindo, Barindra, Upendra Bandhyopadhayay, Ullaskar Dutta, Hemchandra Kanungo, Satyen Bose, Haridas Dutta and others.[15] Satyen was arrested in Midnapore and brought to Calcutta. Later Kanai Dutta and Naren Goswami were also brought under arrest. Thirty-six people were implicated in the famous Alipore Bomb case, which started in October 1908 and ended on 13 April 1909 and judgement was given in May the same year. In the meantime on 1 September 1908 the accused Naren Goswami, who was supposed to have confessed and informed police of the activities of the Calcutta group, was shot dead in Alipore Central Jail by two co-prisoners, Satyen Bose and Kanai Dutta. They were tried and hanged in November 1908. After Khudiram, these two became the next great martyrs of Bengal to the cause of India's freedom. On the other hand, in the Alipore Bomb case, Aurobindo and 16 others accused were released for lack of sufficient evidence against them in 1909. But his brother Barindra and Ullaskar were sentenced to death. However, on appeal their sentence commuted to transportation for life. Another seven were also sentenced to transportation for various terms ranging from life to seven years. Hemchandra of Midnapore was one of them. All of them were sent to the then "penal islands"-- Andaman Islands, in the central part of Bay of Bengal, which was a part of the then British Indian empire.

As the activities of Khudiram, Satyen and Hemchandra of Midnapore had been found, the police soon tracked down the activities of the Midnapore youth and their sympathizers among the educated, the professionals, and the intelligentsia. Almost simultaneously with the Alipore Bomb Case large-scale search and arrests were made in Midnapore in connection with, Midnapore Bomb Case, with a view to curbing and suppressing the then widespread activities of the "extremist" youths of the town. The list of these arrestees was surprisingly long and included not only suspected youths but many elderly and important personalities of the town including well-known lawyers, businessmen, landlords, doctors, government officials and other professionals and several students. Among notable persons arrested were Raja Narendra Lal Khan (of Narajole), a well-known lawyer Upendra Nath Maity, Jagjiban Ghose, son of another well-known lawyer.[16]

The widespread searches led to the discovery of some very crude bombs which ostensibly led to the institution of the bomb case in which over 150 notable persons of Midnapore town were first implicated but actually about 27 were later presented in the first instance including Raja Narendra Lal Khan. They were all kept in Midnapore Central Jail. The case started in September 1908 in the Court of a British Joint Magistrate. All the accused were defended by then highly placed barristers and advocates of Calcutta and Midnapore. On the Government side the Chief lawyer was the then Bengalee Advocate General S.P. Sinha (later he became a Lord). The bail application for the accused was rejected but on appeal the High Court granted bail to some including Raja Narendra Lal Khan. The case, however, in the end fell through against all except three because of lack of evidence. The three accused Jogjiban Ghose , Santosh Das and Surendranath Mukherjee were sentenced to transportation for life for 10 and 7 years respectively. But on appeal to High Court they also were released in the end.

With the end of the Alipore and Midnapore Bomb cases the first phase of the revolutionary struggle for the freedom of India by the combined Calcutta-Midnapore groups of youth led by Aurobindo, Barindra, Satyen and Hemchandra came to an end. With Khudiram and Satyen accepting supreme sacrifice and Hemchandra sent away serving a sentence of transportation for life in the Andamans the Midnapore group of youth became leaderless except for Jnanedra (elder brother of Satyen) who was left alone and largely inactive to the cause of India's freedom. The Midnapore Bomb case further broke the organization, especially its sympathetic circle. Similarly, with Alipore Bomb case resulting in the transportation of some of the leading members of the Calcutta group including Barin, Hemchandra, Ullaskar and others there was a great vacuum. Finally, Aurobindo,[17] who was the main inspirer, philosopher and guide, was also arrested and tried in Alipore Bomb case, was brilliantly defended by the then young lawyer Chitta Ranjan Das and was eventually acquitted. He had an intense love for his country with an urge towards activities to help win freedom from her bondage. Earlier in a short prison life he had started 'Sadhana' (meditation) and study of religious texts. So after his release from the Alipore Bomb case, in 1910 he renounced politics and retired first to Chandernagore and later Pondicherry for meditation. Both these places then were French overseas possessions. In Pondicherry he founded an "Ashram" (which is well-known) and spent his entire life on 'Sadhana' and in reading and writing religious and philosophical texts. In 1926 he entered into seclusion and remained so till his death in 1950.

Impact of the Early Revolutionary Movement

Thus, by the end of the first decade of this century, the most dynamic drama of India's freedom struggle ended. But it left a great impact on the minds of Indians. Briefly speaking, the activities, the writings, and thinking of Aurobindo and the so-called "Extremist" groups in Bengal and elsewhere gave a vital shake-up shot in the minds of the then 'docile' leading figures of the Congress. They also helped to hold before the Indian people, the ideal of complete 'Swaraj' (independence) and the path of struggle through passive resistance, and boycott as well as, if necessary, selected violent activities. The latter were not for any intrinsic love of violence but to convince the rulers of the intense urge of the Indian people to free them from the indignities, oppressions and exploitation under foreign rule and to be able to live in freedom.

However, the revolutionaries or the so-called extremist groups also tried to influence and even "capture" the Congress during the first decade of this century. The spirit and the leadership was again provided by Aurobindo, ably supported by two other contemporary leaders, Tilak and Lala Lajpat Rai, who had then established by their writings, speeches and actions as most sympathetic to the "extremists" views. Aurobindo however remained largely in the background and was ably assisted in public in Bengal by the most fiery speaker of the time Bipin Chandra Pal. The combination of this trio, then reverently called Lal-Bal-Pal, declared their open adherence to radical actions to attain complete freedom, and thus influenced the youth all over India. They ventilated their views very strongly in the full sessions of the Congress at Calcutta (in 1906) and later more pronouncedly definitely at the all - India level in Surat in 1908.

This split between the moderates and the extremists also came to Midnapore as early as 1907.

However, just at the time (1908) as the British rulers in India succeeded in politically neutralizing Aurobindo and his associates by instituting the Alipore Bomb Case, they also tried to eliminate another great and, at least for the time being, a "most dreaded man" in the then Indian politics, Tilak. He had already served two earlier terms of prison sentences on charge of sedition for his "aggressive" writings in his influential vernacular paper "Kesari" in Maharashtrian language. He was again tried in the Bombay High Court in what is known as a historic trial in 1908 to six years' deportation and sent to the prison in Mandalay in Burma which was then a part of the British Indian Empire.

Thus two of the most important guiding spirits and activities of the "extremists" were removed from the political field of India in 1908. Thereafter while Aurobindo retired from politics altogether, Tilak returned only in 1915 and established his famous Home Rule League in Maharashtra. He also joined the Congress and became a great force even as Gandhiji also just came in 1915.

Nonetheless at the beginning of the second decade of this century the thoughts and activities of Aurobindo, helped on the one hand by the services of his devoted and dedicated band of revolutionaries and on the other hand by such great contemporary leaders of most dynamic and vigorous views and minds like Tilak and Lajpat Rai, played a historic role not merely in the political life of India but also in the moral and spiritual upliftment of its people, and upheld their vitality and morals in the most depressing circumstances of the time, further aggravated by the outbreak of World War I.

As a result, notwithstanding the temporary setback suffered by the revolutionareis in Bengal due to the Alipore and Midnapore Bomb cases and the later retirement of Aurobindo, activities among the educated youth and intellectuals not only just continued in Bengal but received an additional impetus both in Calcutta and in other parts of the Province including Midnapore. Important revolutionary groups were formed under the leadership of vigorous and thoughtful youth leaders such as Rashbehari Basu, Jatin Mukherjee and Bipin Ganguli in Calcutta, who were the founders of the "Jugantar" party; Pulin Das of "Anushilan Samiti" in Dacca and Calcutta and eslewhere almost in every district of Bengal. All over Bengal extensive arrangements were made for exercise in discipline and morality, spirit of self-sacrifice, austerity and physical drill and other activities. In these they received great sympathy and even active assistance of many aristocratic families, landed gentry, professionals of different categories and even Government officials.

In 'public' politics the Congress suffered from the impact of the Surat split but managed to continue a divided house. Moderate leaders like Dadabhai Naoroji, Surendra Nath Banerjee, Gopal Krishna Gokhale, Ambica Charan Majumdar continued their activities in organizing public meetings and annual sessions in which they "reiterated their belief that the Congress objective was the attainment by the Indian people of a system of government similar to that enjoyed by the self-governing members" of the then British Empire (such as, Australia, Canada and New Zealand). They also urged "for India's participation, 'on equal terms' in the rights and responsibilities of the Empire". Their approach to attain those objectives, was a peaceful and constitutional "reform in the existing system of administration and by promoting national unity, fostering public spirit and developing and organizing the intellectual, moral, economic and industrial resources of the country".[18]

The first decade of the twentieth century in Bengal and to a lesser degree also in most other parts of India saw besides an explosive burst of political consciousness and resulting activities, massive waves of religious, cultural, educational and social awakening and concomitant activities of utmost importance.

Ramakrishna and Vivekananda : Their National and Global Impact

The appearance in the middle of the nineteenth century, soon after Rammohan Roy, of the greatest of modern sages of India, Ramakrishna Paramahansa Dev (1836-86) was undoubtedly, of greatest significance. His early life, of deep meditation and worship of a universal God, his gospel of love towards all and unity of all faiths, his core idea and earnest preachings of the "divinity of man", regardless of birth, creed, colour, caste and sex, and of service to man, as "man was God",[19] through numerous simple parables told in common peoples' language, helped to create a great religious, cultural and social convulsion in the then static society, especially in Bengal. Ramakrishna, did not have any formal education, but he was well versed through diverse practical lessons, deep and penetrating discourses with roving mendicants, practices of diverse religious tenets and above all his inner realization and intuitive knowledge of the "ultimate reality" whom he called "The Mother", helped to arouse amongst those he came into contact with a deep sense of inner purity, and spiritual upliftment, faith in human dignity and the value of human life and its great spiritual and ethical significance. By his simple preachings he tried to break all religious rigidities and prejudices, all barriers of caste, creed and beliefs. At the same time he tried to dissuade the newly appearing intelligentsia of Bengal educated in Western thoughts with their pursuit of material well being and their isolation from the masses. He tried to rouse them, to the untold sorrows and sufferings of the common man, as a consequence partly of their social and political bondage, and partly of their ignorance. Hence his special message was that service of man was the real service to God. Like Buddha he preached love and charity for all men, and indeed God to him was love and charity, and all men were embodiments of God and therefore brothers.

Ramakrishna lived a simple life in a Ashram at Dakshineswara. Great crowds of people were attracted people from all societies listened to his simple message. Among them was one of the most brilliant, highly educated but agnostic young man who later became his greatest disciple and achieved even greater fame--Swami Vivekananda. Earlier, his name was Narendra Nath Dutta. He came from a highly educated and enlightened family of Calcutta. Having read both eastern and western literature, especially on logic, philosophy and poetry, both English and Sanskrit, he had a profound intellect, a deep, discriminating and penetrating mind. He too like many other was influenced by the French Revolution and by the heroic exploits of Napoleon, as observed by his great French biographer Romain Rolland.[20] He too practised meditation. He had love and sympathy for the poor, the oppressed, the downtrodden, the exploited, and the unfortunate victims of political, social and economic oppression. In his youth he was influenced by the great reformist ideas of the Brahmo Samaj established first by Raja Ramamohan Roy and then further developed and reformed by Keshab Chandra Sen.

Naren came in touch with his great master Ramakrishna, at the age of eighteen. After his death, Vivekananda opted not for the life of a pure mendicant devoting all his life only to meditation and prayer but to seek the means for the removal of the untold miseries and sufferings of his people. In fact, he took this as the principal mission of his life. And in fulfilment of that mission he first roamed on foot the entire length and breadth of India, to see for himself the extent and depth of such misery. He also saw the extent of ignorance, superstition and injustice performed in the name of religion. He strived ceaselessly, for the removal of human misery and the rectification of its ingrained causes. He later travelled to U.S.A. and almost half the world in search of material help for the poor and down trodden of India. He had the heart to appreciate the kindness and sympathy he received from many starting with the first lady Mrs. G.W. Hale he met while sitting lonely and tired and penniless under a tree in then already busy city of Chicago, in September 1893 when he went there to attend, in his own capacity, the first great Parliament of Religons.[21]

In the USA and as well as in Europe, Vivekananda, had a varied contact with people of all ranks. Especially in the U.S.A. and most of the two great American continents were then mostly remote from the "Old World". Vivekananda found in them a fertile ground for the application at least partially of the great ideas e.g. of a universal religion, unity of faith and world brotherhood. In those countries he spoke to many people ranging from highly intellectual and sophisticated to most ordinary. He wrote profusely, and travelled extensively. He had absolute faith in God and in his own mission--that he was a "link" between the ancient East and the modern West. He spoke from a nobility of spirit and a high intellectual plain but in simple language. To a people saturated with "materialism" the young Swami spoke about the "Divinity of man" and men's noble mission of infinite "search of reality, from lesser to greater truth". In the Parliament of Religions he spoke *inter alia* of "science as nothing but finding of unity" through "multiplicity and duality".[22] He spoke of the eternal spiritual principle that lay behind all manifestations, and guiding the destiny of mankind.

Vivekananda spoke with conviction but with modesty. He was not a vaunted preacher trying to convert the world to his own views but was pouring before his audience his soul which saw, through the grace of his Great Master, the Divine `light. He pointed to the West their virtues and vices, as he later, after his return to India, thundered to his own people to shed their slumber, sloth and despondency and arise and awake to a life of vibrant and enlightened activity. Christopher Isherwood says :

> Vivekananda landed in Ceylon (now Sri Lanka)[23] in the middle of January 1897. From there on, his journey to Calcutta was a triumphant progress. His countrymen had followed the accounts of his American lectures in the newspapers..... they quite rightly regarded his visit to the West as a symbolic victory for exceeding in its proportions the mere amount of money he had collected for his cause or the number of disciples he had made. Indeed, one may claim that no Indian before Vivekananda had ever made Americans and Englishmen accept him on such terms--not as a subservientally, not as an avowed opponent, but as a sincere well-wisher and friend, equally ready to teach and to learn, to ask for and to offer help. Who else had stood, as he stood, impartially between East and West, prizing the virtues and condemning the defects of both cultures ? Who else could represent in his own person young India of the nineties in synthesis with Ancient India of the Vedas ? Who else could stand forth as India's champion against poverty and oppression and yet sincerely praise American idealism and British singleness of purpose ? Such was Vivekanandas' greatness.[24]

Yet, amidst "all this adulation, Vivekananda never forgot who he was : the disciple of Ramakrishna and the equal brother of his fellow monks". In May 1897, soon after his highly successful tour of the West, he[25] called a meeting "of the monastic and householder disciples of Ramakrishna" "in order to establish their work on an organized basis". Vivekananda suggested an integration of their work in religious, educational and philanthropic fields in two institutions--The Ramkrishna Mission especially dealing with diverse social service, chiefly in India, and the Ramakrishna Math (at Belur on the other side of the River Ganges in

Dakshineswar near Calcutta) --a monastic order devoted mainly to religious and contemplative life. The latter has now many branches in India, Asia, Europe and America (both North and South). These are the two great practical gifts of the great and acclaimed Swamiji to India and the world, apart from the vast literature of his innumerable speeches and writings compiled by his followers and admirers in India and abroad, first during his life time and then after he passed away in the prime of his life, barely 40 years, in Calcutta in 1902.

Summing up the greatness of Vivekananda, Christopher Isherwood has observed :

> Vivekananda was not only a great teacher with an international message, he was also a very great Indian, a patriot and an inspirer of his countrymen down to the present generation.[26]

At the end I would add "also to generations to come". For, Vivekananda, like his Great Master, spoke of the eternal values of and in man : human dignity, equality and brotherhood, and love and charity towards all. He also believed in the value of science but it must be blended with and result in true human happiness and upliftment for all humanity, not only for selected people and selected races or castes or religions. [27]

The Golden Age of Renaissance

Thus the great spirit of renaissance which originated in Bengal--Brahmaputra and the River Ganges--with the advent of Raja RamMohan Roy and Prince Dwaraka Nath Tagore at the third quarter of the eighteenth century [28] may be said to have reached its peak with the combined personalities of Ramakrishna and his disciple Vivekananda in the second half of the nineteenth century. RamMohan, because of his pioneering activities for religious, social and political reforms, could be "described as the father of modern India."

But it must be said that in their great task of reviving the noble spirit and wisdom of ancient India and energising the activities of her modern sons they were ably assisted by many poets, litterateurs, philosophers and scientists, who were all born or active in the second half of the nineteenth century and continued to do so well into the first half of the twentieth century.

Thus, that period may be said to be the "golden age" of the great and significant Renaissance of the then undivided Bengal, brought about chiefly by "those personalities of genius", sons of her own tender and fertile soil and fragrant air, "who during the last century have sprung up in awakened India, reviving the ancient energies of their country and bringing about a spring time of thought within her borders."[30] The work of each one was creative in each one's respective fields -- language, grammar, literature, science and philosophy. They include besides RamMohan Roy the famous Pandit Iswar Chandra Vidyasagar who was a great scholar, educationist, social reformer, humanist and a highly compassionate person who led a simple life. But he was a very determined and courageous man. He was born in Midnapore but made Calcutta and the whole of Bengal as his field of activity. He was called Vidyasagar or "Ocean of Learning" because of his great scholarship. He was the principal of the Sanskrit College of Calcutta and had a pioneering contribution in the development of the Bengali language and literature. Though a "Pandit" or well-versed in ancient Sanskrit religious texts he fought for widow remarriage and the upliftment of women.

And almost his contemporary in prose literature was another of Bengal's great men Bankim Chandra Chatterjee. He was one of the first two graduates of the Calcutta University after it was founded in 1857. It was the first of the three Universities--the other two were at Bombay and Madras--to be established in that year by the then British rulers of India. He joined the executive service under the British rulers and his second posting was in Contai in the district impressed by Contai's seashores, rivers, forests and sand dunes and wrote one of his famous novels *Kapalkundala.* His famous work has been the politico-historic novel *Ananda Math* wherein he composed his famous poetry-cum-song in praise of the Mother India, "Bande Mataram" or "Ovation to the Mother". This had been the main anthem of the freedom fighters of India until her independence in 1947 and still a favourite song for many. [31]

Unlike the European 'renaissance' that started in Italy in the fourteenth century and remained most concerned with Europe, the fathers and exponents of Indian renaissance beginning with Ram Mohan and Dwaraka Nath Tagore, and continued through Keshab Chandra Sen, Iswar Chandra Vidyasagar, Bankim Chandra Chatterjee, Ramesh Chandra Dutta, Ramakrishna, Vivekananda, Aurobindo and Rabindranath Tagore, took great pains of spreading the ideas of Indian renaissance overseas and especially to Europe. Because they all knew that European Renaissance had brought in a flood of liberal, progressive and democratic ideas to many of their countries from fourteenth century onwards. And India in her quest for her own regeneration had much to learn from Europe. But at the same time India kept its own ancient traditional values.

Romain Rolland, that great European mind who understood India well, writing about Vivekananda, said :

> .... at the feet of simple Ramakrishna the most intellectual, the most imperious, the most justly proud of all the great religious spirits of modern India humbled himself. He was the St. Paul of the Messiah of Bengal. He founded the Church and his doctrine[32]. He travelled throughout the world and was the aqueduct, akin to those red arches which span the Roman Campagna,[33] along which the waters of the spirit have flowed from India to the Europes[34] and from the Europes back to India, joining scientific reason to vedantic faith and the past to the future''.[35]

Notes and References

1. First by the then Balkan States (e.g. Bulgaria, Greece, Montenegro and Serbia) against the Turkish Ottoman Empire for liberation of parts of their respective territories occupied by the Turks, and then amongst themselves for supremacy in the whole area. The area has always been a disturbed one partly bacause of rivalry amongst the local powers and partly due to the intervention and machinations by the then great powers of Europe.
2. Cf. Diggy, William (1901) : *Prosperous British India* (T. Fisher Unwin, London).
3. The most notable among the Indian writers to point this, citing authoritative facts, were Ramesh Chandra Dutta (in his famous books such as the *Famines of India* and *Economic History of India*) and Dadabhai Naoroji (in *Poverty of India*), "a high priest of the economic drain theory".
4. Derozio inspite of being of Indo-Portuguese parentage, was a young talented poet, teacher, social reformer and a political patriot.
5. The list of names is not, as it cannot be, complete.
6. The Province of Bengal prior to 1905 consisted of Bengal proper, Bihar, Orissa and Assam. The partition divided the Bengalee people as such with east and northern districts and Assam forming one province, and western districts joined with Bihar and Orissa. It was practically the dissolution of the Bengalee community or what might be called the proper Bengal.
7. Hume's motive was said to be an "amalgam, of liberalism and materialism, and he found in the proposed plan (of Indian National Congress) an efficacious 'safety-valve', for the escape of great dangers that faced the British Empire" especially from the "Bengali Baboos of "advanced" views Cf. Mehra (1985) : *A Dictionary of Modern Indian History 1707-1947* ; Oxford Univ. Press, p. 149.

8. See later.
9. In his later life he became the private Secretary to Kumar Devendra Lal Khan at Midnapore, who dedicated his life in working for the subsequent generation of Midnapore revolutionaries. See later.
10. Cf. Das, B.K. (1987) : *Role of Midnapore in the Fight for Freedom* (in Bengali) ; (Dey Book Store), Calcutta.
11. Cf. Mehra, Parshotam (1985) : *A Dictionary of Modern Indian History 1707-1947* ; (Oxford Univ. Press, p.48.
12. In those days many young men who had gone to England for higher education with a sense of patriotism, self-respect and dignity could not but be influenced, on the one hand, by the discipline and love of their own country shown by the British people, and, on the other, by the indignity and humiliation they (the Indians) had to suffer at the hands of many of the British people because of colour and India's dependent status.
13. His earlier visits particularly in 1902 (as already mentioned) to Midnapore were for temporary contact with the revolutionary groups there.
14. Indeed he had such faith in this that he later (since 1910 till his death in 1950) devoted his entire life to the pursuit and preaching of this ideal.
15. For the full list, see B.K. Das, *op.cit.*, p. 201-2.
16. See B.K. Das : *op.cit.*, pp.233-34..
17. Although Aurobindo was the main spring behind the coordinated and combined activities of the two groups, he played a very silent role, so much so that the then Viceroy of India Minto in 1910 described him "as the most dangerous man we now have to reckon with", and wanted to deport him. But the British Government in London hesitated as no "fool-proof case could be brought against him". See Mehra : *Op. cit.* p. 50.
18. P. Mehra. *op.cit.*, p. 149
19. "Are you seeking God". Then ask Him in man. The Divinity is manifest in man more than in any object (The Gospel of Sri Ramakrishna, quoted by Remain Rolland (the French philosoper) in his *The Life of Ramakrishna* (English Tr. Calcutta.) p. 182.
20. Romain Rolland, *The Life of Ramakrishna, op. cit.*, p. 224.
21. G.W. Hale, Cf Teachings of Swami Vivekananda (Advaita Ashram Calcutta), "Introduction" by Christopher Isherwood, ix.
22. Selections from Swami Vivekananda (Advaita Ashrama, Calcutta, July 1975), p. 10.
23. After his first triumphant visit to America and Europe.
24. See Isherwood's Introduction to *Teachings of Swami Vivekananda, op.cit.*, pp. xxxiii-xxxiv.
25. *Ibid.* p. xxxiv.
26. *Ibid*, p. xxxviii.
27. Please see also chapter IV Section 7, for further elaboration of their thoughts and ideas and their impact on this author.
28. One could even go back to further three centuries and start with another great Bengali saint Chaitanya (1485-1533) who was an "ecstatic lover of Krishna", the great Indian saint-cum-hero of the Mahabharata time. As Romain Rolland has said of him, "he achieved a great reputation as a theological and Sanskrit scholar and shook off the dust of the old religion with its paralysing formalism. He went into the highways to preach a new gospet of love founded on mystic union with God. It was open to all men and women of all religions and all castes as brothers, and even to those without caste; Moslems, Hindus, beggars, pariahs, thieves, prostitutes, all came together to listen to his burning message and went away purified and strengthened".

    Romain Rolland with his great and intimate knowledge of the Indian history, religion and social systems further observed :"An extraordinary *Awakening* was

heralded during the course of a century by the song
And he named particularly Chandidas and Vidyapati.
was greatly inspired by Chaitanya especially after 1858 and
himself with him''. See his *Life of Ramakrishna, op.cit.*, p. 24 f.n.

29. See Pershotam Mehta; *op. cit.*, p. 595.
30. Cf. Romain Rolland, *op. cit.* p. 2
31. Some Indians have stayed away from it as a sort of 'idol worship'. While respecting their feelings I would say a symbolic worship of the Mother Country and even of God as the ''Mother'' is not new to India but also found almost in every advanced country of the world. The Christian Catholics are essentially Mother worshippers and even the Russians now call their great country as ''Motherland''.
32. Ramakrishna Math and Mission.
33. Means field or countrysides.
34. Signifies collectively Mother Europe and her brood of the Americas .
35. Romain Rolland ; *op cit.*, pp. 281-282.

CHAPTER 2

POLITICAL, SOCIAL AND CULTURAL LIFE IN BENGAL (1912 - 1920)

This was briefly the background of world situation as well as the political, social and cultural atmosphere in Bengal and other notable places of India when the year 1912 ushered in.

The year became noted in history because : (a) internationally, for the Balkan War and the climaxing of rivalry between the then strong European powers e.g. U.K., France, Germany, the Austro-Hungarian Empire, the Turkish Ottoman Empire and Russia, for hegemony in Europe and the Middle East and dominance over overseas territories, and the gathering of dark clouds of a major conflict engulfing large parts of the world; and (b) nationally, for the growing awakening and discontent among especially the educated and the intelligentsia against the oppressive and exploitative foreign domination, in spite of the annulment of the Partition of Bengal. For the annulment (in 1911) did not restore the *status quo ante* (i.e. original position). In place of the former two provinces -- Bengal, Bihar, Orissa and Assam, there emerged three political entities -- Bengal proper in charge of a governor-in-council, Bihar and Orissa under a lieutenant - governor - in - council, and Assam under a chief commissioner. And as if to punish the Bengalees as for their mini-revolt, the capital of the then Indian Empire was transferred from Calcutta to a new place near the old city of Delhi, in the north in 1912, obviously to reduce the importance of the premier city of Bengal.

In addition, the people of Bengal and o realise that the British rulers were playing a 'dirty g the seeds of a permanent cleavage between the majority nity and the Moslems, the largest minority community. Sin 23 "Mutiny" of 1857 both the communities fought shoulder to shoulder in the South, under the command of a Moslem ruler Tipu Sultan against the British, the latter got scared and tried by all means to divide the two communities for good. Its first open expression was found in 1906 when with the first instalment of a very limited constitutional reform, known as Morley - Minto Reform of 1909, the British entered into an agreement with then well known Aga Khan (1877 - 1957), a long time friend of the British and a co-founder of the All India Moslem League, "that the Moslems of India should not be regarded as a mere minority, but as a nation within a nation whose rights and obligations should be guaranteed by statute". And this was done in the Indian Councils Act of 1909 which formed the basis of the first dose of constitutional reform in India. It provided, also for the first time, that the Moslems should have certain number of seats reserved for them in the newly established Legislative Councils both at the Centre and in the provinces, and these members should be elected by the Moslem community only. Thus was introduced the thin wedge of "separate electorate" to divide the Indian communities till it finally culminated in the great partition of India in 1947.[1]

This inevitable future tragedy of the British policy of *divide et impera* (followed by their earlier Roman equivalents with the far-flung Roman Empire in Europe, Asia and Africa) could not but be foreseen by the then British rulers. For Minto's private secretary Dunlop Smith then noted that "Men like the Aga Khan plainly feel that in pressing for large separate treatment for Mohammedans they are fighting our battle much more than their own. We have far more to lose than the Muslims by an 'entente' between Islam and Hinduism."[2]

One cannot forget that even today, after the worst partition in history, of a great and ancient country, with both its most tragic immediate and long-term consequences for the vast majority of peoples in all the three countries - India, Pakistan and Bangladesh, the thinking of a man like Dunlop Smith still determines the attitude of many Westerners with regard to the Indian sub-continent.

situation in the second decade of
al situation for the people of Bengal and
rather gloomy, partly because of a series of
porary immobilization of the leading revolution-
partly for the split and division among the ranks of the
the Indian National Congress.

Nonetheless, the Bengalies during that period kept up their spirit in other ways. Many among them steeped themselves in the great glory of the two of their greatest departed spiritual leaders -- Ramakrishna and Vivekananda, and found time to contemplate their invaluable legacies not only to Bengal but to the whole of India and even to the world. This was greatly helped by the work and energy shown by the disciples of Swamiji through the activities of the Ramakrishna Mission and the Math in India and abroad. Simultaneously, and almost parallel, but not without mutual influence, the ideals of Rammohan Roy, Debendra Nath Tagore and Keshab Sen, as observed earlier in Chapter 1, also helped greatly to bring a new orientation of thought and activities of large sections of educated youth. One of the lasting gifts of Debendra Nath to the people of Bengal, and eventually to the whole of India was the establishment of the now famous Santiniketan in Bolpur[3] in the district of Birbhum, where he spent the last years of his life (he died in 1905) largely in seclusion and on the meditation of one universal God. Later his son the, great poet Rabindra Nath Tagore made it the main centre of his literary, educational and cultural, as well as of many notable constructive, works. He founded his first school named "Brahmacharjyashrama" or a school for the practice of continence, with only five students in 1901, and later (in 1918) the great Visva-Bharati as a centre of World Learning.

Rabindranath Tagore

RabindraNath was in politics during the partition movement. In 1905 he composed his famous patriotic song in Bengali, "Amar Sonar Bangla, Tomai Bhalobashi" ("My Golden Bengal, I love you"), which became very popular with the entire Bengali people, both Hindus and Moslems.[4] Then again in 1911 Tagore composed his other even more famous patriotic song comprehending the then entire India of diverse geographic features, peoples and cultures as one united and integrated country, from Kashmir to Madras and Cape Comorin and from Punjab and Sindh to Bengal, Assam, Orissa. It started with the Bengali words (in fact similar to Sanskrit) "Jana-Gana-Mana-Adhinaya... vidhata" ("Ruler of peoples'minds and Builder o... all seek thy blessings and Victory to Thee.") The so... popular, naturally first with the Bengalees, and later also ... Indians when they came to understand its language and spirit. Afte... dependence its first two stanzas were selected as the National Anthem of India and its tune is played with India's military bands on all national ceremonial occasions.

But in 1908 Rabindranath withdrew from active politics and devoted his genius and time mostly to literary works, but also to several important constructive programmes on education and rural reconstruction. He believed the two were vital for India's regeneration. Education, he considered, must be based on Nature, consistent with his basic 'holistic' view of the entire universe of which man and nature were but two closely integrated entities. So he tried to apply this view in practice through Santiniketan. At the same time, consistent with his all comprehensive approach, he believed in the basic unity of the entire mankind and thus in international brotherhood, peace and international understanding. He, therefore, envisioned Visva Bharati to be the centre of study and research along these lines, with a selected band of teachers chosen from different parts of India and the world, who were in sympathy with these ideals.

As for rural reconstruction, Rabindranath started a separate experiment in certain selected villages of Bengal, particularly near Santiniketan in Bolpur, and established a special vocational institution for it, which he characteristically called 'Sri Niketan' ("Abode of Welfare"), with the help of an English born and U.S. educated youngman Leonard Elmhirst.[5]

During the second decade of the current century Tagore's genius as a Bengali (and even as an English) philosopher-poet and writer was widely recognized in Bengal and abroad. At his 50th birthday in 1912 he was felicitated by the then prestigious "Bangiya Sahitya Parishad" (Bengali Literary Society) and the same year he left for England with a prose translation of his now famous "Gitanjali" (literarlly, 'song offerings'), consisting of -- poems of lyrical and devotional character. Most of them are akin to songs and have been sung ever since their composition in special tunes given largely by Tagore himself and his brother Gaganendra Nath Tagore and known as a class by itself, namely, Tagore Songs and music. In England, Tagore placed Gitanjali before a top circle of his literary friends ... ...rsons as W.B. Yeats, Ezra Pound an... ...hat in 1913 he was awarded the ... Prize in Literature and thus shot into ... and the following year (1913) he undertook ...ited States and England (lecturing at the Univer-... and Harvard in U.S.A. and at Caxton Hall in England). ...elled extensively, both in India and abroad including U.S.A. ... other countries of Europe as well as in the Far East including ...pan and China. He was the recipient of great honour everywhere[6].

Tagore wrote over 1000 poems. But Tagore was not only a great poet and a great composer of songs (nearly 2000), but also a versatile writer of many dramas of diverse character (social, historical and cultural), great novels, and short stories. He was also a great dramatist and musician himself, a great and profoundly intuitive philosopher writing and lecturing in India and abroad on complex texts of Eastern and Western religious and philosophical subjects.[7]

During his full 80 years of life, from almost the middle of the nineteenth (1861) to the middle of twentieth century (1941), Tagore lived an honourable, aristocratic and in many ways an isolated life, for most part in Santiniketan. He was highly contemplative and philosophical. But he also was deeply connected, as already said above, with many practical and constructive works, like his immemorable Santiniketan, Sriniketan and Visva Bharati, where he combined the teachings of high moral, ethical and humanistic principles of ancient India, with knowledge of the acute problems of modern man, not only of India but also of the world as a whole, and particularly of Asia. He symbolized and expressed the feelings of all men, women and children, of all ages and all climes. He was a great creator of words and languages. A genius and a man like him is rarely born even in a thousand years. As another famous poet of Bengal, Kazi Nazrul Islam has said, "he was at once Vyas,[8] Valmiki[9] and Kalidasa[10].

Thus 1912-13, may be said to be a mark of Tagore era in Bengal and also for India.

But apart from the emergence of the great personality of Rabindranath Tagore, the first two-three decades of this century saw many educational and cultural activities in Bengal. Many gifted men of all vocations and professions like, to name a few, Sarat Chandra Chatterjee

(1876-1938), the most popular and humane and prolific Bengali novelist. Dwijendra Lal Ray (1863-1913), the well-known writer, dramatist, poet and composer of inspiring nationalistic songs; Asutosh Mukherjee (1864-1924), a most notable jurist and educationist; Acharya Profulla Chandra Ray, Jagadish Chandra Bose, Professor Satyendra Nath Bose and Meghnad Saha, all eminent scientists; great lawyers and educationists like Gooroodas Banerjee (1844-1918) and Rash Behari Ghose (1845-1921) who was a great philanthropist as well; pioneer journalists like Shishir Kumar Ghose (1840-1911), founder editor of the first English daily paper of Calcutta, the *Amrita Bazar Patrika*, appeared on the scene of Bengal and all of them contributed considerably to enrich and enlighten the life of the Bengaleese in different ways.

In this connection it is important to mention here about two other most notable sons of undivided Bengal, who not only played a very significant role in framing the social, cultural and political course of contemporary history of the Province, but also left a permanent mark for all Bengalees of the future generations, even after the parent province was partitioned in 1947. They were the great poet, music composer, writer, dramatist, patriot and humanist, Kazi Nazrul Islam[11] (1899-1976) and the noble hearted politician A.K. Fazlul Haque, (1873-1962).

Kazi Nazrul Islam

Nazrul was a rare genius as a versatile poet-patriot. He wrote many inspiring and fiery patriotic songs.[12] He also wrote songs for the poor, the exploited and the oppressed on the one hand, and against all sorts of religious, caste and social prejudices and conflicts, on the other. Like Tagore, he too has left great impact on the Bengali-speaking people of the two parts as well as among their compatriots scattered all over the world.

As for A.K. Fazlul Haque, in spite of his somewhat uncertain politics, he was a noble soul, a great lover of Bengal and its people, regardless of creed and caste, and especially of its downtrodden and exploited peasantry. He tried to maintain the Province's unity but destiny and circumstances worked against him.

So, a political slump at the beginning of the second decade was more than offset by a widespread educational, cultural and social activity during that and subsequent decades, which gave a great spurt to political activities again in twenties to forties, i.e., the period of intense struggle and independence.

My Family

My ancestors, both on father's and mother's side came from two aristocratic families apparently from Midnapore district itself my father's side from the Contai subdivision in south west of Bengal bordering the Gangetic delta, and mother's side from the Sardar subdivision bordering Howrah district. The original family surname on my father's side was 'Dev' but for at least the last five generations it had been 'Ray', a title given by the Moslem rulers of Bengal, the Nawabs, with certain grants of lands, for reasons not known to me. On the mother's side, the original family name was 'Ghose' but her ancestors were also awarded by the Nawab of Bengal at one time the hereditary title of 'Ray Mahashaya' with grants of tax free (*nankar*) lands and the office of revenue administration ("*Kanungo*") over certain areas in the village Jakpur and in other parts within and outside the present Midnapore district, in lieu of certain services rendered by them to other contemporary landed gentry in time of their distress.[13] All these rights were recognized by the British rulers under their Permanent Settlement regulations of 1793. In addition my ancestors, both on father's and mother's side, had been given by the Nawab's lands with "Debottar" rights for the maintenance and worship of certain idols (or images of Gods). After independence all these rights of "Zamindary " except "debottar" rights were abolished with the abolition of the Zamındary system.

My grandfather on the father's side, on the other hand, had been among the first batch of students in the then Anglo-Vernacular School[14] established in Contai on 20 March 1857, and was the first recipient of a scholarship soon thereafter. The amount of scholarship was Rs. 4 per month for a period of one year.[15] In 1864 the vernacular department of the School was abolished by the then Director of Public Instruction, and it was converted to a Middle English School. In 1860, Bankim Chandra Chatterjee the great man who had been one of the first two graduates of the Calcutta University in 1857, and later became a famous novelist and a pioneer in Bengali prose writing, came as the Sub-Divisional Office(the chief executive officer) of Contai with his seat of administration at Negua. He arranged to grant an endowment of 3.60 acres of land which "opened up an avenue for the long life and prosperity of the school". The school was allowed to open then what were called "Entrance Classes" (i.e. to hold classes for examination for entrance to the University in Calcutta) from January 1881, when one young British Officer, Mr. Andrew was the S.D.O.[16] That is, it was then converted into a full-fledged High or Secondary English School with English as the main medium of instruction.

My grandfather, Ganga Narayan Ray, being one of the first English educated boy of Contai, was later appointed as an official of the status of "Kanungo" in the then Contai "Neemak Mahal" or Salt Administration in 1860's.

My father and all his brothers after schooling joined the City College, founded by Ananda Mohan Bose in 1879. He was, a "pioneering educationist, social reformer and nationalist" of Bengal, and a co-founder, with another famous man of his time, Sivnath Sastri, of the "Sadharan Brahmo Samaj" in 1878 following the second split from original Samaj "after the parting of ways with Keshab Chandra Sen". Since its foundation Sadharan Brahmo Samaj became the predominant and most powerful wing of all the three sections of the original of "Adi-Brahmo Samaj" founded by Ram Mohan Roy.

Calcutta City College, still one of the major colleges of Bengal, was then naturally highly influenced by the ideals of Brahmo Samaj .

The eldest brother of my father, Satish Chandra, was a qualified lawyer. His sons -- Prem Nihar qualified as an F.R.C.S. of England and a surgeon attached to the Calcutta Medical College, the Presidency General Hospital, and during World War II served also in the Allied Hospital at Southern Avenue. His wife Irene Ray, and English lady still living, became a devotee, of Sri Ramkrishna and Swami Vivekananda and wrote some books on them especially for children. My eldest uncle's second son Benoy Bhusan obtained his B.Sc. in Physics from London University and served at the Central Government Hydel power Dam at Bhakra Nangal. He had also married an English lady and left two daughters.

My second uncle Nibaran Chandra became in his time the Senior Professor of Physics at the Scottish Church College and also a Member of Calcutta University Senate and Syndicate, and for sometime the Inspector of Colleges along with late Harendra Nath Mukherjee (a former Governor of West Bengal). He spent most of his time serving the cause of higher education in Bengal. He was a member of the Liberal Party founded by J.N. Basu and is said to have attended with the latter the First Round Table Conference convened by the British Government in London from 12 November 1930 to 19 January 1931 to discuss about the constitutional reforms in India. It was boycotted by the Indian National

Congress. He died in 1942, when I was a "Security Prisoner" (a political detainee) in Rajashahi Jail during the Second World War.

My third uncle, Surendra Nath was a bachelor and lived in Calcutta practising as a Veterinary Doctor. The fourth uncle, Dr. P.C. Ray, after having obtained his M.B.B.S. degree from the Calcutta Medical College, went to Edinburgh and qualified as an L.R.C.P. (Licentiate of the Royal College of Physicians) and on his return joined the Indian Medical Service in Bihar and acted as a Professor of medicine in Patna College. He married the second daughter of late Tarak Nath Ghose, a former Headmaster of Contai High School, and was initiated in the Brahmo Samaj. He had a son and a daughter. He died at the age of 80 in Calcutta after India's independence. His son was in the Indian military and served as a Major in the British Indian army during World War II.

My fifth uncle was Binode Behari who first practised as a lawyer in Midnapore town and then as the Secretary of Midnapore District Board. He was also a bachelor. He was a great lover of music. My four other brothers, sister and myself lived with him and it was he who virtually brought us up, as our father Barendra lived for the most part of his life in Contai and practised as a lawyer in the Contai Bar and at the same time looked after our share of the ancestral property in and around Contai.

My sixth and the last uncle was Lalit Kumar Ray who was a Lecturer in mathematics under the Bengal Educational Service and served first at Dacca Intermediate College and successively at Chittagong, and Calcutta Presidency and Bethune Colleges. He was also an initiated Brahmo and married the first sister of late Professor Amiya Kumar Sen, a former Principal of the City College.

My father Barendra Kumar was a man of simple habits. After graduating from Calcutta City College he had first joined the Bengal Engineering College to qualify as an engineer. But he later changed to law and obtained a B.L. degree from the Calcutta University. My father married in 1910. My mother's parents and two younger brothers then lived in their Jakpur "palace" -- a huge and extensive old zamindary style two-storeyed house with a vast adjacent temple complex of a central hall for annual "Durga Puja" and twelve surrounding smaller temples of Lord Shiva. Nearby there was a "Rasamancha", a place for the annual ceremony of the union of the legendary gods of Krishna and Radha.

My mother came to Midnapore after marriage, to my father's residence at Ballavpure behind the then Midnapore Town School. The site and the main building were originally the office of Zamindary of the Mahashaya family of Jakpur. It had been donated for the school by one of descendants of the Mahashaya family, Kartic Mitra, who then lived in Midnapore and was a highly educated person. He was the first recipient of the prestigious Premchand Roychand Research Scholarship of the Calcutta University (an award which was later given to me in 1944 for my thesis on "Agricultural Economics of Bengal" while I was a political detenu in Buxa Jail during World War). Soon thereafter my mother's two parents with their two young sons -- Mangala and Bimala -- also moved to Midnapore town for the education of their sons.

It was in Ballavpur house where I was born on 1 December 1912, I was the first child of my parents. There was, naturally a great joy among my parents, my grandparents and my other relatives. Naturally I do not remember the events of early childhood, except that my parents and uncle had moved to another better two storeyed house at Sujagange, belonging to a local merchant family of Kundus,[17] near the Jagannath Temple, an important landmark of the town. The place was more open and airy but on the main road made of red laterite stone chips which were easily available in Midnapore town being situated in the laterite zone of southwest Bengal. North and west of Midnapore were rocky with small low hills covered with forests, through which the river Kangsavati flowed from its source at Chotanagpur plateau in Bihar to its confluence nearly 100 miles down with the Ganges near Calcutta by the south of Midnapore town. The town was of great historic importance because it was often frequented in the past by the officers and the marching army of the Moghul rulers in Delhi from Akbar and south. Moreover, the Bay of Bengal was not very far which washed the Southwest coast of Midnapore district, especially Contai subdivision which was an important sealane for maritime merchant and other ships sailing from Europe and the Middle East to southeast Asia for spice trade in the earlier days. There was a sizable Moslem community, mostly descendants of former Pathan and Mogul army which settled down in Midnapore as well as in other parts of the district. They were peaceful people and many of them were highly cultured, and there was never any conflict with the majority Hindu community of the town. Rather there was a free mixing and mutual participation of the two communities in respect of their festivals and fairs. Many distinguished Moslem personalities of the town used to visit my family regularly in our house and some were invited for dinner and various social functions.

My sister Kamala and my second brother Nirmal[18] were born with an interval of two years from each other -- one in 1914 and the other in 1916. My father who until then had practised as a lawyer in Midnapore town decided to go to our ancestral home in Contai and settle down there. However since my uncle Binode (a bachelor) was left alone at Midnapore, my maternal grand parents with their two sons joined my uncle in the latter's house at Midnapore for the time being (from about 1920 till 1921) and myself and my sister and second brother moved to Contai but in 1922 we returned to Midnapore to join schools there.

My early Education and Environment

My father had told me that my first education was started at home in Midnapore town from about the age of four around 1916, at the time of First World War. My father himself taught me English. He started straight with the words, simplest of course, without teaching me first the alphabet, which was the more conventional method. He also used to narrate interesting stories from our old epics, the *Ramayana* and the *Mahabharata*, and other ancient literature like *Panchatantra* and *Hitopadesha*. He also told me stories from the Aesop's Fables and even the Bible.

However, after about one year, in around 1920, soon after the war my father, as I have said earlier, decided to go back to Contai to live there permanently in our two ancestral houses there, he took my mother as well as me and my sister and other brother. He selected the house by the main road to stay. It was also built of unburnt bricks and thatched roof but big and spacious with a fairly large courtyard inside with lovely plants of Kamini, (white scented flowers). There was plenty of space inside which was used by my mother for gardening. We had also a big farm outside of about one-and-a-half acre of land with plenty of coconut, mango, areca nut, tamarind, custard apple, '*bel*' and other useful fruit trees, as well as a small tank which was full of fish. There was also a much bigger tank neary which was named after my father's grandfather 'Krishnakanta'. The whole neighbourhood once belonged to our ancestors. But in course of time some lands were given to others in lieu of payments of rents. on the basis of long-term leases, where they built their houses. And some lands went out of my grandfather's hand as, I was told, he had borrowed some money from others to meet certain obligations especially when he became sick. But the whole area was well-developed and almost all who lived there were highly educated and belonged to different professions, though mainly lawyers. So the area was called "Ukilpara" or area of lawyers[19]. There were people of different castes but mostly Brahmins and Kayasthas. But they all used to mix and joined together in social and religious functions. In fact the people of the whole area seemed to belong to a larger family. There used to be many Hindu festivals and 'Puja' ceremonies in some houses in which all the neighbours used to be invited and they all enjoyed.

Contai town as a whole was a peaceful and clean place, a small semirural complex which contained minimum facilities of an urban centre, like a civil and criminal court, a post and telegraph office in the centre, one main long road with a few subsidiary roads, population at that time less than 10,000, three English High Schools for boys and two for girls in the centre of the town, plenty of open grounds including several playing grounds. The town was (and still is) located on the ridge of a sand dune but with plenty of clear and cool underground water within 50 yards depth. Water supply was provided mainly through private and public ring wells, and big and small tanks with clear water; later some tube wells were sunk. A graduate college was established some years later.

Majority of people were Hindus of different castes. Muslims also lived there, who were very posperous with cultivable lands of their own. Both the religious communities lived in harmony and peace. Muslims held their own religious ceremonies like Id, Muharam, etc. The Id, a festival of friendship, was held with great pomp and show and a big fair was held every year on an open sandy ground. There were several Shiva and Kali temples. One of the latter was and still is named after "Kapal Kundala", the idol which was supposed to be the central figure in the famous Bengali novel of the great Bengali writer Bankim Chandra who wrote it when he was the subdivisional magistrate in charge of Contai subdivision about 1860.

The town was situated about five miles away from the western shares of the Bay of Bengal. It had a bracing climate in the summer with strong south wind blowing from the Bay. Being on a big sand dune there was very little stagnant water at any place though there were plenty of irrigated tanks for domestic use. The town was relatively advanced in education chiefly because of the influence of the Brahmo Samaj which was relatively strong and lively considering the small size of the total population. Women in general were educated and of progressive outlook and used to come out freely. Common people, mainly independent farmers, tenants and share-croppers were generally happy and prosperous, though there were many litigations on land rights and especially over inheritance of lands.

There was no railway in or near the town. The nearest rail station was 36 miles away -- Contai Road Station -- on the Calcutta -- Puri Line. Originally, in our childhood, a few taxies ferried daily passengers but bullock and camel carts were the more usual means of transport, which took full one or even two days to cover 36 miles. I remember that we had on several occasions to travel in these carts. It was boring but fun, passing and stopping through different villages and even spending nights in road side country style cottages with earth walls and thatched roofs but clean and having facilities for own cooking. And bus service was started some years later.

So I remember to have enjoyed my first stay in Contai, with my parents for about a year during 1920 - 1921. At that time I had my first schooling in a country style primary school called *Pathashala* near our house. But only for about one yeasr and a half. For, towards the end of 1921 I was brought to Midnapore town by my uncle Binode and maternal grandmother, and admitted to the Midnapore Town School straight in the then 6th Class or modern Class V at the age of 9 years.

World War I and its Conseqences

In the meantime, in 1914, the First World War broke out between what were known as the Allied Powers (including primarily Great Britain, France, and the then Russian Empire, on the one hand, later joined by U.S.A.) and the Central Powers (including Germany, Austro-Hungarian Empire and the Turkish Empire). The War lasted for four years until December 1918. The total causalties suffered by the Allied and Central Powers -- the two fighting groups were 37,000,000, of which more than 8 million were killed, 21 million were wounded and nearly 8 million were prisoners and missing. The largest casualties were suffered by then Russia, Germany, Austro-Hungary and France -- all above 5 millions, and the then British Empire and Italy 3 and 2 million respectively.[20]

India alone contributed more than one-and-a half million soldiers and directly supporting personnel, and lost more than 100,000 as dead; besides there were many more wounded. And in cash and commodities including arms manufacture in India, it contributed more than Rs. 10,000,000,000 (Rupees 1000 crores). This was an astronomical figure and had undoubtedly been a great drain, especially on the then largely undeveloped resources of the country.[21] Its economic and social impact on the people of the entire country was very serious.

I was, however then still too young to remember all that, including particularly the effect of the War on Midnapore and Contai. But I guess that Midnapore and especially Contai with rich and fertile soil, and still then relatively much fewer people, with almost every family[22] having some cultivable land, had somehow got over the "hump"; they did not have to face a severe food problem at least. In fact, the then province of Bengal as a whole endowed with one of the largest riverine delta in the world -- the Ganges -- Brhamaputra -- with its extensive rich fertile soil and a criss-cross of many other large and small rivers and streams on the one hand, and with generally been self-sufficient in food and agricultural raw materials such as jute. And also with rich mineral resources like iron and coal, it has been fairly prosperous almost all through its history, except when severe disasters struck as in 1770 and again in 1866-1867.

And during the War, at least in two places, because of scarcity of rains and prevalence of near-famine conditions, farmers were in difficulty to pay their land rents and revenues to the landlords and the Government respectively, namely in the district of Champaran in Bihar, and in Kaira in Gujarat. So much so that Mahatma Gandhi who, after his return from South Africa in 1915 had assumed the leadership of Congress, launched his 'Satyagraha' movement (which literally meant "resort to truth" but in actual fact a recourcse to non-payment of taxes or revenues).

As for the cause of such famines while the then governments attributed it primarily to vagaries of monsoon, most Indian experts such as Ramesh Chandra Dutta, had also blamed the flaws in revenue assessment and collection. While this had been the normal situation, the conduct of the war required a great levy as well as a more stringent collections of land revenues and taxes rogardless of farmer's actual position. This was the case in many parts of India during the four-and-a-half years and a half of the war, including Champaran and Khaira. However, because of Gandhiji's first experiment of non-cooperation and non-payment of taxes in India, the respective governments of Bihar and Gujarat ultimately exempted the protesting farmers for the time being from the payment of land revenues.

World War I and its Political impact on Bengal -- Second Phase of Revolutionary Uprising

During the war and immediately after there had been certain important developments in the political situation of Bengal and the rest of India.

The revolutionary groups, or the so-called extremists, who, after 1910 became largely passive again began to reorganize themselves to take advantage of the War. They resumed their work with new vigour and new expectations, not only in Bengal but also in other parts of India, especially north India. They established new contacts and reestablished old ones with Indians living abroad particularly in U.S.A. but also in U.K., Germany, and other countries in Europe as well as in south-east Asia.

In Bengal, there were many local group leaders but at that time especially two stood out -- Rashbehari Bose and Jatindranath Mukherjee. Rashbehari based him first in the then French Chandernogore, then in Benares. He was in contact with what was then called the Anushilan Samiti (literally meaning "Society for Exercise") which was originally founded in Calcutta in about 1904 by a close associate of Aurobindo, P. Mitra of Calcutta. It later extended its activities to Dacca under the leadership of Pulin Das. Subsequently its activities spread more extensively in Calcutta and to other districts of Bengal and even to many parts of northern India. Rashbehari was a government servant but he carried on revolutionary activities, particularly in northern India, immediately before and during World War I. He is even said to have thrown a powerful bomb on Lord Hardinge, the then Viceroy of India, during the well-known Delhi Darbar held in December 1912, on the occasion of the visit of King George V of Britain.[23] It was done so secretly that the police did not get an exact idea as to who did it. However, they suspected Bose in connection with many other revolutionary activities in north India including Delhi, Punjab, Maharashtra, Bihar, and the United Provinces.

Other revolutionary activities such as the organization of gymnasium clubs, study centres and even political robberies, individual actions against selected police officers and spies, were on the increase. Bose maintained close contacts with them in all important centres -- Calcutta, Benares, Lahore, Delhi. His name came out especially in the Raja Bazar Bomb case of 1913, as well as in the Delhi Conspiracy case of 1914 in which four young men were implicated, tried and hanged in Ambala prison in Punjab in May 1915.[24] Police had suspected also Bose but could not get him. He was as elusive as ever, though always very active.

Rashbehari worked in close cooperation with other major groups in Bengal led by Jatindranath Mukherjee (1879-1915). These groups were collectively called "Jugantar" (as distinguished from the 'Anushilan Samiti' and allied groups working with Bose).

The name Jugantar was derived from the weekly paper of the same name which earlier "served as a rallying point for the Aurobinda-Barindra group of Calcutta "and ventilated" extremist" views about the freedom struggle in India. Its first editor was Dr. Bhupendra Nath Dutta, the celebrated brother of Narendra Nath Dutta (Swami Vivekananda). The actual Jugantar party was said to have been formed later in 1914 or early 1915 by bringing together several groups such as (i) Atmonnati Samiti (Self-Improvement Society) of Calcutta, headed by Anukul Mukherjee, Bipin Ganguli and others, (ii) Mukti Sangha (Freedom Association) headed by Hemchandra Ghose of Dacca, (iii) Barisal Group, headed by Satin Sen, (iv) Madaripur group headed by Purna Das, and (v) Mymensing Group headed by Surendramohan Ghose, and many others. They all worked under the overall leadership of Jatindranath Mukherjee.

At the outbreak of the War all the revolutionary groups of Bengal co-ordinated their activities especially to plan and execute some major joint actions to take advantage of the British involvement in the War. The major action plan was to import large consignments of small and medium arms from Germany, with the help of the German Government, and stage a large-scale uprising within India with the help of certain sections of the Indian army. To carry out this plan, contacts were made through certain Indian residents abroad especially in Germany and U.S.A. and even by sending certain special emissaries from India with a view to opening channels of communication with Germany and other Central Powers. The German Government as well as its representatives in different countries offered various helps and even did actually send some ship loads of small arms and ammunitions for being off loaded by representatives of the Bengal revolutionaries in some prearranged and designated coastal areas of the Bay of Bengal.

The preparations for armed revolution were indeed very extensive involving practically all the important groups of revolutionaries in Bengal, in close cooperation with similar groups all over north India on the one hand and with revolutionary minded Indian residents abroad. Among the latter the largest number were the migrant Sikhs who formed the "Gwadar Party" (revolutionary party) in the United States. Many of them actually came to India to join the army and the peoples, simultaneous revolt against the British rulers of India. For which even a date was fixed -- 4 February 1915. The overall lead by the planned all-India uprising was taken by Rashbehari Bose.

But the plan was finally exposed through the vigil and activities of the elaborate secret service system of the then Indian Government operating in different countries. Actually the plan was too big to remain asecret. Too many people belonging to too many parties and scattered over too wide areas covering India as well as at least half-a-dozen foreign countries, were involved to keep the plan unnoticed by the world wide espionage network of the British rulers. So in the end, before the zero hour they got the hints, partly from the movements of the Indian revolutionaries and their agents and sympathizers in different countries, and partly from the confessions of some army men in India.[25] So large scale arrests and detention were made of many key personnel, both in India and abroad. And the British navy intercepted in the Indian Ocean some of the German ships bringing arms to India. Some other ships which were supposed to come finally failed to reach India.[26]

Rashbehari and his colleagues in India came to know of the exposure of their plan from the large-scale arrests including many in the army, by the Government. So they decided that Rashbehari, their leader, should be sent off to a foreign country where he would be safe and be able to pursue the objective of enlisting continued foreign, and especially German support for future struggle for India's independence. A decision was taken that he should go to Japan and secret arrangements were made for it.[27]

He landed in Japan in May 1915 and visited Shanghai in China in June-July from where he tried to send arms to India through German friends.

Destiny and revolutionary colleagues of Jatindranath Mukherjee assigned to him a different role. While Rashbehari was to organize and prepare for an uprising especially in northern India (first on 4 February 1915 and then the date was deferred to 19 February of the same year) with a simultaneous revolt of large sections of the Indian army, Mukherjee was responsible one of the triple deliveries of German arms, planned at Sunderbans in West Bengal. Two other deliveries planned in Hatia (Sandip in East Bengal), and in Calcutta, were placed under the responsibility of Naren Ghose Chaudhuri and Bipin Behari Ganguli respectively. To take the delivery of arms at Sunderbans from a German ship named "Maverick", Jatindranath with his four selected associates - Chittapriya Raychaudhuri, Manoranjan Sen Gupta, Niren Das Gupta and Jyotish Pal went from Calcutta secretly by road, via Tamluk and Contai with the help of some local friends,[28] to an especially selected post named

"Kaptipoda" in Balasore district in Orissa, near the Bay of Bengal, and bordering Midnapore district. However, the ship did not reach the Sunderbans and had been diverted back to U.S.A. via Batavia (then Dutch East Indies). Another ship was arranged through the help of the German Consul in Batavia but that ship was intercepted by the British after they made arrests in Singapore, Calcutta as well as Balasore. And the police in Bengal were then following the track of Jatindranath and his associates.

They reached Balasore in September 1915 but instead of going to their secret centre at Kaptipoda they were hiking from village to village in the south of the district in search of a safe shelter. But they were soon followed by local people who become very curious about the strangers and suspected them to be criminals or German agents. In the meantime police, especially under the direction of the then well-known Calcutta Police Commissioner Charles Regart, also started following them. Finally, the five came by a river Buri Balam which was then in spate because of the monsoon rains. There they were surrounded on the one side by the villagers and on the other by armed police contingent. This was a crucial and historic moment for all five young fighters for India's freedom. They soon took the momentous decision to fight and not to surrender. On 9th September, by the river Buri Balam there was a prolonged severe but unequal fight between the five brave young men, with their limited arms and the large contingent of police, all well-armed. They had already been tired and hungry over a long march through inhospitable country but yet put up a great fight. As the inevitable result one colleague of Jatindranath, Chittapriya died while fighting and Jatindranath was severely wounded and died in the hospital on the following day of the other three, also wounded in the fighting, all were later tried by the then Government, and two -- Monoranajan Sen Gupta and Niren Das Gupta were sentenced to death, and the third, Jyotish Pal, was sentenced to 14 years' transportation for life and sent to the penal settlement (prison) in the Andaman Islands. He too died later.

This opened the most heroic armed confrontation between a small group of five determined revolutionaries and a large Indian army of the foreign rulers led by British officers in India was the first of its kind to happen after the "Sepoy Mutiny" of 1857. It was by all standards an utterly unequal fight. But the bravery, the determination, the spirit of sacrifice that the five showed, set a noble example to the youth of the country of future generations and, as later history shows, inspired thousands of others to emulate them in the cause of India's ultimate freedom. The five with their blood inscribed on the shores of the river Buri Balam the valuable lesson that no sacrifice was too great to achieve the independence of the Motherland.

With this episode may be said to have been the closure of one of the great chapters of India's long history of fight for freedom. Undoubtedly, a most extensively planned and coordinated collective effort by large groups of Indian revolutionaries, both in India and abroad, led by two most dynamic and courageous persons, Rashbehari Bose and Jatindra Nath Mukherjee, to overthrow the foreign rulers by force ultimately failed. The failures must have caused a great despair among the valiant and patriotic freedom fighters and their supporters and sympathizers in India and abroad. But today, it appears to be a stage, and important one, though, in the way to the final success which came in the wake of the Second World War, in 1947. Its greatest value lay in what it taught to the future generations of Indians -- that a determined, coordinated and concerted action by selected bands of armed revolutionaries, at an appropriate time, can shake violently even the mightiest of rulers which seemed at that time to be absolutely impregnable and irremovable. Later generations also came to know also of certain flaws in the attempts. First, lack of popular support and even knowledge of their activities; second, there were few representatives of the largest minority community -- the Muslims. However, as observed earlier, a better opportunity came during World War II of which full advantage was taken by two of India's modern greatest men -- Gandhiji and Subhash Chandra Bose.

Gandhi's advent

The second major event in Indian political field which occurred during World War I, was the advent of Mohandas Karamchand Gandhi (1869-1948) in India in 1915.[29] Already before coming to India, Gandhi had been known all over India as well as in the world for his non-violent and passive, but courageous and determined, fight in South Africa for nearly two decades, against one of the greatest injustices on and repressions of man by his fellowman, in the name of race and colour, that is, of the "black" Africans and the so-called "coloured" Asians in South Africa by the "white" settlers from Europe.[30] Gandhi brought two major lessons from his long struggle in the country first, a determined and mass based open struggle against the oppressive foreign rulers in India to achieve independence; and, second, the application of what he termed as "Satyagraha" (resort to Truth), i.e., a non-violent struggle.

After returning to India Gandhi came into close contact with Gopal Krishna Gokhale (1866-1915), the great Maharashtrian leader [31] (contemporary of Tilak) who was a well-known educationist, social reformer, administrator, parliamentarian of great repute and very active in political life. He was a dominant figure in the Indian National Congress. Gokhale was chosen as its president at its Annual session in Banaras in 1905 and from then, until 1915, "reigned virtually supreme in the party". He was a great patriot, a great lover of India and its people. He said : "I recognize no limits to my aspirations for our Motherland ... I want our men and women without distinction of caste or creed to grow to the full height of their stature."[32] Gokhale "firmly believed that the economic results of the British rule had been disastrous (for India) and spelt frightful poverty for the country". As a remedy he believed in the most urgent need of education in : "the techniques of administration, the rudiments of public health and sanitation, the skills of advanced technology, the basic principles of communal harmony and social equality, the methods of democratic agitation, and as pre-requisite for learning all these things, an elementary reading and writing".[33] Thus, Gokhale was undoubtedly a great thinker and builder of modern India.

But he was a moderate in his political views and approach. He had great faith in the British system of government, and opposed the Swadeshi Movement and Boycott "as retrogressive measures". He thus came into conflict with other contemporary leaders like Tilak and Aurobindo, and therefore tried to keep the latter out of the Congress. He however did not like non-cooperation and passive resistance, though he supported Gandhi's Satyagraha in South Africa, and "was largely responsible for bringing about an agreement with the South African Government". Nevertheless, Gandhi called Gokhale his *Rajguru*, and on the latter's advice travelled all over India to get an intimate knowledge of its people and their living conditions. During the travel he had an opportunity of visiting Santiniketan and meeting Rabindranath Tagore, through the good officers of the English missionary Father C.F. Andrews, who was a common friend of both the great men.

Gandhi, like Ranade and Gokhale, was basically a pacifist and had earlier believed that by helping the British in their war efforts against the then Central Powers (including Germany) he would be able to persuade the British to grant India autonomy within the British Empire along the lines then enjoyed by the British Dominions like Australia, Canada and New Zealand. With that in view, on his way back home from South Africa in 1914, while in England, he raised an Indian ambulance unit for which, after his return to India, he was awarded by the British Government a Kaiser-i-Hind gold medal. And, during the War he spoke in favour of India's joining the British army and even himself conducted a recruitment drive. But after returning to India in 1915 he established his first famous Satyagraha Ashrama in his home province in Gujarat, on the banks of the Sabarmati river, opposite its capital city, Ahmedabad.

Soon thereafter, as a result of his first 'voyage' of discovery across India, he had a close view of the sufferings of the peasants of India, especially because of the forcible collection of rents and land taxes (called land revenue) by both the landlords (including the British planters and agents of the East India Company which still had its offices in some parts), and the Indian Government, even in years of acute scarcity of rain and the consequent crop failure. To remedy the situations he launched his first two Satyagrahas, or peasant movements for non-payments of land taxes, first, in the district of Champaran in Bihar in 1917 and again in the district of Khaira in Gujarat in 1918. Although Gandhi was tried (his first trial in India) and sentenced for his role in the Champaran Satyagraha, in both the cases the movements succeeded in achieving their limited goals. Moreover they helped considerably to project Gandhi as a new all-India leader wielding a new source of power -- that of the masses -- organized through non-violent means which was quite different from the conventional paths hitherto followed by the Indian fighters for freedom.

Annie Besant and the Home Rule League

Meanwhile during the war years several other major events happened in the political atmosphere of India which had profound effects on the country, both in the short and the long run. One of the most important was the appearance of at least a semblance of unity among the so-called Extremist[34] and Moderate Wings of the Congress following a compromise reached of its annual session at Lucknow in 1916. A further compromise was effected between the Congress and the All-India Moslem League at Lucknow. "The upshot of this latter agreement", as Subhas Chandra Bose has written "was that the Congress and the Moslem League put forward the same demand for self-government and agreed about the representation to be given to Moslems in the legislature under the reformed constitution, on the basis of 'separate electorate'.[35]

Both these agreements -- between the extremists and the moderates within the Congress, and between the latter and the Moslem League, were reached largely through the mediation of Annie Besant (1847-1933), who was predominantly of Irish lineage and a woman of "bold and independent thinking". She was at one time a member of the Fabian Society of England (1885) and later also of the Theosophical Society. She was greatly interested in the Hindu religion and culture, which she believed to be "the fount of all other religions and the 'cradle of civilization'. She came to India in 1893 and became involved in various religious, social, educational and finally, political activities. She wrote, lectured and participated in the struggle for self-government of the Indians within the British Commonwealth (then Dominion). She thus gave for the first time a clear-cut political and constitutional objective before the country and the parties, which she called "Home Rule". She actually founded in September 1916 a "Home Rule for India League" [36] as distinguished from the Congress, to work for this objective. Congress was still not clear about its final objective, that is, whether complete Swaraj or only limited autonomy under the British Rule, largely because it was, then, still under the influence of the Moderates. Outlining the League's objective, Besant wrote that "the cry for Home Rule, swaraj (self-rule) ... is really a cry for that which is most precious in a Nation's life, for the life of its very soul, for the right to grow, to evolve on its own national lines."

But, Tilak, after his release from prison in 1914, and having found the Congress then dominated by the moderates, had found earlier his own separate organization, "the Indian Home Rule League", at a special conference in Belgaum in Maharashtra in April 1915 with his supporters. The objective of Tilak's Home Rule League was more or less similar to that of Besant's League established five months later, namely, "to attain Home Rule or Self-Government within the British Empire by all constitutional means and to educate and organize public opinion in the country towards the attainment of the same".

There was some rivalry between the two Home Rule Leagues but also there was a large degree of cooperation. And while Tilak confined his League's activity primarily to then Bombay and Mysore, Besant to Madras and some parts of the north including Bengal. Both had tried to influence the Congress to adopt the objective of Self-Rule for India but failed initially; so many important members of the Congress joined one or other and some even joined the two leagues, including then young Jawaharlal Nehru. Also many Moslem leaders including M.A. Jinnah, were drawn into the movement. The growing influence and organization of the two leagues caused concern among the then Indian Government. They adopted various measures of suppression of what they called "sedition'', including the arrest and a short-term imprisonment of Besant in June 1917. This led to widespread demonstration and protests all over India, which finally forced the Government to release her. The result was that by the end of 1917 the Home Rulers were in command of the Congress and Mrs. Besant was elected as the President of its Annual Session in Calcutta that year.

This was the highest mark in her career. Being a woman of a foreign country, she loved India and worked for its freedom. She played a historic role in the social and political development of India at a very critical stage -- in the vacuum of leadership between the departure of Aurobindo in 1910 and the rise of Gandhi in 1920. She defined and held before the educated intelligentsia the ideal of Home-Rule and joined hands with Tilak, in many activities. In addition, she also had some lasting gifts to the future generations of India -- the founding of the Central Hindu College in Banaras which later developed into the Banaras Hindu University, the establishment of the Boys' Scouts Association, and the National University of Adyar near Madras in 1918, of which Rabindranath Tagore was designated the Chancellor. She preferred the constitutional method for Swaraj and did not like Gandhi's non - cooperation and passive resistance movements. Hence with the emergence of the latter after 1915, she was gradually eclipsed. Nevertheless, during the first two decades of this century she became one of the greatest personalities in the Indian History.

"Black Years"

The years 1918 and 1919 were "black years" for India. The end of World War I in December 1918 had brought high expectations that India's great contributions in men, money and materials to the conflicts' successful conclusion for the British and her allies would soften the British Government to feel a sense of moral obligation to grant a real and substantial measure of self-government to the Indian people, along the lines enjoyed then by other automous 'dominions' like Australia, Canada and New Zealand. And these expectations were further heightened by the success of the great revolution of the Russian people against the autocratic Czarist regime in 1917, and finally the declaration in January

1918 by then President of the United States of America that "the war was being waged to relieve people (everywhere) from unbridled autocracy". Many people in India took it to be a genuine statement, appreciated the spirit behind it and expected that USA's closest ally Great Brtain would act up to it.

Constitutional Reforms in India

The British Government announced in August 1917, constitutional reform in India, known as the Montagu-Chelmsford Reforms, which later were confirmed by a special act of Parliament, the Government of India Act, 1919. It provided what was known as a "Dyarchical" form of Government at the provincial level. That is, a dual system of government of each province, of which a small part was given to the responsibility of elected representatives in a provincial legislative council, and the greater and more important portfolios, such as home and finance, were reserved to the provincial head, the Governor, and a group of his nominated ministers. The provincial legislative council had both elected and 'nominated' seats. The latter one were to be selected by the Governor, while the former (elected) through limited election on the basis of part 'general' and part 'separate' constituencies delimited on the religious and communal basis as well as of various commercial and other special interests. In all matters of legislation and administration, the Governor of a Province had the last say. In the Centre, a provision was made for a bicameral legislature -- a lower house called the Legislative Assembly and an upper house, the Council of State. Both houses were to consist as in the provinces, in part of members elected along communal and separate lines, and part nominated. There was no transfer of power at the Centre. The Governor-General in Council was responsible for the governance there to the British Parliament through the Secretary of State (for India).

These reforms naturally completely failed to satisfy India's expectations. That the British Government had then no intention of transferring real legislative and administrative powers to the Indian people, were shown by two notorious actions of the then Indian Government. First, the enactment of a new "black" legislation called the "Rowlatt Act" passed in early 1919 by the (Indian) Imperial Legislative Council. The title of the legislation was derived from that of a committee headed by one Mr. Rowlatt appointed by then Government of India on 10 December 1917, and including two High Court judges -- one British and one Indian, and two non-officials -- also one British and one Indian. The full title of the Act was 'The Anarchical and Revolutionary Crimes Act (1919)'. It was meant to reinforce the draconian powers of arrest, detention and other oppressive measures that the Government of India had introduced under the 'Defence of India Act' during the war, to serve then in a peacetime situation after the war, with a view to checking what the Government called "terrorist activities". The main purpose was to dispense with as much of the ordinary procedure of law as possible for the trial of a person accused of 'crime'[37] and to secure his speedy conviction". Amongst its provisions were : (a) a special court from whose judgment there could be no appeal, (b) trial in camera, and (c) consideration of evidence not admissible by the law of evidence. The provincial governments were also given extraordinary powers of search, arrest and demand of security.[38]

The Rowlatt Act was passed in spite of vehement opposition from the Indian Members of the then Imperial Legislative Council at Delhi, the press and the leading public including Mahommad Ali Jinnah who, as noted above, was then a member of the Congress. The Congress itself, then under Gandhi's leadership, declared an all-India *hartal* or stoppage of activities on 8 April 1919. The response to his call from all over the country was unprecedented. Almost all parts of the country joined. And to then India Government, as Mehra has observed[39] "two important portents of danger" became evident -- "the fraternization of Hindus and Moslems and the general excitement among the masses". It resulted in a rash of violence involving public and private property and even against certain personnel including those of the British community, especially in Punjab but also in Gujarat and Bengal (Calcutta). Gandhi, wedded to the principle of 'non-violence', which was still not very clearly understood in India, was "deeply upset", and "admitted that in launching his movement without prior preparation he had committed a 'mistake of Himalayan magnitude' and announced his decision to suspend passive resistance".[40]

It was a momentous decision not only for Gandhi but also for the whole of India, and may be said to have been a turning point in the history of freedom struggle for India. Because, had it been any other revolutionary leader like de Valera (of Ireland), Lenin (of Russia), Kemal Ataturk (Turkey) or Mao-tse-Tung (of China) he would in all probability have assumed control of the events and given an active leadership and direction towards a greater and a more widespread upsurge involving people of all the major communities -- Sikhs, Moslems and Hindus, at a time when both the British Government at home (Britain) as well as the Indian Government were just recovering from the effects of a prolonged and devastating war. But Gandhi must have his reasons. As he himself has said on so many occasions before and after this event, Means was as important to him as the End, and the great mission of his life was Truth and Non-Violence. Everything else was secondary to him.[41]

But neither the British nor the Indian Government was then in a mood to appreciate Gandhi's stand or to trust him in his abiding faith in non-violence. They were determined, first, to take the revenge of humiliation, meted out to some of their fellowmen by the Indian masses in the wake of the latters' "smouldering discontent" against what appeared to be a highly oppressive and unjust legislation, and, second, to give Indian people a lesson as to the might of the Imperial rulers. So especially in Punjab, which has always been in the forefront of India's struggle for freedom against foreign rulers, and had suffered most from the war, for which the peoples' discontent rose to the highest, the civil government was handed over for administration by the military authorities under one Brigadier - General Dyer. They chose one of the holiest cities of India, Amritsar, the site of the most scared temple of the Sikhs -- the Golden Temple, and the occasion was a mass meeting of protest against the oppressive Rowlatt Act by the general people of the city. The place was a small abandoned garden called Jallianwala Bagh surrounded on three sides by tall buildings and on one side a low wall with only a few narrow exits and entrances. There collected nearly 20,000 people -- men, women and children to hold the protest meeting on 13 April 1919 (now a memorable day in Indian and world history). As the people assembled, Dyer came with his soldiers and ordered them to fire at the crowd without any advance warning. Altogether 1,650 rounds of bullets were fired for 10 to 15 minutes until all the ammunitions were finished. Hundreds died, thousands were wounded. Among them many were women and children.

The whole country was aghast to hear the news of this terrible massacre of unarmed men. There were immediate protest meetings all over India and the day ever since became a memorable day of remembrance for a 'mini holocaust', by the entire Indian people. The passive agitation in India and the enormity of the 'crime' as details of the tragedy came out, later moved even the British Parliament. Dyer had to make a statement to the House of Commons on 3 July 1920 in which he observed by way of justifying his action in Jallianwala Bagh that it "was not a fortuitous gathering but a mob which was there with the express intent to challenge Government or defy me; I knew if I shirked the challenge .... there would infallibly follow a general mob movement which would destroy all the European population."[42]

It is also worthwhile to note here the other official versions as to the situation then prevailing in India in the aftermath of World War I and the passing of the Rawlatt Act of 1919. The Hunter Enquiry Committee which was appointed in October 1919 by the then Governor - General, Reading, with British Government's approval, with 5 British and 3 Indian members under the Chairmanship of Lord Hunder, in one of its big report observed that the Government viewed the situation in 1919 was critical; the authority was nervous and was prone to run for the nearest shelter; it felt 'it was not competent enough to cope with the situation'. The British believed 'they were sitting on the edge of an abyss. They were concerned that the story of 1857 was going to be repeated'. "There was information about the wreckage of railway line, the burning of mills' stores, of a great railway strike, the shifting loyalty of Indian troops, Gandhi's plans to overthrow the government and the impending Afghan attack on India. Furthermore, available evidence led them to believe that the army, which held India, was in such a condition of dissatisfaction, that, if Gandhi's satyagraha movement fell into the hands of violent agitators the country would be plunged into a revolution and would no more be amenable to control"[43]

Some Indian writers have observed that the statements in the Hunter Committee Report were an exaggerated view of the situation to justify. Dyer's action. It might be so, but basically they were true. Because, as we have said earlier, the debilitating effect on the British as well as on the India Government, of the War and the contemporary upsurge of revolutionary activities within India during the war, and, furthermore, the explosive discontent that erupted following what many in India regarded as the British betrayal by giving mere shadows of self-rule in the form of Montagu-Chelmsford Reforms, and even that hedged in with the suppressive measures of the Rowlatt Act, must have upset the nerves of the two governments.

Be that as it may, the Jallianwala Bagh massacre may be said to have put British rule in India on a reverse gear. As Gandhi later said "Plassey (in Bengal) laid the foundation of the British Empire (in India); Amritsar (in Punjab) has shaken it". Tagore observed later that what happened at the Bagh was "a monstrous progeny of a monstrous war". And even the celebrated British historian Edward Thomson observed that the massacre ended the British connexion with India. As for its *Impact on India,* it has been well summed up as follows : "It gave a tremendous impetus to the freedom struggle. From now on political activity increased rapidly and thousands of hitherto uncommitted people were drawn into the vortex of political activity. It induced a reappraisal of Congress policies[44] and marked the commencement of the Non-Cooperation Movement."[45]

Montagu - Chelmsford (Constitutional) Reforms

Finally, it led to the emergence of Gandhi as a leading star in the Indian political sky.

But Gandhi, true to his self, in spite of the developments following the Rowlatt Act including the atrocities committed by Dyer and his men in Jallianwala Bagh, had openly welcomed the Montagu-Chelmsford Reforms, knowing fully well that they fell far short of his own and the Indian peoples' legitimate expectations. He wrote in December in his weekly paper *Young India* : The Reforms Act coupled with the Royal Proclamation announcing the assent of the Government of India Act, 1919, "is an earnest of the intention of the British people to do justice to India and it ought to remove suspicion on that score .... Our duty therefore is not to subject the Reforms to carping criticism but to settle down quietly to work so as to make them a success".[46] Gandhi did not confine his views to writing only, but also succeeded in persuading the annual session of the Indian National Congress in its December 1919 session in the city of Amritsar itself in passing a resolution in favour of working the new reforms, against the opposition especially of the Bengal leaders including Chittaranjan Das,[47] Bipin Chandra Pal and others.

Whether this was merely a tactical retreat on Gandhi's part or a genuine attempt to test the British sincerity of ultimately granting the Indian people real self-government, it is difficult to say. But he must have soon realized that the much heralded Montagu-Chelmsford Reforms gave very little substantive powers to the people of India. First, the manner of election both to provincial legislatures and the Central Legislative Assembly and Council of State was greatly vitiated and perverted by splitting the electoral constituencies on lines of religion and special interests, like Muslims, Indian Christians, Anglo-Indians and Europeans, etc. secondly, a large number of members of the provincial legislatures were nominated by the Governor -- among which there were government officials, and representatives of aborigines, backward tracts, depressed classes, labour, landlords, universities, commerce and industry. The same principle was followed with respect to the central legislatures -- the Council of State and the Central Legislative Assembly. In addition their members had to have higher property qualifications. Thus, both the provincial assemblies as well as the central legislatures had little impact on true legislative process. They were clever instruments in the hands of foreign rulers to keep the country perpetually split and divided between communities and interests and to neutralize themselves by conflicts and bickerings amongst them.

Thirdly while in the Centre there was no actual transfer of power to the legislatures, either on the budget or any other substantive matters, in the provinces, special powers vested in the governor severely limited the power of the people in law making and voting the budget even with regard to the "transferred subjects". Too many special powers were given to the Governor to work a truly democratic government.

Gandhi as the Supremo of the Congress

Because of these serious drawbacks of the new constitution proclaimed by the British Government, people in India became skeptical about its working. Many of them felt that it was another clever move by the British of 'one step forward, two steps backward'. It was an award of a semblance of part - responsible government, diluted with a more insidious and extended system of 'separate electorate' and the reservation of real power of lawmaking and administration in the representatives of the British Government in the centre as well as in the provinces. Even Gandhi felt it so strongly that around the middle of 1920 he was thinking already of non-cooperation with the Indian Government in the implementation of the reforms. He was however doubtful if it would be possible for him to effect such a radical change in the position of the then Congress. So, as many think, he tried to ally himself with the leading Moslems then agitating for what was then known as Khilafat Movement.[48] He thus tried to combine the widespread anti-British feeling prevailing then among large sections of the Moslem population of India with that in the Congress, excluding the Moderates like Surendra Nath Banerjee, Pandit Madan Mohan Malviya (1861-1946) and Mrs. Annie Besant.

Tilak, then the most powerful leader of the Extremist or Nationalist wing of the Indian National Congress, died in early 1920. So Gandhi, with his plan for launching a country wide non-violent non-cooperation action, became the "logical successor" to him. [49] Inspite of Gandhi's abortive Satyagraha in the wake of Rowlatt Act, his new action plan (see below) offered an opportunity to the people to ventilate their suppressed wrath and feeling of grave injustice and autocratic authority of the British rulers in India. So at a special session of the Congress in Calcutta in September 1920 he presented his plan of "a policy of progressive non-violent non-cooperation" which would "begin with the renunciation of title bestowed by the Government and with the triple boycott of legislatures, law courts and educational institutions, and would end in non-payment of taxes." The resolution was adopted by the Calcutta Congress held under the presidency of Lala Lajpat Rai of Punjab with a slender majority of votes.[50] The Bengal leaders Chittaranjan Das and Bipin Chandra Pal did not vote as they did not agree with the boycott of legislature. But the Congress leader from the Midnapore District, Birendra Nath Sasmal, supported the resolution wholeheartedly.

However, three months later, in December 1920, at the annual session of the Congress held at Nagpur, the same resolution on "progressive non-cooperation" including the boycott the legislatures, of law courts and educational institutions, was placed. Das who came again for opposing it, but had an understanding with Gandhi and changed position. In fact, he himself moved the resolution which was seconded by Lala Lajpat Rai. Thus Gandhi won the support of two top so-called "Extremist" leaders and the resolution was passed almost unanimously, but still with the opposition from Malaviya, Mrs. Besant, Jinnah and Pal.

Results of Nagpur Congress (1920)

It established Congress as a more unified and homogeneous political party than any time since its establishment in 1885. Although it still had its moderate and more "extreme" wings still they all accepted Gandhi as the supreme commander and agreed to work out the action plan laid down by him. (ii) Jawaharlal Nehru (1889-1964), who was then young and 'came under the powerful impact of Gandhi' after the Jallianwala Bagh massacre in 1919, later described Gandhi as "the permanent super president of the Congress". (iii) It redefined the goal of the Congress from "self - Government within the British Empire" (which many Congressmen did not like to "Swaraj", which literally meant Self-Rule. And it was left to individual Congressman to define the term in his own way. Gandhi himself defined to mean "Self-Government within the Empire, if possible - and outside, if necessary".[51] (iv) There was a change in the constitution of the Congress organization. This has been well summed up by Subhas as follows:

> Before the Nagpur Congress the machinery of the Congress had been a loose one. There were branches only in the big cities and throughout the year no work was done according to a systematic plan. At Nagpur, it was decided to reorganize the the Congress on a country wide basis. The smallest unit would be the Village Congress Committee. Several such Committees would be combined to form a Union Congress Committee. Then there would be formed in succession--sub-divisional (also called Taluka or Tahsil), district, provincial and All-India Congress Committees. The All-India Congress Committee would be a body of about 350 members consisting of representatives from the different provinces. The Committee would elect a Working Committee of 15 members which would be the Supreme Executive of the Congress for the whole country. Further, the provinces were reorganized on linguistic basis ... The basis of the new (1920) Congress constitution was of a democratic and parliamentary character".[52]

(v) It made an important change in the means to be followed to attain Swaraj. In place of what was formerly "constitutional means", in future it would be "all peaceful and legitimate means". This was mainly to enable the Congress to resort to non-cooperation, which could be regarded "unconstitutional".

"Regarding both the goal and the means", as Subhas Chandra Bose has observed, "the decision of the Nagpur Congress represented the golden mean between the views of the Right-Wingers like Pandit Malavia and Jinnah, and the youthful Left-Wingers who swamped the Congress for the first time in 1920. The latter desired the goal of the Congress to be complete independence to be attained by all possible means. It was Mr. Gandhi, however, who by virtue of his tremendous influence and popularity was able to keep the Left-Wingers at bay.''[53]

As for the Nagpur Congress of 1920, it also laid down certain definite plans of action, such as the revival of hand-spinning or 'charka', that is, ancient hand-spinning and hand-weaving, and removal of untouchability among the Hindus.

For all these reasons, Subhas Chandra Bose observed about the significance of the Congress and Gandhi :

> The Nagpur Congress, like the Calcutta Congress (also in 1920 but earlier) was a great triumph for Mr. Gandhi. It was his constitution and his plan of work that was adopted there. The gathering was an unprecedented one, twenty thousand people attending the Congress. Public enthusiasm was at a high pitch and among the distinguished visitors were two labour members of the British Parliament, Mr. Ben Spoor and Col. Wedgwood... It (the Congress) stood for a complete break with the Moderates, but it did not represent a complete victory for the Extremists. The latter ... would have to work for many years before they could bring the Congress round to their point of views.''[54]

Gandhi's plans were not altogether new, since in Bengal, in 1905, to fight the partition, the people had already resorted to the boycott of British goods well as of the state-owned educational institutions. Simultaneously attempts were made to revive national industries and establish national schools and colleges, ''free from the the state interference of everykind''. Also leading lawyers like Bipin Chandra Pal had refused to give evidence before British law courts ''on the ground that they refused to recognise their jurisdiction''. And even with regard to 'non-cooperation', much earlier, around 1850-1860, the indigo cultivator of Bengal who had been terribly oppressed and exploited by the then indigo planters, mostly British, rose in revolt, refused to pay their unjust and exorbitant due levied on them by the planters, and, stopped, cultivating indigo. They actually rose in revolt and even committed certain acts of violence against the planters. The public and the Press including Harish Chandra Mukherjee (1824-1861) of the *Hindu Patriot* and Sishir Kumar Ghose (1840-1911), founder-editor of the *Amrita Bazar Patrika*, took up their cause. And a Bengali drama called ''Nil Darpan Natakam'' by Dinabandhu Mitra (1830-1873) about life on an Indian plantation, and its translation into English by the poet Michael Madhusudhan Dut published by a Christian missionary. Reverend James Long (1814-8' also went greatly in favour of the indigo cultivators. So in the e Government of Bengal was forced to pass a law (Act VI of 1862) a abolish the oppressive system of indigo plantation.[55] This was indeec clear example of what the people could do to free themselves from t oppression of the foreign rulers by their own means.[56]

Russian writer Leo Tolstoy's book *Kingdom of God is Within Yc* greatly influenced Gandhi. Similarly another book by the well-know American writer Thoreau *Civil Disobedience,* which Gandhi had alrea read earlier in South Africa, had also a profound influence on him.

The Nagpur Session produced a number of important results fo the future of India :

(1) The Congress became a real national party encompassing mos patriotic and forward looking peoples of the time, and thus filled great vacum in the history of the freedom struggle of India, espe cially after the failure of the second phase of the Revolutionaries concerted efforts during the 1914-1918 War. Only the so-callec Moderates opted to remain aloof. But many of the Revolutionary leaders and workers found its objective, plan of action acceptable and workable, so they joined it, though most retaining their separate bases.

(2) Subhas Chandra Bose has observed that Gandhi translated the teachings of Christ and the ideas of Tolstoy and Thoreau into actual practices and demonstrated that it was possible to fight for liberty without resorting to violence.[57]

(3) Gandhi, through his immense sacrifice, innate sincerity of purpose, hard work, strict discipline and a high sense of moral values, humility combined with firmness and his almost unending tactical ability, emerged, as Subhas has said "as the virtual Dictator of the Congress". Since 1920 his leadership had been a great unifying factor for the country until his sudden death almost twenty eight years later.

But one of the greatest deficiency in the strength and organization of the Congress was that it failed to draw in its ranks any substantial section of the Moslem community, although there were a few respected top leaders including Jinnah (until 1920). It was why Gandhi decided to take up the cause of the "Khilafat Movement" and thus won over the confidence of its two leaders -- Ali brothers -- Shaukat Ali and Mahommad Ali. That movement also was at its peak in 1920. But Kamal Ataturk's revolution against the Turkish Sultan and the abolition of his Khalifat, gradually led to the dying of the movement.

Thus the first two years after the end of World War I --1919 and 1920 - were very eventful in the history of India. The hope and prospects of peace and freedom were marred by new repressive measures by the Government to destroy both and by the massacre at Jallianwala Bagh, on the one hand, and by a renewed will and determination of the people to enlarge the scope of the struggle for freedom by bringing the masses under the leadership of a now most charismatic leader, Gandhi.

Notes and References

1. The great Aga Khan lived long enough to see this as he has admitted in his *Memoirs* : "Minto's acceptance of our demands was the foundation of all future constitutional proposals made for India by successive British Governments and its final, inevitable consequence was the partition of India and the emergence of Pakistan" (see P. Mehra, *op.cit.*, pp.16-17).
2. *Ibid*, p.17.
3. Which he first started in 1873, with a two-storeyed brick house on a wide barren, vacant land. Rabindranath first went there in the same year with his father at the age of 11.
4. It is now the national anthem of Bengla Desh, the old eastern part of Bengal which during the 1947 partition was made the Eastern Wing of Pakistan and then, as a result of their 1971 war against Pakistan, became an independent country with Bengalee as the official language.
5. This writer had an opportunity of coming into close contact with this great scholar, humanist and internationalist in later years.
6. For details see *Rabindra Jiban Katha* (Life of Rabindranath) in Bengali by Prabhat Mukherjee (Ananda Publishers, Calcutta).
7. In 1940 he was invited by the University of Oxford, England, to give the prestigious Hibbert lecture which was later published as the *Religion of Man* and the University conferred on him the Honorary D.Litt. Degree at a special convocation.
8. Author of the great Indian epic *Mahabharata*.
9. Author of the second great Indian epic *Ramayana*.
10. The celebrated poet and one of the "Nine Jewels" in the court of the ancient Indian Emperor Vikramaditya II of 4th century, A.D.
11. Like Tagore, Nazrul is also said to have composed more than 2000 songs of diverse themes and tunes. Cf. *Nazrul-Geeti* in one volume (in Bengali).
12. His first set of patriotic song, appropriately named as *Agni Bina* (Fiery Flute) in Bengali, was published in 1912.
13. See *History of Midnapore* (in Bengali) by late Jogesh Chandra Bose (see Brothers, Calcutta).

14. Later changed to Contai High School which is the oldest and the leading secondary school in Contai subdivision today.
15. "A Retrospect on One Hundred Years of Contai High School" (A Centenary Celebration brochure of the School, held in 1957), p.3.
16. The S.D.O.s of Contai have long since been the ex-officio Presidents of the Managing Committee of the School.
17. This family later became close friends of our family and one of their sons, Phani Kundu became my close associate in our fight for India's independence in the thirties.
18. Who was also a political detainee in his student days first in the thirties and then again during World War II. After independence he became a Senior Professor of Economics of City College, Calcutta.
19. When the great novelist Bankim Chandra Chatterjee was in Contai as an S.D.O. he used to live in a house there, so in 1977 my four brothers gave away our entire ancestral land there to form a "Bankim Memorial Trust".
20. *Encyclopaedia Britannica* (1959), vol. 23. p. 775.
21. Indeed, it has been said by authoritative sources that Britain fought and won the two Great Wars of this century, especially for the extensive theatres of war east of the Suez (canal), depending largely on the vast potential manpower and material resources of India undivided. With regard especially to World War I, a somewhat more detailed breakdown of India's material and financial contribution to Allied War efforts during 1914 - 18 war, has been given by the notable historian R.C. Majumdar and his two colleagues as follows : India's material contributions included huge quantities of arms and ammunitions, food and agricultural as well as industrial raw materials, and she made "financial contributions to her utmost capacity". For example, "although her troops were employed outside her borders, she paid the normal expenditure for their maintenance, which varied between 20-30 million (Pound Sterling) *per annum*. She also paid the cost of an additional force of 300,000 men and made a *free gift of 100.00 million to the British Government*. See Majumdar, R.C., Raychoudhuri, H.C. and Datta, Kalikinkar : *An Advanced History of India* (Macmillian & Co.) Second Ed., 1958 p.930.
22. Many of them held vast tracts of practically virgin lands across the Bav of Bengal in the Sunderbans area.
23. For more details about Rashbehari Bose, see *Bharate Sashastra Biplab* ('Armed Revolution in India') in Bengali language by B. Rakshit Ray (Rabindra Library, Calcutta, pp. 120-129.
24. Amirchand, Abodhbehari, Balmukund and Basanta Biswas, all close associates of Rashbehari in north India. Balmukunda was married. His wife on hearing the death of her husband fasted herself unto death. *Ibid*, p.130.
25. *Ibid*, p.130.
26. For details, see *Banglay Biplabbad* (Revolutionism in Bengal) (A Mukherjee & Co., Calcutta) 4th ed. 1969. A big trial for conspiracy was held in April 1915 before a Special Tribunal inside Lahore Central Jail in April 1915 against 80 "accused" and the judgment was delivered in September. 24 were sentenced to death and 26 transportation for life. On Appeal, of the 24 sentenced to death, 17 were given sentence of transportation and seven's death sentence was retained. They were hanged on 17 November 1915 in Lahore Jail. They included 6 Sikhs and one Hindu B.G. Pingle, a close associate of Rashbehari.
27. That this was a wise decision is seen from the later events in which Rashbehari had played a crucial role from Japan in organizing first the well-known India League and, finally, to crown all his herculean efforts in the cause of India's independence, in his joining of hands with and giving active support to Subhas Chandra Bose when he

escaped from India during World War II and, in cooperation with Germany and Japan, established an independent Indian Government abroad, the now famous Azad Hind Government with the help of a "free" army "Azad Hind Fouz" consisting of high officials as well as jawans of the British Indian army who surrendered to Germany and Japan during the war in different theatres of war, and also including many civilians living abroad at that time.

28. See B.K. Das, *op.cit.* p.220.
29. He was born on 2 October 1869 at Porbandar, coastal town of Gujarat. His father was the Chief Minister of the then Rajkot State. After having early education there he went to England at the age of 18, to qualify for the Bar. He returned to India in 1893 but left for South Africa to practice law but faced there strong racial prejudices institutionalized through various means. He fought against them for two decades (1894-1914) and then returned to India again.
30. An unfortunate matter which still prevails in a far more vile and vicious form even today. Gandhi had realized the euphemism of the term "white". For "white" technically means colourless, that is, absence of blood. No man can live without blood. And blood is red, so all men are intrinsically of red hue. But red colour is mostly marked in the case of people who reside in or nearer the northern and southern poles. As one moves to equator people are found to become of mixed hue and darker. This difference of skin is the result of the differences of the components of the sun and air, and have nothing to do with the inner attributes of a man. Yet so much fuss has been made, so many strifes have been and are still being caused, and sufferings inflicted on men of one community upon another in the name of an utterly fictitious sense of superiority of one colour over the other.
31. He was a "worthy disciple" of another great Maharashtrian Mahadeo Govind Ranade (1842-1901) who was widely accepted "as the father of the renaissance" in western India. He was a brilliant man of varied interests--an economist, politician, historian and a social reformer. Officially, he rose to be a judge of the Bombay High Court. He was a man of "great massive intellect" as Gokhale himself has said, and "an earnest and dauntless spirit". He was called a "modern Rishi". Mehra : *op.cit.* p.599.
32. Quoted from P. Mehra : *A Dictionary of Modern Indian History* 1707-1947. *op.cit.*, p.274.
33. *Ibid,* p.274.
34. The extremist section was led by Tilak and included Mrs. Annie Besant (an Irish lady who had joined the Indian National Congress in its early days) and, ironically, as it seems today, even Mahommed Ali Jinnah who was still then with the Congress.
35. S.C. Bose : *Indian Struggle* (Thacker, Spink & Co., Calcutta) 1948, p.40. For explanation of the term 'separate electorate' see later.
36. Also an Auxilliary of the Home Rule Leage for India had been formed in England in 1915 in aid of the Indian national movement. see P. Mehra, *op.cit.*, p. 310.
37. The term 'crime' was not defined, and all activities included in the schedule to the Act could be called 'anarchical'.
38. Simultaneously there were amendments to the Penal Code (by another Bill in 1919) providing for greater and stricter control of the press.
39. *Ibid,* p.621.
40. Mehra : *op.cit.*, p.621.
41. It must be mentioned that Gandhi was a *Vaishnava* by birth and conviction and was deeply imbibed with the gospel of love propagated by the legendary God-cum-here Krishna of India's ancient literature, and revived by the great lover-saint Chaitanya of Bengal (1485-1533).
42. Quoted by Mehra, *op.cit.*, p.356.

43. Quoted by Mehra, *op.cit.*, pp. 356-357.
44. Even by Gandhi.
45. Mehra, *op. cit.*
46. Subhas Chandra Bose : *Indian Struggle, op.cit.*, p.57.
47. Das began his professional career as a barrister in early years of this century and achieved great fame in the Alipore Bomb case in 1908 by defending and securing the release of Aurobindo Ghose. Earlier, during the Bengal partition he had been a co-worker of Aurobindo, Surendra nath Banerjee and Bipin Chandra Pal. He was also associated with two leading nationalist journals at that time - *New India* and *Bandema-taram*. His active political life began in 1917 when he presided over the Bengal Provincial Conference in Calcutta where his address was considered as a landmark emphasising the importance of the Bengali culture. For his other activities see later.
48. Towards the end of the War (I) the British and other Allied powers planned to dismember the then Turkish empire which then included the Moslem holiest places in the Middle East, and deprive Turkish 'Sultan's right to be the leader and in control of those places and the *Khalifa* or the Head of the Islamic churches. The Indian Moslems rose in protest nd started a movement, called 'Khilafat Movement' under the leadership of then two famous Ali Brothers, Moulan Shaukat Ali and Maulana Mohammed Ali.
49. Indeed Tilak's death and the failure of the attempts of Indian Revolutionaries within and outside India during the war facilitated the rise of Gandhi as the undisputed political leader of India for nearly a quarter of a century -- from 1920 till his death in early 1948.
50. Out of 2,728 votes, 1,855 were in Gandhi's favour Cf. Bose, *op.cit.*, p.67.
51. Mehra - *op.cit.*, p.187.
52. Bose, S.C. : *op.cit.* p.68.
53 S.C. Bose, *ibid*, p.68.
54. Bose S.C.: *op.cit.*, p.70. Which to speak in respect, they never could do during Gandhi's life-time and even later, partly because the Congress itself adopted some of their views like the "socialist pattern of society" as a goal and therefore many of them joined the Congress as full members, and partly because they themselves "mellowed down" with age and change of the circumstances. Those who could not, left the Congress and formed or joined alternative parties.
55. Cf. Mehra, *op.cit.* pp. 346-348.
56. Indeed this was repeated later (in 1921) in another part of Bengal - the district of Midnapore - by the people refusing to pay Union Board taxes, which they considered as arbitrary. For further details, see later.
57. Bose : *op.cit.*, p.71.

CHAPTER 3

COLLEGIATE LIFE IN A CRUCIAL DECADE 1921-1930

Nationwide Non-Cooperation Movement

The third decade of this century--1921 is well-known in India as the year of launching of Gandhi's first *Satyagraha* or Non-cooperation Movement on a national level, throughout the then British India. Armed by the power and authority given at the Nagpur Congress, Gandhi gave a call to the country's educated intelligentsia to boycott legislatures, law courts, schools and colleges and other professional institutions, and to the masses not to cooperate with different government agencies. The response was enormous from all and there was a great enthusiasm for the movement.

The Congress legislators absented themselves from the 'dyarchic' form of legislature. Courts were boycotted by leading lawyers such as C.R. Das, Bipin Pal and Byomkesh Mitra in Bengal; Motilal Nehru in Uttar Pradesh; Vithalbhai Patel and Ballavbhai Patel (Patel Brothers) in Bombay; Dr Rajendra Prasad in Bihar; and C. Rajagopalachari, A. Ramaswami Iyenger, Satyamurthi Prakasam from the Madras. They all came and stood by Gandhi. Besides them, Shaukat Ali and Mahommed Ali (Ali Brothers) of Khilafat Movement; Maulana Abul Kalam Azad, a veteran Moslem scholar from Bengal; and Dr. Ansari of Delhi also responded to Gandhi's call.

Hundreds of lawyers from different provinces and district courts also gave up their legal practices and joined the movement. From

Midnapore, the lead was taken by Birendra Nath Sasmal, who was a leading barrister in Calcutta Bar and one of the top Congress leaders of Bengal. He was followed by a host of other lawyers from the district, such as, Manmatha Nath Das, Kishoripati Ray, Jawaharlal Adhikari, Umesh Chandra Bera and others. Among the professional classes, the lawyers played the most important part. Many among them not only gave up their practices for good but became important figures in the Congress for their whole lives. They formed a Congress Committee under the presidentship of Birendra Nath Sasmal.

Jawaharlal Nehru, who was then young and had returned from England in 1912 and has been practising at the Allahabad Bar, also responded to the call of Gandhi. Later in 1921, also Subhas Chandra Bose of Bengal, who had passed the Indian Civil Service in England in 1920, "but finding that it would be impossible to serve both masters at the same time--namely the British Government and my country", he resigned from his post in May 1921 and "hurried back to India with a view to taking my place in the national struggle that was then in full swing."[1] On returning to India the first thing he did was to meet Gandhi in Bombay, who after a short discussion, advised him to report to C.R. Das in Calcutta. Das became then already famous all over India, not only by giving up a very lucrative practice at the Calcutta Bar but being also the first to donate his big Calcutta House with all its valuable furniture to the people, having placed on "bonfire" all his foreign made clothes, in response to Gandhi's call to the nation for the boycott of foreign (particularly British) goods, especially cloth.

The third group to respond to Gandhi's call was the student community, particularly in Bengal. Thousands came out of their schools, colleges and the University and joined the Congress and helped actively in the movement of non-cooperation. They were deeply inspired by the message of the then fiery Bengal leader Bipin Chandra Pal: "Education may wait but Swaraj cannot."

Thus the first results of Gandhi's non-cooperation call to the nation showed a great success. As Subhas has said: "Throughout the country there was unparalleled enthusiasm. The 'triple boycott' (of legislatures, courts and educational institutions) had been fairly successful."[2] In addition, the boycott of foreign goods, especially British clothes, assumed a great magnitude. And simultaneously, to fill the vacuum caused by the stoppage of import of the Lancashire and Manchester fine cloth, indigenous cotton mills were started and the ancient Indian art of hand spinning by 'charka' and hand-weaving (of cloth) started. 'Khadi', the hand woven cloth, began to be produced in a large-scale all over India, and all Congress leaders and workers started to use them as constant wears. It soon became a sign of distinction. Thousands of sympathizers also donned Khadi clothing of diverse types.

Through large-scale use of 'Khadi' as well as the revival of cottage industries on a country-wide scale, Gandhi had hoped to achieve two important objectives: economic and political. They could help giving employment to masses of rural people who then lived in abject poverty, andthus wouldgive them a feeling of self-confidence and self-respect. At the same time they would, in due course, affect the then prosperosus cloth industries of Britain, particularly in Lancashire and Manchester.[3] and also other industries whose products had filled in the vast market of India. Gandhi had envisaged that the adverse impact on the British economy, of India's own efforts to have an extensive indigenous system of producing the essential goods, would force the British Government in India to take repressive measures against the Congress. This would further arouse mass awakening and mass protest against the British rule in India, which would ultimately force them to consider conceding greater autonomy or self-rule to its people.

Another aspect of the non-cooperation movement was a mass boycott of the use of narcotics and liquor. The object again was two-fold. First, their large-scale consumption--especially of indigenously produced opium and its derivatives and country-liquor--by the poor peasants and the workers was debilitating and demoralizing the addicted people, and so by their boycott, people would be persuaded to give up an obviously bad habit. Secondly, the Indian Government had levied substantial excise duties on the production and consumption of narcotics and liquor which gave them a sizeable revenue. So, through the boycott, the then Indian Government would be deprived of an important source of revenue.

Another important, activity was the simultaneous start of the anti-untouchability movement to remove one of the greatest weaknesses of the Indian society.

Thus, the non-cooperation movement, as a whole, caught up with the intelligentsia, as well as the masses of India on an unprecedented scale, though primarily amongst the Hindu community. This was, in a way natural, as the Hindus had formed an overwhelming majority, over 80 per cent of the total population of the country. However, the Congress had been started and had always remained a truly national organization representing, and with its doors open to, all the Indians regardless of their caste, creed or vocation. Hence, many among its top leaders came from other communities including the Moslems, Parsis, Sikhs and Christians. But no doubt more could have come from them, particularly form amongst the Moslem community and there could have been a greater participation from among the Moslem masses.

Khilafat Movement, 1921-22

Perhaps realizing this, Gandhi, as observed earlier, allied himself and made a common cause with the Khilafat Movement which was started at the end of World War I against the plan of the victorious Allied Powers including Great Britain to dismember the old Turkish Ottoman Empire (which had aligned with Germany during the War and had lost) and to abolish the institution of the Caliphate held by the Sultan. Caliph was the religious head of all Moslems all over the world. The plan was later affirmed and formalized in the Treaty of Sevres (1920) between the Allied Powers and Turkey. A large section of the Moslem community in India was greatly agitated over this plan and established a separate All India Khilafat Committee to protets againts the British rule in India especially for its policies towards the Moslems. They also adopted the technique of non-cooperation and demanded Swaraj, largely under the influence of Gandhi. In fact Gandhi and many top Hindu as well as Moslem leaders of the Congress participated at important Khilafat conferences and *vice versa,* like the Ali Brothers who joined the Congress. Both the Congress and the Khilafat Committee had agreed upon the triple purpose of non-cooperation, namely, redressal of the Punjab grievances, rectification of the Khilafat wrongs, and the establishment of swaraj or home rule.[4]

From mid 1920 to mid 1921 the combined movement of the two major organizations had assumed a great proportion and there was a widespread feeling of Hindu-Moslem Unity. Which became a matter of serious concern for the British Government of India. Hence they put most of the top leaders of both the Congress and the Khilafat movement under arrest, tried them in court and sent to jail. But Gandhi himself was spared (until 1922). The Government of India was so concerned that they sent special emissaries to Gandhi with some proposals for new arrangements expand to be made for further constitutional advance for India in return for a suspension of the non-cooperation movement by the Congress. Gandhi however did not consider the terms satisfactory and therefore did not agree.

But in Turkey an important event happened. In 1922 the nationalists under their great leader Kemal Ataturk rose in revolt against the Sultan, abolished the monarchy with all its temporal and religious powers, and had established a modern, progressive, democratic and secular state. They established a separate Caliph shorn of all temporal authority. Even this was finally abolished in 1924. This deprived the Khilafat movement in India of its real base, so its followers and members, a majority of whom had joined it not so much for the sake of the achievement of nationalist aspirations in India (like the Congress) as to uphold what they believed the rights of the Moslems of the world, found themselves lost. Many gave up altogether and many others joined the All-India Moslem League which had been established as early as 1906.[5] Only a few came to the Congress. This ultimately proved a great set-back for the Congress and especially to Gandhi in his efforts to bring Hindu-Moslem unity and to offer a joint front in the fight for Swaraj against the British rule.

No-Tax Campaign in Midnapore, 1921

The non-cooperation movement, jointly conducted by the Congress and the Khilafat organizers under the combined leadership of Gandhi and Ali Brothers, was at its peak and the people of Midnapore were also deeply involved in it. An altogether new and even more radical movement was launched by the people of Midnapore district under the leadership of Birendra Nath Sasmal. It involved non-payment of taxes imposed in 1921 in the villages by the newly established Union Boards under a new law, Village Self-Government Act of 1919, passed in Bengal. The object of the Act was to introduce a measure of local government by the village people through the Union Boards. Sasmal and other leading people of Midnapore district, and particularly of Contai and Tamluk sub-divisions, felt that it would lead to increase in the local tax levied on each family, known as 'chowkidari tax' or "village watchman's tax". It was estimated that the tax would be increased seven-fold without giving in return any real power of autonomy or self-government to the people. On the other hand, it would affect the traditional village autonomy, which people still enjoyed, by too much interference by the local agents of the Government in matters of village management and administration.[6] About 227 Union Boards were established in the district (Midnapore) in April 1921, of which the first was in Contai. This immediately created a great stir among the people of Contai with series of protest meetings, demonstrations, etc. in which, besides Sasmal, many other leading figures in and outside the local Congress, especially the students, played an active role. Sasmal himself launched the actual action by refusing to pay taxes levied on him, and he was soon followed by multitudes of others throughout the sub-division. The movement soon spread through the whole district. Utmost repressive measures were taken by the District authorities to suppress the movement by way of 'forcible seizure of property, harassment and prosecution of the villagers, intimidation by military police and by soliders'. This continued throughout the year 1921, but the people of the Midnapore stood firm and absolutely unbending. So ultimately the Government of Bengal gave in and withdrew the Act and abolished all the Union Boards by 1 March 1922.[7]

This no-tax campaign of Midnapore, had been a spontaneous reaction of the people of the district. It had been thought of, planned and executed under the initiative and leadership of B.N. Sasmal independently of the Non-Cooperation movement launched by Gandhi and the Congress. But it had been unanimously approved by the Midnapore District and Contai branches of the Congress. And as B.K. Das has said in his monumental work,[8] the spirit of defiance and the courage to bear severe repression by the agents of the then Government of Bengal, as well as the technique of non-violence used in attaining a political objective, though of limited dimension, were greatly influenced by the doctrines and policies of Gandhi, adopted by the country in 1921 for the much wider objective of attaining country's Swaraj. Nevertheless, the Midnapore movement became known all-over India and earned a great credit for its leader and the entire people. Writing about it in his famous book *Indian Struggle* in 1934, Subhas Chandra Bose, observed: "The success of this no-tax campaign gave considerable strength and self-confidence to the people of Midnapore and popularity to their leader, Mr. B.N. Sasmal".[9] It may be added that this strength and self-confidence stood them in good stead in later years when much bigger fights were launched under the initiative and leadership of Gandhi in 1930-1931 and, finally, in 1942.

To calm down Gandhi's influence on the Indian people, the British Government arranged a visit by the Prince of Wales, the eldest son of the then British King and Emperor George V on 17 November 1921. But his visit too was boycotted by the people everywhere, including Calcutta, on the advice of Gandhi.

The year 1921 was thus a most eventful one in India's history of long struggle to gain independence from the foreign rule. Before launching his mass movement of non-cooperation and boycott Gandhi had been so hopeful of its results that he predicted the attainment of Swaraj or home rule by the end of the year. Indeed because of the great success of the joint massive efforts by both the Hindu and Moslem communities, forming over 90 per cent of the total population of India, under the leadership of the Congress and the Khilafat movement, many people were led to believe that it would be possible to realize, at least in a great way, Gandhi's dream.

However, the year 1921 came to a close without any tangible result toward getting 'swaraj'. There was no positive sign of any constructive movement on the part of the British Government. On the other hand most of the top leaders of the Congress all-over India were put in jails, including C.R. Das and Subhas Chandra Bose in Bengal. So the energy and spirit of the masses showed signs of exhaustion. This was aggravated by an unexpected external situation, namely, the Kemalist upsurge in Turkey and the overthrow, as earlier described, of the Sultan with all his temporal and spiritual powers. This put a sharp damper to the majority in the Moslem community to continue to fight against the British in India.

Suspension of Civil Disobedience Movement, 1922

Gandhi had clearly sensed this and tried to apply his final weapon in his strategy of fight against the British rule, namely, the non-payment of taxes on a massive scale throughout India to severely weaken its financial strength. This created a renewed excitement all over India. The first no-tax campaign under Gandhi's direction was to start in Bardoli Subdivision in Gujarat, then a part of the Bombay province. And the stage was set for a massive campaign all-over India' including Bengal. But suddenly, on 4 February 1922, came the news of outbreak of some violence in a village--called Chauri-Chaura in the then United Provinces, in which the exasperated masses set fire to the police-station and killed some policemen. As soon as Gandhi heard the news he was distressed, as it went against his basic principle of non-violence and, with the approval of the Congress Working Committee, he decided to suspend the entire civil disobedience movement throughout India for an indefinite period.

This was a great disappointment for the country including the top leaders like C.R. Das, Motilal Nehru and Lala Lajpat Rai. Subhas Chandra Bose has thus summed up the situation: "The situation in the country was exceedingly favourable for the success of the civil disobedience campaign. To sound the order of retreat just when public enthusiasm was reaching the boiling point was nothing short of a national calamity".[10] It may be noted that it was second such retreat ordered by Gandhi. The earlier one, as noted before, was when the protests and demonstrations by the people of India against the Government of India's oppressive Rowlatt Act in 1919 had resulted in certain violent incidents in several places of Punjab and elsewhere.

This makes it relevant to note Chitta Ranjan Das's views about "the virtues and failings" of Gandhi's leadership, as quoted by Subhas: "According to him, the Mahatma opens a campaign in a brilliant fashion; he works it up with unerring skill; he moves from success to success till he reaches the zenith of his campaign--but after that he loses his nerve and begins to falter".[11] How far this appraisal of Gandhi's leadership in the earlier stages of his non-violent freedom movement, is true can be judged only in context of his even far greater responsibilities in the subsequent much bigger struggles of the nineteen-thirties and forties, at a future date when the still prevailing red glow in the Indian sky of political events and sentiments, following the death of the great departed leader, become somewhat dimmer. But, notwithstanding what many among his contemporaries as well as his immediate successor generations might think of as his "failings", especially as a political leader, Gandhi's great contributions to the political, social and even economic thinking and activities of the Indian people made a tremendous impact whose effect will last for generations to come, provided they can be interpreted and applied in their true spirit and not either idolized too much or denigrated in the extreme, and, finally, be suitably adapted to the fast developing political social and economic scenarios of the current and future era of India.

Gandhi's arrest and historic trial, March 1922

However, with Chauri Chaura, ended the second stage of Gandhian non-violent struggle for freedom. And he paused for a respite, to prepare the country through various constructive activities, such as spinning and weaving 'Khadi', Hindu-Moslem unity, prohibition of usage of liquor and village upliftment. But, while advising the Congress and Gandhi's own followers to engage themselves in constructive activities, he himself tried to keep up their spirit of revolt by writing in his weekly paper, *Young India*. In early 1922, he wrote some articles which, to use Subhas's terms, were "the finest he has written and which will rank for all time among his inspired writings", which the Government held to be seditious. And after some hesitation Gandhi was arrested on 10 March, 1922 in Ahmedabad and put on trial and sentenced to 6 years' imprisonment on charges of bringing or creating "disaffection to his Majesty's Government, established by law in British India." It is worth mentioning that both the Government prosecutor Sir J.T.Strangman, Advocate General, and the trying judge C.N. Broomsfield, I. C. S., District and Sessions Judge, Ahmedabad, were British nationals posted in India.

The trial has since become a famous history not only because of the great importance and personality of the "accused" but also because of the historic statement Gandhi had made before the court at the end of the trial and before the sentence was passed.

Influence of Ramakrishna and Vivekananda

I was greatly influenced by Ramakrishna and Swami Vivekananda, and read their writings and other important publications of the Ramakrishna Mission. It aroused in me a great respect for the modern Indian saint and his noble and worthy disciple. His writings were fiery, soul-inspiring, patriotic, humanitarian and were both of eternal value and of great importance to the solution of the current social and economic problems of India. His own soul was burning with the sorrows and sufferings of the Indian people and the injustices and repressions of the foreign rule. He however did not think of political solution straight away but wrote, spoke and lectured on the ways of uplifting the masses spiritually, make them feel strong, self-confident and have faith in themselves and their destiny, the destiny of their dear Motherland, the great and ancient country India. But he urged that the new thinking, and activities should be consistent with traditional Indian thought of universality and oneness of the world and of the entire humanity and India as an integral and honourable part of the entire world. Hence Vivekananda thought his work should not be confined to India alone but spread across the world. He realized that there was colossal ignorance in the then world (and even now) about India. He felt intensely within himself that the world should be roused and made aware of the conditions in India. The sympathy and support of other peoples and nations was necessary to solve India's problems -- poverty and degradation amongst the masses, the arrogance and vanity of most of the upper class peoples, the heavy weight of meaningless and blind traditions that bound the people in the garb of religion and social norms. Vivekananda wanted the Indian to adopt rational and scientific thinking of the West and remove vain socio-religious practices from Indian society. By this he wanted India to restore its own ancient rich cultural heritage. He was a believer in one universal God (Vedantist) but with many manifestations, *Ekam-sadbipra bahudha badanti.* He, therefore, like Ramakrishna, believed in the unity of all religions--Hinduism, Buddhism, Islam, Christianity and others.

But Vivekananda was at the same time highly proud and fully conscious of the value of Hinduism and its great contribution and influence to building up India's ancient religious, spiritual and philosophical thought and culture. He felt India could communicate these to the Western world where people at that time were running after the material things but, getting away from the moral and spiritual values. However, true to his own religious and spiritual thinking and upbringing Vivekananda never tried to approach the West politically but morally and spiritually make them aware to his thinking of freedom, justice, and equality of all peoples and lands.

He wanted to mingle good ideas of the West with those of the East and in consequence a mutual respect, tolerance and feeling of brotherhood among all instead of hatred, arrogance, power, feeling of superiority and inferiority complex.

With this great vision he left the shores of India towards the end of the nineteenth century on a voyage of peace and reconciliation with the peoples of America and Europe with two principal objects. First, that of opening the closed shores of India under foreign rule to the outside world and the closed and static minds of the Indian people to the modern scientific thought and ethos of the West. Second, to convey, in return, by lectures and writings, to the peoples of the West, India's message of the divinity of man, the oneness of the universe, the oneness of the spiritual principle that is guiding basically the destiny of the mankind and gives it a deep moral purpose in its origin, evolution and progress. It gives mankind a hope, mental peace and contentment instead of frustration, discontent, depression and lack of mental balance.

Thus, in his approach to the West Vivekananda was not diffident or had a feeling of inferiority. But he was supremely conscious of the greatness of his country and its immense philosophical, moral and cultural attainment over nearly five thousand years of most dynamic history and evolution, and of the importance of the message that he carried from its shores for the West and the world. On the other hand, he was a humble Indian mendicant or sage who realized within him the eternal values of man and wanted to impart them to the willing all over the world regardless of the barriers of their shores, races, colours, religious and material prosperity. He had an immense and magnetic personality about which Romain Rolland, the celebrated French philosopher, said: "His pre-eminent characteristic was kingliness. He was a born king and nobody ever came near him either in India or America without paying homage to his majesty"[12].

So there was no wonder that I was charmed and hypnotized by Vivekananda's ideal, messages and teachings even in my bare teenage. Hence in my spare time and holidays I was a frequent visitor to the Ramakrishna Mission in Midnapore and spent much time in reading in library, attending lectures, speaking to various *swamis,* and some times participated in nursing of helpless patients in the Mission hospital. Also I took an active part in the periodical functions of the Mission in feeding the beggars.

All through my life this early initiation in the teachings of Ramakrishna and Vivekananda have inspired me in all my diverse activities, and given me strength of mind at most difficult and critical times. Vivekananda's speeches in U.S.A. and United Kingdom in the last decade of nineteenth century, his appreciation of the scientific temperament and advancement of those countries during the end of the century and at the same time his criticism of their attendant malaise of crass soulless materialism remain equally even if not more valid even today.

My participation in Scout Movement

In the mid-twenties, as we have seen earlier, the political situation in India, particularly after Gandhi's release from prison in 1924, remained relatively calm. Hence in both Midnapore and Contai we had a fairly quiet and peaceful time.

At Midnapore town my sister and I lived with our uncle Binode Behari and grandmother and two maternal uncles. We had a very close and peaceful atmosphere. My uncle had many professional friends, mostly lawyers practising at the law courts. He was a great lover of music and held frequent gatherings of notable musicians at our home. He was especially a great lover of Bengali songs particularly those of Rabindranath Tagore, Rajanikanto and Atulprasad. He had two celebrated music teachers of Midnapore, a Hindu and a Moslem. Moreover he used to sing on his own early in the morning and also occasionally at other times. He taught my sister Kamala and me to sing some of these songs at our very early ages. These songs have had a profound influence on me all through my life, and not only laid the seeds of my own love for music but also determined, along with the teachings of Ramakrishna/Vivekananda, the future make up of my mind and, in fact, my basic philosophy of life and mental attitude in facing my whole future. They also gave me enormous strength of mind and peace during some of the most turbulent times of my life. At my uncle's home on Midnapore there were often lively discussions of current political situations and developments in the country, which made a deep impression in my mind. There is no doubt that these unknowingly had created in me an intensive love for my Motherland and a desire to participate in the country's efforts to liberate her from foreign rule.

In 1923, Birendra Nath Sasmal, a well-known barrister-at-law of Midnapore who had already established himself as a political, especially Congress, leader of the district through his very determined and successful no-tax (non-payment of chowkidari or local police) campaign in

Contai, was elected as the Chairman of the important District Board, the headquarters of the district Self-Governing administration. He appointed my uncle Binode Behari as its Secretary or the Chief Executive. The latter served in that capacity and the chief development officer of local government activities of the entire district until his retirement in 1950, with considerable efficiency and utmost honesty for which he made a great reputation. So much so that during the thirties when the District Board was superseded by the Government, because of non-cooperation movement of Gandhi in which most of its board members had participated, and the Successive District Magistrates -- James Peddies, Douglas and Burge (all of whom had later been the targets of the revolutionaries of Midnapore)--were in the overall charge of the District Board, my uncle's service as secretary to the Board was retained. In private life my uncle was a litterateur, a member of All Bengal Sahitya (Bengali literature) Sabha. After his retirement, at the persuasion of Dr. Shyama Prasad Mukherjee, the then President of All-India Hindu Mahasabha, he became the secretary of its Midnapore Branch. He was also for long closely attached to the Midnapore Brahmo Samaj and later became its secretary.

My uncle was a great moralist and disciplinarian and led a puritan life. He was a bachelor all through his life and in his private life he took over the responsibility for the upbringing and education of myself as well of my sister and four other brothers. With great affection and care he discharged this responsibility till his death in January 1965. He left a great influence and impact on my life especially.

In 1924, a new opportunity for extra-school work came before me. A unit of the All Bengal Scout Movement, which had been set up at the world level by the Englishman Lord Baden Powell, was formed with Midnapore Town School. Earlier a similar unit had been already established in another High English School, the Collegiate School, which was controlled and financed by the Government, with permission from my uncle I decided to join. Fortunately, the unit commander was our class teacher (of Class VII) Sri Amulya Nandi, a middle aged, well disposed, able and affectionate teacher of English. He had already undertaken a prior training course at the All Bengal Scout Station in Calcutta. He was also a great moralist and well versed in Indian religious texts and philosophy. Under his guidance and direction we in the School Scout Unit practised regular drill, outside excursions in and around Midnapore town, and offered ourselves to services of the poor. During some of these excursions in north of Midnapore which is notable for its rocky red laterite undulated topography intersected by certain narrow streams formed by the seepage of the rocks, he used to hold drills in open fresh cool air in the morning, and during our rest period used to teach us the lessons of the *Gita* and asked us to be truthful and moral. He insisted that we count the number of lies we speak in the week and report to him during his next drill. I thus started reading the *Gita,* the essence of Hinduism, and in fact, the most ancient Indian philosophical text originally written in Sanskrit verses.

This made a profound and lasting impact on my mind and character, as a complement to all the influence that simultaneously was working on me through my uncle's disciplined, moral, austere and dedicated life . It gave me a new urge to develop and improve my own quality of life, and strengthen my will to serve the poor and the country. I used to feel an inner transformation of life. I felt a deep urge to dedicate my life to the service of the poor and the downtrodden, the oppressed and the exploited of my country and to the attainment of her freedom from foreign rule.

A decisive year came next in 1925. An oath taking ceremony and a ceremonial parade by the combined Boys Scout unit of all the Midnapore High English schools was held at the District Magistrate's residential compound in the north of the town. The District Magistrate, R.N. Reid, was the head of the Boys Scout units in the district and administered the oath of allegiance in the parade with our usual formal semi-military Khaki dresses including neck scarves and hats. The allegiance sworn was to "God, King and Country". In a sunny bright and clear morning we all took the oath under the command of our respective Scout Masters. There for the first time, at the age of 13, I saw face to face an Englishman and the chief administrator of the district which was almost as big as a small country of Europe. Reid was a member of the prestigious Indian Civil Service, an original native of Britain and trained for overseas service, like all other recruits to the service--British or Indian, in that country. Usually they were British University graduates especially trained for tough but skilful executive and judicial works in India. They often first started from the sub-divisions and worked their way through the district, divisional and provincial headquarters up to the Central Government in New Delhi. As District Magistrate he was the representative of the Provincial Governor and ultimately of the Governor General and the

Viceroy of the then Indian Empire, the brightest jewel of the mighty and worldwide vast British Empire.

While I felt somewhat elated at my adolescent age to have met and shaken hand with such a person, a prick stuck may conscience immediately after the oath taking ceremony ended with a little speech by the District Magistrate. The big question that raised in my mind was: how in a dependant country under the rule and domination of a foreign country one can owe allegiance of service simultaneously to the King (who was the Emperor and head of the British Empire including India) and to his country (i.e. India)? What disturbed me most was the idea that the Boys Scouts were supposed to work as auxiliaries to the army on intelligence and works behind the line in case of war or rebellion. Suppose there was a war involving the British Government or the then Government of India which was against the interest of India as a country on its own, how could we serve the foreign ruler's interest instead of trying to seek means and ways to utilize the opportunity in the true interest of India? Or, suppose, even worse, if people in India rise in revolt against the forces of the foreign rulers and the Indian army is engaged in quelling it and the Boys Scouts are engaged to aid them, what would be our duty?

With this disturbed thought I came home from the parade. But I kept on brooding over the matter and on what should be my duty--allegiance to my country or to the foreign head of a distant Emperor who obviously forcibly kept my country under subjugation? I spent several days on it. I did not leave the Scout Movement all at once. I liked its semi-military dress, its part military drill, discipline, service to the people at critical juncture and above all our Scout master (who, as I have said earlier, was also our class teacher and teacher of English) Sri Amulya Nandi. He was by all standards a good man. He personally impressed me most and also liked me. I followed his lessons in the class regularly and the drill dutifully. But I loved more, even at that early age, my Mother country. I felt intensely for the poverty and distress of our common people. Whatever literature I had read at that early age of 13 like those of Bankim Chandra Chatterjee, the celebrated Bengali writer of the nineteenth century, especially his *Anandamath,* and the patriotic poems I read and songs I heard particularly of the great poet administrator Dwijindra Lal Roy, Atul Prasad Sen the rebellious and young poet Kazi Nazrul Islam, the elder and world renowned poet-philosopher Rabindranath Tagore, and many others kindled in me a tender flame of patriotism--love for my country.

With this feeling the more I thought the more I felt that services to my dependant country and to a foreign ruler were grossly contradictory. So I finally decided to leave the Scout movement, but waited until I went to the next class (Class VIII) where I would have a new class teacher.

It may be said here that there were no particular political and social activities in Bengal during 1923-1924 except that the controversial Civil Marriage Bill was passed by the then Central Legislative Assembly in 1923, and the Bengal Criminal Law Amendment Act promulgated to arm the Government of Bengal in their effort to clamp down the activities of the revolutionaries of the Province.

Extra-Curricular Activities, 1925

In 1925 I left the Scout movement and thought of alternative actions and consulted some of my socially minded young classmates like Haripada Bhowmik, Saktimoy Banerjee, Pulin Maity, Biren Majhi and Santosh Mishra. All of them were in their teens and belonged to the first ten boys of the class in merit and their class studies. We formed a small literary and cultural club in the school and named it *Milan Mandir* or Temple of Unity with the goal of pursuing amongst students of the Town School extra-curricular studies of selected patriotic and didactic books and magazines, debates and discussions on important historical and social issues and promoting the habit of writing amongst the students. We started a monthly journal in handwritten form with articles and poems from the students. We also staged some short theatrical performances mostly of plays written by some amongst us focussing on the current social and other matters affecting the students. In all these activities we sought the blessings and cooperation of our teachers.

Simultaneously we also participated in various sports, especially football, and organized a small gymnasium in the compounds of the big garden house of a leading lawyer of Midnapore, Upendra Nath Maity. We selected one of his sons, Khagen Maity, a youngman of robust body who had been doing various types of exercises, as our trainer. Besides we took part in various social functions through the Ramakrishna Mission and other *ad hoc* public relief, such as in flood relief operations.

At this time, one day, my uncle took my sister Kamala and me to the house of a well-known friend of his in Midnapore town. Kedan Bose the brother of Jnan Bose, the private secretary of Kumar Debendra Lal Khan, and also of the famous martyr Satyen Bose. They were all nephews of late Raj Narain Bose, the famous ex-headmaster of the Government Collegiate School and a reputed educationist of Bengal about of whom I have mentioned earlier. It was also noted that Styen Bose, along with an associate Kanai Dutta, was hanged till death in a Calcutta jail for shooting an approver, Naren Goswami, in the famous Alipore Bomb Case in 1908. My uncle introduced us to Kedan Bose as well as to her sister who was known to have helped in smuggling a revolver to her brother in Alipore Jail through some fruits (Jack friuts). At our very young age we were very much impressed by her.

Chitta Ranjan Das

In 1925, the eminent Congress leader of Bengal, Chitta Ranjan Das, who had been affectionately called "Deshbandhu" (Friend of the Country) for his great sacrifices for the cause of India's freedom, died. As stated earlier, as a leading barrister of the Calcutta High Court early in the century he had made a great name by defending Aurobindo Ghose in Alipore Bomb Case (1908) and getting him acquitted. He had also acted as a defence Counsel in certain other political conspiracy cases like those at Dacca (1910) and Delhi (1914). He was a contemporary of Motilal Nehru and already a leading figure in the Indian National Congress, not only prior to Gandhi but also during the latter's life, until his death. He had dominated the Congress and political scene of Bengal as also of the rest of India since 1917. In 1918 he became the President of the Indian National Congress and in 1920 he joined Gandhi's non-cooperation movement and took to handspun and handwoven simple *Khadi* dress.

Das brought the Congress movement to realities. He brought it down from its previous high pedestal of an elite and aristocratic organization to the level of the common people including peoples of ordinary means of all classes and religions. He established a good rapport with the Moslem leaders, and with the masses, the peasants, and the revolutionaries of Bengal. He is said to have imparted to the political movement "a distinct type, a distinct character and a distinct law of his own".[13] He believed that government repression alone in Bengal, especially since 1905, had caused the revolutionary movement to develop and the way to remedy it was the grant of substantial freedom (political) to the people. His thinking was mostly along the lines of his renowned predecessors in Bengal like Surendra Nath Banerjee, Bipin Pal and Aurobindo Ghose. He supported Gandhi's non-cooperation movement. But he had been opposed to the second doze of constitutional reform proposed by the British Government under the Montagu-Chelmsford reforms of 1919, as inadequate, offensive and obstructive to the final goal of achieving a complete independent, united and sovereign India. The principles of separate electorate and dyarchy were, in his opinion, laying the seeds of permanent division of the country along religious lines.

Das was initially opposed to Gandhi's non-cooperation movement but later joined it wholeheartedly. And when Gandhi withdrew the movement following violence in some parts of the country, particularly in Chauri Chaura in the then United Provinces, Das was aggrieved. He later formed with Motilal Nehru and the famous Ali Brothers (Mahommed Ali and Shaukat Ali) and Hakim Ajmal Khan, the *Swarajya Party*, with a programme to enter the newly set up provincial Councils under the Montagu-Chelmsford Reforms of 1919. His idea was to oppose it from within the divided and feeble dyarchical form of provincial legislative Council consisting of elected and nominated (by the Governor) members. Even the elected ones, came through the process of 'separate electorate', according to which the Council seats were allocated among separate religious communities and each community elected separately only its own quota of members. In retrospect, it was a *religions apartheid* ingenuously devised by the British rulers in India to lay the basis of the ultimate division of the country, as said above, which they did in 1947.

Das, however, kept a good *rapport* with Gandhi towards the end of his life and they concluded the so-called Calcutta Pact in 1924 under which both the Gandhians and the Swarajyists were allowed to work from the Congress platform but in their respective ways. In 1924 he formulated a 'Communal Pact' to promote what he considered to be permanent peace between Hindus and Moslems. On a broader front he dreamt of a pan--Asiatic Federation of the oppressed nations and advocated India's participation in it.[14]

Apart from his deep involvement in the national and provincial politics Das also took control of the Calcutta Corporation through his

Swarajya party and tried to improve its constitution and function and make it more responsive to the peoples' needs (a thing which remains illusive even today, 40 years after India's independence). He also set an important party organ in 1923, named *Forward,* which in my childhood made a great name in presenting news items and writing editorials from India's national point of view, especially in marked contrast to then leading daily the Calcutta '*Statesman*' which was the main mouthpiece of the British rulers and the British business community in India. The new media's first editor was Satya Ranjan Baksi whose editorials evidenced great elation and appreciation among the Indian intellectuals. Das was also a well-known litterateur and a devoted Brahmo, not of orthodox type, but of broader outlook with a proper appreciation of its goals and functions in the wider context of its parent religious tenets and philosophical doctrines.

Das died in June 1925 at a comparatively young age of 55 (1870-1925) after a brilliant legal carrier, and a hectic and most active political life pursued through all available channels in achieving the goal of India's freedom and of uplifting its poverty stricken masses. He tried in unison with the Congress, the revolutionaries and the liberals, to halt the British machinery of administration in India by legal, constitutional, extra-constitutional means. He adopted the policy of non-violence of Gandhiji but did not leave out the fiery bands of youth of Bengal (or of other provinces) out of his determination to fight against foreign rule. He actually strengthened Gandhi's hand although he opposed the latter on many accounts. Gandhi's regard for Das is shown by his visit to Darjeeling before the former's death.

I had an opportunity of seeing Das when I was very young, at a meeting of the Congress in 1924 at the house of a prominent lawyer and Congress leader of Midnapore, Kishori Pati Roy. Das was then addressing a public meeting. I also saw Birendra Nath Sasmal, the top Congress leader of Midnapore and one of the top leaders of Bengal Congress as well. But Sasmal did not participate at Das's meeting. He was seated in a reclining chair in a side room and was agitated. Some other leaders were trying to persuade him to join Das's meeting but Sasmal was refusing. I was then too young to know the reason. Much later I came to know that there was some dispute between Das and Sasmal over the appointment of the Secretary of the Provincial Congress Committee when Das was its

President and similarly also of the Chief Executive Officer of the Calcutta Corporation when Das was its Mayor.

Das's name very often came in the course of discussions which were held in my uncle's evening gatherings in our Midnapore house. They used frequently the words 'no-changer' and 'pro-changer' but I did not understand clearly their meanings. But they meant those who were 'Swarajyist' or believed in Council entry and those who did not.

Thus the political atmosphere in India and Bengal was very lively in 1925 when I was barely thirteen years old, and its repercussion came to Midnapore in a great way.

Opening of a new Vista

The year 1926 saw an important development towards the fulfilment of that mission--the arrival of Profulla Tripathy as a new student of class IX. A young, tall, handsome and dynamic Brahmin youth about a few years older than I, he was with most tolerant and liberal political and social views and of most dynamic nature. He was the only son of his parents who were very kind and nice persons. He had already worked with Birendra Nath Sasmal in the Non-Cooperation Movement of 1921, and could speak and write well. Soon we became very close friends. He was not of the first batch of students in academic studies in our class but had studied extensively extra-curricular literature, such as general history books, Bengali literature, etc. Soon we two became very much attached to each other, mainly because the similarity of our goals--the priority we gave to the attainment of country's independence before all other activities in our lives, as well as of the views to reach such goals. Prafulla however was basically trained for public political activities, e.g. through the Congress movement and through activities among the youth and students.

For the moment our main task was to inspire the young students to an intense feeling of love and patriotism for the motherland and to organize them through talks, discussions, readings of patriotic literatures, both national and foreign. The former included those of Swami Vivekananda, Rabindranath Tagore, Dwijindera Lal Ray, Sarat Chandra Chattopadhyaya, Subhas Chandra Bose, and many others, while the latter like Trotsky's *Mother,* de Valera's *My Fight for Irish Freedom,*

William Digby's *Prosperous British India,* J. T. Sunderland's *India in Bondage,* etc.

In and out of the school Prafulla and I moved together preaching amongst the students and youth of Midnapore the need for working for country's independence and hence of building our moral character as well as physical strength through drills and exercises and sports.

For the political parties in the wider national field, this was a period of retrospection and consolidation of past activities since World War I and preparation for the future struggle against the British rule. As we have already seen, Gandhi devoted his time mainly on constructive programmes and it seemed he was also planning his next strategy; the revolutionaries were nursing their wound suffered at the hands of the British rulers in their widespread attempt of an armed rising during World War I and regrouping themselves for possible actions for the future. There were not much activities of other political parties. However, there had been two important ones on the part of the Government. Subhas Bose, who was detained in Mandalay (Burma, then still a province of India) for three years for his suspected contacts with the revolutionaries of Bengal, was released on grounds of health in 1927. And the British Government having realized that the Dyarchical form of internal autonomy granted under the Montagu -Chelmsford Reports failed completely to satisfy the Congress and the revolutionaries, announced the appointment of a Statutory Commission under the Chairmanship of Sir John Simon and six members of British Parliament including the Labour Party member Clement Attlee (who later became the British Prime Minister after the end of World War II). The terms of the Commission were however very limited, including *inter alia* "to enquire.... and report as to whether and to what extent it is desirable to establish the principle of self-government or to extend, modify or restrict the degree of responsible government then existing therein...." The composition (all British and no Indian) and its terms of very limited and equivocal nature gave a new incentive for agitation by the people of all shades of political opinion in India.

However, in Midnapore in 1927 I was promoted to Class X, the final year of my school and engaged myself closely to my studies first for the preparation of the school test at the end of the year and then to appear at the first University entrance examination (then called Matriculation) in

1928. But I maintained my activities, in cooperation with Profulla, among students and youths and tried to keep myself informed as much as possible of the wider political developments of Bengal and all-India.

1928 -- An Eventful Year

At the end of 1927 I was duly sent up by the school to sit for the Matriculation Examination of the Calcutta University in early March 1928 and I did. I Passed in First Division with special credit in Mathematics. I decided to join the Intermediate Science course in Midnapore College.

At the College corridor I and my maternal uncle met a young man slightly older than me. We stopped and talked to him and came to know that he was Dinesh Gupta. He came from Dacca and got himself admitted into the College the same day in the second year I.Sc. class just one class above me. We talked for a little while and was greatly impressed by him. Thereafter we met on several occasions at the meetings of the executive committee of the Midnapore Youth Association, which had been organized by Profulla Tripathi and myself with the help of other friends like Haripada Bhowmik, Phani Kundu and others as well as with the collaboration of several other youths and students of Midnapore. We persuaded Kumar Debendra Lal Khan to be its President and Profulla was its Secretary. At the executive committee meeting we used to discuss the policies and programmes of the Association. We had also established through Dr. Subodh Chandra Bose, a brother of the Midnapore martyr Satyen Bose a contact with Subhas Chandera Bose in Calcutta whose ideas and activities especially impressed us. This brought upon us some ire of the orthodox leaders and workers of the Congress in Midnapore who were strict followers of Gandhi's principle and policy of non-violence and passive resistance as the principal tool of struggle against the British rulers of India, and his goal of "swaraj" or self-government in the then British Empire. Subhas on the other hand was in favour of complete freedom from British rule and did not leave out normal historical means to achieve freedom, if required.

We had however established, through the initial introduction by Profulla, contact with individual Congress leaders of Bengal and Midnapore like Dr. Prafulla Chandra Ghose, Dr. Suresh Chandra Banerjee, Basanta Kumar Das, all of *Abhoy Ashram*, an institution set up in Bengal to pursue the political goal and economic ideals of Gandhi through propagation of non-violence, removal of untouchability, and use of *charka* (a simple Indian instrument for spinning) and also hand-weaving at the small rural cottages. There was a good but small library in the Midnapore *Abhoy Ashram* with many books, in English as well as Bengali language, on India's history, culture--past and present, and also on Gandhi's writings. Many of us were regular readers of the Library and we developed a special relation with Basanta Kumar Das of Contai, who was principally in-charge of the library and the *Abhoy Ashram*. He was a devout Gandhiite and follower of the Congress. During 1921 Non-Cooperation Movement of Gandhi he, like hundreds of other students of his time, gave up his education (he was a student of the Presidencey College in Calcutta) at Gandhi's call and joined the movement. He was a person of mild disposition and of very broad and liberal mind. So that although he knew that we cherished more extreme views with regard to the achievement of India's independence, he was very kind to us and assisted in a great way to let us have their library's books. I had developed a special relation with Basanta Das which lasted from that time until his death in 1984 and through completely diverse phases of our lives and activities.

There were several important developments in the general political field in India in 1928, which gave a great spurt to our activities in Midnapore in our restricted field. Two main happenings of historic importance were: first, the visit of the Simon Commission and the country wide protest and boycott by all parties -- the Indian National Congress, the All India Liberal Federation, the All-India Muslim League, the Hindu Mahasabha and even the Federation of Indian Chamber of Commerce and the Indian Mill-Owners' Association. Only a small section of the people welcomed the Commission, including understandably the Europeans, the Anglo-Indians and a certain section of the so-called Depressed Classes (a term coined by the British rulers). Thus the visit of the Commission was the occasion of a great agitation and excitement all-over India. The students and youths throughout India, and particularly in Bengal, took a leading role in the protests, and bore the brunt of police atrocities[15]. "The Commission thus worked in an atmosphere of boycott and non-cooperation." Nor did its report mend matters. When submitted on 27 May 1930, it confirmed in fact the worst fears of the nationalists. *Inter alia,* it omitted any mention of Dominion

Status[16]. Thus the failure of the Commission was a forgone conclusion: It was indeed a "farce", as then described by Motilal Nehru, (father of Jawaharlal Nehru, and a top Congress leader of his time) and as such was ignored by all parties.

The second most important happening in 1928 was the holding of a full session of the Indian National Congress in Calcutta at Park Circus ground. In view of the attendance of all the top leaders of the party from all over India including Gandhi, Jawaharlal Nehru and Subhas Bose and having on its top agenda, the important question of determining as a party its final political goal--complete independence or Dominion Status--there was a great deal of interest and excitement for this session all over India but particularly in Bengal because of the important role that the revolutionaries and leftists played in the provincial Congress organization. The leading spokesman of this latter group was Subhas Bose who was then joined by young Jawaharlal Nehru. They brought before the session a proposal to declare complete independence free from any control by the British Government and Parliament as the Congress' goal. But that proposal was lost and the Congress session, under Gandhi's advice, by a majority vote, accepted Dominion Status as its goal "if granted before the end of 1929".

A notable feature of the Calcutta Congress and of great potential importance for the future political development in India, was the organization of a *Bengal Volunteer Corps* formed and drilled on para-military lines and with full military attire, for controlling and maintaining discipline amongst the vast crowd that collected at the session as participants as well as visitors. It was commanded by Subhas Bose himself also attired in full military uniform and riding on horseback and holding the title of GOC (General Officer Commanding). He was assisted by Major Satya Gupta, Jatin Das and others. The Corps attracted great attention from assembled leaders and the public. But many of the leaders did not like the idea of a military role in what they considered to be a gathering of an organization dedicated to non-violence and peaceful resistance. However, Subhas's main objective in setting up the B.V. Corps was to set an example and provide an inspiration to the youth and students of India to organize themselves militarily so as to play, if occasion required, a complementary role in the fight for independence, to that of non-violent passive resistance by the Congress. Considering later developments it could be considered as a preliminary rehearsal of Netaji's great role in organizing the Indian National Army during World War II.

Another important byproduct of the B.V.Corps was the assumption of the name on a more permanent basis by that section of the Bengal revolutionaries which had a predominant role in the organization of Corps during the Congress. Major Satya Gupta was one of the top leaders of this Section of revolutionaries in Bengal.

I had then been a visitor to the Congress, alongwith two of my uncles and had some feel of the excitement and controversy that was raging within the huge pandal under an especially erected canvas tent, and also seen the B.V. uniformed volunteers active in controlling the crowd. But after joining the Midnapore College I pursued, in cooperation with Prafulla, my activities in the work of the *Midnapore Youth Association.* Our main task still was to create among the youth an urge to work for the freedom of the country, through studies and discussions, building up good health and physique, participation in lectures on socio-political matters by distinguished outside visitors as well as reputed public leaders in Midnapore. With the help and patronage of Kumar Debendra Lal Khan we established a library in his administrative office and a gymnasium in its ground and sought the help of Jog Jiban Ghose who was a reputed athlete and had suffered 10 years' imprisonment mostly in Andaman Islands after being implicated and convicted in Midnapore Bomb case of 1908.

My initiation into Bengal Volunteers Group

During that time an arrangement was made by Haripada Bhowmik, one of my closest colleagues and co-workers, for Dinesh and me to meet in private and talk. When we met Dinesh told me that although he came from Dacca he belonged to a revolutionary group with its headquarters in Calcutta and had been sent to Midnapore to organize a unit in Midnapore. Their object was to work for an eventual violent overthrow of the foreign rule in India. He voiced the skepticism of the group members in achieving freedom through the methods of non-violence and passive resistance. He cited the examples of the French Revolution against the French monarchs, the American War of Independence and the

Irish Rebillion against the British rule and the Russian Revolution against the oppressive Czar. Dinesh was a well-read young man and could speak well. I listened to him in great attention and was impressed by his logic. I was not too sure of Gandhi's suggested methods which were after all novel and were only of experimental nature. The pursuance of violent means for the emancipation of dependent and subjugated peoples was the norm of history. Moreover Dinesh's approach offered us in Midnapore a channel and an opportunity to have a contact with an opening to a wider field that of the entire province of Bengal. Our close integration with this group would increase our resources and capabilities. So I decided to join Dinesh and his Bengal Volunteers Group.

We had already created a good field in Midnapore town through our student and youth activities and collected a band of young men. So under Dinesh's overall guidance we three--Haripada Bhowmik, Phani Kundu and myself--formed a first batch of B.V. unit. Soon we were joined by a bigger group with Amar Chatterjee, Braja Kishor Chakravarty, Kshiti Prasanna Sen Gupta, Naren Das, Phani Das, Kamakshya Ghose, Jyoti Jiban Ghose, Pravangshu Pal, Binode Sen, Prodyot Bhattacharjee, Bimal Das Gupta, Bhupati Mandal, and some others. All of them were in their late teens and intensely attached to the idea of working for, and devoting their lives to the cause of, India's independance. They were all tested and trained by Dinesh. Then came even a bigger batch with Sachin Kanungo, Nanda Dulal Singh, Rabi Mitra, Nirmal Ray and others. And finally, many other groups. There was indeed a great surge and urge of boys to join our first revolutionary group established after a long gap since Khudiram, Satyen and Hem Kanungo early in this century.

The test of 'recruitment' was very severe. Every one had to pass through individual examination of physical fitness, mental aptitude and alertness, courage and above all the dedication to the cause of country's freedom. For example, as a test of courage a rendezvous was often arranged for selected groups to meet in the evening in darkness in the crematorium situated in a deserted place far away from the town. We had to go there on foot and individually. So that we did not arouse any suspicion on the part of even the few passers by along the road leading to the place. For physical exercise, apart from a public gymnasium already set up in the ground of Kumar Debendra Lal's administrative office in the centre of the town, we also established a new rather secret one amidst a set of old and abandoned houses in the south-east section of the town. We did not know who the owner was but we cleaned it and put various exercise gears and practised every morning various forms of exercises including wrestling. Dinesh also took part with us. We also formed a para-military wing of B.V. with boys amongst ourselves as well as with some outsiders under the command of Dinesh who had already been in the Dacca brigade and had his lessons in military drill there.

Congress declares Complete Independence as its goal at the Lahore Session, 1929

Thus 1928 was a most eventful year for us but 1929 was even more notable. In the all-India field the British Government showed no sign of 'granting' Dominion Status to India by the end of the year. But since there was a great deal of excitement and agitation amongst the Congress leaders as well as the people of India on this issue, the then Viceroy Lord Irwin, in October 1929, while announcing a decision by the British Government to call a Round Table Conference of Indian leaders in London on this issue mentioned: "I am authorized on behalf of His Majesty's Government to state clearly that the natural issue of India's constitutional progress as therein contemplated is the attainment of Dominion Status"[17]. However, this did not satisfy the Congress leaders and therefore at the Lahore Congress in December 1929 the organization declared its goal to be complete independence from the British rule and control. Its leaders, including Gandhi, were fed up with the hesitation, prevarication, and duplicity of the successive British Governments of both the Conservative and Labour parties. They also noted with great annoyance and anger that even the limited advances in self-government which had been 'granted' till then were hedged in with blatant divide and rule policies in the form of so-called 'diarchy', separate allocation of seats and elctorates for different religious communities, ethnic and business interests arbitrarily determined and with a plethora of safeguards and reservations to continue British political and economic dominance in the country.

All parties were, therefore, preparing for the next phase of the struggle. The Congress, under Gandhi's leadership, planned to offer a new form of non-cooperation, rather of more active nature. The Revolutionaries, in their turn, were working towards more specific actions. But their difficulty was that notwithstanding their high ideal and devotion there were no unified organization, no agreed and clear cut strategy as to how to carry on the struggle against the British rule. As a result many of them joined the Congress and became supporters of one or the other of the leading figures in the party, both at the all-Bengal level and in district levels. Some believed in mass struggle but had little influence on the masses except through the influence of the Congress leaders they supported. Others believed in violent individual or at best group actions against important personalities or key outposts like armouries, police stations, etc. of the British administration. But they usually should not trust one another for a joint or coordinated action lest the plan of one could somehow leak through any loophole in the organization of others. This is what happened, as we have seen earlier, in the mighty preparations of the great revolutionary leader of India, Rashbehari Bose, during World War I. Then the preparations involved not only different groups in India but also extended to a number of foreign countries including Burma, Singapore, Indonesia and as far as Canada and U.S.A. However, the revolutionaries were not daunted by this failure or by their organizational weakness. They were, if anything, brave lots intensely dedicated to cause of India's freedom and each group tried to accomplish in what in its judgment was the best short-term objective and strategy that its separate limited resources permitted. And even their separate and often isolated violent 'action' started in full swing in 1930 and continued until 1935 especially in Bengal, which we shall presently recount. Indeed this half decade in this province's history was marked by a virtual dominance of the revolutionaries in its political climate.

But already in 1929 certain groundwork was laid first by the well-known Meerut Conspiracy Case in which 31 prominent trade union leaders were tried for conspiracy to "deprive the King Emperor of his sovereignty over British India". They included communists, Congressmen and others. The trial dragged on for four years and created a great impact especially on the revolutionary youths. I still have some memory of it and among the names of the 'accused' that became well-known then, that of Dange was prominent. He is still living and one of the leading figures in the communist movement of India. The second notable incident was the dropping of a bomb into the Central Legislative Assembly in New Delhi on 8 April by two youths from Punjab, Bhagat Singh and Batukeswar Dutta, in protest against the Public Safety and

Trades Dispute Bill and the death of Punjab leader Lala Lajpat Rai as a result of police assault.[18] Third, the death of a celebrated revolutionary of Bengal, Jatin Das, in Lahore Central Jail after 64 days' fast. He was arrested in Calcutta on 14 June 1929 and put on trial with three other youths of Punjab--Bhagat Singh, Rajguru and Sukhdeo, in what is known as Third Lahore Conspiracy Case. The three were later sentenced to death and hanged in Lahore Central Jail on 23 March 1931.[19] I remember that simultaneously with massive demonstration and protest in Calcutta there was a big procession of protest and indignation by the students and youth as well as the public in Midnapore, in which I had also participated.

The fourth important event of 1929 in which I was directly involved, along with Profulla, Phani Kundu and several other young friends of Midnapore, all members of the Midnapore Youth Association, was the holding of the first Midnapore Youth Conference in December 1929 with the charismatic leader of Bengal, Subhas Chandra Bose, as its president. Earlier when we had decided to hold the Conference and to invite Subhas to be its president, the idea was not liked by orthodox Congress leaders of Midnapore who were staunch followers of Gandhi, because of the known differences between Bose and the Mahatma, on the goal and methods of achieving India's independence. But we had the support of many other Congress leaders of the district like Kumar Debendra Lal Khan, Manmatha Nath Das, Jawaharlal Adhikari and Narendra Nath Das, all eminent lawyers.

Subhas in Midnapore--December 1929

Subhas arrived in Midnapore by train on 28 December. A unit of the para-military wing of the Bengal Volunteers, including myself, under the command of Dinesh Gupta, welcomed him along with several Congress leaders. They included Manmatha Nath Das who was his host during his stay in Midnapore. With Subhas came from Calcutta a few other Congress leaders, Dr. Subodh Bose, Subhash's close friend the famous singer Dilip Kumar Ray and Syed Jalaluddin Hasheni. We took them in a route march through the town of Midnapore to the house of Das. There on behalf of organizing committee of the Conference, Profulla and I met Subhas and apprised him of the details of the preparations and the programme. This was my first face to face meeting with him. He was then the idol of the youth of Bengal and had already established his reputation as a top leader of the Congress, and especially for his more radical views on ways of achieving India's freedom and of post-independence reconstruction. He seemed to the youth of Bengal to be a greater realist than Gandhi or Jawaharlal Nehru, although they had the highest regard for them. Subhas wanted to know from us the position and strength of our organization and the attitude of the Midnapore youth towards him. Profulla and I tried to reply to the best of our knowledge. But then I had to leave the conversation to go to the College where the final test on Chemistry was being held at that time for qualifying for the final I.Sc. Examination of the Calcutta University. But next day at the Conference I had the opportunity of seeing and talking to him again, and listening his address before the Conference at the New Bengal Stage theatre hall in the centre of Midnapore town before a well-attended gathering of students, youth and the public of Midnapore.

In a long speech in Bengali lasting over one hour Subhas dealt with many problems relating to the youth movement vis-a-vis the national movements of various types, its true goals, the conflicts and contradictions it has to face in the pursuit of the goals, its relation with the Congress movement and the latter's appropriate role in the country's fight for independence. He emphasised that without political freedom, we cannot achieve the dignity of human being and cannot effectively work for our spiritual, social and economic development. He therefore urged the youth to come forward in the fight for freedom of the country.

Regarding the appropriate goal of the youth movement he observed: "to search for the new... new society, new State, new economics... and introduce them; to instil in men new and loftier ideals and lift them to the higher state of human life. Those who have been inspired by such higher goals of life cannot rest satisfied with the present conditions and realities of life in India but become a rebel and work for their radical change. This can only be achieved by properly constituted youth associations."[20] Further, these objectives and heavy responsibilities could not be performed by the youth by merely becoming appendages to other established political organizations but by having and working for a separate identity through maintaining a close contact with the established premier national organizations like the Congress. Continuing Subhas said: "Our leader Deshbandhu Chittaranjan Das had a 'dream' and we have inherited it from him. What is it? I want a new completely free society and above it a free State. In such a society man will be completely free and will not be crushed by the deadweight of decrepit and degenerated social doctrines and norms--a society where there will not be any caste barriers, where women, like men, will be free and enjoy equal rights with men and be able to engage them in the service of the people and the State, where there will be no sharp differences in wealth, where every man will have equal opportunity of education and development, where there will be a full recognition of the dignity of labour and work, and the idle, the lazy and the inactive will have no place, a society and a State which will be completely free from the influence and dominance of outside countries, a State which will be an instrument of our own indigenous society but will not rest satisfied by achieving merely India's ideals and removing her wants but also regarded in the world's comity of nations as an ideal State and society." "This dream is ever true and wholesome to me. To establish it one can do everything, renounce everything, suffer all pains and troubles and even sacrifice our lives." Subhas then observed with a great touch of dedication and affection: "Oh my young listeners, I have no riches to offer you but only this dream which has given me unlimited strength and unbounded joy, which has given a lofty meaning to my little life. I offer this as my gift and may you accept it".

In conclusion, Subhas said: "We have to build the new society on 'complete socialism}. And "to sum up", he observed: "We want India's complete and all round freedom. Those who will be born in the new free India will be considered as man in the World's comity of nations. India will again be honoured for our excellence in knowledge and science, in action as well as in virtue, in learning and in preaching (nobler spiritual and moral doctrines) and in chivalry and courage." He asked the youth "to come forward and work towards the creation of a new Mother India and instal her on the lofty pedestal of a Goddess resplendent with honour, dignity, self-contentment and self-sufficiency".

Subhash came and had gone. His stay in Midnapore was short. But our objective was more than accomplished by his presence and personal contact. Above all his presidential address to the people and especially to the youth of Midnapore created a great stir, a tornado in the somewhat turbid water of the entire district. It gave substantial food for thought in short as well as long run. It offered a variety of directions in which the youth could act. For myself it held before me the broad perspective of post-independence goals and actions--a vision of the structure of free India, that is, the establishment of a completely free and sovereign polity in which the people, irrespective of the diversity of caste, creed and colour enjoyed an equal share of justice equality, peace and freedom to pursue their vocations as long as they did not interfere with similar rights of others and recognised their essential duties to the State and the society. The speech gave a new meaning to the activities we had already launched among the student and youth fronts and the people at large. It prompted us to go further forward in the pursuit of our final goal--the achievement of India's independence.

Thus the year 1929 and, in fact, the whole decade of twenties which closed helped to lay the basic foundation of my life and to put it on the proper alignment in the wider perspective of the then political, social and economic ambience of my country. They also unveiled before me at my very early age the unbounded and arduous field I had to travel in the future.

Notes and References

1. Bose, S. C.: *Indian Struggle, op. cit.*, p.79.
2. *Ibid,* p.83.
3. That Gandhi was absolutely right in his calculation will be seen from the following passage quoted from an important publication, "*Gandhi a Memoir*" by an American journalist William L. Shirer who accompanied Gandhi during the Second Round Table Conference held in 1932 in England to discuss India's constitutional reform. Gandhi then was invited to visit Lancashire to see for himself the plight of the British labourers in the city and the mills. He writes: "I followed Gandhi for three days through "the Lancashire cotton mill country, the gloomy 'devastated areas' ... *where thousands of looms, millions of spindles and hundreds and thousands of workers had been idled since Indian nationalist boycott of their goods became effective*. Gandhi was visibly moved as he sat at the window of his second class compartment on the late train from London to Manchester after evening had fallen, and *watched mile upon mile of factories, dark and silent, pass by*" After Gandhi had been taken next day through "the silent looms and spindles of the great Greenfield Weaving Mills of Darwin, and later visited *shabby, unheated, overcrowded tenements* where the workers and their families lived like cattle, he told a delegation of textile union workers: "The terrible poverty I have seen here has distressed and depressed me--even more so because I realize I have had some share in causing it" *Ibid,* pp. 180-181.

   Gandhi however reminded his audience--the Lancashire cotton workers and owners--that "the major blame rested on the refusal of the British Government to free India". "My distress", he continued, "is relieved, however by the knowledge that it is the result of a step I had to take as part of my duty toward the largest army of unemployed the world has ever seen, India's starving millions, compared to which British poverty is insignificant." *Ibid,* p. 181.

It may be observed in parenthesis that this writer had an opportunity of seeing the Manchester City in the sixties during one of his frequent visits to England, and of driving through its cotton mill areas. The whole area with its series of tenements for workers and their families looked so dark and dismal and depressing as was unbelievable in any country, and far less in the post-world war "prosperous Britain".

4. Cf. Mehra, *op cit.,* p. 378.
5. In Dacca (then East Bengal) under the initiative of the Nawab of Dacca (Nawab Viquar-ul-Mulk) and the Aga Khan, who wanted a separate political organization for the Moslems to safeguard their interests. In 1906 they led a delegation to then Viceroy and Governor-General of India, Lord Minto, for separate representation in any future constitutional frame of India. The Viceroy found it an ideal opportunity for the British to weaken the Congress and the growing Indian nationalism. The result was the provision of 'separate electorate' for the Moslems in the Morley-Minto Reforms of 1909. It was the beginning of the "Anglo-Moslem Rapprochement" which had been basic to the British Government's policy in India ever since, with overt and covert support to the separatist sentiments among certain sections of the Moslems in India, leading ultimately to the partition of the country.
6. For details of the no-tax campaign in Midnapore, see Das: *op.cit;* Ch. VIII.
7. *Ibid,* pp. 265-266.
8. B.K. Das, *op. cit.,* p. 295.
9. *Indian Struggle.* p. 85
10. *Ibid,* p. 108.
11. *Ibid,* p. 103.
12. Romain Rolland: *The Life of Vivekananda and the Universal Gospel,* Advaita Ashram, Calcutta, Fourth Impression, 1953, p.5.
13. Quoted in P. Mehra's *A Dictionary of Modern Indian History, op. cit.,* p. 186.
14. Cf. Mehra, *op. cit.,* p. 191.
15. This has been well recorded by P. Sitaramayya in *The History of Congress,* p. 330.
16. The term was defined at the (British) Imperial Conference in 1926 to indicate the Status of the "autonomous communities within the British Empire, equal in status, in no way subordinate one to another in any aspect of their domestic or external affairs, though united by a common allegiance to the Crown, and freely associated as members of the "British Commonwealth of Nations". (Quoted by Mehra, *op.cit.,* p.199) It was originally meant for such countries as Australia, New Zealand and Canada, all of whom earlier were British colonies but later granted autonomous equal status with their mother country, Great Britain. India was however considered a dependency with much inferior status. So many in India and even the Congress initially had made Dominion Status as the ultimate aim of their struggle for self-government.
17. Mehra, *op. cit.,* p. 200.
18. B. Rakshit Ray: *Armed Rebellion in India* (in Bengali) Rabindra Library, Calcutta, p.255.
19. This was in spite of widespread protests and demonstrations all over the country against their death sentence and even a personal representation by Gandhi to Irwin for commuting the sentence.
20. This and the following English rendering of selected extracts from the speech are made by the author.

CHAPTER 4

ROARING THIRTIES AND THEIR FALL (1930-1934)

Second Mass Civil Disobedience Movement : Salt Satyagraha

The second half of nineteen twenties burst into the open with much greater fury from the very beginning of the thirties. All sections of the people and especially the two major political groups--The Indian National Congress and the diverse brands of the Revolutionaries--then came to the conclusion that without further struggle and sacrifices the British would not part with real constitutional powers to India. Hence the Congress, at its annual session in Lahore in December 1929, passed with Gandhi's approval the momentous resolution declaring "complete independence from British rule" as its goal. This was acclaimed by the vast majority of the people in India except small sections who basked in the sunshine of the British rule.

But large bodies of peoples were not satisfied with a mere proclamation. They wanted action. Many of them remembered the retreat made by the Congress on previous occasions[1] during the mass agitations started by and carried at the behest of that organization. The Congress leaders, and especially Gandhi, decided to hold the 26th January as the 'Day of Independence' all over India. It was observed for the first time in 1930 at a special ceremony starting with the hoisting of the "national flag,"[2] where assembled people took a pledge of loyalty to the Indian National Congress and "to carry out its instructions from time to time for the purpose to establish *Purna Swarajya*" or complete Independence from the British rule.[3]

The observance of this special 'Independence Day' with all solemnity, was continued ever since every year prior to Independence, under the auspices of the Congress, all over the country with special drills and parades and oath-taking ceremonies and significant speeches by important leaders. And since independence in 1947 it has been observed, as is well-known amongst the present generations, by our Government and people, as an official Republic Day ceremony with spectacular military parades and shows of social tabloids in our national Capital i.e. New Delhi, as well as in the separate State Capitals and in thousands of other places all over the country.

To utilize the vast accumulated steam of discontent of the people of India and, to channel it to predictable and controllable direction, the Congress under the leadership of Gandhi decided to launch a massive non-cooperation and passive resistance movement far greater than any tried before. Gandhi formulated the main strategy as well as the detailed tactics. He took a simple issue affecting every man, woman and child in the country, that of making salt by the *satyagrahis* or leaders and volunteers who willingly participated in the non-violent struggle, by boiling the saline water from the vast expanses of the seas that girdle one-half of the great Indian land mass. The manufacture and sale of salt was then a Government monopoly. Salt was usually imported from abroad at high cost and a tax was imposed on it. That made its price to the people very high, so Gandhi took this issue.

Gandhi himself took the lead and started on 12 March with a band of devoted Congress followers a historic march on foot called Dandi March from his Sabarmati Ashrama near Ahmedabad to a Western Arabian Sea Coast, Dandi, about 241 miles away. It took the party 24 days to reach there. During this period it aroused great enthusiasm all over India. At Dandi the leader himself broke the law on 6 April 1930 and the vast assembled people started making salt under his leadership. Preparations were made all over India, and especially at the coastal places, to break the salt laws and make salt out of sea water. There was a great response in Bengal as well, especially from the Congressmen and their supporters. Many known leaders marched through Midnapore town to the seashore in Contai where large masses of common people joined and started making slats from the waters of the Bay of Bengal. An unprecedented event -- a mass upsurge all over India[4], surpassing all expectations either of the Government or even of many Congress leaders. The Government got dismayed and organized counter forces and applied them ruthlessly against the unarmed people including women and children. There was a worst scene on the Contai seashores. The salt-makers in mass were struck indiscriminately with thick bamboo rods (Lathis) by rushing police forces under the command of the senior police forces, magistrates and even of the District Magistrate himself, James Peddie.[5] The Police and the military even fired in many places, such as Karachi, Peshawar and Madras, and many people were killed. Thousands of participants in the movement or even their sympathizers had been arrested and put in jail. In Midnapore, many known people, including our friends Profulla Tripathy and Sachin Maity, were also arrested. The police served on me a prohibitory order (hung up on the wall outside our house in the town) under Section 144 of the Criminal Procedure Code, not to address or participate in any gathering of 5 persons or more.

Gandhi himself was arrested in May when the movement was at its peak. However, it continued throughout the year with great fury and the forces of law and order tried to counter it with an iron hand.

Chittagong Armoury Raid, April 1930 - Second[6] Major Guerilla action by the Bengal Revolutionaries

While the political atmosphere of India was thus beginning to heat up with nationwide protests, demonstrations, 'illegal' making of salts and non-payment of taxes, at the initial stages of the Salt-Satyagraha movement, the whole country was startled by the news of the Chittagong Armoury Raid in Bengal on 18 April, the most daring revolutionary activity in the then British India after the historic 'Sepoy Mutiny'' of 1857. For the first few days the identity of its participants was not disclosed. But it gradually leaked out that the main raids[7] in Chittagong town (now in Bangladesh) on the night of 18 April on the police armoury and the European Club, were followed by severe and intensive armed fights between the insurgents and the security forces on the adjacent hills of Jalalabad in which many on both sides died. Many other raiders dispersed and staged subsequent fights. All these were the activities of a fiery band of young revolutionaries of Chittagong under the leadership of a mild, elderly school teacher, Surya Sen, and his close colleagues Ananta Singh, Ganesh Ghose and Lokenath Ball.

This incidence had a tremendous impact on the country, and in fact a double one. First, on the youth, particularly of Bengal, in giving a clear signal that it was high time to follow this initial action by a series of other armed activities within their capacities, to weaken the strength of foreign domination at a critical moment. Second, on the general people to whom it showed that public movement and mass demonstrations and protests needed to be complemented by selected armed actions and the attendant display of discipline, courage and the spirit of self-sacrifice on the part of the youth.

Here it may be worthwhile to note a few lines about the true objective, philosophy and the logic of such armed activities of the Indian revolutionaries, as there had been in the contemporary periods as well as since India's independence in 1947 many wrong perceptions among both the public leaders and the historians about these valiant bands of youths. Even among many of the sympathizers and active supporters there have been a tendency to regard the activities of the revolutionaries as reactions or 'reprisals' to the repressive actions of the then Government.[8] But this was only partly so but not wholly. For it was true that the objective of the revolutionaries was to create a panic and disorder among the entire personnel constituting the "iron pillar" of the British administration in India, from the topmost to the lowest levels. But more important, it was to demonstrate to the political parties and the public in Great Britain and also to the people all over the world that the youth in India were not prepared to tolerate foreign rule with all its oppressive and exploitative actions. Though the revolutionaries recognized that there were apparently some benefits of the British rule, e.g. a unified administration of the country, better communications through the railways, postal, and telegraph systems, introduction of modern education, etc. But they, like all other patriotic sections, felt that the latter were designed more for the convenience of administration of a system which was basically anti-Indian (as Gandhi showed in the course of his historic trial in 1922) than for the real benefits of the people. They were especially slanted to serve the cause and interests of the British capitalists at home and the British business in India. So the revolutionaries vowed to disrupt and destroy them by means which would in their opinion be more effective than the Gandhian way of non-violent non-cooperation.

Thus the cause of the revolutionaries was just, moral and human, and the means they adopted, armed action, collective or isolated, were justified by the logic and compulsions of history. They were not "terrorists" as called by the British rulers and their agents, nor blood hunters. They did not want violence for violence' sake, but only on a selective basis and to the extent it was necessary to convince the British rulers of India that it would be impossible to hold India against the wishes of its people. They did not want to physically hurt, or even wish ill of the average British people but to warn all those, both British and Indian, who formed an integral part of the ruling machinery which was alien, exploitative and oppressive. Finally it may be noted that the revolutionaries wére all normal, and some even above normal, persons of great education, intellectual attainments, and mental and moral strength. They had been trained for and keen or sacrificing their lives whenever necessary for their great cause -- the freedom of India, their Motherland.

Thus, while by the end of 1930 the Congress Non-Cooperation Movement had reached its peak and there were signs of some negotiation between Gandhi (then in prison) and the Viceroy, the revolutionaries kept their state of preparedness.

After Chittagong Raid B.V. Group takes the Initiative

It was in the midst of these exciting situations that I sat for the Intermediate Science Examination of the Calcutta University at Midnapore in February 1930. After the results were out I decided to go to the Bengal Engineering College at Shibpore near Calcutta.

Though I was happy to join the college, but at the same time, I was feeling bad at the thought of getting away from Midnapore, the main centre of my political activities -- both revolutionary and in student and youth fronts. Dinesh had already gone back to Dacca having been recalled to work there. His place was taken in Midnapore by Sasanka Sekhar Das Gupta who also joined the Midnapore College but lived at Hijli (near Kharagpur) with his uncle who was an engineer there. While he had the overall responsibility of work of our Midnapore unit, its main work was entrusted to Phani Kundu and myself. The public front was mainly taken care of by Profulla Tripathy. Haripada was sent to Contai in 1929 to start and organize a group there. He took admission in Contai P.K. College and lived in the hostel and was doing good work. I had maintained some links with Profulla in working at student and youth front at Midnapore although my main task was to keep our revolutionary unit in a state of preparedness and necessary 'action', should there be any call. The work of our unit was going on well, thanks to the disciplined help and cooperation of our next group with Amar, Kshiti, Phani Das, Brajakishore and others. Through intensive training and study, secret group meetings and rendezvous among all members of the group we kept our preparedness.

Because of the sincerity of purpose and earnestness of all concerned, our work appeared to be satisfactory to all of us as well as to most senior members of our organization in Calcutta. Phani and I often visited the latter in one of our principal centres at the office of the party's monthly journal "Benu" (the 'Lute') whose main theme was writing nationalistic and patriotic articles, poems, comments and editorials. The paper had made a good reputation under the editorship of one of our senior members in Calcutta, Bhupendra Kishore Rakshit Ray. Among others whom we then used to meet in Calcutta were Haridas Dutta of the fame of Rodda arms loot incident in Calcutta in 1914[9], Prafulla Kumar Dutta who had qualified as an engineer from the Benares Hindu University and started a small factory of his own at Dakshineswar in north Calcutta, Rasamoy Sur, a teacher, and Jyotish Guha and Benoy Sen, two lawyers. Many of them, in return, sometimes came to Midnapore to meet us and also other selected members of our Midnapore unit.

During this period, in the second half of 1930, the revolutionary activities in Bengal, as in several other provinces of India, were continued. A bomb was thrown on the then British Police Commissioner Charles Tegart of Calcutta. But it missed and rebounded and killed the thrower, a youngman named Anuja Sen. In a trial that was held later for conspiracy the 'accused' were then well-known public figures like Dr. Narayan Roy, editor of a journal in Patna, *Searchlight,* and Dr. Bhupal Bose, a medical doctor. They both had contacts with the Bengal Volunteers Group. The second and more daring incident took place on 29 August 1930 in Dacca (then the second city of Bengal). The Inspector-General of Police in Bengal, Lowman, was on a visit to Mitford Hospital with Hodson, the Superintendent of Police of Dacca, when they were fired on by an unknown young man with a revolver. Lowman died on the spot, Hodson was wounded seriously and admitted into the hospital where he was operated and recovered. The assailant escaped. He was later identified as Benoy Bose, a mild and apparently a quiet young student of the Mitford Medical School. The attack was the first major action of the Dacca unit of the B.V. group after the Chittagong uprising. The police could not trace Benoy, so he was declared an absconder.

Daring Raid on Writers' Building,

While there were several minor actions by different revolutionary groups of Bengal in different districts, the third major and even more daring one took place on 8th December 1930, in Calcutta, and within the very seat of the Government of Bengal at what was and is still known as the Writers' Building in Dalhousie Square. In the morning of that day three young men, deluding the squad of strong armed guards, consisting of both British sergeants and Indian armed police, posted all over the building, climbed on to the second floor and started firing from their revolvers extensively. The shooting went on for some time absolutely unchallenged and they raided from office to office and shot at the occupants. Their principal target was the Inspector-General of Prison, Simpson, a senior British administrator of jails all over the province. He was killed instantaneously. Several other British officers were injured while some were reported to have escaped down the drain pipes. The young men had the absolute control of the building for at least half-an-hour. Only after that a strong armed police arrived from Lalbazar, the headquarters of the Bengal Police, located only a few yards from the Writers' Building. By that time the three young revolutionaries, whose identities were later revealed, Benoy Bose (who had shot dead Lowman, the I.G. of Police earlier in Dacca), Dinesh Gupta and Badal Gupta, had successfully accomplished their job which was assigned to them by elders of the Bengal Volunteer's Group to which all the three belonged. Then under previous instructions from their leaders they swallowed the deadly poison of patassium cyanide which they had been carrying, to commit suicide. Although they had ample time to escape, they acted as per their instruction to demonstrate to the people the courage and the self-immolating spirit of the revolutionaries. But while Badal Gupta died immediately sitting on a chair, Benoy and Dinesh survived the effect of the poison because of their excitement. So they shot themselves with their revolvers through their heads and were seriously wounded. The police later removed them to the Calcutta Medical College Hospital, where both were operated and kept under medical care.

Soon after the incident the daring story flashed out through mouth, radio and newspaper, first in Calcutta and then in Bengal and the whole of India. The news was received by the people at large with great excitement and elation, and especially among the revolutionaries. Next to the Chittagong Armoury raid at the beginning of the year this was ranked as the second most serious challenge of the year to the British administration in India.

Before the incident happened, in September 1930 I had already joined the B.E. College at Shibpore, near Calcutta, and was staying as a boarder in one of two college hostels, the Slater House, on first floor. I had been anticipating some such incident. For contrary to all my expectations, when I was trying to settle down in my new academic environment of the academics of the College and in my first hostel life outside my family, I found to my great surprise that in one of the chilly and misty evenings of December appeared the figure of Dinesh right on the first floor of the Slater House. He was dressed in his usual simple 'dhoti' (a loose-flowing Bengali dress) with a short 'Punjabi' and clad in a woollen shawl to protect him against the cold. I was a bit frightened of the hostel authorities because visitors were not allowed after 7 p.m. in the evening. However, I managed to whisk him away to the ground floor and to the adjacent ground and there we talked. He told me that he was not happy that I had left Midnapore as my absence was creating there some problems in the organization at this crucial time when the situation in the whole country was most opportune for harassing the agents of the alien rulers by selected armed actions. So he plainly told me to leave B.E. College as early as possible and return to Midnapore. This was a matter of serious concern to me personally and to my family but I had to think of the country and the party. Dinesh revealed at the end that "this is our last meeting" but, consistent with our training in strict secrecy, he did not elaborate on it.

But I guessed that something was coming. For Dinesh, like Benoy Bose, was already a declared absconder by the Dacca police because of some of his political activities. For some time we in Midnapore, in cooperation with our Contai friends, arranged to keep him undetected by the police at the farm-house of one of our first members of the Contai Unit, Anil Maity, about ten miles outside of Contai town, in a village at the confluence of the river Rasulpur and the river Ganges, near the extensive lower Bengal delta. This was done with the approval of Anil's elder brother and his family who managed that house and looked after their landed property. They all were sympathetic to our cause. After some time Dinesh was recalled to Calcutta and had since been living there.

However, at the B.E. College hostel that evening (about 6th December, two days before the Writers' Building action) I decided not to let him go but served him with a light snack out of my stock and at 9 p.m. when the room lights were off we too slipped in my bed and covered overselves with blanket. We got up early in the morning next day, quickly became ready, and covering ourselves with woollen wrappers set out of the hostel and walked, unnoticed by anybody, to the College compound gate. It was still locked and the gateman was sleeping. Dinesh scaled the gate and quickly vanished in the mist. I gave him a last look with a feeling of love and respect.

In the evening of 8th December 1930, the news of Writers' Building raid got around and caused a great excitement amongst our hostel inmates. Many uttered the names of Benoy, Badal and Dinesh again and again. On hearing the news the meaning of Dinesh's last words to me just two days before became perfectly clear to me. I became both elated and very sorry. Elated because Dinesh carried a most cherished mission of his life; and sorry because he was at that moment hanging between life and death, and also thinking that even if he recovered from his wounds he would be tried and sentenced to extreme punishment by the government. However, he left a specific legacy for me -- to go back to Midnapore and help in the work of our party unit there. So I started thinking.

Next morning at the B.E. hostel bathroom I met another student of just one class above me, who also came from Midnapore and had been in the college there in the same class as Dinesh and knew him well. He suddenly asked me, "Didn't I see Dinesh last night with you on the corridor?" I was taken aback as I thought that nobody noticed us when Dinesh visited me at the hostel. But I controlled myself and promptly replied, "Dinesh? Here! oh no." The matter ended there but it appeared that the other student had not been convinced.

However, in spite of the storm that was blowing within me regarding the Writers' Building act, the fates of Benoy and Dinesh, lying seriously ill at Calcutta Medical College hospital, the future of the revolutionary struggle in Bengal and particularly in Midnapore and of my own activities, I kept my outward calmness and went to my classes as usual in the morning and afternoon. But I keenly felt like talking to my friends in Calcutta and Midnapore and exchange views. I was sure this would have a great impact especially on the boys in Midnapore. They had already been burning for some 'action' of their own. However, I had to wait until the Christmas vacation of the College at the end of December 1930. I was almost convinced that I had to leave the College and go back to Midnapore but I could not do it abruptly so as not to upset too much my uncle and relatives at Midnapore and any parents in Contai, especially as my mother's health was not good. Moreover, I did not want to go to Midnapore immediately as I had already been marked by the police there. They only recently had served a notice on our house under section 144 of the Indian Criminal Proceeding Code forbidding me to address or participate in any meeting on assembly of more than five people. It had been served just before my departure for B.E. College in September.

In the meantime, Benoy and Dinesh were recovering in the Calcutta hospital. But then were Benoy came to his sense he willfully scratched his headwound in the absence of doctors and nurses, and the wound became sceptic. This news came out in papers while I was in Shibpore. Benoy's parents went to see him in the hospital and came out in tears. His end came in a few days. The people of entire Bengal deeply mourned it. But they appreciated in their heart of hearts the tremendous bravery of Benoy, Dinesh and Badal and their self-immolation at the altar of freedom for India. Dinesh was recovering well and the government was getting ready for his trial. At the same time the entire police in the province was put on alert and known members of the B.V. group especially were kept under strict surveillance.

Midnapore boys become restive

When the B.E. College and its hostels were closed for the Christmas holidays I came to Midnapore. The first thing I did after meeting my mother, grandmother and uncle, was to meet my closest colleagues of the local unit of B.V. in secret and discuss the impact of the Writers' Building act and especially of Dinesh' participation in it. They told me that they as well as the entire rank and file were pleased and proud and anxious to follow it up by some sort of activity in Midnapore. They felt that the time was most opportune because, first, the party there had been reached an enough state of preparedness to undertake major single or group actions second, the terrible repression that was unleashed by the government and the police,[10] including the Police chief of Contai and even the District Magistrate, James Peddie, himself on the Salt *Satyagrahis* and their sympathisers in Contai, not sparing even women and children, had created a deep resentment amongst the people against the authorities. Therefore it was thought that though as soldiers of the non-violent struggle for freedom launched by Gandhi they would not think of themselves undertaking any violent reprisal, if the revolutionaries gave a fitting reply it would be highly appreciated. This was also the feeling of the "man-on-the spot", our colleague in Contai, Haripada Bhowmik. Eventually, the sentiments and readings of the Midnapore group were duly communicated to its leaders in Calcutta.

As a first step it was decided to take some measured reprisal against the chief of Contai Police, Samsuddoha, for which a young man in his twenties was sent from outside the Midnapore district. It was considered advisable not to involve directly any of the local boys as that would expose the local organization at its infancy to the wrath of the authorities. The youth came to Contai alone when I was there. Haripada and I met him and introduced him to one of our senior local friends, Jyotish Bera. We four -- Haripada, Jyotish, the youth and myself met in our house and discussed and decided the modalities for an attempt on the life of the Police Chief. Jyotish would follow the latter's movements and try to get advance information and report to the youth. To avoid police suspicion he had instructions from Calcutta to have the least necessary contacts with us. He would have his meals at local hotels and watch the Police Chief and spend the nights outside the town under treeshades. He thus spent about a week but did not get a suitable opportunity to meet or see the Police Chief from close quarters. However, after a week he was recalled to Calcutta. It was then discussed by our party leaders at headquarters that in view of the preparedness of the Midnapore boys something bigger should be tried and hence the attempted action of Contai should be called off.

In January 1931 I returned to Shibpore with the decision that I would leave B.E. College in March and come back to Midnapore and get admission in the local college for B.Sc. with honours in Physics. I had already spoken about it to my mother, uncle and other close relatives before leaving Midnapore at the end of the Christmas holidays. They were all very sorry but did not object. At Shibpore I told two of my class fellows -- Shyamapada Chowdhuri and Sailen Nandi -- both from Sylhet, with whom I developed a special relationship during our first term in the B.E. College. Earlier I had revealed to them my real objective in life and affiliation to a political party.

In January/February 1931, I visited Calcutta several times and talked to some of the elder party members. By that time (on 13 December 1930) Benoy Bose had died. Dinesh recovered from his revolver wound and was put on trial for murder of the Inspector-General Prisons. He was lodged at Alipore Central Jail. Phani Kundu came from Midnapore and joined me in discussions with party leaders. It was then suggested that an attempt should be made on the life of the District Magistrate, James Peddie, who had earned an enormous displeasure of the people of the whole district of Midnapore and even outside for his brutal repression of the Salt *Satyagrahis* including even women and children. Phani and I readily agreed to this suggestion. At the same time we both offered help if required at a suitable opportunity. But the elders did not accept our proposal. They throught that as we two were among the very limited group of the first rank of the Midnapore unit our permanent departure from the scene would seriously jeopardise the future actions of the unit. So the choice fell on the second batch consisting of equally determined, dedicated and mature boys. Although this batch was somewhat larger, the names particularly of Jyoti Jiban Ghose and Bimal Das Gupta cropped up and they became the final choice. The elders had already an opportunity of meeting them in Midnapore during some of their earlier visits there. Phani Kundu was assigned the task of contacting the two on his return to Midnapore and informing them of the assignment and of making the necessary preparations.

I returned to B.E. College after the meeting and passed my time in great suppressed anxiety and excitement. I had to prepare for leaving the College in March. I informed the College authorities and the Superintendent of our hostel, the Slater House. He felt very sorry as he used to love me very much, almost like father. I also informed my two friends from Sylhet who too became very unhappy. But I took the opportunity in the meantime to do some work in the College itself in furthering our party objective. I collected from our headquarters in Calcutta a bunch of red pamphlet written in Bengali, entitled *"Rakte Amar Legeche Aj Sarbaneasher Nesha"* (or "My blood today is intoxicated with a desire for destruction"). It had been earlier distributed clandestinely among the public of Dacca, Midnapore and other places. It urged people to rise in revolt against the British rule in India, and hence was considered by the Government as seditious and banned. On one cold and misty night with Shyamapada I got out of our hostel and walked through the silent ground of the College compound and went to the complex of College lecture halls of different departments. With Shyamapada's help I stuck the pamphlet extensively on the walls and the notice boards all over. After finishing the job we two silently walked back to our hostel and slept. In the morning of the following day we went to our classes as usual. By that time the pamphlets were seen by many people, the bearers, students and later the teachers. There was a great excitement amongst all, as this was the first time in the history of the B.E. College that a seditious leaflet had managed to find its way into the college building. The police had been informed by the authorities and came to investigate. Shyamapada and I then held our breath. But nothing was found and nothing came out of the police investigation. Sometime later Profulla and Haripada came to see me in Shibpore during the day but visitors were allowed at that time, so nobody suspected anything. But we talked about the political situation in Bengal and particularly in Midnapore.

Suppression of the Civil Disobedience Movement and Gandhi-Irwin Pact, 1931

Towards the end of March 1931 I left B.E. College and returned to Midnapore. By that time Gandhi's Salt *Satyagraha* and Civil Disobedience Movement had reached nearly its peak, an unprecedented 'mass upheaval' all over the country. The Government of India as well as of the Provinces had taken strong measures to crush it. Gandhi was arrested soon after he started the *Salt Satyagraha* in March 1930, and kept in prison. So also were almost all the leaders of the Congress at the top as well as the most important Congress leaders and workers down to the village level. Thousands of other participants and supporters from among the common people were either taken into police custody, tried, convicted to varying terms of imprisonment, or beaten and tortured, and even shot and killed, by the forces of 'law and order' with the help of armed police and military fighting mercilessly unarmed civilians -- men, women and children.

Subhas Bose described the grim situation in clear and lucid terms in his *Indian Struggle:* "As soon as the Government realised the serious proportions which the campaign had assumed, they became entirely ruthless and brutal in their attempts at suppression. It is not possible to describe the atrocities committed by the forces of the Crown -- including both the police and the military -- in this connection. It is difficult to say which province suffered most, for each province had its tale of woe. In

Bengal, the Midnapore district suffered most and the sufferings of the people gave birth to a terrorist movement for organizing reprisals against officials.'' Bose also especially mentioned the then United Provinces, Gujarat and the North-Western Frontier Province. In the latter province, under the leadership of the veteran Frontier Gandhi, Khan Abdul Gaffar Khan, the valiant and material spirited Pathans, who pledged non-violence and formed a movement called 'Khodai - Khidmadgar' or 'Servants of God', responded massively to Gandhi's call. The authorities got frightened, particularly in view of the fact that the Province provided the British Indian Army with some of the finest soldiers to help sustain their rule over India as well over the independent spirited Pathan tribes in the N.W.F. Province.

As a result of the combined action of the Indian Government in removing the leaders of the Congress organization at different levels --- central, provincial, district and village, on the one hand, and of the ruthless acts of repression and suppression of the volunteers participating and even of their families and sympathizers, the Salt *Satyagraha* and the Civil Disobedience Movement waned substantially towards the end of 1930. However, the scale of the Movement and the extent of the people's participation, notwithstanding the reservations on the part of the Chiefs of the feudtory 'States',[11] certain sections of the minority communities, vested interests and foreign business communities, showed the extent of the hold of Gandhi and the Indian National Congress on the masses. The British Parliament then (mid-thirties), consisting of a Labour majority and headed by a Labour Prime Minister, Ramsay MacDonold, reviewed the situation in India and came to conclusion that India cannot be denied too long a fully responsible government by the Indians themselves. Therefore they advised the Viceroy, a somewhat liberal and openminded chief administrator of British rule over India, Lord Irwin, (1926-31) to arrange to meet Gandhi. Consequently the latter, along with other members of the Congress working Committee, were released in January 1931. Thereafter the Viceroy met Gandhi and the two had prolonged talks, following which a compromise agreement between the two was signed by the two on 5 March 1931, which came to be known as Gandhi Irwin Pact.

The Pact was however only a short-term truce in which Gandhi, the Congress and the country gained little. According to its terms the supreme leader of the Congress agreed to suspend the Civil Disobedience

Movement and to participate in the deliberations of the Second Round Table Conference[12], to be held in London, "for drafting a Constitution for India on the basis of (a) Federation, (b) Responsibility and (c) adjustments and safeguards that may be necessary in the interests of India." The Congress was also given the right to "forge the demand for an investigation into the allegation of police atrocities in different parts of India." In return the Viceroy, on behalf of the Government, agreed (a) to release simultaneously all political prisoners jailed in connection with the non-violent movement, (b) to restore confiscated property and land to the owners where it had not been already sold or auctioned by the Government; (c) to withdraw emergency ordinances; (d) to permit people living near the sea coast to collect or manufacture salt; and (e) to allow peaceful picketing of liquor, opium and foreign - cloth shops in general and not specifically aimed at British manufactures, with a view to promoting the 'Swadeshi movement'.

The terms of the Gandhi-Irwin Pact, even seen as a temporary truce, were a great disappointment to the people and even to many of the Congress leaders including young Jawaharlal Nehru. Because there was no reference to the declared (in Lahore in December 1929) Congress goal of "complete independence" or even Dominion Status.[13] However, one net result was that the Civil Disobedience prisoners were started to be released but not the thousands of revolutionaries either convicted or detained. So the latter did not accept the truce. To make the matters worse, the three noted popular young revolutionaries of Punjab -- Bhagat Singh, Rajguru and Sukhdev -- who had been earlier tried and sentenced to death for their *supposed* part in the third Lahore Conspiracy Case (10 July - 7 October 1930), a sentence against which the whole country protested and demonstrated and even Gandhi had intervened in talking to the Viceroy (Irwin), were hanged in the Lahore Central Jail on the evening of 23 March, 1931.

Gandhi-Irwin Pact comes as a disappointment to Revolutionaries

This incident shocked and stunned the country. It was contrary to the spirit of the Gandhi-Irwin Pact through which, it was widely regarded, the British Government had showed their intention to develop a peaceful atmosphere in India for the next round of talks on constitutional advances. But the hangings proved that the British were not sincere to part with real power over India, and what they outwardly promised to 'give' they wanted to take away by various ingenuous devices including the alienation of one set of people within India from another and isolating the radical nationalists and the revolutionaries. The latter did realize this and therefore decided to continue their activities against the "iron frame" of the British rule in India, though not against the British people as such, as observed earlier.[14]

That was the definite impression I received from our party elders in Calcutta when I met some of them in late March in 1931 before my return to Midnapore. Some of them had already visited Midnapore and talked to our colleagues there, Phani Kundu and the two boys Jyoti Jiban and Bimal Das Gupta who had been selected for the first major armed attempt on the life of the District Magistrate as a reprisal for his repressive actions against the Salt *Satyagrahis* or civil disobedience volunteers in Midnapore district, especially Contai.

After my return to Midnapore towards the end of March 1931 I had some secret meetings with Sasanka Sekhar Das Gupta and Phani Kundu. I did not meet Jyoti and Bimal, as whenever I came to Midnapore I used to be very systematically watched by the secret service police of the Intelligence Branch. Secondly, among three of us, the frontrankers in the Midnapore Branch of B.V., Profulla Tripathy, Phani Kundu and myself, while Profulla was specially assigned to open political activities and maintain contact with the Congress, youth and student activities; myself partly with activities in the open front and partly with organizational work of the group; Phani, by a tacit understanding, was to deal with practical actions. This was mainly because having come from a business family of Midnapore, of Kundus, and being himself engaged in the business he was not suspected by the police. From Sasanka Das Gupta, and Phani Kundu[15] I came to know that all preparations for the action were complete; Bimal and Jyoti were fully briefed about its details and they were in fine spirits. As a result of my talks with the former two, it was decided that I should leave Midnapore town as soon as possible, go to Contai and remain there for next two to three weeks when the 'action' was supposed to take place. This was to avoid any suspicion by the police that I had been directly involved in it. So, although my mother was then seriously ill at my uncle's house in Midnapore, I had to leave her and go to Contai where my father was living alone.

At Contai I met Haripada and we talked about the impending action We were naturally very excited and anxious about how the thing would go. On the morning of 8th April, while we were sitting in a tea shop came the newspaper with the the great news that the District Magistrate, James Peddie, was shot last evening when he was visiting a Boys Scouts exhibition at the Collegiate School, Midnapore, by two youths who subsequently fled. He was seriously wounded and removed to the local hospital where the doctors frantically tried to save his life but he died in the early morning. Our hearts beat with great excitement and apprehension. Excitement, because of the very success of a first attempt by the Midnapore boys made on the local soil, and hence of the tremendous impact that it would have on the local people. It would show that the district of Midnapore which had taken a key role in two successive non-violence non-cooperation movements of Gandhi and silently suffered to the extremes, opened a new dimension, through armed action, in the history of freedom struggle for India. At the same time it gave a warning to the whole country against a 'false dawn' created by the euphoria of the Gandhi-Irwin Pact signed a few days ago. Apprehension, because it was not certain how the Government and its forces would react, and would there be new oppression against the people? However, we were greatly relieved at the news that the two youths who did the act had escaped.

Police was not sure who was responsible -- boys of Midnapore or outsiders? But they made some indiscriminate arrests and these included our two leading members, Profulla Tripathy and Phani Kundu a close and sympathiser of ours, Sachin Maity, son of the veteran lawyer Upendera Nath Maity, Kishore Dutta of Barisal who was the founder-organizer of a sister revolutionary group of Bengal, the Anushilan Samiti at Midnapore, and many other youths who had been somehow active in public life. At Contai, Haripada and I, on reading the newspapers about the list of daily arrests, thought that our turn might come at any time. I became very worried about my father and mother as well as uncle who had expected me, as the first child of the family, to distinguish myself in life and society through high education and good reputation. But I felt some relief thinking that they never objected to my political activities and even had appreciated them. They knew many of my close colleagues both in public and secret activities and loved them all. But they would naturally be concerned over what would happen to me if I was involved in any major act.

My arrest in Contai and transfer to Midnapore

Five days passed like this. On 12th April (Sunday) when my father went out marketing, I went to Haripada's hostel and together we two went to the bi-weekly market through the main road of the town passing by the law courts, police station, the post office and a series of shops. On our return I suddenly looked back, which was my habit as I had often in the past been shadowed by agents of the Intelligence Branch. I then found a few steps behind me the second police officer-in-charge of the Midnapore, Ashgar Ali, accompanied by a constable. I became immediately suspicious and asked Haripada to move away from me. To test my suspicion I turned back as if to go back to the market. Then Ali stopped me and said: "Don't go, you are arrested". I feigned a great surprise and interjected: "Arrested? Me? Any warrant?" He replied : "why do you ask me that question? You know everything. You are arrested on charge of murder of the District Magistrate under section 302 of the Indian Penal Code, and I do not need any warrant to arrest you." I then thought it was useless to argue further. I was taken to the local police station and told that I would be taken to Midnapore town soon. I asked them to inform my father who was then living alone as my mother and all four brothers were with my uncle at Midnapore. In about half-an-hour my father came walking, as Contai was then a small, beautiful and prosperous town with plenty of big trees and there was no public transport. My father was just about fifty and looked greatly worried. I told him that I was arrested on suspicion in connection with the murder of the District Magistrate and would soon be taken to Midnapore. This was a tragic moment but I tried to hold my mental strength. I bowed to him to bid farewell, with an uncertain future of life and death. But we had been trained for such eventuality. My father slowly trod out of the police station.

I had been treated on the whole nicely at the police station as most of the senior police officers knew my father who was a lawyer practising in the local law court. I was given some lunch on the Indian style and then put on a bus going direct from Contai to Midnapore, a distance of about 70 miles. Ali and his constable accompanied me. We left about midday and the journey took about five hours during the hottest time of the day and in the hottest month in Bengal. The road all along was very familiar to me, as ever since 1922 when I had joined the school in Midnapore I used to travel to and from Contai mostly by bus to visit my parents there. The road passed through the countryside with open fields, at that time largely bare and dry, and through an important railway junction and colony, Kharagpur, and then near the Midnapore town over a road bridge across the river Kangsavati which flowed south of Midnapore town. The bus then passed by our house, where my mother was very ill, and then soon came to the police station. Most officers there were known to me as our house was not very far from the police station.

My life in Police Lock-up

At the police station, first I was treated all right. The officer-in-charge informed my uncle who, with my maternal uncle, came to see me. They were naturally very grieved and upset. I could imagine how much my mother and grandmother must be worried. However, my uncle controlled his emotions and asked the officer if he could send a mat for me to spread on the floor of the locker where I would be kept under police custody for the time being for questioning, and a sheet with pillow and a mosquito curtain to be used for the night. The officer agreed and my uncle, on returning home, arranged to send the articles to the police station. The lock-up was not very bad, was attached to the main office facing the south where I could get some breeze. As evening came I was locked in. Later I was given some meal brought from a nearby hotel. There I myself made the makeshift bed, with no mattress however but just on the hard cemented floor of the cell, and a sentry who was posted at the iron door lined with vertical bars, helped to fix the mosquito curtain. Before retiring I expressed my desire to go to bathroom but there was nothing attached. There were a series of makeshift latrines made of corrugated tins with top of the back open, somewhat away from the police station, for the use of the police constables. One of them tied a thick rope round my waist (lest I tried to escape), like an ordinary criminal, and held one end with his hand, and led me to the latrine. While I was using it he held the rope from outside through the opening in the back. They did the same thing every time I went to the latrine. For the sixteen days, I was kept in the police lock-up for interrogation. However, as I was tired for the whole day's physical exertion and mental tension I slept soundly during the night.

Next morning, on 13th April 1931, from about 8 o'clock a fat and plump Inspector of the Central Intelligence Branch from Calcutta, named Bhujen Sarkar, who had arrived in Midnapore, to carry out the necessary investigations, started questioning me. Among the questions were: where I had been for the last one month? What I knew about the murder? Who were the perpetrators of the 'crime'? Hundreds of the other questions which I do not remember today after a lapse of over half-a-century. But I do remember he was writing page after page recording my replies. He acted very much theatrically, sometimes very pleasant speaking to me in a low and gentle voice and at other times in a highly agitated tone with a great deal of anger and threatening me of the grave consequences of not telling him the truth. Sometimes he was polite to ask me to sit on a chair in front of him, at other times he shouted at me and asked me to stand up. I decided to hold my patience indefinitely. The questionings went on for fifteen days, each day from 8 a.m. in the morning till 12.00 and then again from about 2.00/3.00 p.m. to 8.00 p.m. in the evening. His purpose obviously was to tire me out.

Since the police did not get any clue by questioning me on the first day they shifted me to a lock-up down below, in front, with a barred window in the north and the door in the east. There was absolutely no breeze coming from the north in the summer. Moreover they took away the mat, the sheet, the pillow and the mosquito net and gave me only a dusty woollen blanket to sit, lie down and sleep on the floor, as a punishment for not divulging to the police any information. The inside of the lock-up was terribly hot day and night in April, and at night Midnapore was notorious for its mosquitoes. So, for next 15 days I could hardly sleep in the day or at night. The meals -- two main for lunch and dinner and tea and bread in the morning, brought from a local hotel -- were terrible. So I got friendly with a constable and persuaded him to visit my family quietly and bring some money with which he used to bring me occasionally some tasty sweets and buy some anti-mosquito coils for burning in my lock-up at night. But even that was stopped after a few days as the Inspector paid a surprise visit to my lock-up one later evening, at about 10 p.m., and found an anti-mosquito coil burning. He became very much angy and cautioned the Officer-in-charge of the police station to warn all his constables against any help given to me.

In the lock-up, apart from the time I had to spend during questioning by the Intelligence Branch, as long as I was awake I used to walk up and down, though it was barely 10 feet wide and 15 feet long. One thing, I could see from my barred window the main road in front through which passed every day thousands of people. Most of them knew that a youth suspected of having some connection with the murder of the District

Magistrate was kept in the police lock-up, and so looked to me while passing. One morning the I.B. Inspector came to me with a great deal of excitement and asked "Do you know what the men on the street are saying" I responded "What"? He spurted : "See the way he is pacing to and fro in the cell, he must have done the job (i.e. killed the District Magistrate)!" I smiled and only said : "Is that so?" So in the whole morning he again continued his questionings.

Three notable incidents happened while I was in the police lock-up. One morning they brought my father who, though very sad and worried, kept his poise and balance. The I.B. Inspector repeated his harangues against me in front of my father and wanted the latter to ask me to open my mind. But my father easily could know with his legal brain what it meant. He only said : "I know you do not know anything, but if you know you should speak out". I kept quiet. The Inspector was not pleased but later let my father go.

On another morning the British Superintendent (head of the Police) named Kidd, came in front of my lock-up and watched me for a few minutes. My blood warmed up and a spirit of defiance was roused in me, and I started walking up and down inside my cell without seeming to care for him. Another evening after I had just been let out of the cell to have my evening meal on the floor in front of the cell, and then put back at the end, to my great surprise and shock I found that the barred door of the cell in front of me, which was even worse than that of mine, was unlocked and came out Jyoti Jiban Ghose, also for his meal. Jyoti, as stated earlier, was one of the two of our party members who had been given the task of an attempt on the life of the District Magistrate. So I wondered how did he come. Did the police come to know all about him as well as his associate Bimal Das Gupta? I became extremely worried and could not sleep that night.

My transfer to Jail custody at Midnapore Central Jail

However, even worst days passed, and after sixteen days I breathed some outside air and had a glimpse of the open sky when I was taken out of the little lock-up by a hackney (horse-drawn) carriage, then the usual public conveyance in Midnapore town, hand-cuffed and guarded by a sub-inspector and two armed police constables, about two kilometres away, to the big red-hued Midnapore central jail located in an isolated place in the north of the town. Many hardened criminals from all over

Bengal were kept there, especially in its two notorious blocks of 200 deadly, dark, tiny cells in two separate red stoned buildings. After we had reached there, the huge main front gate of the jail of solid iron bars, was opened and I was led in by the officers and the guards to a closed area where the offices of the Superintendent and the Jailor with other staff were located. There my handcuff was unlocked and I took a swift glance all around. A second huge and heavy solid wooden gate, about 100 ft away, blocked the view of the entire jail. I was led in the outer periphery of the massive jail through a small fly door. I still remember what a great relief (though very short-lived) I felt when I had my first view of a long red-hued clear road that went from the main gate to a high central tower complex from where the sentries kept constant watch over the entire jail. The wards and building complexes consisting of prison cells, and various service buildings were all built of solid blocks of red laterite stones. As I entered I was escorted by two jail wardens and taken to Ward No. 8 where all others, arrested in connection with the murder of the District Magistrate were kept. Among them I met my close friends, Profulla Tripathy, Phani Kundu and Braja Kishore Chakravarty, as well as Sachin Maity, Kishore Dutta, Ramsankar Chakravarty, Tarapada Chatterjee, Sachin Nandi, Nirmal Adhikari and Nemai Pal. Later Jyoti Jiban was also brought from the police lock-up.

My heart was filled with joy after having seen so many friends and aequaintances at such close quarters, and indeed all for a common cause, though only Phani and I had an advance warning of the event. We were about fifteen and all kept in the same ward as under - trial prisoners. Most were in their teens. I was 19 and Phani about the same age; so also all others, except Kishore Dutta in first twenties and Profulla and Sachin were somewhat elder. We all were arrested on suspicion of conspiracy for the murder under Section 302 of the Indian Penal Code.

The Ward was a rectangular big room with several spacious barred high windows and one door with solid iron bars. There was enough space between the bars to have a full view of the entire inside by the sentries from the outside. In one of the far ends there was a little protrusion in bent bars, where for the night, when the ward was locked from outside, there was a big drum for the prisoners to pass water and were supplied with a blanket and a sheet for our bed. Our meals, morning and evening, came from the common kitchen meant for the prisoners and consisted of tea and bread as breakfast, and, for lunch and dinner, 'lapsi' or a crude mixture of rice and lentils boiled together, or 'chapatis' (unleavened Indian whole wheat bread), lentils and some crude curries usually of vegetables and occasionally of fish and mutton. Each of us was supplied with the usual prisoners' aluminium glass, as aluminium dish with high brims and an aluminium bowl. We used the latter for eating 'dal' (lentil soup), bath and other purposes as well. We used to have our bath in the open, from the usual prisoners' cemented long shallow channels built almost at the ground level. Some convicted prisoners used to bring our meals. There was a small open paved yard in front of our Ward where we could walk in the morning and evening. We were allowed to wear our own clothes. We were served with dinner at 6 p.m. in the evening and locked in the ward from 7 p.m. till 7 a.m. in the morning next day. We were not supplied with any newspaper or any reading material. Our life was very hard and austere but we were happy, spending much of our time in talking to one another, for first few days on our individual experience with the police immediately after our arrest, then on the effect of the incident on the country and especially among the people of Midnapore and also the possible course of the case. We knew that the charge under Section 302 of Indian Penal Code might, on trial, lead upto a sentence of death. But we were generally not very much concerned for that, as most of us thought that was a price we had to pay for trying to free the country from the brutal foreign yoke. Some amongst us, like Brajokishore, used to entertain us with singing.

Later when Jyoti Jiban was brought from his town lock-up we all were very happy. He was a jolly and humorous young man in only late teens. He kept his role in the attempt on the life of the District Magistrate strictly secret from all except Phani and me. He gave us a short description of how Bimal and he went into the Scout's exhibition at Collegiate School in the evening, how they found and shot at the D.M. and then escaped. They ran out of the room, came on to the main street in front the Collegiate School, got hold of a cycle from a rider and rode, two together, towards, the north several miles and then stopped at a small station called Salboni and left the cycle. Later they boarded a passenger train and first went to Purulia and then managed to go to Calcutta with their arms.[16] They met some of our elder colleagues who then took charge of them. Both of them were kept hidden from the public but as their names did not come out in newspapers, after about a week they were advised by the central leaders to go back to Midnapore. But here was a mistake. Bimal's name had already came out after about 3/4 days, though incidentally. When the police in Midnapore came to search Bimal's uncle's house nothing incriminating was found. But on questioning, a little daughter of their domestic maid spoke out, without knowing the gravity of her words, that "the brother was not at home for the last few days". This aroused the police's suspicion and directed their investigation of the matter on that basis. They became convinced that Bimal was somehow implicated but did not announce it, lay in wait around Bimal's residence in secret. Just at that time Bimal arrived at Midnapore and went to their house. At this his elder brother got surprised and dismayed; however, he and his family managed to hide Bimal for sometime with the help of friends and then to send him back to Calcutta. The police then declared him as an 'offender' in the District Magistrate Murder Case.

However, the police did not know anything about Jyoti Jiban. So he returned safely to his parents' house in Midnapore and stayed there until he was arrested by the police on suspicion and brought to the town police lock-up and later to Midnapore Central Jail.

In the jail, while we had been waiting for our trial with a great deal of uncertainty and apprehension, we had some new experiences of the atmosphere of the jail and its warders who kept watch on us and other prisoners in the adjoining wards. Other prisoners were mostly criminals, at least in the eye of law. However, with a few exceptions we found in both groups a feeling of sympathy and admiration for us. We used to have often friendly chats with the warders. The convicted prisoners who came into contact with us for various services assured us if we needed anything they would get them for us. They had their own contact with the warders and many used to keep some valuables and even cash secretly in selected hideouts. One day a convict showed us how he kept in his body, actually in his throat, a few coins, which he took out and swallowed when he wanted. The hole was made by placing a piece of warm lead in the throat for some days. In such a hole he could hide not only coins but easily a small gold ring or a watch.

One day, we were greatly touched by the offer of a supposedly hardened criminal kept in one of the 200 'death cells' locked for 24 hours with both hands cuffed and bars and fetters between his legs. He used to shout almost 24 hours in a day. He never saw us nor did we see him. But through the convicts, who acted as service boys like servers of meals and sweepers between different wards, he heard about us and even got the information that we had resorted to a short hunger strike and stopped taking meals. He sent a message to us, through one of these 'go-betweens' offering a share of his own 'chapatis' for us. This moved us greatly. So much so that his feelings gave a great boost to our morale. And it taught me the lesson that no man, however cruel or criminal he may be, should be totally condemned; he may have also in a corner of his heart a hidden store of humanity and softness which might manifest on appropriate occasions.

Outside the prison, vigorous police enquiry went on and our relatives became busy meeting and talking to one another, most of whom were lawyers themselves, as well as to other expert lawyers, about suitable means and ways of our legal defence at the law courts when our trials begin. One day some of them, including my maternal uncle, came to interview us in the office of the jail. However, they were not allowed to contact us direct but separated by bars and watched at a distance by the Intelligence Branch officials. They mostly asked how we were and if we needed anything of personal use. But at one moment Sri Jawaharlal Adhikari, a noted lawyer and one of our great sympathizers and father of Nirmal Adhikari who was a co-accused with us, passed on a message from our ardent supporter and well-wisher, Kumar Debendra Lal Khan of Narajole Raj family, conveying his assurance to us that he would do his best and spend whatever money was necessary for our suitable legal defence. That was a great solace to us. And we were also told that almost the entire people of Midnapore were highly sympathetic to us. This was partly because all of us -- fourteen youths -- came from respectable and educated families of the town and we ourselves had already built up some reputation for our distinctions in schools as well as in public activities.

Towards the end of April 1931, all fourteen of us were taken in a closed van handcuffed, and guarded by a number of armed sentries, to the court of the Sub-Divisional Magistrate (S.D.O.), Sanker Sen (who had been 'notorious' for his part in suppressing popular activities in pursuit of freedom. There we were led, handcuffed and tied to our waist with a long single rope, to a raised wooden enclosure especially made for under trial prisoners, close to the magistrate. The court room was filled with lawyers, many of whom were known to us and we were very happy to see them. Outside the court was a big crowd of the public who came to have a look at us and to see what happens in the trial. The magistrate came with all his usual posture and gravity and was seated. One of the senior lawyers told the court to wait a few minutes as the leading barrister and well-known public leader of Midnapore (and in fact of the entire Bengal Province), Birendra Nath Sasmal, would appear to lead the defence. The magistrate gave that time. Soon Sasmal entered the court with his imposing and impressive figure and there was a great excitement amongst all those assembled at the court. His appearance was a great assurance to us and must have created some apprehension among the opposite parties, especially the police and the Government lawyers. Sasmal looked up over his half-moonsize glasses and had a quick view of the magistrate, the court room and of us. Then he blurted out to the magistrate : "Why the prisoners are handcuffed in the court?" The Magistrate replied : "That is for my safety." Sasmal interjected : "'Oh'. Is that so?" Nothing much more was said by either side -- Prosecution or the Defence. But Sasmal's that one question and the reply were enough to expose the partisan character of the trying magistrate and the hollowness of the trial. However, the Police said that the investigations had not been completed yet, so they prayed for an adjournment. The Magistrate agreed and fixed the date on 21 May (1931). The Court dispersed and we were taken back to the jail and to our ward in the same way as we came. But before leaving the Court there were great shouts of sympathy and appreciation from among the assembled people.

On our return to the jail, Phani and I speculated what could be the reason for the police to ask for an adjournment of the case. Did they already get some evidence against us and expect some new ones? We did not know that Bimal's name had come out in the meantime, as we had not been given any newspaper from the time of our arrest and Jyoti also did not know. He was arrested before the news came out. Later the I.B. people came and interrogated us in the jail about Bimal. But then they were not sure how for Bimal was involved as they had started the investigations from the beginning on the assumption that the 'action' was not the work of the Midnapore youths who, according to the Midnapore police's intelligence, were not organized enough to do such a daring and well prepared act. They had assumed that it was the work of outsiders, in which Midnapore boys were only tools or accomplishes. On that assumption, it appears, they treated us relatively lightly compared to our friends and colleagues later in 1932 and 1933. We were harassed and put under great strains in the police lock-up but no physical violence was applied. However, after we were transferred to jail custody pending trial, not much disturbance was caused to us except the usual rigours of the prison life. Our greatest preoccupation was about the trial, how it would come up and what would be the consequences. How much would the police be able to discover? But one thing about which we were sure. Thanks to our strict secrecy and the fact that only three people in Midnapore knew about the attempt -- Sasanka Das Gupta (who came in place of Dinesh), Phani Kundu and myself, other than Jyoti and Bimal, there was not much such chance of police getting any information which they could present to the trying magistrate as positive proof of conspiracy and complicity against us. Our guess was further strengthened by the fact that four amongst us, including Jyoti Jiban and Brajakishore, had been released on bail in the meantime. The conditional release of Jyoti almost convinced us that the police had not been able to find any clue.

Soon the time taken by the police passed and on the morning of 21 May we were again taken to the Court of the Sub-Divisional Magistrate in the same manner as before. On the way again simultaneous feelings of hope and apprehensions occupied our minds. But we tried to talk these out amongst us. As soon as we reached the Court of the Sub-Divisional Magistrate, fully guarded, big crowd waiting at a distance became agitated and greeted us. We were led into the Court handcuffed. The room was fully packed with lawyers on both sides, Government prosecutors and defence.

The trying Magistrate took his chair. Everybody was curious as to what the Prosecutor would say and what would be the Magistrate's judgment. But the former made only a brief statement : "The Government have not found enough evidence to prosecute the accused; therefore, they may be discharged". He named us in the order : (1) Khirode Kumar Dutta, (2) Profulla Kumar Tripathy, (3) Parimal Ray, (4) Phanibhusan Kundu, (5) Sachindra Nath Malty, (6) Ramsankar Chakravarty, (7) Tarapada Chatterjee, (8) Sachindra Nath Nandi, (9) Nirmal Kumar Adhikari, and (10) Neemai Chandra Pal.[17]

The Magistrate then had no other alternative but to discharge us. The verdict was most welcomed by all present except the police. There was a jubilance among the lawyers and the visitors and we naturally were overjoyed. But this was short-lived for some of us, as the head of the police announced that the first five youths including myself would be held under the then notorious Bengal Ordinance which was later enacted into the Bengal Criminal Law Amendment Act. It authorized the Government of Bengal to arrest and hold under detention people who could not be tried in courts for lack of sufficient evidence.

So five of us waived at our relatives and friends assembled at the Court, from a distance as we were not allowed to meet them. However, there was a marked change in the behaviour of the police towards us. Our handcuffs were taken off and the sentries behaved more politely. We were put in a van and taken back straight to the jail.

From an Undertrial Prisoner become a Political Detenu : Last meeting with Mother

There also a great change in our status in the jail from an ordinary accused in a criminal case to that of a *political detenu.* We were transferred from the big ward to what was known as '10-Cells', a much smaller but neater place. Here each person was locked up from the evening till morning in a small separate cell but the gates were open the whole day and we were allowed to move out of the cell and spend our time together within a walled enclosure. We were provided with regular bedsheets and bed. In the cell, besides the iron barred door in front, in the back there was a small barred window above head for ventilation. But it was then (May) the second hottest month in Midnapore. There was no tree or even grass in the whole walled compound, and the inside of the cell became a hot furnace during the day when the temperature outside rose to around 108/110°F if not more. The nights were not much cooler either with the temperature remaining between 80° and 90°F. Hence the first thing we did after being transferred to the '10-cells' was to have a nice bath with soap, for the first time in two months. As a detenu we were allowed a monthly allowance of Rs. 32.00 for all our personal expenses in jail including the costs of clothing, toilet, etc. and 1 rupee and 10 annas (or Rs. 1.60 in decimal value) per head per day for all our daily meals. We could indicate to the jail authorities the main items of food desired by us. For the first time, also in two months, we were allowed to get at our cost daily papers which were then allowed to the detenus - the *Statesman* and *Englishman* of Calcutta, both incorporated in England and the mouth-piece of the British business and political interests in India, and a Bengali Weekly *Sanjeevani* edited by a well-known conservative public figure Krishna Kumar Mitra, but often censored.

We realized that our stay in Midnapore would only be temporary and we would soon be transferred to one of the three main special jails, called 'detention camps', then set up in Buxa Dooar Hills north of Bengal, Berhampore town, and Hijli near Kharagpur railway junction, to accommodate hundreds of "detenus" (persons detained for suspected political activities without trial) already taken into custody by the Government since 1930. Besides there were 20 to 25 elder detenus, who were mostly the leaders of the various revolutionary groups of Bengal and kept under detention in isolation in two's or three's in different jails all over India. They were all arrested under Regulation III of 1818 and called State Prisoners.

During this period one notable incident happened for me. I was allowed to meet my mother in the jail office. Naturally I got very excited. However, my present condition would no doubt be a great relief to her as well as to other relatives. So I tried to put up a nice appearance so that she, especially in her failing health, would be pleased to see me. I was taken to the jail office one afternoon and given a chair to sit on. There was one more chair for my mother. Nearby a police officer sat to hear our conversation and to check that we did not talk any 'objectionable' matters. Soon my mother came in with my youngest brother, Sukomal, then barely 1 year old. She had to leave my two other younger brothers, Amal and Subimal of 10 and 5 years respectively, outside the jail gate. They were not permitted to come inside with my mother. As my mother, a short, frail and fair figure, entered the office room I stood up, bowed down at her feet and asked her to sit. We both were filled with great emotions but both tried to control ourselves. She smiled and said first: "what all you have done," in a tone of part appreciation and part apprehension. I smiled but changed the topic and told her I was all right. She should not worry about me but should take care of her own health. We talked of various things including the possibilities of my studies in jail. After one hour she had to leave and both felt sorry. She was led to the front main barred gate and let out with my youngest brother to join other two brothers. I saw them for the last time before they left in a hackney carriage for home. Then I was taken back to my cell. That was really the last time I saw my mother for I never saw her again as she died in 1933 while I was still in detention.

In May, 1931 while we were in the Midnapore Central Jail we started receiving after about two months some news about the political situation in India. At the Congress front, pursuant to the Gandhi-Irwin Pact of April, the leaders and others imprisoned in connection with the Civil Disobedience Movement were being released. But sporadic armed revolutionary activities continued all over India and especially in Bengal. And we knew that more were yet to come. But in the meantime Dinesh had been sentenced to death following his trial before the District and Sessions Judge Alipore, Garlick. Somehow, the news got to him about the action in Midnapore.

Transfer to Burdwan Jail

Towards the end of May 1931, an order came out from the government of Bengal, Home Department, for our transfer to the Burdwan District Jail. We were greatly surprised and considered it a sort of anticlimax. We had expected to be shifted to one of the special jails for detenus of our category, where we could have the facilities of mixing with a much bigger community. But perhaps the Government thought we were relatively less 'polluted' and it would be better to keep us in isolation. So at the beginning of June we were taken by rail with armed escorts, via Howrah Station, to Burdwan. In the District Jail, all five of us were lodged in a single separate ward with one big room, a yard in front and a separate kitchen. Our meals and other services were taken care of by a group of ordinary prisoners. The Superintendent was an Indian I.M.S. Officer and good man.

But our stay at Burdwan was only for a short period. In late June we received orders for 'village internment' or transfer to different and distant villages in different districts, away from Midnapore, and to be kept there under confinement in isolation in a special cottage within or near a police station and under the direct surveillance of the police officers. The 'internees' were allowed to roam around certain restricted areas within the village except the village post office, schools, etc. They could also mix with ordinary people excluding the postmaster, school teachers and students. Thus Profulla and Phani Kundu were taken to two separate villages in Jalpaiguri district in north Bengal, Sachin to Mymensingh in East Bengal, and I to Murshidabad in Central Bengal.

Escorted by two armed police guards and an Intelligence Branch Inspector I was taken by rail from Burdwan via Bandel, to Berhampore headquarters of the Murshidabad district. There I was kept for the night in the Circuit House under police guard. Next morning, accompanied by the I.B. Officer, I was taken to see the District Superintendent of Police, H.E. Sabine. From my talk with him, (in English) he appeared to me to be a pleasant man. He talked in general terms and nothing specific, from which I understood he would be in-charge of the general supervision of my stay in the district. I was then taken to see the local bell-metal (an alloy of copper and tin) wares market at Khagra, which was famous for locally made costly domestic utensils. Then I was taken to see the holy Ganges river. Being the peak of the mansoon season the river was in high spate.

In the afternoon I was taken by rail from Berhampore town to a small station to the north-west on Bandel-Barhawra line, called Salar, where I and the accompanying I.B. Inspector, Mohini Sanyal, of the district, and two armed sentries got off. We then boarded two bullock-carts with covers at the top, which led us over the narrow, earthen and muddy village road at snail's speed to the nearby police station, Bharatpur, a distance of about 8 miles or 12 kilometres. But it took us nearly two hours to reach the police station. The view around was very pleasant because of the high green tender rice plants that spread over the adjoining fields on both sides, as far as the eyes could see. After nearly three months, I was able to see nature so much. I felt a great relief and a sense of at least a partial freedom. In the late afternoon, we reached the police station in Bharatpur within the Kandi Sub-division of Murshidabad district. There was no direct rail communication from Calcutta.

On our arrival a plump, fair, middle aged man - the officer in charge of the Police station, (Sub-Inspector by rank) came and led us inside the office. There the accompanying I.B. Inspector formally handed over my charge to the police O.C. by completing the necessary paper works. I then barely 19 years old was treated courteously by all present. Then all of them accompanied me to an adjoining brand new mud and thatch hut, behind the police station, specially constructed to accommodate detenus who were to be kept in the police station. There were hundreds of such political 'internees' then kept in isolated villages all over Bengal, as a policy of the Government to hold suspected prisoners detained without any explicit evidence and judicial trial who, the Government considered, were only mildly involved in political activities. My little mud-and-thatch habitat for the next six months consisted of a small bedroom with two little barred windows, a small kitchen, a lavatory and an inside small ground surrounded around by a mud wall with a wooden door. Outside, in front, there was on the south a small tank with a few private houses. There was no arrangement for the supply of running water in the hut. So an arrangement was to be made for bringing water from the tubewell located within the compound of the police station. It had to be done by me at my cost, so also for food and other personal necessities. For which I would be paid monthly an allowance at Rs. 40.00 (Indian Rupees). Of course, I had been given, at Government cost, a wooden bedstead with sheets, pillows, etc. a mosquito curtain which was essential there, and a set of minimum necessary utensils for the kitchen.

Life of a Solitary 'Village Internee'

I moved alone to the hut towards the evening with my small baggage. Darkness was falling then in a wet day and almost absolute quiet and apparent peace. The O.C. arranged for that evening some water in buckets in the hut and later, perhaps because of a compassion for my age, also for some supply of food for the night. I had been given also two hurrican lights with kerosin oil to burn. This was the first night in my life that I had to spend alone in an absolutely unfamiliar surroundings. However the sentrys' barrack was close by. I was extremely tired after the day's tribulations so I went to bed with intense feeling of novelty, adventure and fear as well as worries for my parents and other relatives. But I tried to take courage by thinking of my sick mother's distressed but affectionate face. Dinesh' determined and solemn face while awaiting the execution of his death sentence in a solitary cell in a Calcutta jail, the plight of the people of my country through sheer repression and exploitation, and above all of my vow and dedication to remove the root cause of these, the slavery of my country. While thinking thus I fell asleep.

I woke up after a deep sleep early in the morning and felt greatly relieved, at least physically. But I had the challenges of a new life to face -- in a way even greater than before. I had to take care of my own household, food and everything. The weather outside was threatening because of dark, dense monsoon clouds. After taking breakfast, in the morning at about 8 o'clock I walked to the police office. There before I met anybody, I saw the frontpage of a Calcutta daily lying on the verandah of the office and its banner headline immediately drew my attention : "Dauntless Dinesh Dies at Dawn". I picked it up and read the details, and was terribly shaken. I felt very lonely in that enviornment where I had been just for one night. I sensed a great urge to talk to and exchange my sentiments and feelings with my friends in Midnapore. But then I pulled up myself. Not only was this the final drama of a life of one of the most dedicated and bravest young man that I had ever come across in my life. I felt it was the most worthy sacrifice of a noble life for our country. Thus having composed myself I retreated to my hut in a continued dull grey day overcast with heavy clouds. I sat silent for sometime, recalled my past days with him and specially my last night together at the B.E. College hostel, Shibpore, and I prayed for his soul.

I endeavoured to do the best out of the circumstances. I felt I had to live and overcome whatever trials might come in my way. So later, I went again to the police station and talked to the O.C., partly by way of personal introduction and partly for some help in managing my 'household' requirements. He seemed to be sympathetic. He was a man of sober disposition and polished in his behaviour. He arranged a young Moslem servant for me, who was a past convict and 'marked' man in the record of the police. But he was then changing and behaved well, and, in any case, was under the complete control of the police. It was also decided that he would help me in outside work like shopping, house cleaning, etc. and would also bring my meals twice a day from his home, cooked by his wife. I agreed to it, as I had no intercommunal prejudice. On the contrary, partly because of my family bearings and partly of my dedication to my country and to the cause of a closely unified and integrated society in future India, of all castes and religions, I felt strongly even at that early age that inter-communal contacts and dealings were absolutely essential.

As the police station was rather isolated from the main section of the village I had practically no outside people to mix with. Nor was I allowed any newspaper, except *The Statesman (*British owned) but which did not come to the village, or even books. Even whatever was allowed needed the prior censor and approval of the I.B. I therefore developed the habit of passing my time by thinking about the future of the country's struggle for freedom, the attempts of the Congress, possible future activities of our group in Midnapore, my own future, and my family's future especially mother's health. But still I felt I needed someone talk to. My nearest and sole neighbours were the police officers and their limited families and the small contingent of police constables. So I often went to the police station, talked to the O.C. and other officers on duty, saw their mode of work, keeping records, receiving first information reports (F.I.R..'s) of crimes committed, interviewing suspected criminals, keeping daily diaries including recording everyday my obligatory attendance at 5 p.m. in the afternoon. I spoke to the constables in the barracks and became quiet close to their personal and official problems. But my special companions were two little daughters of the O.C., Begam and Ayesha, aged 5 and 3 years respectively. They used to call me uncle, come in my hut, hug me. They made me forget largely loneliness.

Then there was a young brother-in-law of the O.C., who often came to see me in my cottage. He was of the same age as I. He often talked to me of Islamic religion and culture, and especially of the Urdu poems of Mohammed Iqbal, a great Urdu poet of north India. He also often brought to me some special food prepared by his sister, the O.C.'wife. A lone outsider, who sometimes came to see me, was a police contractor, who was the son of a former police officer. His father had died, so out of compassion, some of the police building contracts were given to him. He used to make his bills in front of me, and that gave me an insight as to how the building contractors make their estimates and prepare their bills. Estimates he made were invariably augmented by nearly double the amounts of the actual costs. Once while he was with me in an evening I went to the kitchen to prepare tea and saw a little cobra (a venomous species of snake) and I asked him to call the constables. The latter came and killed it. I was always scared of the snakes, especially in the evening. So I sent a small note in writing clandestinely to the Calcutta daily *The Amtrita Bazar Patrika,* which published it. But that made my stay there short-lived. For the District I.B. Officer, Mohini Sanyal, soon came to see me, asked me the details of the incident and before the end of the year an order came from the Home Department, Calcutta for my transfer to the neighbouring police station, Banwan. I was taken there by a bullock-cart under police escort sometime in December, 1931.

But during my short stay of six months in Bharatpur police station I learnt the lesson of self-dependence and self-introspection, the art of mixing with people, of winning their love and affection and even admiration. I got an insight into the characteristics of the ordinary Indian police under the British rule. I realized that they too were human, and most of them were, patriotic. But they were in their jobs and serving their foreign masters to earn a living for themselves and their families. I also learnt some of the mentalities of the Moslem common people. They had their separate religious tenets and beliefs but they too were Indian.

From my brief experiences even at that stage led me to think that the best way to promote intercommunal and inter-racial harmony was to establish and develop as many communication channels as possible between the different communities and peoples, at unofficial levels. This belief was more particularly confirmed by my later experiences with a greater contact with the Moslem community during my detention in the subsequent police station.

Revolutionary Activities break the lull of post-Gandhi-Irwin Pact era

It may be observed that while, following the Gandhi-Irwin Pact of March 1931, the Salt Satyagraha was withdrawn and Gandhi as the sole representative of the Congress was preparing to attend the Second Round Table Conference in September. The revolutionary activities, especially in Bengal, went unabated in the form of bombings and shootings of selected official personnels and centres of official activities such as police stations and law courts, as well as British clubs and commercial establishments, during the second half of 1931 and in next three years. The revolutionaries, and many in the Congress, did not believe much would come out of the Round Table Conference. The reasons were, first, neither the Gandhi-Irwin Pact of 1931 nor the subsequent declarations by the British Government specifically defined the precise goal of the proposed constitutional reforms for India.[18] Second, even after the Pact had been signed, its terms were considered to have been violated by the Conservative elements both in Britain as well as in India, primarily among the British bureaucratic officials. Third, the Pact provided for the release of only non-violent *Satyagrahis* and not, as earlier stated, of the revolutionaries.[19]

Hence in the post-Gandhi-Irwin Pact period of 1931-1932 the situation was simmering all over India. In Bengal, revolutionary activities continued. To cite only a few major activities of the revolutionaries, the assassination of Garlick, the District and Sessions Judge of Alipore in June, an attempt on the life of A. Cassels, the Commissioner of Dacca Division in August, assassination of the Police Inspector, Asanullah, at Chittagong, an attempt on the life of Durno, the District Magistrate of Dacca District in October, an attempt on the life of Edward

Villiers, President of the European Association, at Calcutta, the assailant being Bimal Das Gupta, the lone absconder suspected to have been connected with the murder earlier of the District Magistrate of Midnapore, James Peddie, in April, and, finally, the assassination of C.G.B. Stevens, District Magistrate of Tripura District of Comilla by two school girls, Santi Ghosh and Suniti Chowdhuri, in December.

To name again only a few more of the incidents during 1932-34, an attempt was made on the life of the Bengal Governor, Stanley Jackson, at the Senate Hall of the Calcutta University during the annual convocation address, by an undergraduate girl of the same university, Bina Das in February 1932. Again the same year, in April, the second successive District Magistrate, Douglas, was assasinated at a meeting in the District Board at Midnapore. Of the two young men supposed to be involved, one escaped unidentified, and the second, Prodyot Kumar Bhattacharjee, a student of a Midnapore School, was arrested after a police chase and exchange of fire in an abandoned college hostel nearby. He was later tried and hanged on 12 January 1933. He is said to have faced death heroically.[20] His accomplice was later identified as Pravangshu Pal and also tried but released for lack of evidence.

In July of the same year (1932) the Superintendent of Police of Tripura District, Ellison, was shot; another senior police officer, E.Grasby, was shot at Dacca in August; two attempts in August and September were made in Calcutta on the life of Alfred Watson, the British Editor of the Calcutta daily, *The Statesman*, for its anti-Indian editorials, in his paper.

The year 1933 also was marked by several open armed skirmishes between the police and absconding revolutionaries connected with the Chittagong Armoury Raid, certain Calcutta bombings, and a daring train robbery at the Hill Station in the Dinajpur district. Amongst these, the most notable events were the arrest of the guerilla leader of the Chittagong Armoury Raid, Surya Sen, who had been middle aged school teacher of cool, gentle and kind temperament. He was seized with a colleague Brajen Sen, after a brief skirmish with the security forces in the district of Chittagong in February. In May again, there was an armed fight between another hiding Armoury Raid group with the police in which a young girl, Kalpana Dutta, along with another youngman called Tarakeswar Dastidar, were apprehended. Similarly, in Calcutta another absconding revolutionary, Dinesh Majumdar, was arrested with two friends. He had earlier fled from the Alipore Central Jail for a suspected political murder. He was later tried and hanged.[21]

But the worst incident of all from the administration point of view was the attempt by the Midnapore boys belonging to the B.V. group on the life of the third successive District Magistrate, B.E.J. Burge, in broad daylight at the beginning of a football match on the local police ground, even though he was then surrounded by armed body-guards. The guards shot at the two assailants, later identified as Mrigen Dutta and Anath Panja. Anath died on the spot but only after he had done his assigned job, while Mrigen, a cousin of Phani Das, was seriously wounded and taken to the Midnapore town hospital where he died the next day. While at hospital lying in a semi-conscious state he was interrogated by the police and on being asked why he killed the Magistrate he replied : "For the sake of my country". This incident created a great jubilation amongst the revolutionaries of Bengal and in fact of whole India.

The common people in Midnapore had developed an intense sense of grievance against the district authorities not only for their repressive acts perpetrated earlier to suppress Gandhi's Salt *Satyagraha* movement in 1931 by shooting, 'lathi' charging, house burning and putting thousands of people in jail with nominal or no trials, including those who were only remotely connected or mere sympathizers. But also because of the great sufferings that they had later undergone as a result of reprisals in the hands of the police and special military contingents sent to Midnapore following the assassination of the second District Magistrate, Douglas. A large number of young men, mostly students, had then been arrested on points of guns. Some of them were B.V. members like Amar Chatterjee, Jyoti Jiban Ghose, Pravangshu Pal, Naren Das, Kshiti Prasanna Sen, Phani Das, Binode Behari Sen, Kamakshya Ghose (senior), Sarbari Bhattcharjee (brother of Prodyot), and several others, but many were also outsiders though mostly sympathizers. There were extensive police searches and questionings in the town. While kept in the police lock up, in the town, the arrested youths were almost all subjected to terrible torture during questionings. Phani Das, especially was beaten severely in the very sight of the Superintendent of Police, Kidd, for confession. Phani was strong and tough and above all, had a great strength of mind and a devotion for his ideals. He stood all the inhuman persecutions and did not say a word. He was beaten to the end even when he was vomitting blood and became unconscious. This had been all witnessed by Naren who was in the adjoining lock-up in the police station. Phani was later removed to the Midnapore town hospital where the doctors considered him dead and left him overnight in a corridor, covered with a sheet. But, fortunately and due to his sheer vitality, Phani revived by himself next morning and some signs of life were first detected by a female nurse. From then he was attended by the doctors again and he completely recovered.[22] In the meantime the news about this terrible police repression got around in Midnapore and the people were highly agitated. The police became nervous. To add to their nervousness, the information that Prodyot who had been hit with a stone by the police while escaping after shooting Douglas, and then arrested, and also severely beaten during questioning in the same night (30 April, 1932) further caused a great resentment among the people particularly in Midnapore.

These were the reasons behind the Midnapore peoples' jubilation at the shooting of Burge just one year after the Douglas case. They realized that the revolutionary organization in Midnapore (B.V.) was not shattered by the arrests earlier of nearly twenty young people of the party's first rank in the town Branch following the shootings of the two previous District Magistrates. It had enough resources still to have carried out in succession a third assignment under much more difficult circumstances. For the revolutionaries there had already been a great satisfaction that after two 'actions', there was only one real casualty. That was Prodyot who, as mentioned above, had been arrested while escaping, tried and hanged on 12 January 1933. But, following the previous two attempts on Peddie and Douglas in 1931 and 1932, although there were many arrests the police could not get confessions or even evidence to start any case.[23] There were only about a dozen of detentions *but that without trials*. Even Bimal Das Gupta who had been implicated in the assassination of Peddie was arrested by the police only after he appeared in his second attempt on Edward Villiers six months after his supposed first attempt. He was tried for his second act and sentenced to 10 years' imprisonment for which he was later sent to the then 'penal islands' the Andamans, across the Bay of Bengal. Again, subsequently, he was prosecuted for the second time before a Special Tribunal in Midnapore on charge of the murder of Peddie. But the main prosecution witness turned hostile in the court; so the Government were forced to withdraw the case.

Unsympathetic attitude of British Parliament

Under such conditions there was then a considerable alarm at the official circles in Bengal, and the shockwaves of the developments in the province and particularly in Midnapore during 1930-1933 reached up to Great Britain. There were angry outbursts in Parliament against the inefficiency and incompetence of the police on the spot. Even cries of revenge rose in that august body against the Bengal "terrorists", especially among the conservative elements. In their frights, terror and anger they over-emphasized the symptoms and only thought of eradicating them by the proverbial means of 'tit-for-tat'. They failed to look at the root cause, namely, the intense desire for freedom from slavery and foreign rule that burnt like a subterranean volcano in the hearts and minds especially of the young people who became thus desperate finding no other way of alleviating their inhuman and miserable conditions. And the retrograde and unhelpful feeling and attitudes of British Parliament were given expression in Bengal by the then Governor of the province, John Anderson, in one of his statements to the effect that the Midnapore 'terrorists' had thrown a challenge against the posting of a British District Magistrate in the district, and the Government accept that challenge.[24] He mentioned that already a contingent of British army had been brought to Midnapore, and more would be called for if necessary. This statement was actually followed by a march of the army in Midnapore and Kharagpur town early in November 1933.

However, this demonstration of military strength and the mass repressions of the people of Midnapore that followed the assassination of Burge, including expulsions of hundreds of professional and other families who had been rooted in the towns for generations, causing untold sufferings,[25] failed to daunt the revolutionaries or dissuade their sympathizers. The former were actually pleased on two accounts. First, the repressive measures would help alienate the common people against the administration and intensify the hatred against the foreign rulers. Second, the over-reaction by the administration was an indication of the nervousness, not only of the local administration in Bengal but also of the British Imperial Government in England, over the almost unending chain of attacks taking place in different places of the province as well as in other parts of India during 1930-1934. Above all, the revolutionaries were happy that their actions aroused an awareness among the Parliamentarians as well as the common people in Britain of the fact that all was not well and peaceful about their rule over India as was propagated by the successive British Governments and their agencies in India. Considered by these results the revolutionaries judged that the sacrifices that they themselves and the people in general in India were making were worthwhile.

Some hints of official nervousness were leaked out in contemporary media. For example, after Douglas was shot in Midnapore in April 1932, one of the Calcutta daily newspapers published extracts from a letter he had written to his brother who was a Christian missionary in Madras. He wrote that he had been living under constant police guard and had to keep constantly a loaded revolver on his table while working. He said life was unbearable under such circumstances. Such expressions indicated the fright and the inner feelings of Douglas. He was certainly not as tough and autocratic as Peddie but more human. But in the eyes of the revolutionaries, he, like Peddie, was also the chief representative in the district of a foreign oppressive region.

The fright indeed caught many other British Indian Civil Service officers who, (as it was then further reported in news media) were unwilling to come to Midnapore, and it was a problem for the Government of India to find one suitable for the district. So notice was issued by the British Government in England inviting the services of retired I.C.S. Officers who would go voluntarily to that district as District Magistrate. Thus came P.J. Griffiths, an old retired tough officer, as next District Magistrate of Midnapore.[26]

After the arrival of P.J. Griffiths in the district his main task was to counter the wide impact of the daring and successive revolutionary activities of its youth. Contrary to the earlier suspicions of the police that these were mainly carried out by outsiders with Midnapore boys working mainly as helpers, it now came to be certain that the reverse was the case. The main urge and initiative came from the young members of the Midnapore branch of the B.V. group, while the planning and the general tactics had been worked out by the more experienced persons in Calcutta. Therefore all the violent reprisals of the police and the general administration were directed against the Midnapore youth. Scores of them, mostly educated and belonging to local colleges and schools and coming from respectable families, were arrested. These included several important B.V. members, like Braja Kishore Chakravarty, Ramkrishna Roy,

Nirmal Jiban Ghose, Naba Jiban Ghose (two younger brothers of Jyoti Jiban Ghose, who had been arrested earlier in 1931 but released, and then again rearrested following the assassination of Douglas, again discharged for lack of evidence and then held under preventive detention without trial) and also Benoy Jiban Ghose (eldest brother of Jyoti and then a lecturer of history of Midnapore college), Sanatan Ray (son of a well-known lawyer and Congress leader of Midnapore), Sukumar Sen, Santi Gopal Sen, Nanda Dulal Singh and several others.

Burge murder trial and Triple Executions

This time, heavily pressed and censored by British Parliament in London and also by the European Association in Calcutta for their incompetence and inefficiency not just in preventing the extremist activities but also in getting any trial started against those involved in the supposed conspiracy, the authorities and the police in Bengal cooked up a conspiracy case with the help of certain witnesses. There were again no "confessions" or divulgence of any material information about a 'conspiracy'. The two boys who actually did the job sacrificed their lives as they were shot by the bodyguards of Burge. The police knew fully well that except one or two persons arrested, others were not directly or even indirectly involved.[27] Yet they set up a criminal case of murder against seven of the youths named above before a Special Tribunal early in 1934 under special powers assumed by the Government under the Bengal Criminal Law Amendment Act of 1932, to deal with what were considered as 'emergency' cases. The accused were defended by a large group of distinguished lawyers of Midnapore and Calcutta. But the Tribunal sentenced Braja Kishore, Ramkrishna Roy and Nirmal Jiban (youngest of the three) to death, and Kamakshya Ghose (junior), Sanatan Ray, Sukumar Sen, Santi Gopal Sen and Nanda Dulal Singh to transportation for life. It will be recalled that amongst them Braja Kishore had been arrested earlier, in April 1931, following the shooting of Peddie but was later discharged for lack of evidence. Ever since he continued his revolutionary activities unsuspected by the police. He had been a simple Brahmin priest's son and himself put on a very austere appearance. He was a young man of exceptionally strong mind and highly devoted to the cause of independence for the country. His father did not like this very much but Braja often cited a couplet from the great Indian epic *The Mahabharata:*

Father and Teacher are objects of reverence.

The King of regard

But I cannot forget the Truth.

And he explained that the Truth in his case was the attainment of freedom of his Motherland from foreign domination.[28]

The death sentence of the three were later carried out in Midnapore Central Jail in two days, 25 October and 26 October 1934. Those sentenced for life were sent to the penal prison in the Andaman Islands.

With the supreme sacrifice of three young lives of Midnapore and the virtual exile for life of five others to one of the notorious penal settlements of the time, nearly ended a most glorious chapter of Bengal's and infact India's history of freedom struggle. However, the embers of the burnt out fire still lingered and continued to shed its glow for sometime more. In Midnapore district, particularly in Contai, dozens of youths were apprehended and many obtained without trial under the notorious Bengal Criminal Law Amendment Act. These included my brother Nirmal, Haripada Bhowmik, Anil Maity, Jyotish Bera, Ashoke Roy and others. Another B.V. member of Contai, Bhupal Panda, had been arrested on charge of a political robbery, convicted for ten years' imprisonment and sent to the Andaman Islands. Elsewhere in Bengal, a series of cases of shooting and bomb-throwing against various government personnel and establishments continued through 1933 and 1934. Of these the most notable incident was the shooting of the second Governor of Bengal, John Anderson, in the hill town of Darjeeling in May, in which among the attackers (from B.V. group) was a lady, Ujjala Majumdar. It may be recalled that in February 1932 his predecessor, Governor Stanley Jackson, was shot at in Calcutta also by a young lady student Bina Das.

Governor Anderson had made his name by having been posted previously in Ireland to quell the Irish rebels. Because of his special experience he was sent to Bengal by the British Government in early thirties. He took many measures to curb the revolutionaries, arrested, many expelled all suspected people including youths and elderly persons from their traditional homes and places of professions, ordered detention without trial of thousands of students and other youngmen in several special jails, including one high up on the hills in Buxa Dooars, two in the plains at Hijli near, Kharagpur, and Berhampore, and finally one far way at Deoli in Rajputana, close to the Great Indian Desert of Thar.

Revolutionary Activities in the fight for India's Independence

Summing up the situation about the attempts of armed actions against the British rule in India during the first quinquennium of the 'thirties it may be said that, this had been one of the most successful periods of the revolutionary activities all over the country, and particularly in Bengal. Ever since these activities, first initiated in 1904/1905 due primarily to the initiative and efforts of Aurobindo -- Barin, hundreds of revolutionary groups had been organized all over India, and particularly in Maharashtra, Punjab and Bengal, and armed activities resorted to by them to harass and weaken the British stronghold in India. The activities were of various types and magnitudes -- bombing, shootings, and open fightings -- with groups and individuals of both British and Indian personnel and establishments, like seats of administration, police and army barracks, etc. Some were organized on an all-India basis, like those of Rashbehari Bose, Jatin Mukherjee and their colleagues during World War I, in which elements of the regular Indian army were also involved; others on the basis of individual provinces like those of the actions of the B.V. group in Bengal, in different districts including Midnapore, during 1931-1934 and in one district like the massive Chittagong Armoury Raid of 1930 and its subsequent follow-up actions, under the leadership of Surya Sen.

The activities over a period of three decades, 1904-1934 demonstrated the skill, the organizing ability, the resources, and above all the courage and the patriotism of the youth of India in challenging what was the nerve-centre (i.e. India) of the mightiest imperial power in the world (i.e. the British). These activities, particularly those between 1930-1934, had obviously profound impacts on the Indian people, the Government as well as the Congress. Some of these have already been discussed earlier. As far as the Government was concerned, the draconian measures taken by them to suppress the revolutionary movement have been also earlier discussed. But what is not adequately chronicled or known is that the Government of India during the viceroyalty of Irwin, who was definitely a man of more liberal and democratic outlook, with the help of the then Governor of Bengal Stanley Jackson, did take an initiative to talk to the Bengal revolutionaries, following the Gandhi-Irwin Pact of 1931. This has been lucidly described by Subhas Bose in his *Indian Struggle,* which is quoted here for wider knowledge and record:

> Since the Mahatma confined himself to the cause of the Satyagrahis (in the Gandhi-Irwin Pact), the revolutionaries in prison addressed a letter to Lord Irwin stating that a settlement with Mahatma Gandhi would not necessarily be binding on them and that if His Excellency desired a real settlement of the Indian question the Government should come to a separate understanding with the Revolutionary Party. This letter reached Viceroy's hands through a prominent Indian politician.
>
> This representation was not altogether useless, because a few months later, the Governor of Bengal, Sir Stanley Jackson, made an effort to come to an understanding with the revolutionaries.[29] At his instance the late Mr. J.M. Sen gupta went to Buxa Detention Camp in North Bengal and interviewed some of the leaders. The result was not unsatisfactory. The interviewed prisoners said that they were prepared to discuss terms, but they insisted that the negotiations should be carried on direct with the Government and not through any police-officer. They also gave a preliminary outline of the terms which the late Mr. Sengupta duly conveyed to the Governor. Thereafter, a reference was made by Government to the prisoners through the Superintendent of the Camp, who was a police officer. But they refused to move further in the matter, if the negotiations were not carried on direct with them. As the Government were not agreeable to that, the negotiations fell through[30].

Looking backward to the entire history of subsequent events in India it seems a great pity that the Indian Government then did not pursue this sane and sensible policy which might have led to a healthy and perhaps a more peaceful and desirable transition of power and the development of the Indian policy, and thus saved both India and Britain from the almost unending chains of incidences of utter hatred and violence between them as well as among the entire peoples of this country.

Gandhi and the Revolutionaries

As for Gandhi, perhaps he had left out the cause of the revolutionaries in India from the terms of the Gandhi-Irwin Pact (1931), for his adherence to non-violence. He might have wanted to stick strictly to his principle of 'non-violence' and therefore did not wish to give them an official recognition. But towards the end of the thirties when both the Congress and the revolutionary movements seemed to wane[31] and there was a talk amongst the Government as well as the political circles in India for the release of thousands of *detenus*, Gandhi visited the State prisoners (leaders of prominent Bengal revolutionary groups who had been detained without trial earlier in their special jails) but later brought together in the small special jail at Hijli, and talked to them especially on their future activities. As far as I can recall from the then reports in contemporary press media, Gandhi wanted some sort of assurance that the leaders in future would guide their respective organizations towards a more peaceful line of activities against the Government. But the leaders declined. However, Gandhi was quite impressed by their calibre, the general attitude and behaviour in their talk with him. Again, at the end of World War II, in 1946, when Gandhi, for the second time intervened with the Government of India for the release of thousands of "Security Prisoners" kept without trial during the War, he went to see the revolutionaries in Dum Dum Central Jail and talked to them in 1946.[32]

These gestures on the part of Gandhi obviously proved his recognition of the role of the Indian revolutionaries in the fight for India's freedom, and showed that he was keen on taking them along with him. Gandhi realized that the revolutionaries wanted to strengthen his hands by complementing his mass non-violent upheaval by selected armed actions by their supreme self-sacrifices to instil amongst the people the spirit of courage and conviction. That is why they endeavoured to stage their maximum efforts at the time of mass civil disobediences launched by Gandhi, at least in the later phases of their activities.

My Second Spell as a 'Village Internee' in Murshidabad, 1932

For the whole of 1932 I was kept detained as a 'village internee' in Barwan Police-station in Murshidabad district.

Here too I developed a very good relations with all the police officers as well as the constables. The officer-in-charge, a tough Moslem from

Chittagong, was very hard with the suspected criminals and even with common village people but, I do not know why, he was very nice to me. He reminded me that the village post-office was out of my bounds but he was the first to take me there and introduce me to the postmaster while taking me round in a bullock cart to show me the village. Again, although I was supposed to remain in my quarters from 6 p.m. to 6 a.m. he often invited me to his office and talked to me in the course of work till about 8 or 9 p.m. Then the second-officer-incharge, a pleasant and mild Hindu, became very friendly to me and invited me to his quarters where he lived with his family. He later acted as a great friend of mine in saving me from a judicial trial and conviction and from being sent to the Andamans.

As I used to have my evening walk on the embankment of the big tank in front of the police station, late one evening in January 1932, when a light mist hung over the entire village, I felt somebody was shadowing me from behind. I got somewhat concerned and looked back and saw a figure who walked briskly to me convering his head and face with a woollen *chaddar*, and said in a low tone : "I am trying to contact you for a couple of days". On my asking why, he replied that he was coming from the nearest subdivisional town Kandi. He was a student of the local college, and some of them had formed a small secret group to work for the independence of the country; they wanted to learn making of bombs; they heard that I was from Midnapore and was kept in this police station; so he came to me. Although from his age and appearance he looked to be genuine but I could not trust him at the first encounter, so I said that I did not know how to make bombs and therefore was unable to help them. He went away but reappeared after 2/3 days with a little chit from Nikhil Guha Roy, another detenue who, I had heard, had been brought to the neighbouring police station, Bharatpur, where I was kept before coming to Barwan. Guha Roy wrote to me he was sending the boy who hailed from Kandi and was known to him. He wanted to hold a meeting between him, myself and the boy and one or two other boys, in his cottage at Bharatpur. On a date he specified (I do not now remember but probably in early February 1932), at midnight, and if I would come. I hesitated for a minute and thought it was a challenge to me which I should not shirk. So I said I would come. But on returning to my cottage I thought Bharatpur was about ten miles away and to go there and come back before daybreak would mean walking at least twenty miles at night by road absolutely unknown to me. I decided to speak to the junior Moslem landlord friend -- nicknamed Damad Mian (or son-in-law) -- with whom I had already established enough confidence to discuss the matter.

Next morning after breakfast, I went to see my friend and told him about my problem. He at once agreed to help me. He said he would arrange one of his trusted labourer (also a Moslem) who was an ex-convict[33] and a sturdy youngman who knew the way to Bharatpur, but we had to cross a river on foot at night. The river was at its lowest level because of the dry season. It would take at least two hours to go and two hours to come and keeping one hour for the meeting. So I must leave before midnight and return to my quarters before daybreak, by about 5 a.m. Later Damad Mian introduced him to me. It was a great relief for me. Damad Mian and also his cousin-in-law, Bara Mian, helped me in several other highly confidential matters.

On the scheduled evening I had my dinner and got ready. At about 11 p.m. when the whole police station went to bed, except two guards in the small armoury, Damad Mian's man came with a big bamboo stick and a lantern. I covered myself with a woollen wrapper and put on a flowing dhoti and sandals. Then I set out with him in thick darkness. I asked my boy servant to bolt the door of my yard and also my room, stay inside for the night and not to open the doors to anybody till I was back. We then passed by the police office on to the village road of dust going to the south east. We walked briskly in complete silence. It was a chilly night, there was nobody on the road. Small rural villages were generally far apart but when we approached them the village dogs barked. We, however, went along the road passing through dry bare paddy fields on both sides but almost invisible in darkness. But because of the stars in the sky we were able to see a little.

Soon we reached a bigger village, called *Panchthupi*. I had already heard about it from the Superintendent of our hostel at Shibpore Engineering College. After walking for about an hour in darkness through various types of roads, bare and narrow, and low field embankments, and even on dry rugged paddy fields, we came to the side of a big and broad river which the man said was Mayurkashi, a well-known river of the area. He also stated that if the water was deep we would have to take a small country ferry but if it was shallow we would cross it on foot. We could see a tiny light reflected on the water which my guide said we saw a country boat. We both stepped into the water after rolling up our flowing dresses. My guide, who was 'marked' in the village as a 'criminal' and had a prison life behind him, was completely faithful to me and of immense help at a very critical time where every step of mine could end my life in the unknown depth of the river. But my guide went ahead with his lantern holding high above the water and before every advance step hit the water with his stick and felt its depth.

It took us about half-an-hour to cross the river, then walked for nearly another hour and reached the village of Bharatpur and finally to the police station, a place already known to me, at about 1 a.m. at night. We arrived at the site of the lonely and dark graveyard, climbed the little earthen mound where the quarters of my fellow detenu, Guha Roy, was located. I approached his small window on the north where there was no habitation except that it could be seen from the Police Inspection Bungalow situated to the east closely. I was feeling tired and some aches in my leg. However, I knocked softly at the window which was closed. A voice replied from inside (I had not seen or met Guha Roy before) asking "who are you". I gave my identity. He said again in a very low tone: "Go back to your village immediately. the Inspector of the Calcutta Intelligence Branch, Bhujen Sarkar, has come to meet me and he is lodging in the Bungalow"

So I turned immediately back with my guide and was back on the road for my return walk to Barwan police station, about 10/12 miles away. Today, looking back at this trip of altogether about 20/25 miles at night, it seems that it was a minor "exodus" of the type of Moses with his Hebrew followers out of Egypt to the Holy Land of Israel against the watchful eyes of the Pharaoh's guards. Moses had to cross the Red Sea at dead of night but had powers of miracle and bid the sea to divide in the middle so that there could be a clear path for him and his followers to cross. But in my case I had also to cross the broad river Mayurkashi (or may be one of its tributaries) at night, on foot, wading through the water, as I was a mortal man and had no miracle power. However, walking the rest of the night we reached a narrow stream marking the boundary of my village (Barwan) which was the limit of my area officially prescribed (in the detention order served on me) for me. I felt greatly relieved both physically and mentally. My feet were burning as a result of the long walk and I washed them in the stream which was cool and clear, and then separated myself from the guide and walked back slowly to my quarters feigning as if I was returning from a morning walk.

In the day I met Mr. Damad Mian and thanked him for his great help. But this was not the end of this story. For, about two months later, on 11

March 1932, a bomb was thrown at the quarters of the Sub-divisional Officer (S.D.O.) of Kandi Sub-division, in Kandi town. No body was hurt and none injured. But the very fact that such an attempt was made (on an officer who was Indian) at a place which was politically rather peaceful, created a great sensation. A big hunt for the 'culprits' and a wide net of investigation was cast by the police. Higher officers flocked to Kandi town from Calcutta and Berhampore, and ordinary police contingents led by their officers were requisitioned from nearby police stations including Barwan. Perhaps luckily for me, as it would be presently seen, a contingent under the command of the second officer - in - charge of my P.S. went to join the investigation. I heard of all these news from other police officers and later read in newspapers which used to come to the police station. As a result of the investigations during which the police exerted great pressure on the boys arrested, there was a confession by one of them that they regularly used to visit detenu, Nikhil Guha Roy at Bharatpur who taught them the technique of making bombs. So the police arrested Guha Roy and later started the Kandi Bomb case, in which Roy was sentenced to 10 years' rigorous imprisonment and eventually sent to the Andamans. After knowing all these I thanked God and also the boys of Kandi for not divulging my name. I also appreciated my own wisdom not to have entertained the idea of a meeting at my place of Barwan as suggested by the secret visitor to me from Kandi sometime earlier.

But at that time I did not know that there was another person who had acted behind the scene silently to save me from a sure arrest in connection with the throwing of the bomb. That was the Second Officer -in - charge of the Barwan Police Station who, as said above went on deputation as head of the police contingent sent from there to help in the investigation. When he was at Kandi he was given the charge of interrogating a boy who was the one that came to see me. In course of his statement the boy referred my name amongst those who were supposed to come at Nikhil Guha Roy's place at Bharatpur for a secret meeting. The officer sensed the possible danger that would come to me if this statement was recorded. So he snubbed the boy and rebuked him for telling lies for, as he said, he knew that evening I was with them in the police station. The boy got nervous and retracted my name. Thus thanks to his instant presence of mind and intervention I was saved.

When I look back on this incident I still express my deep gratitude to this police officer,[34] who again like Damad Mian and Bara Mian (my two Moslem friends) came to my help. Otherwise if I had been implicated once again on a new charge of conspiracy I would have been also put on trial and convicted. That would have changed the entire course of my future life. This incident once again confirmed me of the underlying sympathy of many of the then police force if we could establish a proper *rapport* with them.

Because my stay at Barwan P.S. was somewhat longer (about twelve months, from January to December 1932) it was much more memorable for several notable events which had a profound impact on me not only at that time but also for practically my entire life.Two of the major ones I have already mentioned above. Among the relatively minor ones was a surprise visit to my quarters by the Superintendent of Police of Murshidabad district, H.E. Sabine, an Englishman, whom I had earlier met at Berhampore, came to see me in late February 1932, with previous permission from the Calcutta and Berhampore Intelligence Branch people and in the presence of one of them, my uncle Binode Behari all the way from Midnapore, accompanied by my maternal uncle, Bimala Prasad from Calcutta. I was greatly touched by the trouble they took to come to such a remote backward village where there was no direct railway communication from Calcutta. During the interview my friend Damad Mian was also present there on my side (with the permission of the police of course). Though my uncle loved me very much, generally he used to speak to me only a few words. He looked at my bed-cum-living room with a great curiosity. At this the I.B. Officer said : "We have taught your nephew the art of housekeeping", referring to some of the cooking and domestic wares supplied for my use by the Government. My uncle had brought some books for B.Sc. mathematics course and asked me to read them at my spare time. He was very unhappy that my educational career was cut short by my arrest and detention at the prime of my life. But he had never complained either earlier when he found that I was deeply involved in political activities, or later when he was subjected to a great deal of trouble and harassment by the Midnapore police (which is briefly described in the subsequent chapter). I assured him that I would read the books and prepare myself for the B.Sc. Course. One hour sanctioned for the interview was thus over and I bowed to him when, as reported to me later by my friend Damad Mian, tears rolled down his eyes. He left in a waiting hired taxi by which they came from Berhampore, a long distance.

My third visitor, also in February 1932, came with a great risk for him, for my two Moslem friends as well as to me. But all four voluntarily took the risk, although it was I who had initiated the visit. For sometime I was panting for news about the activities of our group in Midnapore. What did it do following the arrest and detnetion of Phani rundu, Profulla Tripathy and myself? So I clandestinely got in touch with our close-friend and colleague Haripada Bhowmick who still then had escaped police dragnet and was leading the Contai group. With the help of Damad Mian I posted to him some letters (as the local post office was out of my officially directed boundary) in which I suggested a visit by him in disguise to Barwan. In his reply sent in the name of Damad Mian he conveyed his agreement. Then after having discussed about the arrangements to be made for the visit so that the police would not know it was suggested to him that on a specified date and time he should come to the nearest railway station, Salar, about sixteen miles away from Barwan, dressed as a Moslem. Damad Mian would be present (the latter's description was given to him) with a bullock cart. After arrival and till his departure after two days he would greet all people he met in the Moslem way. He did all these jobs perfectly and Damad Mian received him at the railway station in due time and brought him to their outhouse and lodged him on its first floor which was seldom visited by any outsider. Bara Mian was also briefed about the visit and he was greatly pleased and took special pains to see that no body went to the first floor of the outhouse. Damad Mian personally brought me the news of Haripada's arrival and it was agreed that I would come to meet him after 10 p.m. when the police station would be closed and all would go home. Accordingly I went to the outhouse of my friends, met Haripada and we two greeted each other with great joy. He was perfectly changed physically because of his putting of fake beard and dress of a Moslem countryman. We talked for nearly four hours and exchanged our information. I came to know that the Midnapore boys were getting ready for another 'action'. I left him at 2 a.m. and returned to my cottage. Next afternoon my two friends arranged a lunch in which we all four participated. After that Damad Mian took Haripada back to Salar railway station, from where he took a train for Sealdah, then met our senior colleagues in Calcutta and reported about his visit to me and finally he returned to Contai. From there he wrote to me informing his safe return. All of us were very pleased and I thanked both the Moslem friends from my heart. Bara Mian was so happy that he made a very important comment which I still remember. "If Hindus and Moslems can work like this in cooperation the future of this country is secure."

Another serious event is worth mentioning here. In the summer of 1932 the whole village of Barwan was under the grip of a severe cholera epidemics with barely any appropriate medicines or hospitals available in the village or in the neighbourhood of the police station. Half the people, notably among the nearby *bagdi* and *muchi* communities, were semi-starved and had hardly any pure water to drink. They had little resistance and no immunities. They fell a helpless victims to the deadly disease. At the beginning, after the initial attacks, some women came to me for medicines as they knew I had some homeopathic phials with which I tried to help them in cases of ordinary diseases. Although I was sure that my homeopathy would not cure them from this disease yet I had to give them the pills for their satisfaction. The whole police station was alerted, drinking water from the lone tubewell in the station had to be boiled. I started cooking my own food as I had asked my boy servant, who came from the *bagdi* village, not to come. However, soon to the great relief of all, came two sanitary Doctors from the District Health office with necessary medicinal kits to the police station. One of the first things they did was to inocculate the entire police staff and their families as well as myself. In the days they were busy, but in the evenings they came to my quarters to play cards and have tea. So, for about a month they were my good companions. After about two weeks, the disease came under control. But the doctors still went on working, visiting houses and treating partly recovered patients at the visitor's bungalow of the police station.

However, as days passed on, the sanitary officers left the village and it was trying to recuperate from the great shock, came the news of the shooting on 30 April 1932, of the second District Magistrate of Midnapore, Douglas, and the arrest of one supposed 'assailant' Prodyot Bhattacharjee, after a police chase. As I have said earlier, Prodyot was known to me. I never personally spoke to him very much but heard much about him from my friends like Amar Chatterjee and Braj Kishore Chakravarty. I saw him from a distance. He was a very fair and well-built youth, a student of Hindu School of Midnapore, and of quiet and mild temperament but with determined will. As the name came out I became sure it was an 'action' again by our group. So I pondered once against its possible effects on the people and our boys. Prodyot carried in his pocket a small slip "A feeble revenge of Hijli". This was a reference to the indiscriminate shooting, some time earlier, on 16 September 1931, by the guards of the Hijli Detention Camp, near Kharagpur, on about 200 detenus without warning while they were protesting against some of the humiliating terms and conditions of the prison life. The shooting led to death of two prisoners, Santosh Mitra and Tarakeswar Sen. It created a great commotion all over India and protests and demonstrations were staged not only against the jail authorities but also the Government of West Bengal, under the leadership of Subhas Chandra Bose and Jatindra Mohan Sen Gupta, and even Rabindranath Tagore added his voice of indignation.

Following the shooting of Douglas, the Intelligence Branch went deeper, this time as compared with their similar investigations after the shooting of Peddie, and adopted different means including severe physical torture of those arrested on suspicion. As a result (although none of our key party members made any admission or confession) police got some additional information about our organization at Midnapore and came to know that Phani and I were the original associates of Dinesh in starting a section of B.V. group there. In this context my name as well as that of Phani came out in the newspapers of Calcutta reporting about the police investigations. When I saw them in the Barwan police station I alerted myself as I could be taken back to Midnapore to face a possible charge of conspiracy for the shooting. But fortunately nothing of that kind happened. But for the authorities of the entire province of Bengal, it was the third successive year of a nerve-racking and an intensive as well as extensive pressure by the revolutionaries.

In early January 1933, I was transferred to the Berhampore Detention Camp. I was thus kept for about one full year in Barwan police station. It was one of the most memorable periods of my life. I saw there the human side of apparently a cruel and impassive police force under an alien rule. I tried to help them as much as possible, e.g. I made some savings out of my paltry monthly allowance of Rs. 40/- and gave the needy who approached me. There were of course many but I had to be selective. I started an evening school of *bagdi* and *muchi* boys in my quarters, which the police did not object. And finally, I acquired an intensive and practical knowledge of the agricultural conditions in our countryside. This aroused in me a great interest in the rural economics of the country and also in the comparative situations in other countries.

And I almost decided to devote in future, if and when I got an opportunity, a greater part of my life to the cause of improving agriculture and the conditions of the rural people of India.

When I left Barwan in a bullock cart, accompanied by the I.B. Inspector, Mohini Sanyal and two sentries, my cart was followed by scores of villagers with tears in their eyes for at least half-a-mile. I still remember their painful fairwell looks, the kindness and warm heartedness of the two Moslem friends, Bara Mian and Damad Mian, and their unquestioning help in my risky adventures at no small perils to themselves and to their families, and also the great help rendered by the Second Officer-in-charge of the Barwan Police Station in saving me from a future 'criminal' trial and conviction.

Life in Berhampore Detention Camp, 1933

When I arrived at the Detention Camp at Berhampore I was received by the Commandant (equivalent to Superintendent), a British ex-military officer, and the Indian Jailor, Pabitra Bose. After I entered inside I found a different atmosphere altogether. Nearly 500 political detainees without trial where kept in two adjacent camps separated by high walls, one bigger holding about 300 persons, the other somewhat smaller accommodating about 200 of them. They all were kept in separate barracks in each of the two buildings by batches. The prisoners were locked inside their barracks from about 9 p.m. till 6 a.m. Most of the inmates were young men and some elderly, picked up from all the districts of Bengal. A great majority of them had been students of schools and colleges, and some were teachers and professors. They actually represented the cream of Bengal's patriotic minded youth, and held not only in Berhampore but also in two other "Camps" or Special Jails in Bengal, Hijli and Buxa and one far away from their homes in Rajputana at Deoli as said earlier.

Inside I was very pleased to meet several close friends and party members from Midnapore like Amar Chatterjee, Kshiti Sen, Jyoti Jiban Ghose and Naren Das, also some friends from Calcutta and Dacca. The former had all been arrested with Prodyot earlier following the murder of Douglas in April 1932 but, like us previously, were discharged in May when their trial was held but the police could not find any evidence.[35] This has been stated earlier. Amar was the first person to inform me that arrangements have been made by one elderly detenu, a former school teacher from Barisal, Dhiren Sen, with the approval of the Camp authorities and the Calcutta University, for detenus to sit for various University examinations as non-collegiate students especially held within the Camp under police guards. Amar suggested that I should enrol for the B.A. examination of that year. (Although I had been previously a science student in my Intermediate Courses it was not possible to study B.Sc. in the camp). As the examination was only three months away, in April, I hesitated. But Amar insisted and therefore I agreed. He took me to Dhiren Sen who was very pleased to see me although I was absolutely new to him. What I had to do was to simply put my signature on one of the University forms for application to register myself as a candidate for the Bachelor of Arts Examination for April 1933. He himself filled in the rest of the form and took it along with some other applications, to the Camp office and arranged to send it to the Controller of Examinations office of the University of Calcutta.

So, while settling down in the Camp life, I started reading the necessary text and reference books of the subjects for B.A. Examination -- English and Bengali vernacular and two optional subjects of Economics and History. I utilized my maximum time on reading. Many of the detenus doubted if I would pass. I told, this would be my trial year only. However, internally I took it very seriously. I borrowed books from friends and procured some on my own. Meanwhile there was a mass fast by the detenus as a protest against the Camp authorities for the then state of our amenities and privileges, for which we were locked up in our respective barracks continuously for three days without food. That hampered my studies for those days but then there was a compromise and we resumed our normal Camp life. I wrote to my mother, father and uncle of my plan to sit for the next B.A. examination and they replied saying they were all very happy. April seemed to be approaching fast and our Admit Cards arrived on due time. We were all very much excited. As the dates for it actually arrived I sat for it. The question papers came direct from the University in sealed package c/o the Commandant and the invigilators were a band of police officers deputed from Berhampore. Our seats were duly allotted according to the University Roll Numbers in a separate and isolated hall which was adequately guarded. I thought, because of my inadequate preparations, I might not be able to answer all the required questions. But actually I found them rather within my capacity and I was very happy. So I tried my hand as best as I could. However, I told all again that it was merely my trial examination.

Before, however, the results were due in June I received from my father a letter from Contai giving the news of the sudden death of my mother. I was terribly shaken and felt that the whole world vanished from before my eyes. I was then barely 20 years old, and my mother died very young. I was her first child. She had been already sick for sometime and my arrest and detention further affected her health very seriously both physically and mentally. Even so, she underwent all sorts of penances, prayers and fasts seeking my early release. In that dark hour my friends in the Camp, especially Amar, Jyoti, Naren and Kshiti, stood by me very closely and affectionately. Inside the prison I observed the Hindu formalities of morning as far as I could.

The results of the B.A. examination came soon thereafter, by about the middle of July and I passed with Distinction. I was naturally very pleased. But I was very sorry that my mother could not know it. Had she been alive this would have given her the greatest pleasure. Almost everybody in the Camp was greatly surprised at my result although I myself had not been totally so because I was fully aware that I wrote all my answer papers fairly well. My close friends were happy too. However my next concern was to prepare myself mentally for the transfer to Deoli. But in the meantime there was a severe disturbance in the second camp one afternoon on the sports ground. There was some altercation between the Pathan soldier guards and some detenus. The guards blew alarm whistle. We in Camp One were all then out on the grounds inside the Camp. The guards there also blew their whistle. Under prison regulations all prisoners were supposed to run back to their barracks which would be locked up by the guards and remain so till the all-clear signals were blown. I was then walking quite away from our own barrack but fortunately a friend living in that area pulled me in his room and the sentries locked us from outside. We were then looking outside through big barred windows and saw Pathan soldiers armed with thick sticks were rushing around and chasing those detenus who still were left outside. Just in front of our window stood helplessly an elderly detenu, Suren Sarkar, of Pabna who was a sickly and mild type of man. At that moment a Pathan guard approached and beat him mercilessly on his head with his stick. The head was fractured immediately and blood gushed out, he fell instantly on the ground. He lay there in that condition for some time. Soon after another posse of guards armed with rifles arrived on the spot accompanied by the Jailor Pabitra Bose; they were ordered to kneel down and hold their rifles ready for firing. We then thought that there would be some shooting and loss of lives like what happened earlier in Hijli Camp resulting in the loss of two lives. However, there was no order for shooting but a great tension prevailed. After some time Suren Sarkar was carried to the hospital. With the arrival of evening and darkness the whole Camp was dead silent except the thumping sounds of boots of the parading soldiers. Then they opened every cell and counted the number of detenus inside in order to ascertain that everybody was all right. And we were all left like that for the whole night without food. Thereafter it took a few days for the normal situation to return.

Transfer to Deoli Detention Jail, Rajputana, 1933

Sometime in August order from the Bengal Government came for the transfer of some detenus in batches to the Deoli Detention Jail. I would be among the first batch. This jail had been built in 1914 far away from all the principal localities of India, in the vicinity of the great Indian desert of Thar in Rajputana, to hold some war prisoners (mainly Germans) of World War I. After that War it was left vacant but again was reactivated in early 'thirties to keep 'dangerous' political detenus from Bengal, long way from their homes and places of work so that they could not communicate with their people from inside the jails, which they were considered to have done while kept within Bengal. About one hundred of the Bengal detenus had already been held there since the Revolutionary Movement revived in the province on a large scale in 1930. Now, because the situation has even worsened, a decision was taken, at the highest level between the Governments of India and Bengal, to send there more detenus from Bengal who were considered to be too dangerous to be kept in Bengal. Deoli was meant for people detained for political reasons without trial as the Andamans was for those judicially convicted for the same reasons. A fresh decision to send more detenus to Deoli was obviously taken because of the continuation of the armed activities by different groups of Bengal all over the province in 1932 and 1933 which as, we have seen earlier, assumed almost the proportion of the large scale rebellion.

In mid-August, 1933 the first batch, including myself, was taken from the Berhampore Camp first to Calcutta Presidency Jail, for the assembly of a larger batch brought in from other prisons of Bengal including Buxa and Hijli. After about 2/3 days nearly fifty of us were taken in closed black police vans to Howrah Station and there put on a reserved third class coach attached to the Delhi Express called "Toofan Mail". At that time the windows of passenger trains in India were not barred but those of our reserved coach were. A big crowd collected at the station to watch us out of curiosity, especially when they saw the large contingent of police escorts and the bars in the windows. We were partly happy, at least momentarily, at the prospect of a long rail journey to Rajputana and Deoli, but we felt at heart very sorry to be going so far away as to have hardly any chance of seeing our relatives, even occasionally, at specially arranged interviews.

We reached Agra next morning of we were detrained there and after some time put on another train, in two smaller coaches because the railway was of meter gauge belonging to the central railways, called the Bombay-Baroda-Central-Indian Railways, which touched the British administered city of Ajmer on way to Bombay. Early next morning, we reached the outskirts of the Aravalli Hills. Our train stopped at a station called Bandikui close to the Aravalli ranges, and some amongst us recalling the heroic exploits of the Rajput chiefs, especially of Mewar, sang a couplet from a song written by the famous Bengali administrator-cum-litterateur-and-patriot, D.L. Roy :

"The Hills of Mewar, the Hills of Mewar

With blood-stained flags

And lofty heads"[36]

After about another ten hours' journey we arrived at Ajmer, which was administered by the Central Indian Government from Delhi to keep control of the surrounding autonomous 'Native States', mostly ruled by the descendants of older Rajput chiefs. Since this was a crowded station we were taken to a nearby smaller station of Nashirabad and made to detrain there. Then we were put on several buses and taken to Deoli.

Life in Deoli Detention Jail 1933 - 1937

We arrived towards the evening at the central gate of the huge complex the Deoli Detention Jail made of low (tile) and roofed barracks, surrounded by a series of barbed wires with high posts of armed sentries built all around to keep a watch over the entire jail. It was under the

Central (Delhi) Government administration and armed Gharhwali soldiers acted as guards. The Superintendent was a senior British police officer of the Indian Police Service, F.P.E.S. Finney. After the necessary formalities were completed we were led inside by Gharhwali guards to the entrance gate of Camp No.2 which consisted of series of two tiled roof barracks, each accommodating about 50 prisoners and with some open ground in front fenced separately to allow the locking of a whole barrack at night. The Kitchen, the dining hall and the lavatories were located at some distances from the living barracks. Within the camp there were some common grounds for walking about, and constructing small playgrounds like tennis and badminton courts. The Number 1 camp was on our west, Camp Numbers 3, 4 and 5 were on our east in a chain and a big playing field was located on our north, each separately fenced with barbed wires. On our south, next to the outer periphery of barbed wire fences with sentry posts, was a wood with tall trees. We were allowed to go to the big play ground twice in the day, morning and afternoon, where we could play bigger games like football, hockey and cricket. Each of the two barracks in our camp consisted of five rectangular rooms and each room had about ten beds. In our room were one of the seniormost detenus, Kali Sen and Bejoy Modak of the Communist Party of India, Manoj Kahili, Nirmal Ghose and Asu Mukherjee of Barisal belonging to Satin Sen's group of 'Jugantar', Asit Ghose of 'Sri Sangha' headed by Anil Roy, myself and two others.

It may be mentioned here that most of the top leaders of all revolutionary groups of Bengal, including the Anushilan Samity, various subgroups of Jugantar and Sri Sangha and B.V. had been kept, as earlier stated, separately in other jails as State Prisoners. A next batch either in seniority or in proportion to the danger they were supposed to pose to the Government or arrested first, were kept in Camp No.1. The third batch including myself were held at Camp No.2. Three other batches were later brought successively to camps No. 3, 4 and 5. To name only a few of the more prominent detenus kept in different camps : Hem Chandra Ghose, Satya Ranjan Bakshi, Manindra Kishore Roy, Prafulla Kumar Dutta, Rasamaya Sur, and Nikunja Sen of the B.V. group; Biren Chatterjee, Purnananda Das Gupta, Pannalal Das Gupta, Sudhir Aich, Durgesh Bhattacharjee and Amulya Mukherjee of the Anushilan Samiti, Shyamananda Sen, Phani Mukherjee, Manoj Kahili, Nirmal Ghose and Asu Mukherjee of different sub-groups (Mymensingh, Faridpur, Barisal, etc.) of the Jugantar group; then Kali Sen, Bejoy Modak and Bhabani Sen

Gupta of the Communist Party; and Bhabesh Nandi, Sailesh Roy of the Sri Sangha. From Midnapore, besides myself, were Haripada and Naren.

The inter-group of party relationship was good, partly all being long way from Bengal and partly because of the uncertainty of the future of all due to the fact that revolutionary activities still did not show any sign of abatement in 1933 compared to those in previous three years, 1930-1932. Moreover, the general mass of people all over India, though had quietened down considerably following the Gandhi-Irwin Pact of 1931, were sulking in the absence of any tangible sign of progress towards further self-government, not to speak of independence or even Dominion Status.[37] Thus a close community of life grew up between all the inmates of the five camps. There were various sports and inter-camp matches of football, hockey, cricket and tennis, of great excitement; a general craze for studies of a wide expanse of literature, social, political and economic, philosophical and historical -- both Indian and foreign and particularly Marxist, and, finally, those who had the energy to prepare for the various examinations of the Calcutta University, a facility also extended to Deoli by both Government and the University. The question papers came prior to the examinations from the University direct to the Jail Superintendent's office and packets were opened just before the examinations and distributed by the police invigilators brought from Ajmer. I took an advantage of the examinations for the Preliminary, Intermediate and the Final Bachelor of Law Degree in three successive years, 1934, 1935 and 1936, securing a First Class in all. Because of my obtaining a First class in the first two examinations, I was allowed by the University to appear at the Final Law examination after six months instead of having had to wait for a full year.

But I also joined the classes held on Marxism and Communism by the veteran Communist leader Kali Sen in our room, along with a number of others including Bejoy Modak. The classes were absolutely voluntary for both the teacher and the student. Sen's objective, of course, was to spread the doctrines of Communism, and the educated boys and youths from the middle class who mostly filled the rank of detenus, were the ideal objects of recruitment. It may be noted that the Communist Party in India in early 'thirtees was very small with representatives mainly of labour or those few who then worked in the labour field, and some affluent young lawyers who had an opportunity of mixing with expatriate Indian or foreign communist theoreticians during their studies in England. So thanks to the untiring efforts of a very few communist theoreticians amongst the detenus in Deoli and other special jails including the penal prison in the Andamans, the doctrine of communism spread fairly rapidly amongst the inmates of these jails. Apart from this initiative taken by the communist minded fellow prisoners two other major reasons could be attributed to this. First, the easier availability of old and established literature on communism by well-known foreign writers like Karl Marx (*Das Capital* in two volumes,), Nikolai Bukharin (*Historical Materialism*), Engels and Lenin presented logically and consistently, with a wider historical, social, and economic perspective, the theories of historical materialism and class struggle, and of various political and social conflicts, including the domination of one class or caste by another, one country by another (i.e. colonialism and imperialism), and thus set for the revolutionary minded youth a clear-cut ideology and path for the attainment of a society free from all domination and exploitation. This was in great contrast to the situations of the 'nationalist' revolutionaries who did not have the benefit of any similar comprehensive and consolidated literature dealing with the ultimate objectives, after freedom was won for the country and clear strategy and a set of tractics for attaining these. Hence the result was almost the creation of an avalanche in the minds of young detenus sweeping away almost all the earlier thinking about the goal and strategy of achieving the country's freedom.

The second and even more direct reason for the spread of communist doctrines amongst the political prisoners all over India, and especially in Bengal, was a deliberate and systematic policy of the Government including the Intelligence Branch people as well as the jail authorities to allow the supply, at the prisoners' own costs or as gifts, of communist literatures as much as possible, with a rather liberal 'censoring' prior to their entry into the jails. The idea was that the theory of communism was basically international and was contrary to nationalism. Hence its spread would counter the spread of strong nationalistic ideas and thus bring a conversion of the tough nationalistic minded revolutionaries. This objective became clear to me when in one of the periodical interviews that the I.B. people used to have with the detenus in jails. I was asked by an officer if I read communistic literatures. I had not then known the main reason behind this question, and I thought that the Government and the police were even more against the doctrine of Communism than Nationalism.[38] So I replied that 'no', I had no read the communist literature, but I was surprised with his comments on this. "Oh, that's why your ideas remain so narrow and parochial. You must read communist literature." That gave me a clear insight of the then mind of the police and the government on the matter.

Of course, I did not tell the truth. For I had been one of the first and regular attendants of Kali Sen's classes. Because I wanted to have a good knowledge of the theories of communism. Like all young boys and youths of our time I was highly impressed by the Russian Revolution of 1917 in which Lenin and Trotsky with many of their other colleagues fought against the Carist oppressive reign, and established a peoples' government. I, like many other youths of our time, thought of establishing an egalitarian society in India after we attained independence from the foreign rule. And the basic theory of communism, as I then understood, was the establishment of such a society. So I voluntarily joined Kali Sen's classes as I had thought they would help me in acquiring a knowledge of the basic theories of communism. But at that time I did not want to tell all these to the I.B. Officer who was interviewing me in the Deoli Jail.

But frankly speaking, although I profited enormously from my classes by Kali Sen and, throughout my life, have been greatly influenced by the final goals of communism, I never thought of joining the Communist Party.

The Deoli Camps were retained until about the end of 1937 and I was kept there until then, that is, for a period of four years-and-a-half. Within a month of our arrival there came the news of the assassination of Burge, the third District Magistrate of Midnapore in succession, in early September, and the attack on Hill Railway Station in north Bengal bv an armed band of about fifteen youths.

In 1933, however, there were on the whole a fewer armed actions in Bengal as well as in the rest of India than in previous three years. This trend continued in 1934 when the momentum was kept up to a certain extent, especially in Bengal, by a number of relatively smaller incidents. Among these the more notables were an attack on the European association in Chittagong in the cricket ground in January, and, as mentioned, earlior, the shooting of the Governor of Bengal, John Anderson in the hill station at Darjeeling in May.[39] Thereafter these types of revolutionary activities in Bengal and elsewhere practically stopped.

It was not however, a defeat for the revolutionaries, (as many, especially the Government, at that time thought and many writers later seemed to have interpreted). There were some sacrifices on the part of the revolutionaries, but also greater for the Government. However, the revolutionaries were as much cautious as the Congress. They did not want to shed blood unnecessarily. Their strategy was to convince the alien rulers that they could not stay in India without the full support and willingness of the Indians. Hence while the momentum of their activities in 1930-1934 slowed down they already looked to the future and to their joy found that signs of favourable clouds were already looming in the international horizon by the rise of Italy, Germany and Japan. So they started to think of the likely future developments and the nature of their future strategy. That is how we passed the rest of our time in Deoli.

Notes and References

1. First the much heralded Satyagraha campaign launched in April 1919 as a mark of protest against the oppressive Rowlatt Act of 1918, and, second in 1922 following the outbreak of violence in the country during Gandhi's Civil Disobedience Movement.
2. The national flag was first designed in Paris by a group of non-resident Indians and was later modified by the Congress.
3. Mehra, P. : *A Dictionary of Modern Indian History 1707-1947, op.cit.*, p.328.
4. Even in the North-Western Frontier Province, under the leadership of the tall great Pathan leader Khan Abdul Gaffar Khan, a devoted disciple of Gandhi all through his life, the Pathan tribesmen joined in "an intensive anti-Government movement", including the non-payment of taxes. As the Khan himself has said : "In Haripur prison alone about ten to twelve thousand *Khudai Khidmatgars* ("Servants of God"--his followers) were locked up" and they were met with "innumerable cruelties". Cf. An Autobiography of Badshah Khan, *My life and Struggle* (Orient Paperbacks, New Delhi 1969), p. 145.
5. All these have been chronicled in numerous publications since before and after independence in great detail. It is not this writer's intention to go into them in details. He only describes the main events which had special impact on his mind. Incidentally, the events in Contai and Midnapore were well chronicled in a report of a public committee headed by B.N. Sasmal. Law and Order in Midnapore, (1932).
6. The first, as chronicled earlier in Chapter 2, was on 9 September 1915, in Balasore district of Orissa, led by Jatin Mukherjee.
7. These were preceded by a systematic and planned cut off of communications, such as telephone, telegraph and even railway lines between the Chittagong town and rest of the province (Bengal).
8. E.g. see Bose, S.C. : *Indian Struggle* (Thacker Spink & Co. Calcutta) 1948, p. 259. Regrettably even Tagore made a greater mistake in his little Bengali novel *Four Chapters* (Visva - Bharati).

9. In that year, at the beginning of World War I a consignment of arms of 50 Mauser pistols with hundreds of round of bullets were delivered at Calcutta from a ship to a hand cart engaged by the consignee, Rodda & Co. of Calcutta. On advance information received by the revolutionaries two groups headed by Hemchandra Ghose founder of the then "Muktisangha" (predecessor of B.V. group) and of "Self-Improvement Society" headed by Bepin Behari Ganguli, decided to whisk away the arms by a joint action of the two groups working in disguise. Haridas Dutta along with another colleague carried out this daring act. The arms were distributed among various revolutionary groups. Cf. B. Rakshit Ray : *Armed Rebellion in India* (in Bengali), Calcutta, pp. 144-146.
10. When the Satyagraha movement was launched by Gandhi on 12 March, 1930 this author had then been living in Midnapore and visited several times Contai. So he came personally in contact with many *Satyagrahis* and also heard the detailed accounts from many others. The Police repression was chronicled later in details in a report of an investigation Committee then headed by the Contai barrister and leader Birendra Nath Sasmal "Law and Order in Midnapore (1932)" as stated earlier.
11. Of which there were nearly five hundred at that time, from very small to very big, which enjoyed by and large a greater degree of internal autonomy than the provinces.
12. The First Round Table Conference was held in London on 12 November, 1930 under the Chairmanship of the then British Labour Prime Minister, Ramsay Macdonald, with especially picked-up 'representatives' from the Indian States administered by the Princes and from the British administered provinces. The Congress was unrepresented. It was therefore a foregone conclusion that the Conference would bear no fruit. On January, 1931 the Conference was adjourned *sine die*. Hence for the future the aim of the British Government was to enlist the support of the Indian National Congress and Gandhi in any future discussions on constitutional matters relating to India, but with due hedgings and safeguards to protect the continued British interests in the country.
13. The U.S. journalist William Shirer who accompanied Gandhi during his talks with Irwin at the end of 1929 and early 1930, has written the following, while commenting on the pact: "The Gandhi-Irwin truce .... marked a turning point in the Indian revolution and in the affairs of the British Empire. Not that Gandhi won much. I was surprised that he conceded so much, and Nehru was bitter. Not even his eloquent defence of what he believed he had achieved,.... convinced me that he had not, to an amazing extent, surrendered". But Shirer then concedes that Gandhi "actually had achieved a great deal". "For the first time since the British took away India from the Indians", they had been forced ... to deal with an Indian leader as an equal, to acknowledge that Gandhi represented the aspirations and indeed that the demands of most of the Indians for self-government, and of the Indian National Congress he dominated, would have to be dealt with seriously. Then Shirer concluded : "The Congress might be outlanded again and Gandhi jailed -- this would happen. But they could no longer be permanently suppressed. *From now on it was a question not of whether the British were willing to grant independence to India but of how and when*". William Shirer, *op.cit.*, pp. 55-56. But this was obviously subsequent rationalization by Shirer of Gandhi's action in 1931 much after events that took place.
14. It had been fully realized by the revolutionaries that the ordinary British people were completely kept in the dark about the oppressive and exploitative acts of the successive British and Indian Governments in India, and that many public leaders in Britain, like Wedgewood Benn, Fenner Brockway, Sorensen, all long time M.P.'s of British Parliament, were strongly in favour of ceding at least Dominion status to India.
15. Those who can read Bengali language can find the details of the preparations from two contributions made by Phani Kundu and Bimal Das Gupta in the book *Rakter Akshore* or "In the letters of Blood" by Sailesh De (Biswas Publishing House, Calcutta 1971).

16. The thrilling episode of their escape with the help of a surprised but sympathetic cyclist of Midnapore has been lucidly described by Bimal Das Gupta himself in his contribution to the Bengali language book *Rakter Akshore* (In the Letters of Blood), already referred to earlier, by Saliesh Bose, pp. 132-162.
17. A short news of the trial with the above list of names came out in the then Bengali daily *Ananda Bazar Patrika* of 23 May 1931. Five others had already been released under bail.
18. Cf. Bose, S.C. : *op.cit.*, pp. 302-303, where he observes : "No changes in the official attitude was visible at all in Bengal after the truce and in India, as a whole, signs of goodwill on the official side was lacking."
19. Mehra, : *A Dictionary of Modern India History 1707-1947, op.cit.*, p.200.
20. For details, see Bose, Sailesh : *Rakter Akshore.* (In Letters of Blood), especially the submission of his close colleague, Phani Das, *op.cit*, pp. 163-176.
21. While these incidents have been in my memory from those days, for their confirmation and specific dates I am indebted to the well-known publication in Bengali language *Banglai Biplobad* (or the Story of Revolutionism in Bengal) by Nalini Kishore Guha, *op.cit*, 4th ed., Calcutta 1969.
22. It may be noted that almost exactly at the same time another political suspect in Dacca town Anil Das also kept in police lockup, was similarly severely beaten and he finally died.
23. Following the murder of Peddie, as earlier noted, altogether fourteen young men were arrested including this author, and put on trial but no case could be sustained by the police, so all were released, but later five were again including this author had been rearrested and detained without trial. After the assassination of Douglas, altogether 33 young men were arrested in May 1931 but all were later discharged in trial for lack of evidence and some were rearrested and kept as *detenus*.
24. Cf. Sailesh Bose, *op.cit.* p.110
25. My younger sister Kamala and four other minor brothers were also threatened of harassment and my uncle, who was their guardian, was asked to send them away from Midnapore.
26. The situation in 1931 arising out of "revolutionary terrorism" in Bengal has been well described in a recent publication in India, *Bengal 1928-1934*, by Tanika Sarkar (Oxford Univ. Press, Calcutta), 1987, pp. 120-126. She quotes relevant official documents and observes : "Home Member Prentice confessed 'that terrorism has taken a serious toll of the services and reduced considerably the number of officers available for dealing with it'. He referred 'not just to the dead and the wounded, but more to those who could not cope with the constant nervous tension ..... The strain is telling on the service.' A judge declared that if he was put on the tribunal that was to try the Peddie assassination case, he would immediately leave the country, with or without leave."
27. For example, when my second brother Nirmal, who was a student at Contai (Midnapore) at that time, had been arrested in March 1934 in suspicion of complicity in various activities of the Midnapore group, and a senior I.B. Inspector, Mohini Sanyal, admitted they knew that Ramkrishna and Nirmal Jiban were innocent yet they had been arrested and later executed on charge of conspiracy to murder.
28. This information was given to me by my younger brother Nirmal who worked closely with Braja Kishore.
29. Italics are of this author.

30. Bose, S.C. : *op.cit.*, pp.297-298.
31. For which see next Chapter.
32. For details see later, Ch. 9.
33. My personal contacts with those types of people, both inside the prisons and outside in the villages, led me to believe that they, whether Moslems or Hindus, were not real criminals ; they mostly committed murders or assaults on the spur of the moment during quarrels connected with lands and were thus convicted by law courts.
34. Whose name regrettably I do not remember after a lapse of 56 years (at the time of writing this).
35. Prodyot as said earlier was arrested for his faulty pistol which failed to fire, and later tried by a Special Tribunal and sentenced to death.
36. In Bengali : *Mewar pahar Mewar Pahar*
    Rakta pataka
    Uchcha Shir
37. For more details see below.
38. Actually there was never a real contradiction between the two, as Stalin had demonstrated it for Soviet Russia after the Russian Revolution of 1917, and later again after World War II by different East European countries and, above all by China.
39. A more comprehensive list is given by Malini Kishore Guha in his Bengali Book *Revolutionary Movement of Bengal* quoted earlier.

CHAPTER 5

STORM RECEDES BUT A NEW ONE LOOMS LARGE (1935-1938)

Second Round Table Conference, 1931

Gandhi's *Satyagraha* Movement of 1930-1931 was called off at his instance by the All India National Congress following the Gandhi-Irwin Pact. Thus a comparative calm came in the general atmosphere of the country. But people continued to sulk and fret. The British as well as the Indian Governments realized this and were working towards a further instalment of constitutional advances they would propose for India. They had already initiated the first measures by calling the First Round Table Conference in London in November 1930 with a few nominated members from among the leading Indian public men and the British business interest in India, from the then Native States, as well as with some representatives of the British Parliament. However, Gandhi and the Indian National Congress had refused to participate. This time, having announced the assembly of a Second Round Table Conference in 1931, the British Government wanted to have Gandhi's participation on behalf of the Congress, but Gandhi refused on grounds of differences on the basic issue of discussion. The Congress wanted the goal of Dominion status to be discussed first and then the mechanics of achieving it, that is, the details of the Federal and State structures, the constituents of the Federation including the Native States, the manner of representation at the various legislatures, especially wheather it should be on the communal, caste and business interest lines. But the British Government continued to stress on the prior discussion of the communal question and to sidetrack the main issue of the Dominion Status. But in the later part of 1931 there were some last minute discussions between Irwin, who was the Viceroy, and Gandhi. After that Gandhi agreed to attend the Second Round Table Conference in London.

Gandhi reached London on 12 September 1931 from Bombay by ship, 'S.S.Rajputana'. The Conference, however, opened earlier on 7 September and closed on 1 December 1931. The British Government, even under a Labour Prime Minister, Ramsay MacDonald, evaded the issue of Dominion Status and went first to the questions of mechanics and especially the 'Communal Problem', including 'separate electorate' that is, separate representations not only for the Moslems and other minority communities but even for the socially backward classes within the Hindu community, ('Depressed Classes'), to divide that community legally and constitutionally forever. Gandhi was firm in not to be carried away from the main issue. So at the ceremonial opening of the Conference in the majestic St. James's Palace, in the presence of all the participants, (British and Indian) and the top dignitaries of the British Parliament and the Prime Minister, he made his second historic statement[1], and the first before one of the highest and most august gathering in Britain[2]. In a fairly long speech, delivered while sitting, in a low, soft tone, Gandhi made the following points: (a) that he was the lone representative of the Indian National Congress: (b) that the Congress was the only real *national* political organization of India with membership from all the major communities -- Hindus, Moslems, Sikhs, Christians and Parsis, (c) that the mandate given to him by the Congress, prior to his departure for England, was to ask for nothing short of "complete independence" with full and immediate control over the army, foreign affairs and finance, and a 'scrutiny' of how much of the Indian National debt each of the countries (Britain and India) should shoulder[3] and (d) the "right for India to secede from the (British) Empire or the commonwealth if she desired". He however, observed true to the spirit of his creed of non-violence; "If we are intent on complete independence, it is not from any sense of arrogance, and not because we want to parade before the world how we broke away from the British. We contemplate only a partnership."

Gandhi had already established his reputation as a great strategist and even as a master tactician. He knew that the British Government would not then agree to grant 'Dominion Status' and far less 'complete independence'. But in attending the Round Table Conference he wanted to avail himself of an opportunity of presenting to the British public a clear view of the situation in India under the British rule, of her goal to attain complete political, social and economic freedom from that rule to be able to formulate and guide her own destiny, but without hurting the legitimate and justified interests of other[4], and, finally, of the reasons for this goal. Gandhi also had in mind the idea of propagating before a much wider public all over the world, India's case for independence in London, the heart of the then mighty British Empire. But his repeated attempts at the Conference to get even a mere commitment for the future from the British Government failed. Instead the British Government gave top priority to relatively less important issues in the deliberations, especially to the Communal Problem. So, finally, having been disappointed he left the Conference and went for people-to-people contact, to the two cotton mill centres of Lancashire and Manchester[5], which were, severely affected primarily by the boycott of British cloth by the Indian masses at the behest of Gandhi and the Congress. He also visited Oxford and Cambridge.

On his return from the cloth mill country of the north of England he again went to the R.T.C. session and tried to persuade the British Government to take up the fundamental issues, and at the same time his fellow Indian delegates to arrive at an agreed and sensible solution of the communal problem. But both the attempts again failed. For the British Government, in spite of the many adverse problems they had to face in their own country,[6] were not in a mood yet to transfer real power to the Indian people. And, as for the Indian delegates who were all British Government nominees under the leadership of the then multimillionaire and expatriate the Aga Khan, their selection was, as it was meant to be, a stumbling block and an adverse guarantee of the failure of the Conference.

Expressing his views at the failure of R.T.C. and commenting on the composition of particularly the Indian delegation Nehru has observed in his *Autobiography:*

> It was fitting that in this assembly of vested interests-imperialist, feudal, financial, industrial, religious, communal -- the leadership [illegible] Indian delegation should usually fall to the Aga

> Khan, who in his own person happened to combine all these interests in some degree. Closely associated as he has been with British imperialism and the British ruling class for over a generation, residing chiefly in England, could thoroughly appreciate and represented our rulers' interests and view-point. He would have been an able representative of Imperialist England at that Round Table Conference. The irony of it was that he was supposed to represent India.[7]

Gandhi had realized it from the beginning but tried to do his best, with all his sincerity, to persuade all the participants at the Conference to be sane. He appealed to the British to see the injustices and sufferings from what Gandhi himself had said at the beginning of the Conference, their 'misrule' in India, and with the Indian delegation he pleaded for presenting a united front and holding the dignity of their great country and its people. But since there was no sign of any progress, it was a great disappointment for Gandhi but a matter of the greatest satisfaction for the British Government. The Prime Minister Ramsay MacDonald adjourned the conference on 8 October 1931 with a parting hit to Gandhi. He said: "If the British Government forced a constitution on India before a communal accord is reached, our friend Mahatma would probably at once launch another passive resistance movement."[8] The implications of this statement could not be missed by Gandhi with his exceptionally sharp mind and a penetrating look at what he saw and listened.

The British role[9] (behind the scenes) has been well recorded by the U.S. journalist William Shirer.

> I knew that, behind the scenes, the British were doing their best to prevent an understanding between the two great Indian religious groups. My dispatches to that effect were not pleasing to the government (Great Britain) especially the India Office, but one day, on the twenty eighth (October 1931), the liberal *News Chronicle* came out to confirm what I had written.
>
> 'Powerful influences' it wrote editorially, 'are at work in this country which would make the Indian communal difficulties an effective excuse for breaking up the Conference altogether'.

> The influences became bolder and more public. On the evening of October 1 there was strange scenes in one of the committee rooms in the House of Commons, where members of both the houses, mostly Tory, gathered to convince an invited group of Indian Moslems that their future would best be served in an India still ruled by the British *raj* and not by the Hindus. All the arts of flattery, at which the British ruling class was so good, and to which the loyalist Moslems were so susceptible, were generously employed.
>
> Led by Lord Lloyd and Lord Brentford, the Tory members of Parliament assured their honoured guests that they regarded the Moslems as the salt of the earth, or at least of the British Empire. ...If the Moslems of India remained loyal to the Crown, they would be properly rewarded. They were the 'fighting race' in India (actually all but a handful of them were from the same racial stock as the Hindus) and would be given an increasingly important part in building up the Indian Army. They would receive a greater role in the central and provincial governments.[10] The British would never let them down, never permit them to be dominated by the Hindus. And so on. It was pretty strong stuff. The Moslems led by Sir Mohammed Shafi and Shaukat Ali, were overwhelmed.
>
> "You grant us our Moslem demands in India and we will remain loyal subjects of the King and Emperor', said Ali. . . . . . ."

Then William Shirer added: "As I had begun to suspect the last months in India, Shaukat Ali, ... had strayed far from the days when he served as a right-hand man of Gandhi and went to jail with him for demanding that the British get out of India. "I want to be a friend of the British", Ali roared, stopping to smile at and almost embrace Lord Lloyd, who, as Governor of Bombay, once had jailed him. There was loud chorus of Hear !Hear! Splendid! Splendid! from the Tory members. They must have thought that it didn't take much to split the Moslems from the Hindus and doom Gandhi's chances of getting the Round Table Conference to grant India *anything*."[11]

Gandhi was naturally very much disappointed and depressed at such an outcome of the Conference. But he was a man of infinite patience and unbending determination. For, in his birthday party arranged *impromptu* by his friends and admirers on 2 October, 1931 in a hall in the East End of London where about 500 guests, both British and Indian were present, he has reported to have made one of his harshest and most determined statement amongst all the numerous speeches he made at or during the Conference. He said: "What you English don't realize is that freedom is our birthright, as it is yours. *We are ready to pay any price for it.* It is true we do not wish to spill blood in winning it. I believe in non-violence and I insist on practising it. *But I must tell you frankly that if any sacrifice can win our freedom, we will not hesitate to let the Ganges run red with blood to obtain it.*"

At the same time, Gandhi observed: "I entertained no illusions when I came here. But the more I stay here, the more I realize how difficult is our task. It has become almost superhuman. And to make matters worse, there is much ignorance among you about India and why we are here."[12]

Shirer reports that since many of Gandhi's statements were not fully reported in British papers (as most were controlled by the Conservative Party or interests), many present at the birthday party were shocked at these expressions of Gandhi whom they considered him to be the modern apostle of Non-Violence. Indeed they failed to realize that behind Gandhi's veneer of culture, spirituality and humility lay a hard rock of patriotism, courage and determination, all of which combined to help Gandhi, in his loin cloth, to tower above all the assembled glittering Lordsand Commoners and other distinguished guests and participants of the Conference. And Gandhi's spirit, and, even an implied warning to the British rulers, became evident from the brief statement he made on the concluding day of the Conference on 8 October, 1931. He said: "I speak with deep sorrow and deeper humiliation. But my failure does not mean at all my utter defeat. There is no such word in my vocabulary."[13]

This was again the expression of a dedicated fighter and virtually the same as we have spoken earlier (in Chapter 4) about the Revolutionaries' feeling after the great momentum of their activities during 1930-1934 nearly came to a halt at the end of the quinquennium.

Furthermore, William Shirer, following his constant coverage of the entire Round Table Conference and his almost continuous closeness and contact with Gandhi, gave a valuable summing up impression as follows:

"Gandhi was gloomy, but not surprised. He was too astute a politician and revolutionary to say, when questioned, what he would do now. I gathered from my farewell talks with him that he *had concluded, as had the American revolutionary leaders by 1775, that he could never win independence for India purely by negotiation.*"[14] Shirer finally observed that he had no doubt that Gandhi after his return to India would resume the struggle.

This again vindicated the stand taken early by the Revolutionaries in India that the Gandhi-Irwin Pact of 1931 was a ploy employed by the British Government to persuade, through the Viceroy, Gandhi and the Congress, to halt the countrywide Salt Satyagraha Movement and to get Gandhi to attend the Round Table Conference for discussion of a British devised and conjured up constitutional reform for granting a further instalment of dubious autonomous power to the Indian people.

However, Gandhi himself felt that he had been out manoeuvred by the British official trickery and the behind-the-scene activities of the conservative elements that have always stood against all progressive developments even in Britain and not to speak of their colonies and dependencies. And Jawaharlal Nehru felt the same way as he later put in his *Autobiography*:

> There was no question of failure or success of this Round Table Conference itself. Little was expected of it, and yet it made a difference. The previous conference, the first of its kind, had attracted very little attention in India or elsewhere for the Civil Disobedience Movement absorbed attention. ...But in 1931 all was different because Gandhi went as the representative of the Congress and as a leader whom millions followed. This gave prestige to the Conference, and India followed its career with far greater interest; and any failure, whatever the cause, redounded now to the discredit of India. We understood then why the British Government had attached so much importance to Gandhiji's participation in it....[15]

Continuing Nehru has observed·

> The Conference succeeded in diverting world attention from real issues in India, and, in India itself, it produced disillusion and

depression and sense of humiliation. It gave a handle to reactionary forces to raise their heads again.

However, it should be repeated, as has been said earlier, that there was no 'disillusion', 'depression' or 'humiliation' on the part of those Indian peoples like especially the Revolutionaries, who saw through the British game from the beginning and had no expectations for India from the Gandhi-Irwin Pact and the Round Table Conference. The Revolutionaries, therefore, in Bengal and elsewhere, went ahead with their plans of actions initiated in 1930, long before the Pact and the R.T.C. and continued these long after the R.T.C. was considered by all in India as a failure.

In October, 1931 I had been taken as a 'village internee' to Barwan Police Station in Murshidabad district from Bharatpur, and was trying to adjust myself to the new surroundings. Like other revolutionaries, I had no concern for and much less faith on, the Gandhi-Irwin Pact or the R.T.C. But what we were concerned with only was the possible effect of its success or failure on our status condition as a 'detenu'.

Failure of the Round Table Conference and its Aftermath

Gandhi returned to India on 28 December, 1931, and told a vast mass of people who came to receive him at Bombay dock that he had come back "empty handed. But he had not compromised the honour of my country." He found that the whole country was then in the grip of a severe repression carried by the India Government under the direction of a new and a more conservative Viceroy, Willingdon. Most Congress leaders as well as thousands of his followers were in jails. The provinces of Bengal, the United Provinces, and the North-West Frontier placed "under virtual martial law". Gandhi wanted to see the Viceroy before deciding on whether to resume the Civil Disobedience Movement or not. But the Viceroy refused. The main reason was, as it was then reported in papers, that unlike Irwin, Willingdon was a weak man and of set views; he had no liberal ideals or an initiative of his own, and was afraid to meet Gandhi who was reputed to be a man of great persuasive manner of talk, Gandhi, then finding no alternative, decided to resume the Civil Disobedience Movement and was arrested again in Bombay on 4 January 1932 and lodged in his old prison, Yervada, in Poona. With him were also arrested all members of the Congress Working Committee including Nehru, and the Congress was banned.

This time the Government of India succeeded in crushing the movement. For lack of central leadership and direction, it virtually collapsed soon. Of course, out of a sheer momentum and the mass discontent and disaffection that then spread throughout India, it went on for some time, under local leadership and with additional local issues like the non-payment of taxes(as adopted specially in Midnapore district) but these too were severely crushed with the help of 'demoniacal measure' like free shooting, lathi charging, house and furniture burning, imposition of mass collective fines on villages and even outraging women's modesty, by mostly Indian soldiers and police constables, but at some places by British soldiers as well, such as in Pichchaboni village in the Contai Subdivision on Midnapore district, where the local people showed an unprecedented determination, courage and tenacity in carrying on both the Salt Satyagraha and the No-tax campaigns.[16]

From the middle of 1931 the Congress movements gradually came to a halt, but the Revolutionaries, as described in the previous chapter, kept their fight on throughout 1932, 1933 and even in part of 1934. Its severity and the losses on both sides have already been described. And it has also been said that by the end of 1934 both the movements -- of the Congress and the Revolutionaries -- lost their momentum after an almost continuous and intensive challenge thrown against the then powerful Indian Government, helped by various types of vested and communal interests in the country. However, both the Congress and the Revolutionaries were not depressed or dejected. They considered their respective activities as a further major step in their struggle towards independence from the foreign rule. They knew that the struggle would be hard and long. So both again decided for the time being to concentrate on new preparations for what the considered to be another phase of the struggle which would be enevitable in the future.

But in the meantime the British Government finding the 'field' rather open, endeavoured to push down the threat of the Indian people their own scheme of 'reform' -- an even more bitter pill of their consistent policy of 'divide and rule', pursued from the days the East India Company set their foot on the Indian soil in early seventeenth century. In

August 1932 they announced in the British Parliament a '*Communal Award*' with regard to what they called "representation of the British Indian communities" (i.e. other than the then Princely ruled 'Native States') in the Provincial Legislatures, under a proposed new constitutional reform scheme for India, which later emerged as the Government of India Act, 1935. The Award, leaving aside composition of the future Central Legislature, proposed that the new Provincial Legislature, to be introduced under the Act, would consist of separate representatives of Moslems, Sikhs, Christians, Anglo-Indians and Europeans elected from separate electoral constituencies; and voters not belonging to all other communities including the Hindus would form the 'general constituencies'; and special constituencies with separate communal electorates were to be constituted for women. Furthermore the 'Depressed Classes' (i.e. the backward sections of the Hindu communities) "were assured separate special constituencies with a right to vote in the remaining general; constituencies also. There were also certain other special representations."[17] Ironically, there was no mention of the Hindus as such although they constituted about 80 to 85 per cent of India's total population. And the Award retained weightage for the Moslems in the minority provinces.

As Gandhi and other Congress leaders then were in jail that organization could not take a stand on the Award. But Gandhi, acting on his own, staged in the Yervada prison in September 1932, a fast unto death as a protest against the British plan of dividing even the Hindu communities into two major sections, the so-called 'Depressed Classes' and others. As a result, when his condition became critical, the leaders of the Congress as well as from the Depressed Classes including Dr. B. R. Ambedkar rushed to Poona, met Gandhi and arrived at an agreement regarding the seat allotment to the members of the Depressed Classes within the "general communities" meant for the Hindus. The agreement came to be known as the Poona Pact and the British Government accepted its provisions as "an integral part of the Communal Award"

Gandhi resorted to another fast in the prison in May 1933, when he was released. In the meantime, in November-December 1932 a Third Round Table Conference was held in London without the participation of the Congress, but again with a limited number of people from India selected by the British and the Indian Governments. It considered further proposals for the coming constitutional reforms which were then (1933) published as a White Paper. The British Government obviously had decided to go ahead with such 'reforms' as would please at least certain sections of the Indian people, but retaining their vital interests in India, and would further accentuate the internal differences among the Indian people, which would be a major card for them in the future to keep India under their control.

New Constitutional Proposals under the Government of India Act, 1935

Gandhi was released in May 1933 and again in that year he was rearrested and released finally on 23 August of that year. In the middle of 1934 the Civil Disobedience Movement was also finally 'countermanded' and the Government of India withdrew the ban on the Congress. Gandhi started his new weekly *Harijan* in place of the earlier *Young India*, and reverted back to his 'constructive activities'. Congress was by then sufficiently weakened and unable to launch any other new activities in pursuit of their declared goal of independence. It was even unable to stage any protest against the Communal Award which was blatantly contrary to India's unity and integrity. In a resolution of its Working Committee on 13-15 June, 1934 it said: "It can neither accept or reject the Communal Award as long as the division of opinion lasts".[18]

After the release of Gandhi and the legalization of the Congress, the latter decided to function as a constitutional organization and to contest the general elections to the new proposed Central and Provincial Legislatures under the Government of India Act of 1935. The main provisions of the Act were: (a) institution of a bi-cameral Federal Legislature -- the Council of State or the Upper House, and the House of Assembly or the Lower House -- in Delhi, the former with representatives of both the British ruled Indian Provinces and the Native States ruled by the Indian princes; (b) a Dyarchical form of Government at the Centre with division of subjects into 'transferred' and 'reserved' (as it was in the provinces until then) with the latter being completely under the jurisdiction of the Governor-General and the Federal Legislature having no power to make laws, (c) abolition of dyarchy at the provincial level, that is, the Provinces would have no more any 'reserved departments', but there could be 'Excluded Areas' or 'Partially Excluded Areas', the administration of which would be beyond the control of the Provincial Legislatures. The elections to both the Federal and Provincial Legislatures were to be held under separate electorates with constituencies delineated on the basis of the major religious communities, depressed classes amongst the Hindus, Europeans, business and other special interests such as landlords, labours, etc. At the Federal level the representatives of the Native States would be nominated by the Rulers of the States. The special power--legislative, executive and judicial, given to the Governor General as well as the Provincial Governors, 'pock marked' the whole plan of constitutional advance, with reservations by and on behalf of the British rulers in India.

Gandhi after his final release in August 1933, dissociated himself from the Congress and in 1934 retreated to his newly established *Ashrama* at Sabarmati in Gujarat and, as already said, devoted his attention to social questions and 'constructive activities'. He, however, still remained the *de facto* supreme guide and mentor of the Congress and all the top leaders, including the new heads of the Congress governments in the provinces after the elections, used to flock to him for advice on complicated issues.

The elections to the Provincial legislatures as well as to Central Legislative Assembly were held in 1936 and the results were highly satisfactory for the Congress. It emerged as the single largest party in the Central Assembly and secured a majority of seats in the Assemblies of eight out of eleven British ruled Governors' Provinces, e.g. in Bihar, Orissa, United Provinces, Central Provinces, Assam, Bombay (including Gujarat), Madras and the N.W.F. Province. In 1937 the Congress formed governments in these provinces. In Bengal and the Punjab, leaders of other two parties, A.K. Fazlul Haq of the Krishak Praja Party and Sir Sikandar Hyat Khan of the Unionist Party respectively formed the governments. In Bengal, Haq was against Jinnah and the Moslem League (although in 1906 he had been one of its founder members) and offered to form a Coalition Ministry with the Congress but the latter was then reluctant to join in a coalition government. So later Haq joined hands with the Moslem League to form a Government in Bengal. History would judge if the Congress made a mistake and sealed the future fate of Bengal[19] towards an eventual partition.

The Congress governments ruled the provinces until the beginning of World War II (1939), and the organization was the single largest party in the Central Assembly.

Operation of Provincial Autonomy and Relaxation of Restrictions on Detenus

In July 1935 and January 1936, I appeared for the Intermediate and Final Law Examinations for the Bachelor of Law degree and passed both with First Class. By then the position in India with regard to agitation by the Congress was very quiet, and armed actions by the revolutionaries had practically stopped. And with the initiation of a new experiment by all political parties of working out the new scheme of Provincial Autonomy, the centre of popular attention shifted to what could be obtained from no doubt a very unsatisfactory scheme.[20] So the restrictions on detenus and even on convicted prisoners were being relaxed gradually.

From the end of 1936 prisoners from Deoli Jail were started to be slowly repatriated to special Jails in Bengal. I was brought back to the Berhampore Detention Camp at the end of 1937 after spending four years and a half in Deoli. There I met my brother Nirmal Roy amongst my other friends and co-workers from Midnapore. Nirmal had been arrested in March 1934 from Contai after the third District Magistrate of Midnapore, Burge, was assassinated in September 1933.

With the formation of the Congress Governments in the provinces headed mostly by the leaders of the Congress Party, the organization settled down to a period of relatively quiet and constitutional activities. This brought a rather peaceful atmosphere throughout the country except there were some serious agrarian unrests in many parts of India, especially in the *Zamindary* areas of Bengal, Bihar, Orissa and the United Provinces, where under a most unjust system of land tenure system introduced in India by the British Government - the Permanent Settlement Regulation of 1793, peasants at the lowest levels as well as the tenant - cultivators, had to bear a heavy burden of land rent and other miscellaneous levies. These became specially unbearable for most of them due largely to the great slump in agricultural prices in the early 'thirties resulting from the world's worst Economic Depression of this century. The result was a serious political discontent amongst the vast multitude of small and marginal peasants and farmers who constituted nearly three-fourths of the rural population of India. The Congress Governments in the provinces were deeply concerned from the beginning but as the Congress Party itself was largely constituted by leading zamindars, big and small landholders and *zotedars*, these Governments were generally unable to undertake any real solution of the land problems.[21] But this is another major issue by itself about which I have already said and written several articles in different media since independence[22] both in India and abroad.

In Bengal, in 1937 the new coalition Government of the Krishak Praja Party and the Moslem League, under the leadership of A.K. Fazlul Haq a dynamic though somewhat mercurial personality, also followed the gradual policy of relaxation of the restrictions on the political detenus and their eventual release. And later in the year when some of us were transferred from Deoli to Berhampore Detention Camp, the newly appointed Home Minister Khwaja Nazimuddin, of the Haq Ministry, came to see us in the Camp. He told our representatives at the Camp Office that the new Government had taken the question of the release of the political prisoners in right earnest. We then naturally became jubilant as we could then see, as they say in English, a distant streak of light at the end of the dark tunnel through which we had been traversing past seven to eight years. While some of us were indeed lucky to be actually released in the next few months, my colleagues from Midnapore as well as my brother and myself had to go through another and ultimate phase of detention, that is, in distant villages and police stations in different districts away from our home district. Thus, towards the end of the year (1937) my brother was sent to a police station in an island village in the district of Barisal in East Bengal at the great confluence of two of India's mighty rivers--the Ganges and the Bramaputra. And three of my friends, Kshiti Sen, Jyoti Jiban Ghose, Phani Das, and myself were despatched with armed Pathan guards to four different police stations in the Mymensingh district in north-east Bengal, across the middle stretch of the River Brahmaputra.

A short visit to Calcutta, August 1938

The scene there now was completely changed. Because of almost continuous heavy rains since I left, the floodwater level had further gone up and invaded the entire high ground of the police station and that of my quarters as well. So much so that there was no ground for me to land from the boat. But fortunately the floor levels of my bed room and kitchen were still above water. That made it possible for me to land and be back in my room. But all was wet and humid and I had to wade through knee-deep water to go to my kitchen and the toilet. It was nearly the end of July and was still raining heavily occasionally and lightly almost all the time. It was another entirely novel experience for me. I had never seen so much water or lived right in its midst. I could see from my window heavy torrential rain lashing against the flooded water and creating ripples and even bigger waves but at the same time bringing nearer the more serious danger of water coming into my bed room. Actually, one night while I was asleep the floor under my bed subsided because it was hollow underneath due to the nests built there by the indomitable ants, as a result of seepage of water.[23]

But even in those conditions I tried to keep up my spirit. But some mails from my home in Calcutta brought me the news that my grandmother, who had brought us up in Midnapore from our childhood was seriously ill. So I thought of writing to the Government of Bengal for a short leave to enable me to go to Calcutta and see her. I sent the letter through the usual channel, that is, the O.C. of Ghatail P.S. to the Superintendent of Police, Mymensingh and then to the Home Department, Government of Bengal. And much to my surprise an official permission came around the middle of August (1938) to visit my grandmother at Calcutta for a week. I was overjoyed at the prospect of visiting my grandmother as well as close relatives including my sister Kamala and three brothers Amal, Subimal and Sukomal. My second brother, Nirmal, was still detained as a 'village internee' in police a station in Barisal district.

Necessary arrangements were made by the district police authorities again for my travel to Calcutta, first by the country boat to Pingua steamer station, then by steamer to Sirajganj Ghat on the west bank of the Jamuna-Brahmaputra Rivers from there by rail to Sealdah station. Finally, in late August, I reached our newly rented Calcutta house. This was what my grandmother and maternal uncle hired after they came with my sister and three brothers from Midnapore following an order by the Police to my uncle in Midnapore, Binode Behari, that he should send my sister and brothers away from that town because of the suspected political activities of myself and my brother Nirmal. The police officer who escorted me showed the house from a distance. At the entrance, two young boys were standing but I could not recognize them. The Intelligence Branch Officer told me that they were my youngest brothers. I had seen them nearly eight years back, in 1931, when they came with my mother during her interview with me in the Midnapore Central Jail. But

I could then have only a glance of them, as even then they were not allowed to come and see me in the jail office. I was now seeing them for the first time after the death of my mother in Contai in 1933. Only my uncle living at Midnapore, who, all through his life, had helped to bring us up as his own children, was still not allowed to visit me, and my father was living alone in Contai. I narrated to my grandmother all my experiences of seven-and-a-half years of my jail life and heard from her as well as my maternal uncle and sister their ordeals at the hands of the police in Midnapore after my arrest and detention in 1931 and later after the arrest of Nirmal. Naturally I enjoyed my stay and association with them, but it was very short.

India's internal Political Situation

At the end of the week the police came to our house and again brought me back to my place of internment at Ghatil P.S in Mymensingh district which was nearly 500 miles away from Calcutta. My mind then became largely unsettled. But the political situation in India as well as in Bengal, following the initiation of the Provincial Autonomy in which the main political parties actively participated, quietened down considerably. It was apparently all quiet on the Congress front. Gandhi was busy with 'constructive' and social activities like Basic Education and the removal of the various age-old religious, social and economic disabilities of the Backward classes amongst the Hindu community. The Congress Working Committee was busy with planning, organizing and monitoring the works of the Provincial Congress ministries. The Revolutionary Front also became passive, for many of their top leaders were still in jails in late August and early September. And those who had been let off were busy in adjusting themselves to the new situation. But there was amongst many of them a keen awareness that with the new situation in India and the world and the possibility of a world armed conflict breaking out at any time, there was a need for a radical change in their strategy and tactics of fighting the British rulers. This awareness was further intensified by the thinking that the future global conflict would be for hegemony in the world amongst the Colonial - Have and Have not Powers, and it would also draw in the first Socialist State (Russia) established in the world in the late 'thirties', and eventually also India.

So the activities of the revolutionaries underwent a great transformation. With a wider perspective they sought for new and wider fields and bigger organizations for their activities. In the absence of not too many of such organizations dedicated to the cause of a completely independent India with a progressive and secular government, they mostly aligned themselves in the Congress. But some joined the then well established Communist Party of India thereby enhancing the latter's strength. In Bengal, one group joined the official section led by Gandhi and Nehru, but a great majority aligned themselves with Subhas Bose who had always considered Non-Violence as an 'expedient', rather than as an inviolable doctrine, for achieving India's independence. As the prospects of a global conflict heightened towards the end of 1938 there was a great spurt of activities among the followers of Subhas and on the part of the leader himself. He led a campaign among the Congress as well as the masses on the need for the Indian people of getting ready to play a decisive role in a situation likely to be created by a War. Both as a member of the Congress Working Committee and as a charismatic personality he had tremendous influence on the Congress organization as well as on masses. This resulted in the warming up of the political situation in the whole country and particularly in Bengal.

The news of such a situation in the country percolated to some extent to me in Ghatail P.S. through all the barriers of official censors, and influenced my own thought. However, I preferred to wait to take any decision till I was released and had a chance to study the situation myself first hand. In the meantime I tried to work out a balance sheet of my losses and gains during my incarceration of nearly eight years in different jails in India and detention in some of the most backward villages of Bengal. Without burdening the reader with the details, the main accounts could be summed up as follows : *On the loss side* I missed a career of a full fledged engineer and had some retardation of my educational attainments, and also suffered a great deal of ordeal due to arrest for suspected complicity in a 'murder case', then in a judicial trial and the prolonged detention. Furthermore, my family too had to suffer considerably through police harassment. But these were perhaps the *minimum* price I should have paid for my earnest desire and sincere efforts to gain my country's independence. *On the gain side,* I had a great opportunity of coming into contact with a good section of the cream of Bengal's dynamic youth and having an intimate knowledge of their thinking and dedication to the cause of the country's freedom, and, secondly, an intimate contact with some of the Province's backward villages and peoples and to see first hand the extent of their poverty and backwardness, the deprivations and sufferings they went through, exploitation they were helplessly subject to, and the natural hazards and disasters they had to face in their day to day life. Indeed the latter had so much impact on my life that it largely led me to take in my later life after independence, the cause of the rural people and of agricultural development as an essential component of future India's economic, social, cultural and even political achievements. And the first result of my thinking was the preparation, during my second detention at the time of World War II from 1940-46, and easy on the 'Agricultural Economics of Bengal', which was submitted to and approved by the Calcutta University for its distinguished P.R.S. Scholarship in 1944. The University later published it in 1947. In its Preface I had mentioned: "I was as an 'internee' during 1931-38 that I had the privilege of seeing the interiors of many important districts of Bengal. I had then the opportunity of coming into close contacts with the villagers of those districts and of knowing first hand the different problems of agriculture and of the agriculturists. It was during my stay in a very backward village in the district of Mymensingh in 1938 that the idea of taking up the cause of agriculture as well as of the agriculturists took a definite shape in mind. And I plunged myself into the job in right earnest."[24] And in that pursuit I spent the next 40 years of life, through the opportunities available to me as an official of the United Nations, on study, research, writing and actual advice to various countries in the development of their agricultural sectors. When I think of these I feel that the two years of my early life spent in some Bengal villages as a political 'internee' did not go barren.

Around the middle of September 1938, finally the order for my release from detention reached the police station at Ghatail. I became naturally very happy. So in a few days time I packed up my belongings and left the police station, but this time absolutely on my own unaccompanied by any policeman, as a free man. What a pleasure it was! But also a responsibility, for I had to arrange myself the necessary steps for the complicated travel first by a small country boat to the steamer station Pingna, nearly 30 miles away, then by a steamer to railhead at Sirajgange, from there by rail to Calcutta, I was very happy to be finally back to my family but my happiness was to a large extent subdued by the fact that my mother did not live the ordeal of my long imprisonment to welcome me. My first task was then to go to Midnapore to see my uncle and then to Contai, my father. My next major preoccupation was to think of having some avenues of earning at least my own livelihood, without having to depend any longer on my father or uncle. In Midnapore, after consultation with my uncle I enrolled, primarily as a stop-gap as a probationer for Advocateship of the Midnapore Bar. By that time I had received the news of my passing the M.A. Examination of the Calcutta University.

My next most serious concern was what sort of political activities I should have and to what extent. There was no question of withdrawing as the country was not yet free and the oath that my several friends and I had taken by the bank of the river Kangsavati in Midnapore town in 1925 had not yet been redeemed. However, like many other revolutionary friends I felt that the days of activities of the sort we had so devotedly pursued in the thirties and in which so many of the precious young lives were sacrificed, were over. I recognized that was a phase, a very important one, in the struggle for independence. But new situations have arisen, both nationally and internationally, which called for new strategies as already felt by many even prior to their release in mid-September 1938. We felt the need of a wider contact than that of small localized revolutionary groups. Such a contact was possible only in the Congress and with the section led by Subhas Bose. He had, from the very beginning of his joining that organization in 1921, taken an uncompromising stand in favour of complete independence and did no rule out means other than Non-violence as Gandhi had done. I had always a tremendous regard for Gandhi, and still have. He was an astute saint-politician, a great moralist, a man of superhuman courage and conviction, and a master strategist in his own ways of struggle against the foreign rulers. He was by all accounts a great man, perhaps one of the greatest in history. But Subhas appeared to me to be a more realist, more in line with history and had a charismatic personality. He had been a great force in the Congress in 1938 and was elected its President at the Haripura session in February that year. There "he made a bold statement of unqualified Swaraj and the use of force against the British, `if necessary."[25]

So, I thought my best course would be to join the Congress[26] where Subhas was then a great force. Subhas's presence in the organization would give its activities a more realistic content than Gandhi's more doctrinaire and Nehru's visionary and idealistic approaches and make them more balanced.

Notes and References

1. The first, it may be recalled, was made by him, during the course of his trial, before the trying judge in a sedition case filed against him in Ahmedabad in 1922, in which he was sentenced to six years' imprisonment.
2. The full text was never released by the British Government but the US correspondent William Shirer, who accompanied him, took notes which he has presented in his book already quoted : *Gandhi, op.cit.*, pp. 165-174.
3. *Ibid*, p. 171
4. Shirer has reported that after the meeting Gandhi told him: "he was appalled at the ignorance of the M.P.'s of the history of the British in India and of the current situation there. He had expected to find more knowledge in members of Parliament. He said he had to tell them that they had been raised on false history." *Ibid*, p. 175.
5. See Chapter 4.
6. Such as a sagging economy largely from the effect of the worldwide economic Depression of the 'thirties with falling international markets, huge internal unemployment, closure of industries, even a naval revolt at Inverness in Scotland, devaluation of the pound and a serious governmental crisis involving the dissolution of Parliament and the Government.
7. Nehru, J.N.: *An Autobiography* (Oxford Univ. Press), Calcutta, etc., 1982, p. 293.
8. Quoted by William Shirer, *Gandhi, op. cit.*, p. 196.
9. A role which has been well-known to all the countries and peoples in the world who had perforce chances to deal with them, particularly the United States of America, Jews and Arabs, and Ireland.
10. In spite of the fact that the Hindus then consisted of about 85 per cent of the total population of India.
11. William Shirer, *op.cit.*, pp. 186-187. The reporting of the details of the momentary happenings benind the scenes at a vital official high level Conference in London to determine the fate of a great country like India, by an impartial but sympathetic foreign (U.S.) journalist has been an important historic document.
12. Italics are of this author's. It is quoted to show to the current and future generations Gandhi's sincere and keen urge for freedom for his country from the foreign rule. For this author is well aware that his critics were often ignorant of many an original statement of Gandhi partly due to their non-availability, and partly because of the omissions and colourings by his critics and admirers respectively. *Ibid*, p. 190.
13. W. Shirer, *op.cit.*, p. 194.
14. Italics are this author's. *Ibid*, p. 196.
15. Nehru, Jawaharlal: An *Autobiography* (Oxford Univ. Press) 1980 edition, p. 295.
16. These are fully described in the Bengali book: *History of Freedom Struggle in Midnapore*, V. II by B.K. Das, *op.cit.*, Ch. XVI-XX, and also in *Fight for Freedom in Midnapore 1928-1938* by N. Das.
17. Cf. Mehra, P.: *op. cit.*, pp. 147-148.
18. Mehra, *op.cit.*, p.148. Three years later, in October 1937, Congress at its AICC meeting in Calcutta, condemned it.
19. Whether partition of the Province could be avoided in 1947, after the British finally left India, may be debatable but at least Haq was reported to be against it.
20. Referring to its highly undesirable features from the Indian point of view, Nehru has said: "There was going to be Provincial Autonomy, but the Governor would be a benevolent and all powerful dictator keeping us in order. And high above all would sit the All-Highest, the Supreme Dictator, the Viceroy, with complete powers to do what

he will and check when he desires. Truly, the genius of the British ruling class for colonial government was never more in evidence, and well may be the Hitlers and Mussolinies admire them and look with envy on the Viceroy of India." Nehru: *An Autobiography, op.cit.*, p. 386

21. Which unfortunately largely hold true even today, after 40 years of India's independence, in spite of many ostensible land reform meaures introduced in these years by the various State Governments to alleviate the conditions especially of the small farmers and tenants, largely because there has been no radical change in the character of the Congress leadership in many of the present Indian states.
22. The *Mysore Economic Journal,* the *Calcutta Review* (Calcutta University), The *Forward Block* (est Subhas Chandra Bose,) The First U. N. *Report on Agrarian Reforms in Developing countries* (ed. Dorin Warriner) 1951., etc.
23. Studying the land, water and agricultural problems of Bengal, and even of India, I have often thought of this experience and felt that at times we have so much water in this country (now including also Bangladesh) yet we often complain of scarcity and drought. Now I know it is primarily a question of proper distribution by space and time and thus of management and investment.
24. Ray, P.K. : *Agricultural Economics of Bengal,* Univ. of Calcutta, 1947, p. vii.
25. Mehra, P. : *op.cit.*, p. 104.
26. See also later, Chapter 6, for further elaboration on this.

CHAPTER 6

GATHERING OF INTERNATIONAL STORM AND ITS IMPACT ON INDIA

The Indian National Congress and The Impending War: Subhas's views

However, the issue was more pressing, especially for the dependent countries like India at that time, in late 'thirties. If war broke out then, what would be the option of the Nationalist India? And which side would India take, considering its political interest? But the All-India National Congress, then under the leadership of Gandhi[1] and Nehru, was not certain. Its views varied from pacifism to some sort of Civil Disobedience. But a clear cut and realistic alternative was laid down by the traditional 'dissenter' Subhas Bose. Even when he was elected as the Congress President at Haripura Session in February 1938, he made a bold stand "for unqualified *swaraj* and the use of force against the British, if necessary". But Subhas did not necessarily mean violence. For, regarding "the method which the Congress should pursue in the years to come as well as its role in the national struggle," he observed in his presidential address: "I believe more than ever that the method should be satyagraha or non-violent non-cooperation in the widest sense of the term, including civil disobedience. It would not be correct to call our method passive resistance. *Satyagraha* as I understand it, is not merely passive resistance but active resistance as well, though that activity must be of a non-violent character."[2] Subhas then cautioned his partymen that "the acceptance of office in the provinces (following the introduction of limited provincial autonomy in 1937) as an experimental measure should not lead us to think that our future activity is to be confined within the limits of strict constitutionalism''. And he stated categorically: "It is necessary to remind our countrymen that Satyagraha or non-violent non-cooperation may have to be started again.''[3]

During the Haripura session of the Congress Subhas was at the peak of his popularity in India, and also in the Congress. For, with the shadow of a new major war already cast all over the world, most of its leaders, barring him, were still not sure, of their policies and approaches *vis-a-vis* the Indian and, finally, the British Governments. They were still brooding whether these should be qualified cooperation, or struggle, and in the case of the latter what should its form and extent be. Subhas, on the other hand, was more categorical about the need for struggle. He was more outspoken the following year, when he was reelected Congress President for the second time against the 'official' opposition of that organization led by Gandhi, but with the help of left-minded members from all over India Gandhi, though not then even an ordinary member, yet having the key role in all its major decisions, unfortunately took it as his personal defeat and said in the course of a public statement issued soon thereafter that "after all Subhas is not an enemy of the country.'' Gandhi apparently was worried that the leadership of the Congress would pass into hands of the 'extremists' in the party, thereby taking things out of his control.

At Tripuri Congress session (1939) Subhas attended as a sick man and delivered his presidential address from a stretcher. He forecast that following the Munich Pact of 1938 and the collapse of the Republican Government in Spain, the power of the "so-called democratic powers, Great Britain and France, weakened considerably. Moreover, there was a possibility they would join Germany and Italy through "a Four-Power Pact or through some other means'', against Soviet Russia.[4] He then forecast an imperialist war in Europe within months, and therefore urged the Congress "to submit our national demand to the British Government in the form of an ultimatum, and to give a certain time limit''. If no reply was received within this period or if an unsatisfactory reply was received, "we should resort to such sanctions as we possess in order to enforce our national demand''. This was too drastic for Gandhi and other top leaders of the Congress. They were not prepared to give any form of ultimatum to the British Government. They still had pinned their faith on a possible 'amicable' settlement with the latter on the issue of India's independence. Moreover, during that period, as happened at the beginning of

World War I, they thought it was not in the spirit of non-violence to embarrass the British Government at their great moment of crisis. So Subhas's proposal was rejected at the Tripuri Congress. There was a clear cleavage between the so-called Rightist leaders headed by Gandhi and Patel, and the Leftists led by Subhas. Nehru, in spite of his many differences with Gandhi, remained with him.

'Forward Bloc' and its Role

Subhas had for long an idea of forming within the Congress a formal leftist block to bring together "all radical anti-imperialist and progressive elements on the basis of a minimum programme which would represent the greatest common measure of agreement between all radicals of all shades of opinion". At an informal conference of all Congress leftists and other radicals held in Calcutta in January 1939 it was decided that there should be no further delay in forming such a block, which would be given a new name, the 'Forward Bloc'. "It will not be a party as ordinarily understood, but a platform for rallying all those who accept the programme of the Bloc. Besides the unorganized elements in the Congress, members of the existing Leftist parties will be free to join".[5] It was hoped that with the progress of time, the Forward Bloc will draw into its folds all radical and Socialist elements and parties in the Congress.

It may be recalled that already a separate block, named the Congress Socialist Party, had been formed in 1939, within the Congress, with a band of highly intellectual and educated young men under the leadership of Jaya Prakash Narayan, Ashoka Mehta, Achhyuta Patawardhan, Minoo Masani and others. It had been working smoothly within the Congress with many top Congress leaders including Nehru. It had taken a lead in propagating especially amongst the students and youths of India the ideas of anti-imperialism, democracy and socialism. But its organizational effort had not, as Subhas said, kept pace with its agitational endeavour. "That is one of the reasons why, though we (the leftist elements) had a majority at the Presidential election (at Tripuri), we failed to have a majority in the All India Congress Committee."[6]

Subhas, however, made it clear: "The Forward Bloc will function as an integral part of the Congress. It will accept the present constitution of the Congress--its creed, policy and programme. It will cherish the highest respect and regard for Mahatma Gandhi's personality and complete faith in his political doctrine of non-violent non-cooperation. But that will not mean that the Forward Bloc will necessarily have confidence in the present High Command of the Congress."

Subhas was very much aware of the critical time through which the whole world and especially India were then passing. He foresaw a clear approaching external crisis, even more acutely perhaps than Gandhi and Nehru, and felt deeply about creating, as he said, 'an internal crisis' within the Congress organization by forming the Forward Bloc. But at the same time he observed: "I am of the opinion that an internal crisis (within the Congress) today or tomorrow, is inevitable in view of the uncompromising attitude of the present High Command and their failure to move with the times. We can avert the internal crisis today only by surrendering completely to them. But what shall we gain by postponing the crisis through a surrender? Why put off the evil day? We are fast approaching an external crisis. It will be disastrous to have an internal crisis when the external crisis overtakes us. It would be much more desirable to face the internal crisis now, go through it and emerge out of it before the external crisis seizes us."[7]

Subhas had envisaged that the Congress Socialist Party would ultimately merge with the Forward Bloc and the latter would comprise members of socialist and non-socialist radicals and progressives and work together within the Congress platform. To him Socialism was not an immediate issue. The more immediate task for all Indians was to achieve independence at the shortest possible time. And the next war, which would be fought on a global scale, would provide the greatest opportunity. The Congress being the premier nationalist organization should be adequately prepared to take this opportunity. Hence he laid down *two-fold tasks for the Forward Bloc:* first, to instil life and revolutionary impulse into the existing programme of the Congress, and, secondly, to prepare the country for the coming struggle through country-wide agitation and through an advanced radical programme. This advanced programme the Congress will be persuaded to accept.

In May 1939 the Forward Bloc of the Indian National Congress was formally inaugurated following a momentous session of the All India

Congress Committee (A.I.C.C.), and a first session of the All-India Conference of the Bloc was held in June 1939 in Bombay. It is well 'known now that Subhas had framed and activised the Forward Bloc as a leading instrument in the fight for India's independence, till his mysterious disappearance from India in 1940-41 (December-January) one-and-a-half years later. By then the Second World War of this century had already started in September 1939, almost exactly six months later as he predicted at Tripuri Congress (March 1939).

In India, despite Nehru's forebodings and Subhas's open warnings, the Congress was not prepared for the war. All attention given by the top leaders, including Gandhi, was against Subhas and his followers. Subhas had to quit the presidentship of the Congress in April 1939 and, in May, he formed a separate group within the Congress--the Forward Bloc. But even this was getting too powerful in the opinion of the top Congress leaders. So Subhas was removed from the presidentship of the Bengal Provincial Congress Committee, in August 1939, and debarred from holding an elective office for three years. In march 1940, after the War had started, Subhas convened an Anti-Compromise Conference at Ramgarh in Bihar under the joint auspices of the All-India Forward Bloc and the All-India Kishan Sabha. Later, at the Nagpur session of the F.B., he demanded the immediate establishment of a Provisional National Government in India.[8] In July 1940, Subhas Chandra Bose was arrested.

I decide to cast my lot with Subhas

It may be stated here that in early 1939 I came from Midnapore to Calcutta and transferred my probationership for Advocateship from the Midnapore Civil Court to the Calcutta High Court, Original side. My main objective was to be close to the political developments in the country, and particularly in Calcutta, at that momentus situation. I was to take counsel also from my erstwhile political friends and to take a decision as to my own future political activities. I felt that in these completely changed circumstances as compared to the 'thirties, there was practically no role for small revolutionary groups and their limited activities, though taken together and over a longer period (1930-1934) they were impressive. Especially if a major World War broke out there would be a great global as well as national upheaval. Hence there would have to be actions on a vastly wider front, engulfing practically the whole country. Which could only be provided by a bigger but solid party dedicated to the cause of India's freedom and the establishment in India of a true peoples' government on democratic, nationalistic and, at the same time, socialist goals, and also with an appropriate and clear cut strategy and programme to achieving those goals.

So, the choice before me was to join either the Communist Party of India, as did many of the former political detenus whom I had met and known very well during my long years of detention; or the Congress and especially its socialist wing; or the Forward Bloc. As for the first, although I liked the goals and long-term objectives of Communism, particularly its vision of a future exploitation-free society of equal socio-economic opportunity and privilege for all, I was not convinced of the infallibility of its theories of 'historical materialsm' and 'class struggle', and its means of achieving the goals of communism, viz, 'the dictatorship of the proletariat'. While reading communist literatures in the prison I thought and felt that the human society was too complex a matter and the human mind was too deep to be examined and fathomed respectively by one principle or instrument alone. I agreed that there were great elements of truth in all these theories, but felt that no theory could be totally fault-free and sacrosanct, for all peoples around the world and for all times to come. Purely an economic or materialistic interpretation of history can go a long way in explaining human activities of particular peoples and particular countries. But it would be wrong to deny the impact of such major factors as race, religion, language and the geographical location. A classical example of the affinity of race over all other bonds is the Jewish people, who having originally driven from Israel more than two thousand years ago and being scattered during all this period in different countries, from the United States of America to Russia, from the North Pole to the South Indian coast, and having lived under entirely different socio-economic conditions, had and retained a strong racial affinity. So much so that they all combined, from their different backgrounds, in their fight for returning to their 'Holy Land' (Israel). As a result of their persistent and relentless efforts they finally succeeded, at the end of World War II in 1946, in establishing their state in Israel.[9] Among some of the more recent examples or race playing a major role in influencing human activities and shaping human history are the current (1988-1989) ethnical violences in the U.S,S.R. and Romania, both of which have long been under communist rule and supposed to have only one class of people.

Many other examples of the overwhelming impact of religion, language, etc. could be cited from history to prove that the path of historical events is not a single or straight one. To observe in statistical terms, it is through a 'scattered diagram' consisting of a series of dispersed points isolated from each other but showing a common trend. It is man who, with his limited reasoning power, tries to see a uniform pattern and draw a single line as a median of the various points. But this 'median' in no way reflects the actual situation.

However, to be back to my position about joining a bigger political party in 1939, I thought of the Congress as well but I could not fully agree, as I have said earlier, with its doctrinaire approach and its totally pacific way of struggle. Moreover, I had a great reservation on its overdependence on the path of compromise. From my readings of history I felt that no power, and not even a privileged man, wanted to willingly abdicate or give up its or his privilege, and far less the British would part with the real power over India from which they had already benefited enormously, economically and politically; they would continue to do so in the future unless they were compelled to leave. Again, unless any negotiation or compromise from the Indian side was based on some strength, the initiative and option would always rest on the stronger party. So, India, to gain total freedom from the British rule, must show unmistakably its strength compared to the other party, no matter whether it be through non-violent or more violent means. Of course, there was no question of personal or ethnic animonsity against the British, as I have already said. But it was a question of realism. But here was one of the crucial point where I found the Congress deficient. For one thing, it had earlier launched civil disobedience movements but when the latter got a momentum, the organization hesitated to pursue to their logical conclusions. Second, just at that time, at the beginning of 1939, the Congress was not sure of its leadership (as Gandhi had retired from its active leadership), nor was a clear-cut strategy laid down as to how to face a war situation. It has been said that "in 1940, he briefly assumed leadership of the Congress but gave it up the following year when it became painfully clear that, to the party, his non-violence was an expedient, not a creed".[10]

For these considerations I did not think it appropriate to join the Congress although I had a great regard for Gandhi, for his strict moral principles and his adherence as a man to truth and non-violence. After mature consideration I thought it more proper to join Subhas with whom

I came into close personal contact, as earlier said, in my early youth, at the age of seventeen, during the Midnapore Youth Conference in 1929. Ever since I have followed closely his actions, lectures and writings from numerous platforms, and above all his lucid presentation of his views on the future goals of a free India, his ideals of a completely independent, democratic, socialist, progressive, non-communal and a liberal state, and, finally, as laid down in his presidential addresses to the Haripura and Tripuri Congresses, a systematic and step-by-step approach to a consistent strategy to fight against the British rule in India. He was strongly against any form of supplication and unnecessary humility which ran the risk of being interpreted as weakness. At the same time he was more pragmatic in his approach to foreign countries. In Haripura Congress he observed: "In connection with our foreign policy, the first suggestion that I have to make is that we should not be influenced by the internal politics of any country or the form of the State. We shall find in every country men and women who will sympathize with Indian freedom, no matter what their own political views may be". Subhas's main concern was, thus, a country's sympathy and support for the cause of India's independence. If it was positive and supported by active help, he was not in principle against accepting such help provided it was unconditional and free from any strings. So, finally, bearing in mind all these considerations I joined the Forward Bloc early in 1939.

Subhas Meets the Writers of "The Forward Bloc"

My main work in Forward Bloc was to clarify and propagate its socio-economic thinking through writing in the chief media, of the same name, that is, *The Forward Bloc* under the editorship of a veteran journalist and devotee of Subhas, Satya Ranjan Bakshi. I used to write special articles on the economic issues facing the country and the ways to solve them. As a regular writer, one day, during the second half of 1939, I received an invitation to attend a meeting of some selected contributors of the paper at 38/2, Elgin Road, Calcutta, Subhas's residence. As I went there one late evening I was led to the first floor in a fairly big room well furnished. There I found four others including the veteran writer Gopal Haldar. The names of three others I do not remember today. After being first welcomed by a gleaming and smiling Subhas in his milk white *khadi 'dhoti'* and *'punjabi'* (the usual dress of a Bengali gentleman) he invited us to an adjoining round table for tea. After we all were seated, Subhas started talking about the current political situation in the country and the world, his disputes with Gandhi and the 'official' group of top leaders in the country, his justification behind forming the Forward Bloc first as a separate group within the Congress and, then when forced out of it, as a separate party. He had no rancour but only regrets over these developments. He had the highest regard for Gandhi, and also respect for the leadership of Nehru, Patel and Azad. He, however, felt, they all were being unrealistic in relying too much on passive and non-violent non-cooperation by the Congress. He was sure a great war involving Britain was coming in Europe, and Japan and Italy and finally even U.S.A. and Russia might be involved. In his foreign policy analysis, he observed that Hitler was against the Jews, who had long ago emigrated from their original land Israel, forced by the Arab conquerors, and came to Germany as to many other countries including Russia, U.S.A., and Britain. The Jews were very clever and active people[11] and helped to build up the economic and scientific power of Germany. But they were very much ethnically oriented, and had extra-territorial allegiance and strong community of feeling with their compatriots, Jewish settlers, in countries all over the world, particularly in Britain, France, U.S.A. and Russia. By virtue of their enterprise and skill many of them rose high up in the politico-economic hiererchy in those countries. He gave the examples of Reading and Simon in Britain. For their extra-territorial allegiance and economic domination in the German society, Hitler did not like them and tried to force them out of Germany. But Subhas had great respect for Jewish scholarship and intellect and particularly mentioned the names of Marx, Einstein and Laski (of then London School of Economics) for their epoch-making discoveries and liberal and progressive views. Subhas was referring to the Jews, particularly of Britain, who had a strong influence on British political decisions. And they were mostly conservative in approach as they had close interests on the contemporary commercial and industrial establishments in Britain. These Jewish lords would definitely block any negotiation by the British Government with the Indian leaders in giving any political concessions which might affect their vested interests.

Continuing Subhas said that, like Nehru, he had also been in close touch with the current international developments, and felt that a war was inevitable; so India must be prepared to take the opportunity. He felt that the main Congress body was not being directed towards such preparations. Too much initiative was left to the British. Instead, he wanted the

Congress to take the initiative and launch a nationwide struggle. Even a non-violent civil disobedience on a countrywide scale would upset the British war efforts. Subhas was sure the British would not be able to fight a war, as it had been demonstrated in earlier battles and wars like World War I, without the manpower and the material and economic resources of India. So even a massive civil disobedience struggle would force the British to come to a compromise with the real Indian leaders like those in the Congress, and also compel them to desist from proposing 'fake' and diluted schemes of constitutional advances for India.

Subhas also reiterated his view that in our new and more intensified struggle for freedom we should cultivate friendship with nationals and governments of other countries, who were sympathetic to the cause of India's freedom, regardless of whether such sympathy arose out of a genuine love for the Indian people or out of a feeling of self-interest. He emphasized that Indian leaders should take a realistic stand and learn by the experiences of other countries. Even the United States of America, in its formative stage and fight against the British Colonial Government in the 1770s, took the help of France, and Lenin, the great revolutionary leader of Russia, was helped by Germany towards the end of World War I.

In the economic field, Subhas wanted an exploitation free fabric, abolition of landlordism and a redical land reform measure, a balanced and scientific agro-industrial development, centralized economic planning under State initiative and control but with devolution of powers to the states and the people. He had envisaged a planning commission as early as 1938, and dealt with it in his presidential speech at the Haripura Congress. And towards the end of that year, during his presidency of the Congress he had actually set up a National Planning Committee with Nehru as Secretary and himself as the Convenor. He also envisaged a new social structure on the basis of village communities, as it was in ancient India, in the form of *Panchayats*.

Subhas wanted all of us to develop and propagate these ideas through the new national medium, *The Forward Bloc*.

I felt quite elated by hearing from Subhas's own mouth his ideas about the goals and the strategy of the new fledgling party.

After I came home that evening from Subhas's place I started thinking over its contents, and how to propagate them according to my capacity. I was most gratified that I had been invited to the talk. I followed up in having further clarification and exposition by holding a series of discussions with various persons who had been in closer contacts with Subhas for a much longer time, such as, Satya Ranjan Bakshi, at his home in Preonath Mallik Road, Calcutta, Kumar Devendra Lal Khan of Narajole at his residence in No.3 Minto Park, and others. I used to hold some discourses, at the residence in Ballygunge in South Calcutta, of Bhupendra Kishore Rakshit Ray, an elderly and senior B. V. member who also had joined the Forward Bloc. The participants were mainly ladies. The subjects were often the current international issues and their impact on India and our activities. Side by side with these activities I continued my probationership for Advocateship in the Calcutta High Court.

The Congress decides to act after the War breaks out

When the war broke out on 3 September 1939 we looked both to the Congress and the Forward Bloc leaderships as to what directives they issue to their party members and the countrymen. The Congress leaders, with Gandhi's retirement from active politics, then were seriously engaged in constitutional activities and worked in eight out of eleven provinces of then British India the limited Provincial Autonomy under the Government of India Act of 1935. It had then, as observed above, no policy or programme and no long-term strategy of struggle, except perhaps what were in the minds of Gandhi but not yet revealed. He being out of Congress activities, its main responsibility was on Nehru. But he too, as far as then known, had no clear cut strategy of fight. Analysing his whole career one would be constrained to say that Nehru was undoubtedly a great son of India, an intense and sincere patriot; he loved his country intensely and passionately. He was a great scholar, a dreamer and an idealist but never a master strategist for fight. This was shown later during his seventeen years' rule over new India (1947-1964) as the first Prime Minister of the country. As far as fighting strategy and tactics were concerned, he was almost entirely dependent on Gandhi. So when the signs of the war were clearly looming on the horizon and even when it actually broke out the Congress did not know what to do. The opinion of its top leaders varied from active cooperation with Britain's war efforts to mass civil disobedience once again.[12] But then they found to their dismay that India and its people were automatically drawn into the vortex of the war after Britain had joined, by a declaration of the Viceroy on his own, and recruitment for the army and mobilization of resources went apace by the then Government of India, at the behest of the British Government.

So, Congress was later forced to take some actions. The Working Committee, by a formal resolution passed at Wardha on 8-15 September 1939, "demanded that Whitehall categorically declare how far its professed war aims of protection of democratic rights were applicable to India."[13] But the British Government refused to commit. So Congress decided that the Congress Governments in all the provinces would quit in protest against the British ruluctance.[14] It also decided "to organize a mass campaign to galvanize the country politically". In April 1940, at its Ramgarh (Bihar) session, the Congress reaffirmed its goal of complete independence and demanded the convening of a Constituent Assembly with elected representative of the people.

Defence of India Act, in Calcutta 30 April 1940

Before proceeding further to an analysis of the impact of the war, in its earlier phases, on the political events in India, it may be said that since the British entry into the war on 3 September 1939 we, in the Forward Bloc, were apprehensive of the Indian Government taking some action against us, as we had already deep red marks on their books. And, ever since my release from long years of detention, the spies of the Calcutta Intelligence Branch had been my almost constant campanions, following me from behind, wherever I went. They were closely watching all my movements; clandestinely but not totally hiding from me, they were doing their job almost twenty-four hours a day. Sometimes I smiled at them, and sometimes became angry. Sometimes even I spoke to them and admonish them. Then they often apologised and replied that they were doing this job for their and their families' livelihood. However, the Governments of India or of Bengal did not take any action against us for next six months when the war situation was about even between the Allied and the Axis Powers. But in April 1940 when it turned definitely against the former by the fall of the low countries, Netherlands and Belgium, and the occupation by Germany of the two Scandinavian countries, Denmark and Norway, and when the British Navy made an attempt to land at Trondheim north of Norway they were rebuffed by the Germans, the two Governments (of India and Bengal) promptly took action against us. On the hight of 30 April, in the early hours of the morning, around 2 o'clock, we could hear outside our house in south Calcutta the rushing and cracking of boots. My second brother, Nirmal, who was then awake, and preparing for his M.A. Examination of the Calcutta University, guessed what it was and at once woke me up and other inmates including my old grandmother. I promptly removed some confidential papers behind my large collection of books stocked in a shelf. Armed police knocked at the door and, when we opened it, they quickly moved in headed by a senior I.B. officer, and conducted a thorough search inside. They found nothing incriminating. However, the officer told me that they have orders to take me to the Alipore Central Jail, one of the two main prisons of Calcutta, for jail custody. I asked the officer, once again in my life, if they had any specific charges against me. He replied, no, the arrest was made under the Defence of India Act for the security of India in war conditions. I saw no point in arguing furher. So I asked my grandmother, maternal uncle and next brother Nirmal to arrange some of my personal necessaries in a suit case. When that was done I took leave of them not knowing how and where in the end I shall be kept, and for how long and in what conditions. But I felt it all would depend on the course and the fate of the war and its effect on the British Empire.

When I was taken to the office of the Alipore Central Jail I realized what a great problem I was to the jail officials. For they had no advance information of my going there. Apparently the order to arrest me and, as later I heard, another twenty and odd persons under the Defence of India Act at the same time, came direct from the Government of India in Delhi through the Government of Bengal and it was kept absolutely secret till the arrests were actually made. The jail officials had no idea what would be my status--an undertrial prisoner for any supposed political 'crime', or a detenu without trial as earlier under the Bengal Criminal Amendment Act of 1932, or a War Prisoner. However the prison authorities sent me inside the prison to a small ward with a few single cells in a separate walled enclosure. It was a special ward where important personalities had been kept before, including Nehru, J.M. Sen Gupta, M.N. Roy and others. There I found to my great joy two very well-known persons --

Dr. Bhupal Bose who during the 1930's had been convicted as a suspect in a Calcutta bomb case and had been sent to the Andamans and later released, and Bhupendra Kishore Rakshit Roy, an ex-leader of B.V. who had also been detained as a State Prisoner for a long period in the thirties. Beside three of us there, all from South Calcutta arrested on the same day, there was in another cell Soumyen Tagore. Roughly another twenty people mostly belonging to the former B.V. group, arrested at the same time from Calcutta, were lodged in Presidency Jail. These twenty-five people were the first batch to be arrested under the Defence of India Act in the whole of India. Later we were informed by the jail officials that we would be kept as persons detained without trial for "security" reasons[15] and treated as "Security Prisoners". The Government would bear the expenses of our food and personal requisites and no cash would be paid, as was the case when we were detenus in the thirties. We were, however, left relatively undisturbed by the police. We were allowed the English daily, *The Statesman,* as in the thirties, and we used to literally scan through its news, particularly relating to the war and to the actions taken by the Government of India in support of the Allied Powers and Britain, but also about the activities of the Congress and other political parties.

Behind our ward in the Alipore Central Jail, in another ward were lodged the Chittagong Armoury Raid prisoners including Ganesh Ghose, Ananta Singh and Lokenath Ball and several others who had been repatriated from the penal-settlement of the Andamans in the later thirties as a mark of leniency on the part of the Government of India. We often used to communicate with them from our ward over the wall which separated them from us.

Subhas calls upon the Nation to launch a mass struggle

The war situation in the early 'forties has already been described earlier. So also the Congress position of "wait and see". The only actions the latter took in 1939 and 1940 were a decision to quit the provincial Ministries formed by it in eight out of eleven provinces in 1938 as stated earlier, the passing of a resolution at Ramgarh session (Bihar) in April 1940 reiterating its demand for complete independence and for convening a Constituent Assembly "where the rights of all recognized minorities will be fully protected by agreement as far as possible between the elected representatives of various majority and minority groups, or by arbitration if agreement is not reached at any point''.[16] The Congress was still indecisive whether to launch a mass struggle against the British rule in India. It was more inclined to the path of ''constitutionalism and compromise''. Even the more leftist elements, such as the Communists, the Congress socialists and M.N. Royists, all of whom had earlier participated with the Forward Bloc in June 1939 to form a Left Consolidation Committee, boycotted the Anti-Compromise Conference held at Ramgarh in March 1940.[17]

Hence at the beginning of 1940, while in Alipore Central Jail, we were looking with great interest at the activities of the Forward Bloc under the leadership of Bose. Actually the struggle against the British Government was launched by it since the Anti-Compromise Conference in March 1940. Subhas referred to this in his Presidential address to the All-India Forward Bloc Conference later at Nagpur on June 18, 1940:

> We can claim that at Ramgarh we launched our struggle with such strength and resources as we possessed. During the last three months a large number of our fellow-workers, including men of outstanding influence in the country, have been arrested and incarcerated. Nine members of the All-India working Committee of the Forward Bloc are at present in prison or internment. In addition to them, leaders of the Kisan Sabha headed by Swami Sahajananda Saraswati, Prof. Ranga and others, are behind the prison or internment. [18]

> The national struggle we launched at Ramgarh has been steadily gaining in strength and volume. The campaign has made considerable headway in Bihar and the United Provinces. In Bengal, the struggle was launched as early as January 1940 over the question of civil liberty, which had been violated by the drastic ordinances promulgated by the Government in September 1939...

Subhas then referred to the fact that only the Bengal Congress at that time, contrary to the official policy of the All-India Congress, decided to launch a civil disobedience movement of its own, for which the Provincial Congress Committee ''was disaffiliated''. Continuing Subhas pleaded with his countrymen for intensifying the struggle against the British rule in India. He said:

> Shall we not consider what posterity will think of us 20 or 50 years hence if we do not acquit ourselves manfully today? What do people today think of the leaders who mismanaged the affairs of the country between 1914 and 1919? I, therefore, make bold to say that if we do not rise to the occasion and join the struggle without delay, neither history nor posterity will ever pardon us.
>
> Twelve months ago when the Forward Bloc was formed we were, obsessed, as it were, with the idea of coming struggle and how to prepare for it in advance. At that time we did not know how far, if at all, outside events and international developments would aid us in our efforts to win *Purna Swaraj*. Consequently, we had to make "self-reliance our motto in life and action."
>
> Today the situation has altered to some extent. In the war between rival imperialisms, the old ones have been fairing very badly indeed.....
>
> What has been happening in Europe in a kaleidoscopic manner has had its inevitable repercussions on India.
>
> The wheels of history are grinding on, quite regardless of what we may be doing in India. But in order to fully utilize the opportunity which international events have presented to us, we must have sufficient unity and solidarity ourselves. If India could speak with one voice today, our demand would indeed be well-neigh irresistible. It follows as a consequence, that while we should think of intensifying the national struggle and widening its scope, we should at the same time try to develop national unity and solidarity to the maximum limit.[19]

Subhas envisaged first unity within the Congress "on the basis of dynamic programme of struggle" and then between the Congress and other organizations such as the Moslem League. He expressed categorically the view: "If we develop sufficient unity and solidarity among ourselves in good time, we may very well hope that even if the country passes through a struggle and even if catastrophic events take place in Europe, the transference of power from the hands of British Imperialism to those of the Indian people will take place in a peaceful manner".

Subhas then expressed the view that "it is not necessary that the Indian revolution should be a bloody one or that it should pass through a period of chaos. On the contrary, it is desirable that it should be as peaceful as possible, and a peaceful transition can be ensured if the people are united and are determined to have their freedom."

However, Subhas was not doctrinaire in his approach to the winning of India's freedom, as he forcefully observed: "But we are not so much interested in a particular method as in the basic principles of action. And we are not to be dissuaded from pressing home our demand for the admission of our fundamental rights by a clouding of the issues and the cry of 'saboteur!' We have too long been taken in by the clever imperial propaganda."

In conclusion, he stated: "India must in this grave crisis think of herself first. If she can win freedom now and save herself, she will best serve the cause of humanity."

This was a clear exposition of what should be the goal of India and the appropriate approach and strategy to achieve that goal. This appeared to us certainly more realistic and consistent with history. But the Congress's hesitation to launch any struggle at that critical period of Britain's and India's history, was partly doctrinaire and partly perhaps of a feeling of uncertainty, as experienced in the Civil Disobedience movements of 1921 and 1931, as to how far a countrywide mass upheaval could be controlled by the party and its leaders. Moreover, Gandhi and other top Congress leaders were perhaps also concerned with the then strong and wide spread feeling of inter-communal and inter-party suspicion, rivalry and even jockeying for power in any form of new constitutional frame of India. At this point it should also be a point of note that a great failure of *all* the political parties was to enthuse the great majority of the ordinary people of the various minority communities and castes in the fight for India's independence. How far this was due to the deficiencies in the approaches and the organizational abilities of the different parties, and or to the inherent cleavages, such as religion, language, caste, and the mores and customs of the different peoples constituting India, may be debatable. But that there was a large chasm between the parties and the ordinary people, in spite of Gandhi and other leaders' untiring attempts to reconciliate different communities, could not be overlooked. And the British rulers took full advantage of it. Perhaps the more cautions among the top Congress leaders were more taken by these problems and thus less secure of the course and the result of a mass struggle in such a huge country like India. Subhas, on the other hand, felt that the unity would be secured through the path of actual struggle, which he called --a dynamic programme of struggle''[20]

Be that as it may, there was thus, in the earlier stages of the war, a clear cleavage of views and approaches between Gandhi and the top Congress leaders including Nehru on the one hand, and Subhas and other top leaders of the Forward Bloc on the other. In this, at that time, the sympathy of most of the ex-revolutionaries of Bengal were with Subhas. That explains the arrest of a first batch of the Forward Bloc supporters in April 1940, and a second and large batch in May of the same year. Finally, Subhas was arrested in July 1940.

Notes and References

1. Though Gandhi had officially ceased to be a member since 1934 because of some difference of policies with other leaders like Nehru and Patel, he remained in reality its supreme leader all through.
2. Mehra, P. : *op. cit.*, p. 104.
3. *Selected Speeches of Subhas Chandra Bose,* Publications Div. Ministry of Inf. & Broadcasting, Govt. of India, New Delhi, Rev. ed. 1974, p. 73.
4. *Ibid*, p. 95.
5. *Ibid,* p. 101. Lecture on ''Genesis of the Forward Bloc''. From a speech delivered by Subhas at Shraddhananda Park, Calcutta, May 3, 1939.
6. *Ibid,* p. 102.
7. *Ibid,* p. 102
8. Mehra, P. *op. cit.*, p. 104.
9. This author, in his extensive travel to Israel as an FAO official in 1972, found an intensive effort by its Government to integrate and consolidate the Jewish immigrants coming from all over the world, including India, with diverse socio-economic and cultural backgrounds. A similar intense feeling of racial affinity is to be found in modern times amongst the Arab Palestinians who have been scattered (especially after World War II) in different countries but are jointly striving to establish a separate state of their own in parts of old Palestine territories.
10. Mehra, *op. cit.*, p. 257.
11. This the author later realized fully when, more than 30 years after, in 1972 he had the privilege of visiting Israel, as an FAO official, for a European Conference Organized by FAO, Rome.
12. As Abul Kalam Azad observed: ''As on various other issues, the Congress Working Committee was divided on this as well...''. It ''considered the issues' of joining or not joining the war ''without coming to any decision.'' Cf. Azad, Abul Kalam: *India Wins Freedom* (Orient Longman), Calcutta, 1959, p. 25.

13. Mehra, P. : *op. cit.*, p. 150.
14. It is debatable whether this was a right approach, or the Congress Ministries in the provinces should have remained to hamper the war efforts of then British controlled India.
15. Not security of India, of course, but of the British rule in India.
16. Mehra, P. : *op. cit.*, p. 150.
17. From a speech delivered by Subhas Chandra Bose at the All-India Forward Bloc Conference, Nagpur, June 18, 1940.
18. *Selected Speeches of Subhas Chandra Bose* (Publications Div.), Govt. of India, Rev. 1974, p. 111.
19. *Ibid*, p. 113.
20. The truth of Subhas's contention has been demonstrated in various ways in the subsequent developments in the Indian political scene.

CHAPTER 7

MY SECOND INCARCERATION(1940-45)

Our Detention at Hijli Jails as 'Security Prosoners', 1940-1942

It is in place to note here that after our arrest under the Defence of India Act on 30 April 1940, we were first kept in the Alipore Central Jail for about two months. Towards the end of June or early July, all the twenty-five persons apprehended in the first batch were sent to Hijli, near the railway city of Kharagpur in Midnapore District. During the 'thirties' there were two jails there--one in an old two-storeyed building with a central tower, built by the Government of Bengal earlier when there was a plan to divide Midnapore District sereral years back. That building was meant to accommodate the law courts of a new district. But later the plan for a new district was abandoned and the building was lying un-used. In the 1930's it was used for the first time to accommodate a section of large political detenus suspected to have been connected with the revolutionary movement of that time. Nearby, there was another small place, intended to be the district jail of the new district, with high walls around. It was used during the 'thirties' to keep women detenus. Towards the end of the 'thirties', with the release of all detenus, both the jails were closed. But after our arrest in 1940 the small jail was first reopened and we were sent there. Apart from all twenty-five of us, mostly members of the Forward Bloc, there were a few others including some from the Communist Party of India like Sisir Ray, Mohammed Ismail and Soli S. Batliwala, and one outsider, Tejesh Ghose who had a German wife. His wife, like many other German residents of India, was also kept under detention in another jail. The jail Superintendent was a retired Senior police officer whom we knew very well. His name was Pabitra Bose. He was the jailor at the Berhampore Detention Camp during the thirties and a tough and rather aggressive officer. I had already an occasion to refer to him earlier in this volume. Long years back while he was a police officer in Mymensingh an attempt was made on his life by the revolutionaries. But now he was a completely changed man, very pleasant in talk but giving away little as the head of the new jail.

A majority of prisoners there were old members of the B.V. and included Hem Chandra Ghose, Rasamaya Sur, Bhupendra Kishore Rakshit Ray, Satya Gupta, Jyotish Chandra Joarder, Nikunja Sen, Benoy Sen, Prafulla Kumar Dutta, Bhupal Bose. We were a small community in a much smaller place. The place was quiet. The jail officers and guards all behaved with us with a modicum of respect and even sympathy. We used to manage with our meals four times a day, breakfast, lunch, tea and dinner, but with help of ordinary convicts brought from other jails. They had a special ward to live inside the jail. There were no arrangements for sports as, we were told, this jail was only a temporary place of detention for us. But we arranged our own small games like Badminton, a tennis-ball, and then to walk in the open space in front and behind our one single long barrack-type ward which used to be locked up from 9 p.m. in the evening till 6 a.m. in the morning. There were makeshift arrangements for easing ourselves, if necessary, at night inside the ward. There were two rows of 25 beds, one after another.

We used to pass our time mainly by reading. First reading the daily *Statesman* of Calcutta, which was then considered the only 'non-national' and non-offensive (from the British point of view) paper, and therefore allowed to us, and then some books brought from home but censored and passed by the Intelligence Branch.[1] We also played some indoor games like Chess and Cards, and then talked amongst us over the day to day developments of the War, and discussing its future courses and possibilities.

In these discussions Jyotish Joarder, a fair, short and sturdily built elderly young man, who had earlier obtained his M. Sc. degree in Physics from the Dacca University, studying under two world famous scientists, Professor Satyen Bose and Jnan Ghose, and had also studied military history and science quite well, was our constant companion. With his background, also as an officer of the Dacca Unit of Subhas's Bengal

Volunteer Corps, he used to have quicker and clearer grasps of the day-to-day war situations, and he explained these to us. He often quoted parallels from the First World War, and especially the various battles in France like in Somme and Verdun valleys, which were decisive for the then Allied Powers of Europe. He had great admiration for military generals like Marshal Petain (France) and Hindenburg and Ludendorf of Germany. He had however special respect for the German military technology and for its father Clausewitz, whose treatises are a still must for anybody wishing to go up in the hierarchy of the army in any country. Joarder had an exceptional memory and used to speak very well. In his military discourses, though very informal, he kept us all greatly enthralled.

Joarder, however, not only studied military theory and history; he had, as said above, a good background of military training and temperament. He was also a good trainer. Later, during the whole of our second phase of detention (1940-1946) in different jails, when the war situation turned unfavourable to the British and the Allied Powers, he used to hold regular military parade in muftis for us inside the jails, of course, undetected by the jail officers or warders. This was to prepare us for any eventual action which might be necessary in the future.

Joarder's second major hobby was science. He was a great admirer of his two science teachers--Professor Satyen Bose and Jnan Ghose. He often mentioned their names to us. He was greatly elated by the then comparatively new theories of Einstein (Relativity) and Max Planck (Quantum Mechanics). He also often spoke of three eminent British Scientists of his times--Lord Rutherford, Whitehead and James Jeans. He also spoke of many others but I do not now remember their names. In explaining their scientific theories and the related theories of creation he used to often get lost and became meditative. From my long and close association with him in various prisons, Deoli (at Rajputana), Hijli (Midnapore), Rajsahahi, Buxa (in Jalpaiguri Dooars) and Dum Dum, he appeared to be not only a genuine patriot and freedom fighter but also a man with an absolutely pure and unalloyed mind. Incidentally, he was the political *guru* of Dinesh Gupta, a very noble and worthy student indeed. Joarder was essentially devoted to God the Almighty, the Infinite and Absolute permeating the entire universe. To him, well versed in both classical and modern Physics, the difference between matter and mind was only conceptual resulting from the limitations of the human mind.

The two were ultimately clusters of waves. There were nothing tangible or material about them. But the big question then still remained: waves on what? Probably it was some form of massive and all pervading energy.[2] But no body yet knew its character except perhaps, as the modern U.S. scientist Fritjof Capra says, the mystics of ancient India and China.[3]

Thus, we had a very interesting and lively time in the Hijli small jail though we were entirely cut off from all outside contacts, and even with our close relations. The place was still mostly isolated and about 2/3 miles away from any locality. On its south side was a deep forest of principally *sal* trees which extended scores of miles up to Orissa and was the habitat of many wild animals including specially snakes, scorpions, wild bears and even elephants. But our stay in the Hijli small jail was only for a short period for about 2 to 3 months. For, sometime in May another big batch, as earlier said, of suspected political activists were arrested, this time comprising mainly of former members of the Anushilan Samity, like Trailokya Chakravarty, Rabi Sen, Jnan Majumdar and, among the younger groups, Naren Das, and Tridip Choudhuri. Besides, a large number of other suspected persons were also arrested from Calcutta. They included my brother Nirmal. Others arrested from all over Bengal included my friends Haripada Bhowmic, Naren Das, Kshiti Sen, Phani Das and Bhupati Mandal from Midnapore. For the time being they were all kept in their respective jails. But they were further followed by successive waves of other arrests. This created a problem of space. So the Government decided to reactivate the big Hijli Jail built around the old court-building, which had been earlier used for the same purpose in the thirties. This bigger special jail meant exclusively for the war-time "security prisoners", was opened sometime in June/July 1940. In July Subhas Bose, the leader of the Forward Bloc was also arrested and kept in isolation in the Presidency Jail. But he threatened a fast in the jail and was let out in December under strict surveillance. By that time we all were taken from different jails including the small Hijli special Jail to the bigger one nearby.

This was a big and spacious building with two floors, with a high central tower and two wings leading out of it to the direction of east and west. On the south and the west was the Hijli forest, on the east about a kilometre away ran the main railway from Calcutta to Puri (in Orissa) passisng through Kharagpur, the big railway junction with workshops, officers quarters etc. It was a planned and comparatively decent small town laid with trees and gardens. The residents were mostly British, Anglo-Indians and Indian people from South India. The massive main building of the improvised jail and its annexes like kitchen, hospitals, offices etc. were fenced with barbed wires, and even its big balconies and verandahs were fenced to prevent escape. There was a big play-ground somewhat away within the compound. The big tin-shed community bath hall with long cemented shallow channels of reservoir as well as the toilets were also somewhat away from the main building. Here we had more numerous people to meet, talk and exchange our views.

War's developments and the attitude of the Congress, 1940-1941

Our main discussion at Hijli jail centred on the developments of the war situation. The massive German campaign in the west and north Europe was then almost concluded, and German troops also occupied most of south-east Europe. Hess had flown from Germany to Britain on a mission of separate peace with Britain but was held. Japan had attacked U.S.A.'s Pearl Harbour's combined air and naval base in the Pacific (in December 1940) and the next day China, which had already been heavily engaged in a massive but undeclared war against the invading Japanese army on its own main land since 1931, declared formal war against Japan, Germany and Italy.

We were then all looking at Subhas, the leader of the Forward Bloc, and also to the Congress leaders including Gandhi to see what actions they recommend to their respective organizations and to the countrymen, to take in those critical conditions of the world.

It was reported in newspapers that since his release from prison in December 1940 and during his 'house arrest' in his Calcutta home at 38/2, Elgin Road, Subhas had almost completely retired to an inner room. He hardly saw any body, even among his own close relations, except some very limited personalities, such as his eldest sister-in-law (wife of his elder brother Sarat Chandra Bose) and one of his nephews. He was attired in a sannyasi's dress and spent most of his time on meditation. We did not know how far the news were true. And we were not inclined to believe them. To us it appeared, that knowing Subhas as we did, however little it might be, he would be the last person to retire from politics altogether and opt for a sannyasi's life. We knew that no body was more passionate than he in his love for his country and his dedication to redeem her from the shackles of slavery. He had been in fact as we have already seen, expecting a new world war to come, and urging the Congress and his countrymen and later his own party, Forward Bloc, to prepare for it adequately. After all these, that he would abdicate everything, seemed to us as utterly absurd. We recalled then that one of his closest followers and our friend Nalini Guha from Madaripur later told us that in one of very confidential meetings with selected people Subhas had said "Create chaos and then leave to me". Subhas thus had taken upon himself the full responsibility of taking the most appropriate action to utilize the opportunity of the war for the case of Indian freedom. We consoled ourselves with all these thinkings and were holding our breath to see what came out of Subhas's 'meditation'.

As for the Congress, it was still uncertain what action they would take. There were at least three clear-cut cleavages of views. Gandhi was unmovable in his opposition to take any action for against India's participation in the war. To join the war, even if it brought later some political concessions from Britain, would be against his creed of non-violence. To go against would also be contrary to non-violence as it would embarrass the British at one of their critical moments. Gandhi expressed these views in a meeting of the Congress Working Committee held at Bardoli (Gujarat) in December 1941. Reporting on this meeting in his *India Wins Freedom* Maulana Azad later said "Gandhiji stood firm in his view that non-violence was a creed and must not be given up in any circumstances. As a corollary to this, he could not, in any circumstances, approve India's entry into the war."[4] However Gandhi had believed in the statement then issued by the British Government in London, headed by the Conservative Prime Minister, Churchill, that the former "was ready and willing to recognize India as free if India offered full cooperation in the war effort". On the other hand, the view of Azad, then Congress President, was different. For he said: "My own reading was completely different. I thought the British Government was sincerely anxious for our cooperation but that they were not yet ready to recognize India as free." Azad had no objection to India's joining the war for the British and the Allied Powers provided, as he put it in a press statement in Calcutta, "only if the bonds which shackle our hands and feet are removed". Referring to the Congress Working Committee meeting,

Azad observed: "I repeated my earlier view that Congress must place greater emphasis on the freedom of India than on non-violence as a creed."[5] Azad was thus in favour of starting some negotiation with the British Government. But he was at the same time, unlike Gandhi, doubtful if the British Government would then go to the extent of "recognizing the freedom of India". As later events proved, particularly after the Cripps Mission (1942), Azad was right and Gandhi was wrong. The British Government wanted to have the full and willing cooperation of the Indian people without giving anything in return. And, it seemed, there was a third group within the Congress leadership which believed that India should cooperate in the war efforts without any precondition.

Eventually, however the Congress Working Committee is said to have drafted a resolution which made a compromise between Gandhi's and Azad's views. It resolved, *inter alia,* "to offer full co-operation to the British war effort if conditions were created in which Indians could fight with honour and dignity for the cause of freedom and democracy".[6] It was in effect, a repetition of its earlier Poona offer to the British Government that "should a genuinely representative national government be constituted at the Centre, it would cooperate fully in the war effort".[7] But in reply the British Government had offered much less in its, now well-known, offer of 8 August 1940 with a very limited role to the Congress in the current war efforts but with no commitment for freedom even in the future. In September of that year the Congress had rejected that offer and decided to launch, very reluctantly and haltingly, "individual civil disobedience restricted to a limited *satyagraha*". It was at the same time decided that the first to offer *satyagraha* would be the closest disciple of Gandhi, Acharya Vinoba Bhave. The Indian Government's reaction was a mass-scale arrests of all leaders and members of the Congress Working Committee, ex-Chief Ministers and the Ministers of the erstwhile Congress Governments in the provinces and other prominent members of the Congress Party. These were in addition to those thousands of others who had earlier been arrested and already detained as 'security prisoners' under the Defence of India Act.

Subhas's Disappearance, 1941

So in the early phase of the war, 1939-1940, while the Congress had been thinking not in terms of struggle but gaining political concessions from the British by repeated offers of cooperation with Britain's war effort, suddenly loomed on the horizon of India and world the Subhas phenomenon. The announcement on 26 January 1941 about his disappearance from home in Calcutta[8] created a sensation all over India and a feeling of consternation amongst the British rulers of the country. There were all sorts of speculation as to where he could go or might have gone. But all these were set at rest when it was stated that Bose arrived in Berlin in November 1941. And he made his first historic broadcast to India in March 1942. This brought an entirely new factor in the muddy and more or less stagnant water in the then political lagoon of India, where the British Government was adamant not to part with real power to the Indian people, and the Congress was all the while dilly-dallying not knowing for certain what to do at that time. This was later (in 1941) clearly realized by the then Congress President, Azad, after his release from the prison, along with Nehru, in December 1941. He has himself recorded: "on this occasion I felt that even though the war had been going on for over two years, we have not been able to take any effective steps towards achieving Indian freedom. We seemed to be the victims of circumstances and not the masters of our destiny.[9] While this was very sad indeed, as all the contemporary politically conscious people in India, including this author, realized, it was even sadder that Nehru, still then an idol of the youth, did not seem to have any positive and decisive role in the matter.[10]

Subhas, on the other hand, was consistent and steady in his approach to India's freedom. In escaping from India he actually pursued lonely his mission to free India from foreign rule taking enormous personal hazards. It showed his great courage and conviction and his devotion to the cause of complete independence. His first broadcast from Germany was in March 1942. In this and subsequent broadcasts, he made it clear that he had escaped so as "to supplement from outside the struggle (for independence) going on at home."[11] The main theme of his speeches were that Britain would never grant real freedom to the Indian people, whatever they might profess to say in the open. His task was "to lead the final struggle for India's emancipation." He mentioned that he had two-fold objectives in departing from India: "first, to find out for myself the truth as to what is happening in the world, and, second, to see if India has any allies in her fight for freedom". He emphatically assured his people in India that "whatever I have done since leaving India or whatever I do in future, has been and will be done with the sole purpose of bringing the speedy emancipation of my country and I shall never do anything which will not meet with the approval of nationalist circles in India." Continuing he observed: "I stand for obsolute self-determination for India where her own national affairs are concerned and I shall never tolerate any interference in the internal affairs of the free India." It may be noted that in none of the broadcasts Subhas ever made any personal attack against any Congress leaders in India. On the contrary he always spoke in great reverence to Gandhi. What he criticised was the congress policy of compromise, and he appealed directly to the general Indian people not to trust the British Government's promises as they would never grant freedom to India on their own. He told people that the only way to get it was to fight, even on a non-violent way.

So in the circumstances of Congress inactivity and Britain's reluctance to part with real power to India, Subhas's daring escape and subsequent broadcasts from abroad made a profound impact on the people of India. Even Gandhi was impressed. As Azad has written: "I also saw that Subhas Bose's escape to Germany had made a great impression on Gandhiji. He had not formerly approved many of Bose's actions, but now I found a change in his outlook. Many of his remarks convinced me that he admired the courage and resourcefulness Subhas Bose had displayed in making his escape from India. His admiration for Subhas Bose unconsciously coloured his view about the whole war situation."[12]

So the U.S. President F.D. Roosevelt felt that the willing cooperation of India's vast manpower and material resources was essential for the Allied victory over Japan. This cooperation could only be had by the British Government coming to terms with the Indian leaders. So Roosevelt first secretly advised Churchill about this. I remember when we were in big Hijli Special Jail about the middle of 1942 a report on this came out in some of the Indian papers. Churchill of course did not like this advice but could not altogether counter the argument and advice of his closest and most powerful ally. Roosevelt had already been well-known in Indian knowledgeable circles for his liberal and progressive views and for his New Deal programme initiated as the President of the United States of America for the amelioration of the sufferings of the farmers and other relatively indigent people seriously affected by the Great Depression of the early 'thirties'. By his advocacy of India's freedom during the War he became especially popular to the Indian people.[13]

Another person of then worldwide importance who took up India's case for independence was Generalissimo Chiang Kai-shek, then Kuomintang leader and the President of the Nationalist China. He had long been known to India as the successor to the father of modern China--Sun Yat Sen, and himself already engaged in opposing a major war of conquest by Japan. He too pressed the British Government to recognize India's independence.[14] The Generalissimo visited India in February 1942 to meet the Viceroy and the Commander-in-Chief to discuss a common strategy of defence against the Japanese. But he also met Maulana Azad, the Congress President, and Jawaharlal Nehru to ascertain their views about India's participation in the war. As Azad has reported, during their meeting with the Generalissimo he said that "if during the war the British Government offered Dominion status and agreed that Indian representatives could work with a sense of freedom and responsibility, the Congress would not refuse the offer."[15] It was reported that before returning home, the Generalissimo warned the British Government that "if the Indian political problem was not immediately and urgently solved, the danger will be daily increasing. If the Japanese should know of the real situation and attack India they would be virtually unopposed". He also told Roosevelt that "the British policy was tantamount to 'presenting India to the enemy and inviting them to quickly occupy India.' He confessed to being 'both worried and alarmed."[16]

Pressed by these two powerful Allies (U.S.A. and China) in the war as well as by the approach of the Japanese right to the backdoor of India, the British Government, under the two most diehard Conservative Party leaders, Winston Churchill and Julian Amery, Prime Minister and Secretary (Minister) in charge of India respectively, announced the decision in March 1942 to send a single man mission headed by Sir Stafford Cripps, Lord Privy Seal and a member of the British coalition War Cabinet. He was a man of pro-socialist temperament and was already reputed to have a sympathy for India. Earlier he had visited India at the outbreak of the war, and met Azad and other Congress leaders and discussed with the latter the conditions and possibilities for India to join the war.[17] Later he returned in March 1942 as head of a one-man mission carrying the new British proposals for constitutional advances for India, and held discussions with the Congress leaders as well as with the representatives of other organizations including the Moslem League, the Hindu Mahasabha and others.

Cripps Mission and its failure

It is not my intention to go into the details of these proposals, nor of the verbal and other statements that Cripps made to supplement them or the various arguments for and against them put forward by various parties. I can only say that I followed the reports of these discussions in 1942 from the jail at Hijli and noted them with my comments in writing. But these are not found today after the lapse of over four decades and with so many changes occurring in my life. However, the contents and results of the Cripps Mission have been well documented and are available in the form of various publications. My objective is here very limited namely, to complete the chronology of events that I had to pass through in my life. Therefore I mention below only its main proposals, and try to sum up the principal reasons why it failed.

Perhaps I could start with the end and say that the failure of the Cripps Mission was inherent in the genesis and character of the War Cabinet proposals. They were, as it has been said, the statement of a policy determined and laid down by the British Government. They were not strictly proposals which could be discussed and altered. Secondly, Cripps was chosen to be the leader of a single-man mission because of his popularity in India for his socialistic affiliations, his sympathetic views about India's political aspirations, and, above all, his personal contacts with the Indian leaders. But he was essentially a British and had to look to the immediate interests of Britain during the war. Third, Cripps' hands were tied as his terms of reference were mere to 'explain and clarify' the proposals and 'not to negotiate the terms of an agreement'.

As for the proposals, there was no specific declaration as to the Congress's demand for independence or even Dominion Status in the short or long terms. Actually, they put, as it is said in English idioms, the cart before the horses. They outlined in some details the procedures for framing a 'Dominion type' constitution at the end of the war. There was practically nothing for the present, during the continuation of the war. There would be no change in the legal position of the Indian Government. His Majesty's Government, that is, the British Government would remain responsible for the governance for India and the direction of the defence of the country with the assistance of the British Viceroy and the British Commander-in-Chief posted in New Delhi. They would be in full charge of the conduct of the war. Some Indian members would be taken in the Viceroy's Executive Council. And an Indian member could be in charge of Defence. But as Azad later recorded; "he (the Indian Member in charge of defence) would have responsibility but no power. He would be in charge of Canteens, Commissariat and Transport, but would have little about the fighting forces.''[18] This was not acceptable to the Congress. They wanted real power to make important decisions regarding the war though its actual conduct could be left to the Commander-in-Chief. Secondly, the Congress wanted that the new Interim Executive council consisting of Indian members should have the freedom to work as a Cabinet of a free country but Cripps could not give any answer.

As for longer terms proposals to be effective after the war, that is, the procedures for framing a Dominion type constitution, Cripps' proposals stated that first fresh election would be held in all provincial legislatures on the basis of the communal electorate. The persons thus elected, together with the representatives of the Indian Princely States,[19] would constitute an electorate college, which would then elect a constitution-making body, whose function would be to frame the appropriate constitution of the ''Dominion type''. But in the final stage ''if a province expressed its unwillingness, through a vote of its legislature, to accept the constitution, it was free to refuse accession to the Indian Union.'' It would then proceed to formulate its own constitution which would have the same status, powers and functions as that of the Union of India.

The Congress took objection to almost the entire procedures. Its first and the most serious point was that the power given to the provinces to opt out of the Union would mean an advance guarantee of partition of the country. The same power was also given to the Indian States. There were nearly 600 such states, big and small, and each would have this power. So, as Nehru said: ''The whole background would be of separatism''[20], and there might be no unified country. In fact, the Congress saw in it a sinister move on the part of the British Government to 'balkanize' the whole country which even the Moghul rulers of India had never thought of when they ruled the country for centuries. The other major point of Congress objection was the selection of the representatives of the Indian States by their ruling chiefs with no say of their people who then constituted about 90 million of India's total population of about 300 million. In the proposed new constitution making process these people would have no voice "while decisions vitally affecting them are being taken."

The Congress Working Committee met on 11 April 1942 under the chairmanship of Maulana Azad and considered all aspects of Cripps' proposals and his verbal clarifications and explanations given during his talk with Azad, as the sole representatives of the Congress. They came to the conclusion that they were unable to accept the proposals. The Committee passed a formal resolution giving in details the reasons for their decision. In it the Congress clearly pointed out the major deficiencies and the dangers of accepting the proposals and reiterated its earlier view that "it is only the people of India who, through their popular representatives, may shoulder the burden of war worthily. But that can only be done by present freedom, and full responsibility being cast upon them.".[21] But there were no provisions for that in the proposals.

It may be noted that while Gandhi was opposed from the beginning to India's joining the war on grounds of his creed of non-violence, from his very first and only talk with Cripps after the latter's arrival in India, saw through the spirit behind the proposals and their present significance and the potentiality of danger for the future. He therefore made a terse and caustic remark soon after coming out of his meeting with Cripps: The proposals were a "postdated cheque o a crashing bank". Thereby he had, first, expressed his dissatisfaction that the proposals had nothing to meet the demands of the Congress for some immediate action by the British to ensure for India an independent and equal status to fight the war as a free nation, and, second, as for the future, he even voiced his doubt about the very survival of the British Empire after the war. That Gandhi, after having only one meeting with Cripps, made such a bold and frank statement seemed to have surprised even many in the Congress includisng Azad. And the latter implied by statement, already noted earlier, that Gandhi's "admiration for Subhas Bose (following his daring escape from India in 1941) unconsciously coloured his view about the whole war situation."[22] How far this was true it is difficult to say. But Gandhi was famous for his sharp intelligence and an extraordinary capacity to see through things at the first glance, and, therefore, there should not be any doubt that he himself was convinced, right at the beginning, of the hollowness of the British War Cabinet proposals.

Azad himself realized after his initial two talks with Cripps that "the British Cabinet was not prepared to transfer power to India during the War." This was the first point of a statement he made before the meeting of the Congress Committee on 2 April, 1942.[23] He, however, tried to put the Congress view before Cripps clearly and firmly and, for all his personal view that India should participate in a war to save democracy, he sincerely felt that she could do it only as a free and independent country and not as a slave or dependency of the British. So he had stressed the need for India's freedom right at the beginning. But the British were reluctant and adamant. Of course, for many in India, and particularly the followers of Subhas this was but natural for a British War Cabinet headed and led by Winston Churchill.

As for the reactions in the country and the leaders of the Congress to the failure of the Cripps Mission, the ordinary people were not much disappointed as they could not imagine that the British would ever leave India on their own will. The educated and informed middle class who bore the brunt of the struggles against the British rule especially since the beginning of this century, were even more skeptical about the Mission from the beginning and therefore felt no sense of disappointment at all. Regarding the Congress leaders, Gandhi might have some expectations at the beginning that the British would voluntarily part with at least some power; but certainly he could not be disappointed because he did not want the Congress or the country to put pressure on Britain at her gravest hour of adversity. Azad himself was disappointed as India could not join in a war, which he sincerely thought was being fought by Britain and her allies for democracy. But he was firm on his stand over India's freedom. But it seems the most unhappy were Nehru and Rajgopalachari, the veteran Congress leader of south India. Azad, in his autobiography, has clearly described about the feelings and activities of these two top loeaders of the Congress.[24] While all other leaders and members of the Congress accepted without questioning the final resolution of the Working Committee in rejecting Cripps' proposals, Nehru felt very unhappy and distressed. He had a great abhorrence for Fascism and Nazism, and regard for the principles and practices of democracy. His whole outlook about the war and the possible role of India was framed on this basis. He had always been, by education, training and temperament a devout internationalist rather than a staunch nationalist.[25] Azad has recorded: "Jawaharlal has always been more moved by international considerations than most Indians. He has looked at all questions from an international rather than national point of view."[26] So Nehru had been keen that India should fight, what he thought, in a war to save democracy in the world. He felt about it intensely. So when the Congress resolution precluded this, he is reported to have suffered from a serious mental strain. This was perhaps natural for a person who could not apply one of his life's basic principle to practice. Nehru's feelings for democracy were so strong that, as Azad has put it, his discussion with Nehru after the Congress resolution, "convinced me that he was in favour of accepting the Cripps' offer even though there was no change in the British stand". Nehru, in his goodness, wanted to believe in the verbal assurances of Cripps that Britain would grant India independence after the war. And even after the Congress rejection Nehru tried, in an interview to the British press, "to minimize the difference between the Congress and the British. He tried to represent that though Congress has rejected the Cripps' offer, India was willing to help the British."[27] He would have perhaps continued along these lines if Azad had not realized his mental agony and given him the friendly advice to desist from such a course.

It must be said that Nehru himself had fully realized both the immediate and long-term deficiencies and dangers of the Cripps' proposal, and he has described these in great details in his *Discovery of India*. But he admits that when he "read those proposals for the first time he was profoundly depressed", and that depression was largely due to the fact that he "had expected something more substantial" from Cripps "as well as from a critical situation that had arisen".[28] This was rather unfortunate, for it showed that even though he had enormous personal knowledge and experiences of the contemporary international political situation and an apparent expectation for India and himself to play an important role in its future course and development, he was not fully informed of the depth of minds especially of the Conservative British elements and far less of Churchill. In short, his initial depression and subsequent 'frustration' at the failure of the Mission showed again that he was essentially a visionary and saw only the seamy side of life, and not a practical realist to look simultaneously at the darker sides. This was indeed very sad for a great leader like Nehru.

But, even a greater misfortune for India was that Nehru, by his own accounts, admitted that "under stress of dire necessity or some compelling disaster, one has to agree to many undesirable things. *Circumstances may force a partition* of what logically and normally must not be divided. But the proposals put forward on behalf of the British Government did not deal with any definite and particular partition of India.''[29] This showed a great defeatist attitude and indeed very dangerous. It actually indicated to the British Government a qualified acceptance of partition of India, that is, the proposal would have been considered by the Congress if it was put in more specific and concrete terms. Instead of, what was expected of him as a great nationalist leader, indicating his opposition to partition of our great country at any time and at any cost, Nehru gave the world, and particularly the British, the picture that the communal problem in India was intractable and could be solved, if required, by a partition.

But the saving factor was that Nehru kept his ideas mostly to himself and expressed it much after Cripps had departed from India (12 April 1942) openly for the first time perhaps in his otherwise brilliant book *The Discovery of India,* completed in March 1945, during his detention in Ahmednagar Fort, Bombay for the "Quit India" movement of Gandhi (see later). But still it was well before the British Government headed by Attlee, the Labour leader, had sent, after the end of the war, a Cabinet Mission to India in March 1946 with specific proposals to leave India and, before leaving, to have the country divided into two independent states, India and Pakistan, but in three segments. Azad, then (in 1942) as President of the Congress, had already felt embarrassed by the trend of Nehru's mind after Cripps's failure and told the latter that this "was against our best interests". Nehru assured him that notwithstanding his own thinking he would abide by the decision of his colleagues (of the Congress Working Committee).

However, a more difficult situation for the Congress was created not only by the attitude but even by an almost unilateral action of C. Rajagopalachari, then leader of the Madras Congress Legislative Party and a member of the Congress Working Committee.

He had for long time thought that the British delayed granting independence to India because of the communal differences. So to remove this obstacle he persuaded the Congress dominated Madras legislature to pass a long resolution recommending that the Congress "acknowledge the All-India Moslem League's claim for separation should the same be persisted in when the time comes for framing the future constitution of India.'' Prior to this most vital resolution which went absolutely contrary to the concept and dream of a free and united India and to the just passed Congress Working Committee resolution on Cripps Mission, Rajagopalachari had not consulted either Azad or other members of the Congress Working Committee before taking such a fateful action. Later when Azad questioned this 'act of indicipline' against the Congress by one of the topmost leaders Rajagopalachari resigned from the Congress Working Committee but insisted that ''he was unable to withdraw the two resolutions, as they represented his considered view.''[30]

Thus, at a critical moment of India's history, the top leadership of the Congress, the premier political party in the country, was riven by doubts and disarray. However, during the whole Cripps Mission, Subhas played an important role by his repeated broadcasts from Germany over a Free-India Radio advising the Congress and the people of India not to be enticed away by the dubious Cripps' proposals, and even asking Cripps how he being an active member of the British Labour Party and a socialist by conviction, could agree to head the Mission which gave nothing away to India towards the real independence.

However, during all these unfruitful talks the Congress and the country lost more time in taking any decisive action against the British rule over India. So the common people became very restive. They were getting highly discontented with the indecisions of the Congress. At the same time continued broadcasts by Subhas first from Germany and later from Tokyo (after his arrival in Japan in February 1943) was having great influence on the common people. Subhas said in unequivocal terms that real freedom could not be obtained through mere negotiations with the British. This would inevitably lead to partition and disaster. He cited the cases of Ireland and Palestine. He urged people to rise in revolt against foreign domination, and the war provided a great opportunity for that.

'Quit India' Movement, 1942

By the end of March 1942 Japanese invasion on India was imminent and they already dropped some bombs from air in some parts of south India, and the India Government were reported to have made some contingency plans of evacuation of Government offices and establishment from Calcutta to the west, beyond the Hoogly River (Ganges). The A.I.C.C. (the All India Congress Committee), then, at its session held at Allahabad on 29 April, resolved "*inter alia* that the Indian people should offer complete non-violent non-cooperation to the invading forces (of Japan) and refuse to render them any assistance."[31]

Gandhi, then at the age of 73, and still the unquestioned leader of the Congress (in spite of his many differences with Nehru and some other top leaders of that organizations on many important issues), sensed the pulse of the people and felt that they might take some far reaching actions on their own against the Government of India.[32] So he ultimately decided to launch a nationwide Civil Disobedience on a far greater scale than at any time before.[33] Immediately after the failure of the Cripps he wrote several articles in journals especially in the *Harijan*, to tone up their morale.

The Congress Working Committee met on 14 July, 1942 and finally passed a long resolution which began with a firm statement that "events happening from day to day, and the experiences that the people of India are passing through, confirm the opinion of Congressmen that *British rule in India must end immediately*". Reiterating the reasons which Congress had already elaborated before Cripps and other fora, the Working Committee said: "not merely because foreign domination, even at its best, is an evil in itself and a continuing injury to the subject people, but because India in bondage can play no effective part in defending herself and in affecting the fortunes of the war that is desolating humanity. The freedom of India is thus necessary not only in the interest of India but also for the safety of the world and for the ending of nazism, fascism, militarism and other forms of imperialism, and the aggression of one nation over another."

Referring to the Cripps proposals, the resolution stated: they "showed in the clearest possible manner that there was no change in the British Government's attitude towards India and that the British hold on India was in no way to be relaxed". The frustration of the people resulting from the failure of the Cripps Mission led to "a rapid and widespread increase of ill-will against Britain and growing satisfaction at the success of Japanese arms". As for the future, the resolution noted: "On the withdrawal of British rule in India, responsible men and women of the country will come together to form a Provisional Government, representative of all important sections of the people of India, which will later evolve a scheme whereby a Constituent Assembly can be convened in order to prepare a constitution for the Government of India acceptable to all sections of the people''. As to the future relations with Great Britain, the resolution expressed the view that ''Representatives of Free India and representatives of Great Britain will confer together''. The representatives would also discuss ''cooperation of the two countries as allies in the common tasks of meeting aggression''. Finally, the resolution assured that ''in making the proposal for the withdrawal of British rule from India, the Congress had no desire whatsoever to embarrass Great Britain or the Allied Powers in their prosecution of war.....''[34] The Working Committee decided to meet on 7 August, 1942 in Bombay for its approval of the resolution.

In discussing its details Gandhi had explained, as Azad writes: "that the movement also would be on the basis of non-violence. But all methods short of violence would be permissible.'' And Gandhi termed it ''open non-violent revolution''.[35] This was ''a big step forward in Gandhi's thinking. He called it a ''final struggle'' and gave the cry ''Do or Die'' to the people. There had been immediately a tremendous effect on the whole country. It ''created an electric atmosphere throughout its length and breadth.'' As President of the Congress Azad himself writes that the people ''felt that, at last, Congress was launching a mass movement to make the British quit India''. Indeed, as Azad has said: "it is the people and the Government of India who described it as the 'Quit India' resolution, Gandhi, however, did not work out in full the detailed strategy and course of the movement but preferred to wait till the reaction of the Government of India was known. He had expected that the latter, considering the critical conditions faced by the British Government regarding the War both in Europe and in Asia, would come forward with a new offer of some new forms of negotiations to the Congress. But instead, the Government of India, at the direction of the British Government, decided to come down with a heavy hand on the Congress and its leaders."

However, the A.I.C.C. convened in Bombay on 7 August and, giving the detailed reasons for the justification of the 'Quit India' proposals, resolved: ''to sanction, for the vindication of India's inalienable right to freedom and independence, the starting of mass struggle on non-violent lines on the widest possible scale so that the country might utilize all the non-violent strength it has gathered during the last twenty-two years of peaceful struggle.'' It was also stated that Gandhi was to be in charge of the new mass movement and requested him to take the lead and guide the nation in the steps to be taken. Anticipating a stage when the Congress may be unable to issue instructions because of government reprisals, the resolution noted that in such a contingency ''every man and woman who is participating in this movement must function for himself or herself within the four corners of the general instructions issued. Every Indian who desires freedom and strives for it must be his own guide urging him on along the hard road where there is no resting place and which leads ultimately to the independence and deliverance of India.''[36]

The resolution was approved by all members of the A.I.C.C., ''except a handful of communists who opposed the move''.[37] Because, it appears, that the communist thinking was that the character of the imperialistic war was then charged to 'peoples war' following the invasion of the U.S.S.R. by Germany.

Our transfer to Rajshahi Central Jail, 1942

By the time the Quit India Movement was launched from 9 August we had been transferreed to the Rajshahi Central Jail. At the beginning of 1942, following the dramatic escape of Subhas Bose to Germany, the conquest by the latter of the major parts of north, west and south-east Europe, and the severe reverses of all the three segments of the British forces--army, navy and the air--at the hands of Japanese, including the fall of Singapore, the number of Security Prisoners (that is, suspected detainees without trial) in Bengal alone exceeded a couple of thousands of which about five hundred were lodged in Hijli Special Jail. But soon thereafter a decision was taken by the India Government to convert it into an army camp. Therefore the Bengal Government was directed to transfer the security prisoners to different jails in Bengal, temporarily pending their final destination to the Buxa Special Jail.

We had by then fairly settled down in Hijli jail even though we had been passing through periods of one excitement after another because of the fast changing pictures of the war situation in Europe and, even close to the very doors of India, of the escape of Subhas, and also of the sad death in Calcutta in 1941 of the world famous and much loved poet-philosopher-dramatist, Rabindranath Tagore, one of the greatest figures of the mid-nineteenth till mid-twentieth century, who, by his vast writing of multiple types, dominated India's music, art and intellectual life like a colossus. Perhaps never in my life (of now nearly four scores) so many exciting situations came in so short a period (of barely two years 1940-1942). Luckily, I was young and thus able not only to stand them but also to pursue even some normal activities. These included mainly studies on various subjects, rather serious, like the complex land problems of India, the theories and history of communism, socialism and capitalism, the history of the pre-British economic, political and social systems of India and their radical changes, mostly for the worse but also with some beneficial results, and, above all, some readings of astrology, which is a common human weakness, and also of astronomy including frequent star-gazings at nights to identify various planets, stars and constellations.

A special thing for worry to me suddenly loomed in an attack of serious fever with pain in abdomen for my second brother Nirmal who was then also lodged in Hijli Jail. The jail doctors including the Civil Surgeon could not make a proper diagnosis of the disease even after he had been suffering for over a week. He was removed to the jail hospital where my close friends including Haripada nursed him twenty-four hours by rotation. Finally, the jail authorities called in a specialist and reputed doctor, Sachin Sarvadikary, from Midnapore town for consultation. He was well-known to our family in Midnapore and especially to my uncle Binode Behari Ray. He at once recognized us but did not disclose his feelings to us in front of the jail authorities. On examining my brother he came to the conclusion that it was a serious infection of kidney which might need a major operation. So he recommended transfer of my brother to the Medical College Calcutta. That was a great relief for me. In the meantime, my father Barendra Kumar, who since my mother's death in 1933, had been living alone in our Contai house, dreamt one night that mother appeared to him and said "you are sleeping quietly but Nirmal is seriously ill in jail; so you should go and see him". I deliberately had not written to my father at Contai about my brother's prolonged illness as he would worry too much. So I was greatly surprised when my father, at his old age, took all the trouble in hastening from Contai to Hijli jail and meet my brother at hospital. The jail authorities were nice to have allowed my father to see my brother there. Nirmal was then slightly better under the new treatment of Dr. Sarbadhikari, and was soon transferred to the Medical College, Calcutta. There, I came to know, he was placed under the care of then one of the best surgeons, Dr. Panchanan Chatterjee. Nirmal was at the Calcutta Hospital for a long time during which Dr. Chatterjee decided to cure him by treatment and not remove his infected kidney at the young age in twenties only.

By about July 1942 orders came for our mass transfers out of Hijli Special Jail, in batches, to three Central Jails, at Midnapore, Rajshahi and Dacca. I was in the batch of about 125 prisoners, sent to the Rajshahi Central Jail in north Bengal. In this group was included many of those who had been arrested with me in the first batch in April 1940, like Hem Chandra Ghose, Bhupendra Rakshit Ray, Bhupal Bose, Nikunja Sen, Jyotish Joardar, Benoy Sen Kshiti Sen, Naren Das, and also many others, such as, Aurobindo Bose a nephew of Subhas Bose, two Communist Party members, Sisir Ray and Promode Sen Gupta; also many ex-members of the Anushilan Samiti including Trailokya Nath Chakravarty, Rabi Sen, Jnan Majumdar, Naren Das, Tridip Chowdhuri, Durgesh Bhattacharjee and many others. At Rajshahi jail, we all were placed in a long separate ward divided into two or three big rectangular rooms, rather spacious halls. With us also was another noted person, Dr. Atindra Nath Bose of Sri Sangha headed by Anil Ray and Mrs. Lila Ray. Bose was well-known for his high educational qualifications, a holder of Premchand Roychand Scholarship as well as a Ph. D. degree from the Calcutta University. He belonged to a very cultured family of Dacca. I had often discussed with him some problems of higher education and was myself an aspirant for the distinguished P.R. Scholarship as well as a Ph.D. degree. The other much younger Bose, Aurobindo, had then been preparing for his B.A. Honours degree in Politics and used to have occasional lessons from me in classical political texts, such as, Aristotle's *Politics*, and Plato's *Republic*. But I kept my special interest in Land Problems of Bengal and India.

We were kept in Rajshahi Jail for about six months, from July to November 1942. We knew that this jail was a sort of 'transit camp' for us and we would soon be transferred to the old Buxa Detention Jail in the Dooars region in north of Bengal, located about 2, 500 ft. high at the foothills of the Eastern Himalayas, near the Bhutan border. It would be much more spacious there and the weather would be cooler in summer and very cold during the winter. But during our stay at Rajshahi Jail several important events took place for which we had to pass very exciting moments. First, there was the rapid collapse of the British army in East and South-East Asia and the approach of the Japanese army close to India's border in the east, as close as near Kohima; the occupation by the Japanese army of the Andaman and Nicobar Islands and the free movement of the Japanese navy in the Bay of Bengal; air bombings by the Japanese of some of the major cities in the east coast of India and Ceylon such as Trincomalee, Cocanada and Vizagapatnam; the despatch by the British Government of the Cripps Mission to India to negotiate a possible political settlement with the Indian National Congress, and its eventual failure due mainly to the reason of Britain's unwillingness to transfer real power to India; and, finally, the resolution of the Congress Working Committee asking the British to widraw from India and its preparations for a 'final' mass Civil Disobedience movement under the leadership of Gandhi.

The second most important event during our stay at Rajshahi Jail, was the launching of the Quit India movement itself on 8 August 1942 with the approval by the A.I.C.C. of the Congress Working Committee resolution. In reality, the actual movement may be said to have been started by the Government of India itself. For before the movement was formally launched by Gandhi, as in 1930, the Government made a sudden and massive arrest on 9 August 1942 of Gandhi, all members of the Congress Working Committee, even Gandhi's wife Mrs. Kasturba, and Secretary Mahadev Desai. Gandhi, with his wife and secretary, was taken for detention to the Aga Khan Palace at Poona, and the members of the Working Committee to the Old Fort at Ahmednagar. Simultaneous arrests of Congress leaders and workers were made all over India--at provincial, district, town and even village levels, and thousands of people were put in jails.

Being thus leaderless there was a spontaneous mass upsurge of feelings against the Indian and the British Governments. The long simmering antipathy burst with a great ferocity all over the country, largely "unorganized, uncoardinated and undirected". People from almost all shades of nationalist opinions--the Congress, the Forward Bloc of Subhas Bose, the Socialist Party of Jayaprakash Narain, the Revolutionary groups and many sympathizers joined the masses. In the process many local leaders came forward to take the leadership such as in Contai and Tamluk in the district of Midnapore. Then there was an overall direction and guidance from Subhas Bose from over the German radio. It was surprising how things had been reported even in Germany and other parts of the world. Subhas made a series of radio broadcasts from Germany in which he urged and inspired people to continue what he said, the mess "non-violent guerilla warfare", in spite of the leaders' imprisonment, till the British left. He gave detailed instructions to the people what to do in a non-violent way.[38] In jail then we did not know all these detailed instructions. But we were told by many arrested during the movement in Rajshahi and brought in the jail, and also through our contacts inside the jail, about these broadcasts and how the Indian people listened attentively Subhas's broadcasts and acted accordingly.

Devoid of the guidance of the central leadership of the Congress, the spontaneous movement assumed a sort of general rebellion, though generally in a non-violent way but at times leading to sporadic violence, all over the country and especially in Bengal, Bihar, U.P., the North-West Frontier Province, Bombay and Madras. Railway tracks were uprooted, tele-communications were cut, roads breached. Furious crowds attacked government offices, buildings, stores and even, at places, injured many officials and killed some. As in 1931, students were foremost in the struggle. Many abandoned their studies; schools and colleges were closed. Even at some places, like Tamluk in Midnapore district, 'independent' local governments, with all the paraphernalia of administration like police, jail etc., were set up by people under the guidance of local leaders. In Tamluk, for example, the names of veteran local Congress leaders like Ajoy Mukherjee [39] and Satish Samanta, became prominent. For days they held the entire sub-division put out of the fiat of control of the then Provincial Government of Bengal. In another neighbouring subdivision of Midnapore, Contai, which had always been in the forefront of Gandhi's non-violent struggle, also the 'Quit India' movement spread like a forest fire. The police stations of Khejuri, a big tract of prosperous land in the Ganges delta, and of Ramnagar in the south-east by the sea, become especially marked. The former being almost like an island, was seized by the local people and the local police officials were held and barricaded. The police had fired at the people but the latter faced the last bullet bravely and then when the police exhausted their ammunitions, people seized them and held them as prisoners. In Ramnagar, some police personnel were injured, so the Government brought in a platoon of British soldiers and stationed them there.

Among other provinces, the places which were then most disturbed were the northern districts of Bihar and the eastern U.P. In the Ballia district in U.P., the people broke open the jail gates, cut off communications for several days and established 'panchayat raj' of their own. In then Central Provinces and Berar, the situation in Ashti and Chimur, got absolutely out of control of the authorities. In Madras presidency, long distances of railway tracks were uprooted. In Bombay, there were large scale strikes of mills and factories in the city and a 'parallel government' was set up in Satara district.

The British viewed the situation as a grave challenge to their rule over India. The Viceroy wrote to the British Prime Minister describing the situation as "by far the most serious rebellion since that of 1857, the gravity and extent of which we have so far concealed from the world for reasons of military security."[40]

Throughout the entire period Subhas kept up his broadside through broadcasts from the German radio from the beginning of the 'Quit India' movement in mid-1942 till April 1943, and then again after his mysterious arrival in Tokyo in June 1943, from the Tokyo Radio and subsequently from Malaya, Singapore and Burma, after these were occupied by the Japanese and Subhas had established his Azad Hind Government (Free India Government) and Azad Hind Fouj (Free India Army) in exile.

However, the British reprisals against the movement and the people were most severe and cruel. It has been well summed up in the following words:

> Every canon of morality, of human decency was violated in the name of preserving law and order. Mobs were dispersed by lathi charge, by rifle, pistol and occasionally machine gun fire from the air. Men were mercilessly flogged, beaten and subjected to inhuman torture. They were cross-examined throughout the day and not allowed to sleep at night, kept hungry, thirsty and humiliated. Women were stripped, assaulted, raped, even children were not

spared. In a village numerous houses were razed to the ground many were burnt down. People were undressed, tied to trees and beaten. Large numbers were thrown into prison without trial and long terms of imprisonment were awarded. Imposition of collective fines was the order of the day; what was worse, these were ruthlessly realized. The objective was to terrorize the people, teach them a lesson and efface from their minds all thoughts of defiance.[41]

Though leaderless and devoid of a central leadership and planning and direction, the movement went along on its momentum, for nearly two years-from mid-1942 till mid-1944. But as it happens in all popular uprisings, after a peak had been reached during its first six months, it lost its fury but still the fires were smouldering for the entire period even though the Government repression continued unabated. Sporadic mass actions and activities of intense pockets of resistance continued throughout the second year. Parts of these activities were carried on especially by members of the Revolutionary groups and of the Congress Socialist Party under the leadership of Jayaprakash Narain, who went underground. Narayan himself then escaped from a Bihar jail where he had been kept as a prisoner.

It may be said that apart from the Indian Police, a large contingent of army, 8 British brigades and 57 Indian batallions, were engaged by the Government to crush the revolt. As a result, the civilian casualties, in the movement, according to official estimates, were 1,028 killed and 3,125 seriously injured. But this was then regarded by knowledgeable persons as gross underestimates. Indeed according to unofficial figures, the killed alone might have come to about 10,000.[42]

The devastating Cyclone of Bengal, 1942

However, besides the British debacle in south-east Asia and the subsequent 'Quit India' Movement in 1942, one more serious event happened while we were in Rajshahi Central Jail--the great cyclone of Bengal in October 1942 causing widespread loss of life and property especially among the coastal districts of Bengal, particularly in Midnapore, and the most severely affected was Contai. On 16 October we felt its serious impact as far north as in Rajshahi. A combination of incessant rain, tidal wave and a cyclonic storm of utmost intensity took the entire people and the government (or whatever of it was left following the August Movement) were taken by surprise. Two factors which enhanced the loss of life, particularly in the coastal areas, were the War and the Civil Disobedience Movement. First, because of the occupation by the Japanese of the Singapore, Malaya, Burma and even the Andaman and the Nicobar Islands, the India Government had thought the Japan's next target would be India proper and particularly Bengal. So the Government of Bengal, under a directive from the Government of India, confiscated or immobilized all the country boats in the coastal areas including those in Contai. As a result, when the typhoon and the tidal wave crossed over the high sea-embankment in the south of Contai town and spread swiftly over the entire flat land inside for a stretch of 5 to 10 miles, up to the sand dunes over which Contai town was built, hundreds of concentrated but prosperous villages, and their residents at night, were caught in the flood without having any shelter; all trees and thatched roofs collapsed before the surging water. The unlucky people had nothing to hold or stand on and most were swept away and perished. Even those who survived had no means to escape death as there were no boats, and no succour came from the Government for days and even weeks. Rather, the leading spokesman of the Government, the District Magistrate of Midnapore, N.M. Khan, was then reported to have commented that "the cyclone was a divine vengeance on the people of Midnapore".

The second factor for the heavy loss of life, particularly in Contai, was that because of the terrible repressive activities of the Government forces particularly during the night, most people--men, women and children, used to take shelter at night on the outer side of the embankment, in bushes on the seashore, far away from their homes. They were the first to be caught and to perish at the first onslaught of the cruel sea.

This was indeed a sad tale and a heavy blow on the otherwise peaceful and relatively prosperous people of Contai.

A further incident during our detention at Rajshahi Central Jail in the second half of 1942, which needs mentioning, was the reported air bombing of Calcutta by some isolated planes of the Japanese intruding airforce. This created a great sensation amongst us in the prison, as most of our relatives were then in Calcutta. There was a lot of rumours about loss of life and damage to property. But later we heard there was nothing serious. Probably it was a mere trial hit by the Japanese to test the British air defence (which was then very meagre indeed).

Transfer to Buxa Dooar Detention Jail, 1942

However, by the end of 1942, all of us were moved out of the Rajshahi Jail and sent to the Buxa Detention Jail. We were taken in batches with police escort by rail up to Buxa Dooar rail station at the northern most point of Bengal amidst tiger and elephant infested deep forests of the eastern Himalayan *terai* region. From there we were taken by jeeps for about $3^1/2$ miles up the lower elevations and then the remainder $2^1/2$ miles we had to climb on foot through steep hilly slopes. After having been practically immobile for nearly three years in different jails in the plains, that walk on foot was rather exhilarating though somewhat tiring. While walking up through bare forest tracks (as no roads were there) we had to go through the deep forests with tall high trees interspersed by bushes. I met for the first time some blood-hungry leeches with their single red tentacle pointing upward seeking fresh and warm human and animal blood. We had a pleasanter side too. We passed by and over many mountain streams coming down from higher hills and flowing to the plains or merging with bigger fountains or streams on the way. It was winter, so they were relatively dry then but still carried cool fresh pure water for use by human beings living nearby.

Buxa detention jail was on the spur of a hill flanked on two sides by two mountain streams coming down from higher mountains in the north and the east. The streams sloped down in steep gradiants with occasional flat stretches in steps. They were thin in the winter but full and rushed down in great force during the rainy season. The jail buildings were at three levels--top like a plateau, intermediate and lower--from north to south--with one separate block of building for the prisoners at each level. There were some flat grounds at the top level which was paved and we often used to have some games and at times our short and clandestine parade in military style. Just to the north was a deep valley on which was built a playfield. Beyond was a forest road going up to Bhutan border over low mountain peaks. But one rather higher peak--called Sinchula--towered high in front which separated Bhutan from Bengal. In the east was also higher hills and in the south-west lay at a distance the dusty and smoky flat plains of Bengal. But during the monsoon dark black rolling and curling clouds, originating from the Indian Ocean thousands of miles away, rushed over the Bay of Bengal and the entire length of the flat plains of Bengal, and then reached us to the hills over our head touching our body and splashing our feet. The rainy season was long and heavy; winter was real cold and the summer was mild. It was on the whole a pleasant place but after all a jail, surrounded on all sides by a series of high barbed wire fences and in side a chain of barracks each containing several rooms. The rooms were locked from 9 p.m. to 6 a.m. by guards. The Superintendent was an English and Urdu speaking Moslem but from a cultured family of U.P. He was fairly old, tall and handsome and a pleasant man. The jailor was a Bengalee and there were some deputy jailors, office staff and a platoon of guards mostly from Bihar. Being long away from localities the jail authorities were liberal in their behaviour. But outside, there was all dense forest over the hills and narrow passes. The place used to be frequented at night by wild animals like gazelles and sambars, and occasionally by tigers. Elephants could not climb up to that height. The place was electrically illuminated at night. Our water supply came from the mountain streams. There was no transport or means of communication. Everything from heavy furniture to a pin had to be carried on the back of the Bhutanese porters, most of them women of young and old age. They were all fair with flat and depressed cheeks. They wore usually thick smelly coats and gowns, were poor and famished with porterage as the only source of living. Normally they would be only occasionally employed by local forest offices of the Government of Bengal and the timber marchants and contractors who were engaged in felling trees and making timbers for commercial scale. But the porters were all very jolly and pleasant people in spite of their deprivations of most things of a civilized life. In the jail and in the surrounding hills and valleys there was absolute silence in the day and night except the sonorous ripples of the two adjacent streams running close to the jail in the winter and their loud roars during the monsoon. In the winter the entire hills used to be covered with occasional dense fog.

We found the natural surroundings very pleasant and the almosphere inside much more relaxed compared to the austere and rigorous climate of the big jails on the plains. From the very beginning I considered it an ideal place for study. But I also used to take part in sports, especially football, on the big playground outside the main jail, on a relatively bigger flat piece of land down below, which was opened for us in the morning and afternoon for long walk and sports. Once settled in the new life I resumed my intensive study on the land and agricultural problems of India, and particularly of Bengal, which had a most complex and unsatisfactory land system, called the permanent settlement or a feudal type of zamindary system introduced by the British in 1793 to consolidate stheir social and economic hold on the people of Bengal. It created a series of feudal lords between the Government and the actual cultivators, quite contrary to the old Indian community village system where lands were held mostly by communities in groups with individual families having the right to cultivate and enjoy the fruits of their labour subject to the payment of one-sixth of the produce of the land to the king. My objective was to study not only the land system as such but also its long term social and economic consequences, on the agricultural productivity which had ultimately a major effect on food production and supply. So I extended the scope of the study to the diverse but interrelated aspects of the entire agricultural economy of Bengal.

The Great Bengal Famine, 1943

In the meantime came the great Bengal Famine of 1943. According to the Famine Enquiry Commission which was later appointed by the Government of Bengal, between July and December 1943, that is in six months, nearly 1.5 million people died of hunger in the province. Unofficial estimates by Indian experts put the figure much higher, in the range of 3 to 3.5 million. It was then said to be more "man-made" than natural. Ever since the British took over the administration of India, famine in one part or another had been almost a recurrent factor. The then official quarters then put the blame mostly on two factors--the vagaries of monsoon and the ignorance and the inability of the farmers to take advantage of the mordern technology applicable to agriculture. The impact of the then Government's economic policy and their incompetence and inefficiency were hardly recognized. If this had been evident from the occurrence of past famines.[43] It was equally so in the 'forties. Vagaries of monsoon may be attributed as one of the factors behind the Bengal famine 1943. But even they were not irremediable provided adequate steps had been taken earlier to meet the uncertainty of rainfall. As the following footnote would show, the traditional remedies taken in pre-British days were excavation of irrigation canals, storage of water in tanks and ponds in villages during years of excessive or even normal rains to be utilized in scarcity years. But these had been neglected by the British rulers in India for a long time. So also the old canal system. The end result was shortage of water, drought, frequency of scarcity, failure of crops and repeated famines or mass starvation.

Partly because of these long-term problems but mainly for lack of timely care on the part of both the then Central and Provincial Governments, and of an effort to deal with pre-famine conditions in the province, as well as the wrong policies of the procurement and control of food distribution during the war, the situation got out of control. Even then the Government stocked huge quantities of paddy in its stores and godowns in anticipation of the imminence of Japanese invasion on the province and also because of the policy of its attaining a monopoly of food distribution so as to be able to use food as an instrument of political control and thus to suppress the 'Quit India' movement. Finally, there was private stocking of food by hoarders and profiters unchecked by the Government. The overall result of all these factors was mass starvation and death in the entire province and even on the streets of Calcutta. These grim and most tragic conditions lasted for almost one full year from June 1943 till June 1944 until after the assumption by General Wavell, a military man, of the office of the Viceroy of India in early 1944 and the appointment by the latter of an Australian politician, R.G. Casay, as the Governor of Bengal. Only, then the Government introduced, among other means, a better system of food control including the rationing of food.

All these affected my mind severely in the Buxa Detention Jail and I thought it useful to utilize my time in studying both indepth and extent the entire agricultural economy of Bengal---its past and present position and problems, and future possibilities. And it had long been a habit of mine to write something or other everyday whenever I had an opportunity. So I started writing, sitting quietly in a small temporary cubicle made of thick curtains on a portion of the verandah attached to our jail ward from where at times I could see the changing hues of the plains at Bengal with alternate of sun and cloud. By about the middle of 1943 I wrote about 100 pages of a text and gave it the title "Agricultural Economics of Bengal", and showed it to one of our friends, Benoy Sen from Dacca, who was a well read man. He suggested that I try to prepare it as a thesis for the highly distinguished Premchand Roychand Scholarship of the Calcutta University. I had often thought of this for a long time in a vague way. But then the idea struck deeply in my mind. From the middle of 1943 I started getting direct from the Calcutta University, by writing, information about the rules and regulations of P.R.S. Then I tried to collect reference books from the Imperial and Commercial Libraries of Calcutta; wrote to the Calcutta University to send me some of their relevant publications and to my uncle at Midnapore to buy and send me in jail some books. At the same time I also wrote to important professors and notable economists for their views in short on the agricultural problems of India. They included Professors K.T. Shah of Bombay, Dr. V.K.R.V. Rao of Madras, and Professor Haricharan Ghose of the Calcutta University. Luckily for me, I found good responses from all of them. And I also took the courage of writing to the then Vice-Chancellor of the Calcutta University, Dr. Shyama Prasad Mukherjee. He had been a close friend of my two uncles--Professor Nibaran Chandra Ray, a member of the Calcutta University Syndicate, and Binode Behari Ray of Midnapore.

Shyama Prasad Mukherjee's encouragement

It may be noted that all our correspondences--both incoming and outgoing--were read and 'censored and passed' by an official of the Intelligence Branch, posted at the jail; so also were all books and papers which were allowed to us. From these the I.B. officer as well as the jail officials had a very clear idea about the individual prisoners--their inclinations, state of minds and their work inside the jail. I must say, however, that I had never any problem of getting my books and materials required for my research from outside. The jail officials were all very kind and sympathetic to me, mainly because they all knew that I used to spend most of my time on studying. In a few days' time I got a short reply from Dr. Shyama Prasad Mukherjee acknowledging my letter, encouraging me to submit a P.R.S. thesis from Buxa Jail. He suggested me that I should send a preliminary draft of my thesis for comments to Professor Haricharan Ghose in Calcutta, who himself was a P.R. Scholar. So I prepared a copy with the help of some of my close friends. I did not let many people know about my project except only a few close friends. A spare copy was ready before the end of 1943 and handed it over to the jail authorities, and a forwarding letter, with a request that, after both were duly 'censored and passed' by the I.B. officer, they be sent by registered post to Professor Ghose. All this was done in a smooth way, because of the cooperation of both the I.B. Officer and the jail officials.

While waiting for Professor Ghose's comments I carried on my studies on different aspects of Bengal's agricultural, economic and food problems including the need for agricultural planning within an overall plan of a countrywide economic planning, largely on the Russian model. Because of my contacts with Professor K.T. Shah of Bombay, the then Secretary of the Congress National Planning Committee (set-up in 1938 by the then President of the Congress, Subhas Bose, with Nehru as Chairman) I received some important papers and information relating to agricultural planning. In course of my detention in Buxa until the end of 1945 I had collected so much information that I thought of preparing another thesis on "Agricultural Planning for Bengal" for a possible Ph.D. degree. Besides, I also participated in other normal activities of a prisoner in our conditions--in discussions about the possible war situations especially in the background of Subhas's arrival in the Far East and forming the Indian National Army mainly with large captured Indian prisoners of war who had been serving with the British Indian army in the Far East, and partly also with volunteers from Indian residents in different countries of that region. We also discussed what would be our position and should be our role in the event Japan or Subhas's army decided to attack India's eastern borders *en masse*.

We used to hold in the early mornings, even in rain and mist, regular military parade and training in 'guerilla warfare', under the guidance of Jyotish Joardar. I also took part in sports regularly, especially in the afternoon. In the mornings I went to the big playground outside the main jail and used to walk briskly for physical exercise. Then in the evenings, we used to hold some dramas, to which jail officials were also invited. One of the main themes was the terrible famine situation in Bengal. Attempts were made to depict the gruesome pictures and peoples' pathetic conditions through the dramas. Besides, there were occasional visits by the Central Intelligence people, asking questions about the war, our attitude to Subhas, and if we had any information about him. We of course flatly denied having any such information.

Time thus passed, and after about three months came back from Professor Haricharan Ghose the draft of my thesis with his detailed comments, and also a letter encouraging me to finalize it and officially submit in three copies to the Controller of Examinations, Calcutta University by 1944. Before that I had to obtain the permission of the University Syndicate for submitting the thesis so that they could make the necessary arrangements for its examination by one or more specialists. So immediately I did two things: Wrote to the Syndicate for a formal permission for submitting a P.R.S. thesis in Arts, and also to my uncle, Binode-Behari Ray, at Midnapore, to arrange through my youngest uncle, Professor Lalit Kumar Ray, then a Lecturer at the Bethune College, Calcutta, to deposit with the University the necessary examination fees. The second thing I did was to revise, finalize and prepare three handwritten copies of the thesis. Because typing was not possible in the jail

While these were being done, again with the help of my friends (whose handwritings were clear and legible) Kalipada Banerjee, Mrityùnjaya Roy and Abinash Das, I decided to write again to Dr. S.P. Mukherjee in Calcutta requesting the University to submit my P.R.S. thesis in three handwritten copies. I got a prompt reply from him saying that I was allowed to submit my P.R.S. thesis in handwritten special case.

I was naturally overjoyed at this very sympathetic attitude of the Calcutta University and especially of Dr. S.P. Mukherjee. Meanwhile I also received the official approval of the Calcutta University Syndicate. By 1944, the three copies were ready so I requested Jailor, Bimal Dutta, and Deputy Jailor, Gouri Prasanna Mukherjee, to arrange to send the copies by registered post direct to the Controller of Examinations, Calcutta University. They readily agreed. So, without telling other people I sent Malu Babu with three copies of my thesis and my forwarding letter, to the Deputy Jailor personally. The latter then, without much delay, arranged to send them in next few days to the University.

Situation in India after World War II

As for India, the Quit India movement, being leaderless from the beginning, quietened down but simmered in various parts of the country. Subhas's continued broadcasts from different capitals of South-east Asia, his assumption of the direct command of the Indian National Army in Malaya in August 1943, and his proclamation in October 1943 of the formation of a provisional Free India (Azad Hind) Government and the acquisition in 1944 from Japan of the Islands of the Andaman and the Nicobar as the nucleus of a the first 'free' Indian territory, his repeated urge to the Indian people to continue the struggle against the British rule sustained, the Quit India Movement. But by the middle of 1944 with the Allied Powers in Europe and North America turning the tide of war and also the action of the Chinese army against Japan, the prospects of Subhas and the I.N.A. gaining an effective foothold in India proper became dim. But nonetheless, Subhas kept his broadcasts right up to August 16, 1945, that is, even after both Germany and Japan had surrendered to the Allied Powers.

By that time, people turned towards the Congress leaders for guidance. With the war turning in favour of Britain and the Allied Powers from early in 1944, and Churchill being continuously pressed by Roosevelt to come to some sort of understanding with the Indian leaders, Gandhi had been released in May 1944, 21 months after his arrest. And in the second half of 1944 the Government of India took steps to relax restrictions on other top Congress leaders detained in Ahmednagar Fort. They were later sent to the usual civil prisons in their respective provinces. And Azad, the President of the Congress was sent to Bankura in Bengal and kept in house internment outside that town. But before leaving Ahmednagar Fort, the top Congress leaders had no idea or talk about the continuation of the struggle. They, in fact, all thought of taking some rest after their release and already seemed to have been 'tired' because, first, of the 'frustrations' arising out of the British refusal to grant freedom to India during the war, and, second, of the rigours of the long detention.

The British in their calmer moments, and especially the newly appointed Viceroy of India, Lord (General) Wavell, realized that though the Quit India Movement had almost withered out, being leaderless, for nearly two years, on the one hand, and the joining of the large contingents of the Indian army who surrendered to Japanese in East Asia, with Subhas Bose's 'Indian National Army' on the other it would be difficult to hold India subjugated for long. Wavell felt that some sort of understanding would have to be made with the Indian leaders, to share power. This was especially necessary when, after the war, Britain was considerably weakened by the heavy loss of men and materials at home and abroad as a result of the war.[44] So, in May 1945, Wavell, after a short visit to England and returning to India, announced the holding of a special conference at Simla with representatives of all political parties including the Congress, the Moslem League and others. He also announced that all top Congress leaders would be released soon. This was done.

The purpose of the Simla Conference was to discuss what had been then known as Wavell Plan, after the name of the then Governor-General. Its main contents included: (a) the immediate reconstitution of the Governor General's Central Executive Council with all Indian members except the viceroy and the Commander-in-chief; (b) an Indian member would be in charge of the foreign affairs (but not defence); (c) the Council would consist of an equal number of 'caste' Hindus and Moslems, and a separate representative each from the Scheduled Castes and the Sikhs, and (d) the representatives would be selected by the Governor General from panels of names to be submitted separately by the Congress, the Moslem League, Scheduled Castes and other communities represented at the Simla Conference. The main functions of the new Executive Council would be to (a) prosecute the war (against Japan); (b) to carry on the government of India; and (c) to consider ways and means whereby a new permanent constitution may be agreed upon and a long-term solution may be effected.

Although the Wavell Plan did not mention any definite British commitment to the future independence of India, a vague verbal assurance was given by Wavell to the Congress President Azad that Britain envisaged a Dominion-type constitution, as earlier by Cripps. And no immediate responsibility for defence was given to an Indian member pending a final settlement, which had been demanded by the Congress earlier at the time of the Cripps Mission. But even then the Congress was not totally opposed to accepting the plan. It wanted certain clarifications from the Governor General and insisted that "if there was a settlement and a new Executive Council formed, it must have the right to refer the question of India's further participation in the war to the Indian Legislative Assembly. India would participate in the war against Japan not as a result of British decision but by a vote of her own representatives."[45] However, whether even such a qualified acceptance by the Congress of the Wavell Plan was correct, although it appeared that it was basically no different from the earlier Cripps proposal as to the future status of India and also to the interim arrangements, can be a matter of judgment. But what was the alternative? If the Congress leaders then had refused totally to accept the Wavell Plan it would have had to launch or at least prepare for a new struggle for independence. Was the country prepared for it, or the leaders of the Congress, or any other political party within India? It appeared, and as even Nehru is reported to have later admitted that the top Congress leaders, who were mostly old, were already "tired". Perhaps these considerations might have dictated the Congress Working Committee to decide on a qualified acceptance of the Wavell Plan.

But the Congress was saved from this embarrassment by Jinnah's intransigence on the question of representation of Moslems on the Executive Council. He wanted them all to be League nominees. But Azad, as the sole representative of the Congress, refused to agree. He said the League represented only a section of the Moslems, as in no major Moslem majority provinces had the League become majority in 1937 provincial elections. It was the Krishak Proja Party led by A.K. Fazlul Haq in Bengal, the Unionist Party under the leadership of Sir Sikandar Hyat Khan in Punjab, and in the North West Frontier Province the majority party was the pro-Congress *khodai khidmatgars* (servants of God), headed by Dr. Khan Saheb, brother of the greatly respected and a most devoted disciple of Gandhi, Khan Abdul Gaffar Khan, and a member of the Congress Working Committee. In Sind and Assam also, there were non-Congress ministries with Congress support.[46] Jinnah further had insisted that the Congress representatives should all be from Hindus. But Azad also rejected it. He said the Congress was the only organization representing all religious and peoples, so it might send a representative from any community. Jinnah was adamant. So there was no agreement between the parties on communal representation, and the result was the failure of the Simla Conference. Critics have said that the very idea of the Round Table Conference, with its British proposed representation of diverse parties with no common basis and the manner of the suggested way of nominating the representatives, presaged the failure of the Conference. Azad thought, and even told Wavell that Jinnah's intransigence was due to his belief that whatever he asked for would be supported by him (Wavell). As he has noted in his 'Autobiography', "I told him clearly that an agreement with the League seemed very doubtful. Those who were in control of the League seemed to be under the impression that they had the support of the Government and they would not therefore accept any reasonable terms."[47]

Subhas's last broadcast, 1945

Subhas in the meantime, throughout the first half of 1945, went on with his radio broadcasts to India successively from Burma, Bangkok and Singapore urging the Indian people to continue their struggle until full independence was conceded by the British. He told them in his last broadcast of 16 August 1945 not to be cowed down by the 'temporary failure' of their fight both within and outside India but to regroup and carry on. He was last reported to be in Taipeh, Taiwan, the earlier Chinese island of Formosa, which was still under Japanese occupation. And after sometime came the news about his death in a mysterious plane crash while it was taking off at Taipeh for what appeared to be an unknown destination. The people of whole India were shocked. However, the facts relating to his death have ever since remained a great mystery.

Our last days in Buxa Jail

In Buxa Jail, in 1945, we had been closely watching the developments in the international and national situations, their ups and downs, and finally the surrender of Germany, the dropping of first atom bombs in the history of the war by U.S.A. on Japan and their devastating effects, the subsequent Japanese surrender and the occupation of Japan by the U.S. army, the failure of Subhas's long and herculean efforts to organize a 'free' army of the Indian residents and found abroad, in synchronization with the massive internal struggle of the Indian people under the 'Quit India' movement, Britain's persistent unwillingness to recognize India's independence and its dubious successive proposals for limited rights towards a diluted self-government for the Indian people vitiated by the communal virus. But in spite of all these, the news, at the end, of the Viceroy's agreement with the Congress proposal to declare a general amnesty for all the political prisoners, was received by us with a great sense of relief. Many of us thought that our release, though might be for a temporary period, would at least give us an opportunity to recover from the effects of already six years of detention and prepare for a new struggle. But we were informed that our release was not imminent and we had again to go through a gradual process of relaxation by being first transferred to a jail in the plains.

In the meantime came my much expected news regarding the results of my P.R.S. thesis which had been submitted to the Calcutta University a year earlier, towards the end of 1944. The first information came in a rather mysterious circumstance. Towards the end of 1945 when we had been waiting for our orders from the Government, in an early misty cold morning, a messenger guard of the jail authorities came with a cryptic message to me from the Deputy Jailor that "the matter is serious, please come and see me in the office immediately". I could not guess what it was all about and, frankly speaking, felt a bit nervous. I thought: would the Government transfer me alone to some other place? Any way, I tried to put up a courageous face and went with the guard to the jail office. As soon as the Deputy Jailor saw me he gave a big smile, put his hands on me and said "congratulations: see this letter". It was a little postcard written in hand by a well-known Professor of the Calcutta University, Makhan Lal Ray Chaudhuri, who was close to both Dr. Shyama Prasad Mukherjee and Professor Haricharan Ghose. He wrote: "I have seen unofficially your Examiner's recommendation to award you a P.R. Scholarship and the Calcutta University has accepted the recommendation and has approved such an award for you".[48] I was naturally overjoyed but tried to conceal my feelings, and thanked the Deputy Jailore for his early message. He told me that he deliberately sent me a scary note, because the award of P.R. Scholarship being regarded as a memorable event, I would for ever remember the circumstances in which I received the message and above all his name. Indeed I have remembered it since and do think of it even today, after nearly 45 years. His name was Gouri Prasanna Mukherjee. But I am sorry that I do not know what happened to him after I was transferred in one of the batches in December 1945 to the Dum Dum Central Jail.

Notes and References

1. I have still many old books of the time in my Library at Calcutta bearing the stamp of "Censored and Passed" by the Intelligence Branch.
2. As the ancient Indian text *The Geeta* has said, (see Ch. XI, especially Verse 12) : "If there be the effulgence of a thousand suns bursting forth all at once in the heavens, even that would hardly approach the splendour of the mighty Lord". This verse is said to have been cited by the German-American scientist Oppenheimer when he watched the explosion of the first experimental atomic bomb made by U.S.A., in the Nevada desert in 1945.

3. Fritjof Capra: *The Turning Point* (Flamingo-Fontana), U.S.A.-London, 1982/85, Ch.3, "The New Physics", pp. 63-89.
4. *Op. cit.*, p. 40
5. *Ibid.*
6. Cf. Mehra. P. : *op. cit.*, p. 160.
7. *Ibid*, p. 150.
8. We don't try to give any details of how Subhas escaped the most severe security net of the India Government then cast around him. First because we did not know at that time; second, because this has since 1947 been well described and documented by Bose's nephew, Sisir Bose, and Bose's close surviving associates.
9. Azad, A.K. : *op.cit.*, p.. 39.
10. For example, in describing in his *The Discovery of India* (The Meridian, Fourth Ed. 1946, p. 456), he refers to this internal crisis within the Congress, which cropped up first in 1940 and 1941, and the dispute between Gandhi and Azad about the possible role of the Congress during the war, but he does not give any of his own views.
11. Mehra, P. : *op. cit.* p. 104.
12. Quoted from Bose's radio broadcast from Berlin on 17 June 1942. See *Selected Speeches of Subhas Chandra Bose* (Publications Div., New Delhi), pp. 136-137.
13. Many other important personalities in the United States of that time had also held the view that India's willing help was *essential* for the Allies to win the war in Asia. They included the then U.S. Under-Secretary of State, Summer Wells, and General Eisenhower. Cf. Mehra, P. : *op. cit.*, p. 161.
14. Cf. Azad, *op. cit.*, p. 42.
15. *Ibid*, p.44
16. Mehra, P. : *op.cit.*, p.160
17. These have been set out in details by Azad his in book *India Wins Freedom, op. cit.*, Ch.1
18. Azad, A.K.: *op.cit.*, 57.
19. To be selected by the Chiefs of the states but not elected by their peoples.
20. Nehru, J. *The Discovery of India, op.cit.*, p.464.
21. The full Congress resolution was a historic document; it is quoted fully in Maulana Azad's *India Wins Freedom, op. cit.*, pp. 61-63.
22. It may be noted that ever since his arrival in Germany Subhas, since March 1942, had been appealing, through his radio broadcasts, the Indian people and leaders not to join Britain's war efforts till they parted with real power of administration to the Indian people.
23. Azad, *Ibid*, .
24. *Ibid*. pp. 64-69.
25. This was the personal impression I had already formed about him even at that early age, and was later (before and after independence) confirmed from my hearing of his various speeches in India and England at many closed meetings of the A.I.C.C. and at other place.
26. *Ibid*, p. 65.
27. *Ibid*, p. 64.
28. Nehru: *op.cit.*, pp. 463-474.
29. *Ibid*, pp. 465-466. Italics are this author's.
30. Azad: *op.cit.*, pp. 67-69.
31. Mehra, P.: *op.cit.* p.572.
32. As Azad has noted: "The failure of the Cripps Mission led to widespread disappoint-

ment in the country." *op. cit.* p.70. In Calcutta, he found "deterioration in the situation all round. The majority of the people were now convinced that the British would lose the War..... There was great bitterness against the British....."*Ibid*, pp. 71-72.

33. First Azad and also Nehru were opposed to it but Gandhi was insistent and stood firm in this decision. It is believed that Sardar Vallabhbhai Patel had influenced Gandhi on it. *Ibid*, pp. 72-75. But finally Azad also came to the conclusion that "something must be done to keep up the people's spirit".
34. Quoted from Azad, *op.cit.*, pp. 77-78.
35. Azad: *Ibid*, p.77. This was later contradicted by a statement from Gandhi's well-known private secretary Mahadev Desai. He said there had been some misunderstanding about Gandhiji's statement as he did not mean "an open non-violent rebellion against the British." However, people had come to know that the "Congress was now resolved to force the Government to give up their power by adopting all methods short of violent insurrection." Cf. Azad, *op.cit.*, p.81.
36. Quoted from the full text of the historic resolution passed by the A.I.C.C. on 8 August 1942. See Azad, A.K.: *op.cit.*, pp. 238-241.
37. *Ibid*, p. 83.
38. His radio broadcast from Germany on Azad Hind Radio on August 31, 1942. Quoted in *Selected Speeches of Subhas Chandra Bose*, *op.cit.* pp:142-148.
39. In post-independence period, he became one of the Chief Ministers of the partitioned statel of West Bengal in India.
40. Quoted in P. Mehra: *op.cit.*, p. 574.
41. Mehra., P.: *A Dictionary of Modern Indian History, 1707-1947*, *op.cit.*, p.574.
42. Mehra, *op.cit.*, p.575.
43. As a modern English writer has put it: "When the British East India Company was founded in 1600 India's resources were already famed and widely coveted in Europe. In 1660, before the break-up of the Moghul Empire, the French traveller Bernier, wrote of Bengal in these terms: 'The knowledge that I have acquired of Bengal in two visits inclines me to believe that it is richer than Egypt. It exports in abundance cotton and silk, rice, sugar and butter. It produces amply for its own consumption of wheat, vegetables, grains, fowls, ducks and geese. It has immense herds of sheep and goats. Fish of every kind it has in profusion.' And, 'from Rajmahal to sea is an endless number of canals, cut in bygone ages from the Ganges by immense labour for navigation and irrigation'." Again, "In 1757, the year of the Battle of Plassey, traditionally taken as the beginning of British territorial rule, Robert Clive said that Bengal's capital, Murshidabad, was as 'as extensive, populous and rich as the city of London." The writer then asks "why did India fall to 'so disastrously behind'. "In answer he quotes from William Fullharton, a British M.P. "writing about Bengal at the end of the eighteenth century when Britain's industrial revolution was about to take off: `...such has been the restless energy of our misgovernment that within the short space of 20 years many parts... have been reduced to the appearance of a desert. The fields are no longer cultivated; extensive tracts are already overgrown with thickets; the husbandman is plundered; the manufacturer oppressed; famine has been repeatedly endured; and depopulation has ensued". The writer further notes: "India became the source of raw material and labour because that suited Britain's germinating industrial ambition". Then pointing out the then British Government's policy of discrimination against India's export of fine qualities of cotton and silk goods, the writer observes: "It was not, as the school text books are apt to suggest, the rise of technology that fired Britain's industrial revolution, so much as the fact that India's wealth enabled us to pay for it". Colin Tudge: *The Famine Business*. Faber and Faber, London, 1977, pp. 13-14.

44. There was also the continued pressure of the U.S. President Rooservelt on the British to settle the constitutional issue with the Indian leaders. Although the war in Europe had then ended with German surrender Japan had not yet capitulated. And U.S.A. thought without Russian and Indian cooperation Britain alone, even aided by U.S.A. and China, would not be able to win against Japan.
45. Azad. A.K.: *op.cit.*, p.108.
46. *Ibid*, p.116.
47. *Ibid*, p.106.
48. It may be said that the P.R.S. is a highly respected and coveted scholarship awarded by the Calcutta University to advanced students and lecturers for a period of two years on an initial submission of a paper which would have to show some original thinking and research on a new subject. It is highly competitive as often there are more than one candidate in either arts or science subjects, and only one is selected for each of the two streams each year. The total amount of scholarship at that time was about Rs. 10,000, which was split up into two between the two awardees each year. At the end of two years a research scholar is required to submit a final thesis. When this is approved by an external examiner, the scholar is given a Gold medal called 'Mouat Medal'.

CHAPTER 8

DAWN OF INDEPENDENCE AND AGONY OF PARTITION

Our Life at Dum Dum Central Jail, 1946

After my arrival in Dumdum Central Jail in December 1945, I had first to adjust myself in new surroundings of a new jail but also had an opportunity of meeting some old and many new friends. Then there were my brother Nirmal, and several close friends and colleagues from Midnapore like Amar Nath Chatterjee, Kshiti Prasanna Sen, Narendra Nath Das, Benoy Jiban Ghose and his brother Jyoti Jiban Ghose. There were many others, the total number being around 200. We were all lodged in a separate wing of the jail with four or five separate blocks of two-storeyed buildings, each containing a number of separate cells on each floor accommodating single, two or three prisoners in each cell.

Award of P.R.S. Scholarship

The general atmosphere in the jail was relaxed as we all knew we were on our way to final release after nearly six years of continuous detention. Soon after my arrival, two important events occurred -- one concerning me alone and the other also our friends in the jail. By January 1946, the news of my being awarded one of the most distinguished scholarship -- the P.R.S. Calcutta university had come out in most of the leading papers in Calcutta. Hence I received maney letters of congratu- -- from my relatives and friends and many came to see me in the jail. : in Contai and uncle in Midnapore were obviously extremely ınd a most unexpected letter I received was from Bimal Kumar

Singhe of Calcutta, a well-known educationist and public figure of Bengal. The subject of my P.R.S. dissertation was "Agricultural Economics of Bengal", and Singhe was especially interested in the agricultural economic problems of India. Therefore, he had been already a member of the All-India Society of Agricultural Economics, headed by Sir Manilal Nanavati of Bombay, and consisiting of the important academicians and experts in the rural economic problems of India. Singhe wrote to me that: "after your release from the jail you come and become a member of the Indian Soceity of Agricultural Economics". I was grateful to him for suggesing this as a I welcomed the idea very much. And indeed I became its member after my release and have ever since remained so and even today, for over last forty years. I have always been actively associated with its activities, from India and abroad.

Gandhi's Visit

The second and even a much more important event in Dum Dum Jail, was a visit to us by Gandhi. Soon after our arrival, we were informed of Gandhi's visit. All of us as well as the entire jail staff were highly excited. Earlier in 'thirties, he had met the top leaders of the revolutionary parties in Hijli Jail, prior to the release of all political detenus so this visit, too, was a part of his programme to consult with the leading "Security Prisoners", who according to the then Governments of India and Bengal, were of 'extremist' views and were mostly the supporters of Subhas Bose. Gandhi wanted to have a personal appraisal of our views as to what our future course of action would be, especially in the context of the Indian National Congress's policy of an honourable settlement of the question of India's independence in the post World War II years, through peaceful negotiations. Gandhi and the top Congress leaders as well as the Government of India headed by the then Governor General, Wavell, were all concerned about the policies and activities which the ex-revolutionaries and supporters of Subhas Bose would take after their release. It will be recalled that already Wavell had agreed with Maulana Azad as Congress President, to order a general amnesty for all war-time prisoners, convicted or detained, in connection with the war and the Civil Disobedience Movement to create a "proper atmosphere" for conducting negotiations with the British Government. The prospects of such negotiations largely brightened as a result of a new election in Britain in the winter of 1945-1946, and especially the assumption of the Prime

Ministership by Clement Attlee, the well known Labour leader. Therefore the Congress wanted to ensure that a right atmosphere prevailed in India for negotiations with the new British Government. This was the main reason of Gandhi's visit to Dum Dum Central Jail and also to establish a personal rapport with the Revolutionaries.

On our part, we too were anxious to meet Gandhi. First, because, in spite of our differences with him on many issues there were no two opinions amongst us about his greatness as a man and the importance of the role that he had been playing for over three decades in framing the present and future destiny of India. 17 January 1946 was fixed as the day of his visit. From the morning of that day, the whole jail was cleaned by the jail authorities and all jail staff, ordinary prisoners, political detenus as well as the guards, behaved in a disciplined manner. An air of great expectation prevailed throughout the jail. But from around 4 p.m. we, the detenus, all had assembled in our big common meeting hall especially rearranged and decorated by the jail authorities for Gandhi's visit. By about 6.30 p.m. when darkness had set in a short wintry day, suddenly from inside the jail we could hear the shouts of hundreds of people outside the jail acclaiming : "Gandhiji ki jai" ('victory to Gandhi'). It was the usual slogan of the people throughout India in expressing their loyalty and devotion to Gandhi.

A low dias in front was prepared for Gandhi and his party to sit. It was known that Gandhi, because of his age and frail body, was a to address meetings while seated. As he entered the jail gate the entire jail staff were in full alert and in attendance on him. The guards all stood in great reverence. For the common opeople of India Gandhi was already a saint and an incarnation of God.

As Gandhi entered the meeting hall, accompanied by a limited number of his retinus and several Intelligence Branch people, we all stood up in reverence until he was led to and seated on the dias. I sat right in front facing the dias and the visiting speaker. I could see already, in the rather faint electric lights of the hall, Gandhi's gleaming face, perfectly calm and serene. Before starting to speak he asked us whether he should speak in English or Hindi. There was almost a spontaneous reply : "Hindi". That seemed later to be something strange as very few of us understood the Hindi language very clearly though most of us could speak and follow the usual colloquial Hindi. However, already many in jail, realizing the need for approaching the vast non-Bengali speaking massės in India for their future political activities, had started learning the language. Some amongst us presented to him some bundles of their own hand-spun threads on which throughout his life he had given so much stress as a means of attaining India's economic self-sufficiency and therefore a potent weapon of India's fight against foreign domination. Gandhi was highly pleased with this introduction. There was a speical significance in handspinning by educated and revolutionary people like us, and with our cooperation he could perform many acts. He pleaded with us to follow the path of non-violence. This was a much more powerful weapon than violence. He said that mighty rulers like Hitler, Mussolini and Tojo had been finished but he still kept his head high. Bengal's main problem was that there were too many political groups among the revolutionaries and also in Congress. There was a lack of a real outstanding leader. According to him there had been in the past one outstanding leader of Bengal who had considerably influenced the social, religious and cultural life of whole India--Chaitanya.[1] Gandhi spoke for about an hour and observed that at the beginning he wished to speak only for 15 minutes but later when he found that we all could understand Hindi he was so overjoyed that he spoke for more than an hour. Then he asked us all to learn Hindi more, as it was a national language and could one day supplant English, a foreign language, as the official language of free India. Moreover, he said, to learn a new language was always an asset to a man. He said even at his age (78 years) he was learning the rich Bengali language. We asked him if he could cite a poem from Tagore. He replied that he revered Tagore very much as the latter was the living embodiment of Indian past and present culture and an ardent exponent of universalism and the brotherhood of all nations and peoples of the world--the ideals on which Gurudev's Santiniketan and Visva Bharti were based. Then he cited two lines from Tagore's poem[2]. Then he asked if we had any questions.

I had been waiting for this moment. Therefore I stood up and asked: "Do you consider the 1942 Quit India Movement a success or a failure?" Gandhi replied calmly and softly in his usual demeanor: "My reply is yes and no. Yes, to the extent it aroused mass consciousness; no, to the extent it had deviated from non-violence".[3] Gandhi told us at the end that he wanted to live for 125 years and serve the cause of India's freedom and development. After our meeting with him he was in a very lively and happy mood. At the jail gate he was met by an old inmate of the prison, Binode Behari Bera of Midnapore who had been tried and sentenced in the case of murder of a sub-inspector of police during the salt *satyagraha* movement of 1930, to transportation of life. He had since been in jail, for nearly 15 years.

These two events marked only the beginning of 1946. A chain of fast moving developments subsequently occurred in quick succession in the course of that year, both in my personal life and that of India, which made that year one of the most fateful year and a critical turning point for me personally as well as for the entire country.

Release from Dum Dum Jail, March 1946

My release from Dum Dum Jail along with that of my brother Nirmal came soon, in March 1946, after almost six years. My brother and I both were confused by the considerable changes at the approaches to the new permanent Howrah bridge over the river which was constructed during the war years, replacing the old pontoon bridge which connected Howrah Station (main railway head to Calcutta.

We arrived at my uncle's house at Midnapore in the evening. He had no advance notice of our arrival and release; so he was greatly surprised though extremely happy. I told my uncle my plan to go to Contai to meet my father and then to Calcutta and try for jobs, especially as a lecturer in a college. In Midnapore I met some old Congress leaders and workers in the local Congress Office separately and in their meetings. Largely because of the news of my getting the P.R.S. from the Calcutta University, but partly also because of somewhat changed atmosphere in the country and attitude of the Congress leaders and workers following the baptism of fire that they had to go through in Midnapore during the Quit India Movement, everybody welcomed me. Gone was their old apathy and suspicion of my being an active member of the Midnapore Revolutionalry group. I had a long discussion especially with the veteran Gandhite Basanta Kumar Das as to my future course of action. I had also met other leaders of the Midnapore Congress which was then a very powerful organization with an extensive mass base, particularly in the Contai, Tamluk and Ghatal sub-divisions. In Sardar and Jhargram sub-divisions there were also important and powerful local leaders. Most of them had gone through three successive Civil Disobedience Movements of Gandhi of 1921, 1930 and 1942, and had suffered imprisonment and many deprivations as a result of repeated police actions. Among those I met in the District Congress meetings were Pramatha Nath Banerjee, Basanta Kumar Das, Iswar Chandra Mal, Nikunja Behari Maity of Contai; Kumar Jana, Ajoy Mukherjee, Satish Samanta, Sushil Dhara of Tamluk; Jyotish Chandra Ghose of Ghatal and Mahendra Nath Mahato of Jhargram. My main purpose of meeting them was to get to know personally all the top leaders and their views about their future plan of action in the pursuit of achieving finally India's independence. They were all sincere and dedicated people wedded to the doctrine of non-violence. They all used to wear *Khadi,* the handspun and handwoven cloth, and many used to spend their spare time in hand spinning in indegenous *charkha.* I was invited to attend their meetings and listen to their deliberations. I gave them a hint of my intention of joining the Congress but I did not yet make any final commitment. From the local Congress library I used to borrow and read books on Gandhi's philosophy and constructive programmes of social and economic reconstructions. At Midnapore I also met Dr. Prafulla Chandra Ghose who was then all-Bengal and even an important all-India Congress leader, a strict follower of Gandhi, and a great friend of Basanta Kumar Das.

After spending about 2-3 weeks at Midnapore, I went to Contai to meet my father and also various local Contai leaders and workers. I thought if I were to join the Congress I should make Contai as my base and slowly porceed up through Midnapore to Calcutta. I wrote to my father at Contai about my intended visit. One early morning in March 1946 I took a direct bus from Midnapore to Contai. A direct bus service was then feasible because of the construction of a bridge over the river Kangsavati (Cossai in common usage) which flew by the south of Midnapore town. The bridge connected Midnapore town to the main highway to Kharagpur railway junction and then on to the Orissa trunk road which led up to Puri. For going to Contai one had to go upto Contai Road on the main Calcutta--Puri railway and then to turn left for Contai which was 36 miles or about 58 kilometers to south-west. Then, seven miles before Contai, passed the Orissa Coast Canal which cut across the Contai sub division from east to the west, starting from the Kangsavati near Tamluk and ending in Orissa. This was a narrow stretch of water then without any bridge. So all vehicular traffic along the Contai Road to Contai town had to stop before the canal and the vehicles had to be carried over flat botton country barges to the nearside of Contai, from where they then came to Contai. Hence during my travel to Contai by bus I had also to stop before the canal.

But soon after crossing the canal by the boat I found to my big surprise a large crowd from Contai, mostly students and also many from the public who had come there to welcome me. They came with a car to drive me to Contai town. They shouted many welcome slogans. I was greatly overwhelmed by this pleasant surprise. It appeared that the entire people of Midnapore including those of Contai had followed the detailed news of my arrest on suspicion in connexion with the assassination of the District Magistrate of Midnapore in 1931, with the judicial trial and subsequent long detention in different jails and finally of the news of the Calcutta University awarding me its distinguished P.R.S. scolarship, for my thesis.

The warm and affectionate welcome touched me deeply. But more was waiting for me at Contai town. As soon as I entered through the market crowds of people came out on the streets to see me. I was then being carried in an open-hooded private car supplied by a very public minded Congress leader of Contai, Satish Dinda. On our arrival at the centre of the town, near the main post office, the procession stopped.

It was then in a quiet place as there were very few motorized traffics on the road and nearby there were the complexes of various law courts and their offices on the sand dunes, lined up with a series of tall tropical pine trees around a big play-field. There were waiting some of the leading Congress figures and representatives from the public to welcome me. They included the vateran and old Pramatha Natha Banerjee who had lost in his younger days his left arm in the explosion of a bomb which he was handling, while he was a member of a revolutionary group in Midnapore. In his later years he had become a follower of Gandhi, participated in all the civil disobedience movements launched by the Gandhi in 1921, 1931 and 1942, and suffered successive periods of imprisonment under the British rule. Then there were another vereran leader Sri Iswar Chandra Mal. In addition, there were several other Congress leaders including Basanta Kumar Das, Sudhir Chandra Das and Balai Das Mahapatra, as well as Congress workers. They all embraced me warmly. And, finally, there was a large batch of students from the Contai College as well as three schools of the town.

All this welcome and expression of a deep love and affection towards me touched my heart. And especially the welcome by the Congress leaders. For all of them knew that in the fight for India's independence they and I and my friends were following different paths, they that of non-violence while we the one of limited armed struggle. Formerly there had been little contact between the two groups, although many close relationships on individual basis were there. For example, Pramatha Banerjee was a very close friend of my father and practically all others knew my Contai family and especially my father very well. He first gave me the information that as our house in the south-east of Contai town was totally demolished in the great cyclone and flood of 1942 and my father was living alone (since the death of my mother in 1933) in a small rebuilt cottage, arrangements had been made for my stay with Satish Dinda. He had a nice two storeyed brick built house and often distinguished visitors who used to come to Contai used to be accommodated there. With some reluctance I agreed for two main reasons. First, I did not want to embarrass my father with additional trouble for me; and second, Dinda's place being more central in the town it would be easier for me as well as those who wanted to come to see me and talk about our future activities. I was given there a warm welcome and a very kind hospitality by the whole family of Sri Dinda.

I stayed there for a few days and later, finally, moved to my father's place. During this period I had a series of talks with the local Congress leaders including Pramatha Banerjee, Sudhir Das, Balai Das Mahapatra, Iswar Mal and many others. I visited their offices at Contai including an important centre of constructive activities at the National School at the outskirts of the town, set up and run by the Congress leaders and workers. During Gandhi's Quit India Movement, in which the school played a large part, it was dismantled and occupied by the police. I heard firsthand from all of them the sad and gruesome stories of the police repression of the entire people, especially in the countryside, including shooting, lathi charging, burning of houses and destruction of property, imposition of collective fines and widespread molesting of women by the forces of 'law and order'. Then there was the typhoon and the great inundation of October 1942. Finally, to add to all these were the impact of the Famine of 1943. Although Contai, being agriculturally very rich and prosperous, had never suffered from famine or even large-scale scarcity, these recent successive 'beatings' of man and nature had brought untold sufferings to the masses, especially in the villages. In the wake of severe and widespread devastation due to the flood of 1942 there was no succour from the Government. On the contrary of latter's policy of denudation on the whole coastal belt of Midnapore and Contai of the essential means of water transport and even of food grains, partly out of a fright from the expectation of an imminent Japanese invasion, and partly to weaken the people by depriving them of their main source of food, paddy-rice, against their participation in the Quit India Movement, greatly aggravated the situation.

As a consequence of all these the general mass of people in the whole of Contai subdivision (of the district of Midnapore) were ruined physically and financially. And the police and the military repression had brought widespread depression, scare and demoralization, so among the Congress circle at Contai there was feeling that something ought to be done to rouse the people from this scare and feeling of insecurity, and depression.

There an idea was mooted that a party of selected Congress leaders and workers should conduct a march on foot, under the banner of the Congress National Flag, for some key villages, during the ensuing 'national week' observed by the All-India National Congress every year from 6 to 12 April. I liked the idea very much as it would give me a good oportunity to get acquainted with the local people in the villages, to know their problems and also to hear from them their stories of repression at the hands of the Government forces. It was decided to undertake a root march of a total of 100 miles under foot, on an average of 14 miles a day going from village to village, lecturing to people about the need for waking up, to restore their courage and try to come to nromal life, and to continue their fight for independence till India was free. So a band of about 15 to 20 people set out from Contai on foot carrying a high flying national flag on a pole. These included, besides myself, such veteran leaders as Pramatha Banerjee, Sudhir Das, Balai Das Mahapatra, Abinash Maity, Trailokya Pradhan (who had lost all the members of his family during the flood of 1942, and many others. During the seven days we covered many villages. To our great satisfaction we had received a very sympathetic and receptive crowd everywhere. People flocked to see us and hear us. Important people offered us their cooperation and hospitality and served us all our meals, and provided us accommodations for the night. It was an exhilarating experience for me. It was a real contact with the people, to know first hand their problems, their weals and woes and above all the immense sufferings that they had voluntarily suffered while participating in the freedom struggle. It benefited me enormously in getting to know their problems and to place them in wider arenas, in both national and international fields, whenever I subsequently got an opportunity. I had to speak in all the meetings arranged on our route, along with other known local leaders who were with me. I spoke to all types of villagers and people of all religion, castes and creed. I told them we had to pursue our efforts to achieve complete independence for our country and to have the right to frame our own destiny. Our task was to revive the people from the effects of cruel repressions and great natural calamities.

During this tour I realized how true it was that the people as well as the Bengal Famine Enquiry Commission had said it was a "man made" famine. Not only was there the unpreparedness, callousness and apathy of the Governments of India as well as of Bengal then headed by a Moslem League Ministry, but there was their deliberate policy to procure and stock in government godowns as much of the staple paddy-rice of their basic foodgrain during the war and the Quit India Movement. While travelling through many Contai villages we found heaps of rotten, decomposed, fungus-ridden paddy spread across the ground near several village stores which were used to stock the crop by the Government during the war in the early forties. All such paddy was lost as a result of long storage in humid and unscientific conditions, while people were starving and dying of starvation in the villages and on the roads of Calcutta and other metropolitan towns. It was a most tragic, situation. I thought how was it possible under a modern 'civilized' government.

However, at the end of one week we returned to Contai. It was a great success as our personal contact with the masses brought back their confindence as well as trust in the Congress organization. This was further helped by certain important new developments in the political atmosphere of the country after the war, especially because of the establishment of a Labour Government in Britain and its new attitude and policies towards India as compared with earlier primarily an unsympathetic Government dominated by Churchill and his Conservative Party. But, nevertheless, the political situation in April 1946 was uncertain. While there were thoughts and ideas of some new initiatives on the part of the new British Government towards negotiation with the Indian leaders on the issue of their demand for independance, we had to organize the masses for a new struggle. So in our deliberations in the Congress circles in Contai,[4] we were actually thinking of preparing ourselves as well the people for two alternative courses--the path of negotiation and constructive political and social as well as economic activities, and the path of struggle in a non-violent way.

A Call from Sarat Bose

Just at that time I received a telegram from my uncle in Midnapore quoting another telegram he had received from Kumar Devendra Lal Khan then in Calcutta, saying "send Parimal immediately to see Sarat Bose". I was greatly puzzled by this message. For, although I had, met Subhas Chandra Bose previously and had an opportunity to work for him on various occasions, I had never any personal contact with his elder brother, Sarat Bose a well-known barrister of the Calcutta High Court and also an important personality in the hierarchry of the Congress leadership, both in the province of Bengal as well as in the All-India National Congress. I knew then that after the release of Gandhi in May 1944, from imprisonment during the Quit India Movement in August 1942, and with the war conditions turning notably in favour of Britain and the Allied Powers, the British Government pursued a gradual policy of relaxation and of some settlement with the Indian leaders on the issue of India's independence. So, even under the Conservative Government and the Viceroyalty of Wavell (1943-1947) new elections were, as said earlier, held under the old Government of India Act of 1935 in the Provinces as well as in the Centre in the winter of 1945-1946. After some hesitation the Congresses had participated in the elections and won absolute majority in eight provinces as well as emerged as the single largest party in the centre.

Sarat Bose then was returned to the Central legislature from Bengal, and was elected as the leader of the Congress Party members in the Central Assembly. Considering this I thought that it was very significant that Sarat Bose would want to see me.

At Contai, I was then just settling down in my new Congress environment and building confidence among my friends in the Congress circle. Many of them were staunch followers of Gandhi while others were supporters of Subhas Bose. They all were then working in the local

Congress which was a very powerful unit with roots all over the subdivision. Several veteran leaders had been working since 1921, after having given up studies at the Calcutta University and several graduate colleges at Gandhi's call of non-violent non-cooperattion. There were also a large batch of sincere workers devoted to the organization. They were committed to the ideals and policies as laid down by Gandhi and the official Congress line. There was a small batch among them, who, though also worked equally for the official objectives of that organization, were more inclined to support Subhas Bose's views. However, there was never an open conflict. The latter group especially followed Subhas's activities abroad after his escape from India during the war. So, early in 1946, the latter formed a group of volunteers and imparted to it regular drill and parade under the Congress national flag. The group was named "Azad Hind Volunteers". It consisted of young students from the local colleges and schools as well as some outside young boys, and dedicated to the cause of achieving India's independence. But their main work then was social and cultural and to prepare themselves as well as the common people for possible future struggles for India's freedom. The section of the Congress which organized and conducted the affairs of the Azad Hind Volunteers, associated me with their work in this respect. But at the same time I tried to develop contacts with all groups of Congressmen and was regularly invited to all their joint meetings.

Although I too had my natural inclinations towards Subhas's ideals and activities I did not think that at that critical period of India's struggle for independence it was wise to take any partisan view. Rather my idea was to attempt for the integration of Subhas's strategy with Congress's overall goal and stratgey. That is, to carry on a united fight atgainst the British rule in India even by non-violent means till complete independence was achieved. So I did not take an offensive attitude against anybody.

Partly for this, and partly considering that great changes that were expected in the political field of India in the near future following any new initiative that might be taken by the British Government in solving India's demands for *swaraj*, a decision was taken by some in the Congress to elect me, in the then coming Congress elections after the war, to the all-Midnapore District Congress Committee and then to the Bengal Provincial Committee of the Congress. So, on hearing that the veteran all-Bengal Congress leader Sarat Bose wanted to see me. All my Congress friends were happy.

So, I left Contai in early May 1946 and came to Calcutta. There I first saw Kumar Devendra Lal Khan at his residence enquired from him if he knew anything about the purpose of Sarat Boses call although he had not seen me earlier. Khan told me that the elder Bose needed a special political secreteary to help him in the conduct of his special responsibility as the leader of the Congress party in the Central Assembly. So Bose was looking for me, when my name was recommended to him by Satya Ranjan Bakshi, the well-known journalist of Calcutta who had been all through his life a close associate of Subhas Bose and the editor of the latter's daily paper *The Forward Bloc*. Sarat Bose therefore asked Kumar Devendra Lal Khan to contact me. Perhaps because I had been a long admirer of Subhas, and earlier (in 1938-1939) had been writing regularly in *The Forward Bloc* and finally because of the recent award to me. I was pleased because I thought it would place me at the centre stage of the coming political scenes. But on a second thought I considered that I should not tie down my hands in the work of a single person however distinguished and exalted he was. I wanted to keep my options open.

Moreover, I recalled that the University had granted me the P.R.S. distinction with its substantial monetary benefit on only a part of the results of my research work on 'Agricultural Economics of Bengal." Under its terms I was to conduct further researches for a period of two years and to submit the results at the end of each, which would be again considered by an external examiner to judge whether they were upto the prescribed standard. If it was found satisfactory, the Calcutta University Syndicate would award me the prized gold medal named after Mouat. So, finally I came to the conclusion that I could not accept the elder Bose's offer. I could see that my decision would upset many of my well-wishers and close friends, especially Devendra Lal Khan and Satya Ranjan Bakshi. But I thought that it was the only sensible thing to do, taking into the long-term interest of my country.

However, I did not want to take a final decision immediately but wanted to think over the matter further. In the meantime I requested Devendra Lal Khan to make an appointment for me to see Sarat Bose at his residence at No.1 Woodborn Park. It was sometime in late April 1946.

Meeting With Sarat Bose

I found the house in a quiet area; it was big and located in a wide compound with a well maintained garden. I walked into his big visitors' rooms where people of all sorts--his ardent political supporters and admirers, Congressmen, legal clients were assembled.

When I got an opportunity to meet him, I politely introduced myself and told him I came to see him on being asked by Kumar Devendra Lal Khan. He told me to go upstairs to his study and wait there. Bose then with his big bulky body in a milk white *khadi* (hand spun and woven) *dhoti* and Punjabi, came up and met me. I greeted him duly, and then he sat with me in a big sofa. He opened the conversation first and said he had great responsibilities and work as the leader of the Congress party in the newly constituted Central Legislative Assembly and he needed help of a person with suitable experience and background. I was ready with my reply and said: I was awarded a Premchand Roychand Research Scholarship only recently while I was still in jail; under its terms I would have to conduct research on my subject for two consecutive years and then to submit a thesis at the end of each year to the University, so I would have hardly any time to spare. Bose at once got the hint and did not pursue. I then changed the topic and asked him what he thought of Subhas's reported death from air accident at Taipeh. He knew that I was an admirer of Subhas, so unhesitatingly replied: from his lalk with Colnonel Habibur Rahaman (who had been originally in the British Indian Army and later joined the I.N.A with other Indian military officers after the fall of Malaya and Burma, was a close confidant of the INA leader, and who was travelling with Subhas on the same plane and reamained uninjured) who had come to see him sometime earlier, he was led to believe that Subhas had died of the plane accident. Habibur Rahaman showed him the burnt marks on his wrist as a result of the fire which engulfed the plane following the accident, and also gave him the watch which Subhas had been wearing then. We then exchanged a few more words. But I did not think it wise to stay long as I knew Bose was an extremely busy man. I took leave of him after greeting with all politeness.

But on coming out of Bose's house I thought of whether I lost a great opportunity in my life, especially when I was not still settled properly either careerwise or financially. Bose later became a member of the Interim Central Government set up in September 1946 following the Wavell Plan and the Simla Conference. Much later, in 1948, in Oxford, I learnt from Prafulla Chakravarty that after having sounded me Bose had selected him as his additional secretary. Chakravarty then had been a lecturer in a college. It may be said, previous to Bose's calling me, his principal political secretary was Nirad Choudhuri who became a well-known writer later and settled down in Britain.

Important Political Developments in India, 1946

It may be recalled that by that time, several important steps had been taken by the British Government as well as the new Governor General of India, Archibald P. Wavell, since the latter's arrival in India at the beginning of 1943. He had been for long a General in the British Army and was a former Commander-in-Chief of India. Earlier, during World War II, he had served for some time as the G.O.C. - in-C of the Allied forces in the Middle East, and again as the Allied Commander in the South West Pacific. When the war was passing through its critical phases for the Allied Powers in 1943 and 1944 Wavell, in his capacity of the Governor General of India felt the need of a willing participation by the Indian leaders and the people in Britain's war efforts. This was also a particular point which had been pressed by the Governments of U.S.A. and China on that of Britain. Though by the end of 1944 and at the beginning of 1945 the tides of war definitely showed signs of turning in favour of Britain and its allies, still Japan, their major enemy in the Far East, remained yet undefeated. So the concern of the U.S.A. and China was that to defeat Japan cooperation of the Indian people was essential. Hence Wavell on his own as well as, first, the British Coalition Government dominated by the Conservative Party, and then by the Labour Party, after its landslide victory in British general elections in June 1945, took a successive series of measures to break the Indian political and constitutional deadlock. First there was the Wavell Plan, (1945) which was amended and approved by Churchill's government in Britain, and finally announced by the British Secretary of State for India in Parliament in London on 14 June 1945. It was essentially a revamp of the Cripps proposals and dealt with the immediate reconstitution of the Viceroy's

Executive Council with mainly Indian members except the Viceroy and the Commander-in-Chief, with "equal number of Muslims and Caste Hindus." There was no clear commitment or reference to the intended future constitutional status of India.

Secondly, main as a follow up of the Wavell plan, a conference would be held with leaders of all main political parties including the Congress, the Moslem League, the representatives of (Hindu) Scheduled Castes and Sikhs, the then Nationalist Party (of M.S. Aney), and the European Group in the Central Assembly. There were to be a few other special invitees. The conference met at Simla on 25 June 1945, where Gandhi was also present in a non-official capacity, to be available for consultation if required. Maulana Azad was then the President of the Indian National Congress and was delegated by the Congress working Committee to be their sole representative. Accordingly he had met Wavell before the Conference (which had since been known as the Simla Conference) and had detailed talks about its intent and goals. Wavell assured him that although "no far-reaching constitutional changes would be carried out for the duration of the war", "the Viceroy's Executive Council would be completely Indian and he would endeavour to set up a convention that the Viceroy would always act on the advice of the council". And further, as Azad has recorded: ''He appealed to me to trust the Government. It was his sincere desire that the problem of India must be solved after the war was over[5]. Wavell also said that the war was approaching its end; hence it ''would be to India's advantage to accept the offer and cooperate with the British in bringing the war to a victorious close''. But at the end Wavell referred to the Moslem League and said ''it would be necessary that there should be an understanding between the Congress and the League''. At this Azad replied to Wavell that ''an agreement with the League seemed very doubtful. Those who were in control of the League seemed to be under the impression that they had the support of the Government and they would not therefore accept any reasonable terms''. The Viceroy then said; ''There was no question of the Government supporting the League''.[6]

Azad was impresed by his talk with Wavell and became convinced that the ''Viceroy was sincere and genuinely desired a change in the atmosphere''. He therefore advised the Congress that ''we should participate in the Conference with a view to accept if the terms were suitable". So the day before the Conference met on 25 June 1945, the Congress Working Committee therefore, in principle, agreed to Azad's suggestion, that is, accepted Wavell's and the British Government's proposals. But they sought certain points of clarifications. It may be said that this was a big departure for the Congress compared to its rejection earlier of the Cripps' proposals. For, like the latter, in the so-called Wavell Plan there was no provision for a long-term solution of the India's constitutional problems, no promise of complete independence, no transfer to Indian hands of the Defence, and no surrender of the Viceroy's veto or other powers. And the new proposals were even worse than those of Cripps in that they treated the Congress and the League on terms of equality. They were, in fact, against all that Congress stood and asked for, and even one of its basic claim from the very beginning that it was a 'national' organization with representations from all religious communities and all interests, where as the League was merely a communal organization.

Indeed it was most unfortunate that relying on mere verbal assurance and hope of the Viceroy that "it was his sincere desire that the problem of India must be solved after the war over".[7] The Congress agreed, on principle, even "to cooperate with the British in bringing the war to a victorious close". Explaining this *volte-face* on the part of the Congress, some people later commented that "in accepting Wavell's offer, Congress leaders had demonstrated that they were tired of the political struggle and were anxious to arrive at a settlement on the terms proposed".[8] Both the Viceroy and the Moslem League leaders were fully aware of this weakness of the premier 'nationalist' organization and took full advantage of it. For, Jinnah having got the parity of representation of the 'Caste Hindus' and the Moslem League in the newly proposed Viceroy's Executive Council, pressed his demand that all the five Moslem members must be selected by the League while the Congress would choose only the Hindu members. The Congress, of course, did not accept it, and the Viceroy then cleverly left the matter to be decided between the Congress and the Moslem League.[9] In their meeting held between the Conference sessions, the two organizations failed to agree on the matter. Once more the attempts by the British representative in India and the Indian leaders went along a blind alley and the Conference continued in this suspicious atmosphere for a few days more. On 14 July, in less than three weeks, the Viceroy announced the failure of the

Conference. Once more the blame was on a lack of communal agreement, which had always been a ruse and stock argument of the British Government.

When this drama was being played we were still in Buxa Detention Jail. As earlier, in the case of Cripps Proposals we did not have much faith in these negotiations as we skeptical of the British intentions as to the granting of real freedom to India, especially as long as the Conservative Party had the predominant say in the Government. We had also doubts on the policy of the Congress in leaving most of the times, the initiative in such negotiations to the British Government. Part of their difficulties was that the Congress Leaders at that time had not thought of an agreed alternative strategy of their own, especially for a new struggle even in a non-violent way, should the negotiations with the Government or with other major political parties on the basic demands for complete independence, unity and integrity of India not materialize. Perhaps it would have been even better if after their release from prison in 1944-45 the Working Committee had met and made a clear declaration reiterating their basic demands and at the same time to advise the people to prepare for a new struggle, should those demands not be met by the British Government in a given time. This was indeed most tragic and, the critics might say, was the beginning of the tragic story of ultimate partition of the country though with independence for the separated segments. Even Azad himself has recognized that "The Simla Conference marks a breakwater in Indian history".[10]

It may be noted here that during the Simla Conference, as earlier said, Gandhi was not a participant but was present at Simla to be available for consultation. But, as Azad has recorded, at the Working Committee Meeting to discuss the Wavell proposal, Gandhi did not raise again the question of violence and non-violence, while the Committee agreed to participate in the British war efforts.[11] Critics have said that this was because Gandhi's influence in the counsels of the Congress waned perceptibly after 1945. This was evident both in the events leading to as well as consequential on the Simla Conference.[12]

However the landslide victory of the Labour Party in the British Parliament in June 1945 brought in July a new Labour Government with Clement Attlee, long time regarded as sympathetic to India's freedom, which brought a new hope in India, particularly among some of the top Congress leaders. But, as subsequent events proved such hope was misplaced, at least overoptimistic. It lulled most congress leaders as well as large sections of the people into complacency. The Congress President Azad was so enthusiastic that he sent a telegram of congratulation to Stafford Cripps who was included as a member of the Attlee Cabinet. This, however, as Azad has stated, was not liked by Gandhi and Nehru both of whom "were skeptical about the Labour attitude to India".[13] The Labour Government, however, took up the thread of the chain of activities which their predecessor the Conservative Labour coalition Government had earlier started with regard to the constitutional advances in India. It was after the Labour party had assumed power in July 1945, as already stated, the Viceroy of India, Wavell declared that a General Election would be held for the Central and the Provincial Legislatures in the winter. We have already seen that these elections were held as suggested by Wavell, in which the Congress came out as the largest party in the Central Legislature, and also got the absolute majority in all the provinces except Bengal, Punjab and Sind. In the latter three provinces the Moslem League became the single largest party but not the absolute majority. "In these provinces", as Azad has said, "the majority population was Moslems, and the Moslem League had carried on propaganda to arouse religious fanaticsm and communal passions".[14] In the N.W. Frontier Province, though also a Moslem majority area, the Congress got the majority and formed the government, largely due to the devoted work of Abdul Ghaffar Khan and his brother Khan Saheb.

Also in the winter of 1945-46 (in January-February 1946) a British Parliamentary Delegation, led by a Labour M.P., visited India to study the then political situation. And, as far as I remember, a young British M.P. who was a member of the delegation came to visit us as far as in Buxa Jail in December-January 1945-46. The delegation then made a good impression on the Congress leaders as well as to most people by their sympathetic understanding of the Indian problem. "They were convinced that the Indian freedom could not long be delayed." On their return to British they must have reported along these lines to the Labour Government.

Soon thereafter (on 19 February 1946), the new Secretary of State for India (Lord) Pethick Lawrence made an important statement in Parliament with regard to setting up a new constitution making process in India, and announced that with that end in view a speical three-man Mission of Cabinet Ministers would be visiting India soon. The mission was to consist of himself, Stafford Cripps and A. V. Alexander, then First Lord of Admiralty, and would "act in association with the Viceroy - (Wavell) in this matter".

On 15 March 1946 the British Labour Prime Minister made an important policy statement in Parliament that the situation in India had completely changed and demanded a new approach. He said that "he did not wish to stress the differences between Indians, for in spite of all differences and divisions, Indians were united in their desire for freedom".[15] It was indeed a frank and fair diagnosis of the Indian situation made by a ruling Bristish Prime Minister. It was no doubt an expression of a feeling of a real man behind Attlee who professed all his life the ideals of socialism and therefore was dedicated to the principles of justice and equality amongst all peoples[16]. Clarifying the role of the Cabinet Mission Attlee observed: "His colleagues were going to India with the intention of using their utmost endeavour to help her to attain freedom as speedily and as fully as possible".

The Cabinet Mission arrived in New Delhi on 24 March 1946, and the leader of the Mission, Pathik Lawrence declared that their primary objective was to set up "an acceptable machinery" whereby India would realize her 'full independent status' as determined by herself, and also to make 'interim arrangements' for this purpose[17]. This was obviously a clear statement of the goal and policy of the new British Government and went a long way, and after a long time, in meeting the aspirations of the Indian people. But the snag lay in how the terms were interpreted by agents of the British Government in India (most of whom by their past, current and immediate conducts showed that they were not very sympathetic to the idea of India's gaining independence), the various political parties, especially the Moslem League, and by different special interests. The Mission conducted discussions with the leading representatives of various bodies for nearly five weeks and at the end, 12 May 1946, put forward their own proposals which were then called the Cabinet Mission Plan.

Disaffection among Indian Armed Forces

Following the surrender of Japan in August 1945, it was inevitable that the mission of Subhas Bose and his Indian National Army to free India should fail. But that time the INA had already showed its organizing and fighting capability by establishing the first free 'Indian Government' on the Islands of Andamans and Nicobars, and by temporarily attacking the mainland in the north-east and being in a position of occupying Imphal, the capital of Manipur. However, after the Japanese surrender, the British soon recaptured Burma and therefore many of the INA officers wer taken prisoners by the British. But they did not repent for having joined the Indian National Army under the leadership of Subhas. The British put some of them to trial for treason. The most important trial that took place was of three senior officers--Shahnawaz, Sahgal and Dhillon, Moslem, a Hindu and Sikh respectively, all of whom had been earlier in the British army, then taken prisoners by the Japanese in Burma-Malaya region during the War, and finally joined the INA under Subhas's call.

The Congress then, having come to know their courage and dedicattion to the country, took up their defence. The trial was held in the historic Red Fort of Delhi. It aroused a great excitement and commotion all over India and a countrywide sympathy for the prisoners among all communities. The impact was far reaching than the British and the Indian Governments had realized when they put these officers into trial. In fact it affected even the regular Indian armed forces who were then still serving. The trial continued for several months and in the end all the officers were released. But its effect remained.

Earlier there had been two serious naval revolts among the Indian officers of the Royal Navy in Bombay as well as in Karachi. There was complaint of racial discrimination by the British officers against them but more clearly the revolts were due to a new sense of patriotism and of duty on the part of these officers to their motherland. Similarly there was a widespread disaffection also among the Indian Air Force and finally, even among the ordinary police, as Azad has said: "All the three branches of the Armed Forces--the Navy, the Army and the Air Force--were inspired by a new spirit of patriotism.[18] And, again, all these convinced the British that they could no longer rely on the Armed Forces unless the political problem of India was satisfactorily solved[19]". These events, no doubt, persuaded the British Government to take some serious and tangible steps with regard to the solution of the Indian problem. But as far as the Congress was concerned, although they had found in late 1945 and early 1946 that clearly "the country had undergone a complete transformation" and absolutely a new India, "fired with a new desire for freedom" for India, had been born, there was unfortunately hardly any attempt on the part of its (Congress) leaders to keep this spirit alive. From Azad's clear descriptions of the then politcal situation given in his "Autobiographical Narrative," it appears the entire people of India--the general public, Government officials, Indian Army, Navy and Air Force and even the Police--then expressed their readiness to respond to the call for a new struggle against the British rule, from the Congress. But the latter devoted their almost entire energy on negotiations trusting completely the declared intentions of the British Government and their Viceroy in India, and also without taking due regard of the difficulties that would inevitably crop up on the attempts to reconciliate what were almost irreconcilable, that is, the professed goals and activities of the Moslem League with those of the Congress as the premier nationalist organization. While the stand then taken by the Congress leaders that during the period of negotiation with the British Government, there should be no new movement by the Congress was perfectly reasonable, did not political foresight and acumen require that there should at the same time be kept an alternative approach ready, if the attempts to arrive at an agreed settlement with the parties and therefore with the British Government failed? If that was done, then there would have been perhaps no frustrations among some of the top Congress leaders at the failure of each political mission that the British Government sent to India after the Cripps' Mission. Which frustration, it seems, finally led them to accept Jinnah's proposal for partition with most disastrous consequences for the entire people of India. The irony was that although Azad talked of the need for the Congress to follow a dual policy" of keeping "the spirit of sttruggle alive among the Indian people, and "refraining from any precipitate step"[20] it appears that the Congress as a whole relied more on the latter than on the former. This point is made not with a mere spirit of criticism but in a sense of great anguish and sorrow.

Meeting with Shyama Prasad Mukherjee

The entire country was then in a most critical phase of its long history and the people were waiting for fresth developments with new expectations from the Congress leaders' policy of wait and see and of a negotiated settlement with the British. But there was simultaneously a great apprehension amongst many as to the increasing aggressiveness of the Moslem League and its demand for partition. People's apprehension and disappointment were further aggravated by the British policy of no independence for India till the communal question was settled to the satisfaction of both the Congress and the Moslem League.

However, even at that time of severe stress I had first to look for a decent means of income not only for my own living but even to continue my part in the coming political events with a view to achieving the still unattained goal of India's independence. But I first thought of meeting Shyama Prasad Mukherjee who, as far as I remember, was then no longer the Vice-Chancellor of the Calcutta University but still the most influential man in the University and also a very powerful leader of the Hindu Maha Sabha.[21] I felt greatly indebted to him for his assistance in clearing the way for the submission of P. R. S. thesis from the Buxa Jail. So I went to see Shyama Prasad in late May 1946 at his residence at Ashutosh Mukherjee Road, Calcutta. His reception room-cum-library was on the first floor. I went there and found a large crowd already waiting. I stood outside on the balcony and watched the traffic on the road below. Then when I saw Shyama Prasad entering his reception room I went in. Later as he sat in front of the other end of the room facing the people assembled, he looked at me but perhaps did not recognize. Because prior to that I had only one chance of seeing him before in between my two prison terms, from October 1938 till March 1940 after I had obtained my M.A. and B.L. degree, during my first term in prison as a detenu from 1931 to 1938. He knew very well my two uncles - Nibaran Chandra Ray, then Senior Professor of Physics of the Scottish Church College, Calcutta and a member of the Calcutta University Syndicate, and Binode Bihari Ray, Secretary, Midnapore District Board. However, at the suitable opportunity I Introduced myself to Shyama Prasad and he at once expressed his congratulation for my obtaining the P.R.S. award from the jail. And he asked me if I would be interested in accepting a lecturership in Economics which was than available at the Ashutosh College, Calcutta. On my agreeing to it he asked me to go and see the principal, Panchanan Sinha. Accordingly I went one day to the college and saw the latter but he did not seem to be much helpful.

However, at that time I also took an opportunity of seeing Professor Haricharan Ghose, Vice principal, Bangabasi College, Calcutta, and also a post - graduate lecturer in Economics at the Calcutta University. I wanted to thank him also for having helped me in the preparation of my thesis from jail. When I met him at his residence in Calcutta he asked me if I would take up the post of a lecturer in Economics in Bangabasi College. I told him that Shyama Prasad had already asked me to join his college. Then Ghose said S.P. was sick at that time but he would tell the fomer about me and he asked me to see the principal P.K. Basu of Bangabasi College the next day. Soon after I met Basu in the college. Ghose was also present. After talking to me, they asked me to join as a Lecturer of Economics from June. I was very pleased. It seemed to be a god-send and perfectly what I had wished for. For this would enable me to work in the education and academic lines, pursue my P.R.S. research, and at the same time leave me some time to devote to politics. At the College I started lecturing on Economic and Political theories and practices at both I.A. and B.A. classes from June 1946.

Elected as member of B.P.C.C and A.I.C.C.

Having thus secured my footing in Calcutta, I went to Contai and informed my friends in the Congress about my joining Bangabasi College as a lecturer. While they expressed happiness they seemed to be a bit disappointed that I could not be available as a whole-timer to help to reorganize and revitalize the Congress in Contai. But I assured them that I would do my best. They then told me of their wish to send me to the Bengal Provincial Congress Committee and later, if possible, even to the All India Congress Committeee (the A.I.C.C.). Soon came the Congress organizational elections first to the Midnapore District Congress Committee, then the B.P.C.C. and finally to the A.I.C.C. My Contai and Midnapore friends put my name successively in all the three levels of the Congress organization, and by the beginning of July 1946 I found myself to be elected, through the long chain as a memebr of each Congress Committee at the four levels. Thus, within three months of my release from the jail I was thrust with two responsibilities at the same time. One at the Bangabasi College as a full time lecturer with responsibilities for lecturing to Intermediate and Graduate students on Economics and Politics, and the other as a member of the Congress Committees at the Contai sub-divisional, Midnapore District, Bengal Provincial and the All-India levels. I took the two most seriously and tried to do my best in both.

The Cabinet Mission Plan

The Cabinet Mission proposals[21] consisted essentially of three parts: (i) the basic elements of the shape and constitution of a future free India; (ii) the manner of setting up a constitution making body and the details of its functions and suggested procedures; and (iii) the setting up of an Interim Government at the Centre and the manner of its composition.

As for the first, the future shape of India, (a) there would be the Union of India comprising both the then British Indian Provinces and the Indian States, which should deal with only three subjects : Foreign Affairs, Defence and Communications; (b) the Union should have an executive and a legislature consisting of representatives chosen from the Indian provinces as well as the states; (c) all subjects other than the three Union subjects and all residuary powers should vest in the provinces; (d) the States would retain all subjects other than those ceded to the Union; (e) the Provinces should be free to form Groups (sub-federal) with executives and legislatures and each Group could determine the provincial subjects to be taken in common; and (f) the constitution of the Union and the Groups should contain a provision whereby any province could by a majority of vote of its legislative assembly call for a reconsideration of the terms of the constitution after an initial period of ten years, and at ten-yearly intervals thereafter.

In other words, although designated as a 'Union' the constitution would be essentially of a federal character with Centre having specified powers with only three major subjects while all the residuary powers would be left with the provinces and the states. This, it may be observed, was in lines with Azad's own thinking which he had earlier put it into writing and discussed with the Congress Working Committee as well as Gandhi.[22] The only additional provision that Cabinet Mission proposals had was the idea of the formation of the three Sub-Federal Groups of provinces : Group A, consisting of Bombay, Bihar, the Central Provinces, Madras, Orissa, and the United Provinces, all with a Hindu majority population; Group B, comprising the Punjab, the N.W.F. Province, Sind and British Baluchistan, all with Moslem majority populations; and Group C with Bengal and Assam with a total population of slightly Moslem majority. These groupings were no doubt intended to assure the Moslem League as well as the entire Moslem community of a maximum autonomy for each Moslem majority province as well as for groups of provinces with a combined Moslem majority, but only within the framework of a united India. But any province would have the power to opt out of any Group "as soon as the new constitutional arrangements came into operation", with a decision taken by its legislature after the first general election under the new constitution.

As for the constitution making body, there would be a Constitutent Assembly comprising of 292 representatives of the Provinces as well as of the States. The former would be elected on communal basis -- Moslem (78 seats), Sikhs (4), and the General with all others (210). The elections from the provinces would be on the basis of provincial assembly elections but by a system of proportional representation with single transferable vote. Apart from framing the Union Constitution, the Constituent Assembly would negotiate the treaty contemplated between the Union Assmebly and the United Kingdom "to provide for certain matters arising out of the transfer of power".

Since the arrival of the Cabinet Mission in Delhi on 24 March 1946 prolonged, and detailed discussions were held between the Mission members and other leaders of all major political parties, groups and interests including especially Azad as the President of the Congress, and Jinnah, President of the Moslem League. The Congress, in principle agreed with the main contents and the principal proposals, but reserved judgment on the details.[23] The League at first demanded partition and a separate state, to be called Pakistan. The Cabinet Mission, as Azad has recorded, "was not prepared to concede the demand". So, finally, the League accepted the scheme and the Moslem League voted unanimously in its favour.[24]

Thus the basic proposals of the Cabinet Mission were accepted by both the Congress and the Moslem League, and, to use Azad's words, this "was a glorious event in the history of the freedom movement in India" and "throughout the country there was a sense of jubilation and all the people were united in their demand for freedom."[25] However, this joy was only short-lived, for differences between the Congress and the League over the third item of the Cabinet Mission proposals the formation of the Interim Government, that is a new Executive Council of the Viceroy. The latter, after preliminary discussions with the major political parties and finding no agreement, himself proposed on 16 June 1946 an Executive Council of 14, of which 6 would go to the Congress, including a Scheduled Caste representative; 5 to the Moslem League; and one each to the Sikhs, the Christians and the Parsis. Jinnah, claimed that the Moslem League would nominate all the Moslem members and the Congress only the Hindus. But the Congress opposed this claim as well as the principle of parity with the Moslem League. The Congress had originated and worked as a 'national' organization and had members and important leaders from almost all communities including millions among the Moslem population. But the British Governments had always worked on the basis of parity of the two organizations. So, at the end, the Working Committee, while "accepting the Cabinet Mission's Plan for the future, found itself unable to accept the proposal of the interim Government."[26]

Thus, while both the Congress and the Moslem League accepted the longterm proposals of the Cabinet Mission Plan, both had their reservations, especially with regard to the composition of the proposed Interim Government at the Centre, that is, the Viceroy's Executive Council. The Mission members tried to reconcile the almost unbridgeable gaps, and failed. So, finally, the Mission left India on 29 June 1946.

Yet there was no formal announcement of failure and the Congress seemed to be under the impression that the Mission's Plan would still materialize. It therefore called a meeting of the A.I.C.C. on 7 July 1946 at Bombay to approve the decision taken earlier by the Working Committee. I was then a member of the A.I.C.C. and attended this session. There was strong opposition from the leftists in the Congress, especially, the Congress Socialist Party. But finally after explanation and exhortation of Azad, then Congress President, the A.I.C.C. approved the Working Committee resolution accepting the Cabinet Mission Plan. Later, however, the Moslem League withdrew its acceptance on the plea that Nehru in a press statement, after the A.I.C.C. session, had made a reference contrary to the terms of the Cabinet Mission.[27] And in its session of 27 July 1946 the Moslem League reiterated once again its demand for Pakistan.

This upset the Congress very much, and especially Azad, and the Congress Working Committee in its subsequent session of 8 August 1946 confirmed once again its acceptance of the Cabinet Mission Plan and clarified further its position with regard to the constitution-making process laid down in the plan. But this did not convince Jinnah. Thus all hopes and efforts of the Congress were dashed to the ground. And, finally, the Cabinet Mission Plan ended in failure.[28]

However, it is necessary to state that all the people in India were not necessarily happy with the Cabinet Mission proposals. For example, the Sikhs were reported "to be against the division of India, of the grouping of provinces and a weak centre".[29] The Scheduled Castes were divided into two factions : one led by B.R. Ambedkar, opposed the framing of the constitution by a sovereign assembly, while a rival group led by Jagjivan Ram accepted the Congress point of view. Moreover, the Assamese perhaps would have objected if they had studied the possible consequences of their being grouped in a Moslem majority area. Finally, the Cabinet Mission Plan for grouping of provinces by Moslem and Hindu majority areas had great potential difficulties. It all would have depended on the spirit of cooperation and understanding among all participants who were to operate within the various provincial "groups". With the then outlook of the Moslem League and Jinnah it would have been very doubtful if such cooperation and understanding would have come forth. Critics actually saw in this grouping plan of provinces an incipient Pakistan with two wings, west and east (as finally turned out under the Mountbatten Plan).

So, even the Cabinet Mission Plan, with all Attlee's sincerity in solving India's problem of independence through negotiation with all political parties and interests in India and with the approval of both the Congress and the Moslem League had, infact the seeds of failure within it. However, the general people in the country then did not realize fully the Plan's complexity and problems; they met with another disappointment of their chance of seeing India free in their life time.

League's 'Direct Action Day', 16 August 1946

I returned to Calcutta after attending the A.I.C.C. Session in Bombay on 10 July, 1946 and resumed my lectures at the Bangabasi College. I was then staying with my uncle Lalit Kumar. (Lecturer of Mathematics at the Bethune College), at their residence at Ballygunge Place. There were rumours that all over India the Moslems were collecting arms, mainly daggers and swords, for mass and concerted attacks on the Hindus. There was then still the Moslem League Ministry in Bengal, headed by H.S. Suhrahwardy.

One day my another uncle, Dr. P.C. Ray, who had retired from his Professorship of Medicine at the Patna Medical College and settled in Calcutta, asked me:' "The Moslem League supporters are collecting arms. Boxes of arms coming from outside Bengal have been intercepted by the police. What is the Congress doing." I could not give any satisfactory reply to him, as I was not aware of the Congress then having any clue of this development and issued any instructions to its members all-over India as to what to do, should the rumour materialize. Indeed, as I still remember, there was great apprehension among the people in Calcutta as to the likely performance of the Moslem League after the latter had repudiated the Cabinet Mission Plan on 29 July.

Wavell, however, as the Governor-General, working in accordance with the Cabinet Mission Plan, invited Nehru, on 6 August 1946, to form an Interim Government and asked him to consult Jinnah. But the latter declined to join such a Government unless certain terms laid down by him were satisfied of which one was that a Nationalist Moslem would not be included. But Nehru was unwilling to accept this condition.

Earlier, towards the end of July 1946, the Moslem League had already decided to launch what it called 'direct action', in pursuance of which Jinnah declared 16 August as the "Direct Action Day". Nobody knew what it meant. But, as said above, I found that the rumours and apprehensions of the Hindus in Calcutta were highly intensified. As Azad has also noted that : "In Calcutta, I found a general feeling that on 16 August the Moslem League would attack Congressmen and loot Congress property. Further panic was created when the Bengal Government decided to declare 16 August a public holiday".[30] It had been clearly an indication that "the Government was giving effect to a party decision through the use of Government machinery". And "there was a general anxiety in Calcutta which was heightened by the fact that the Government was under the control of the Moslem League and Mr. Suhrawardy was the Chief Minister".

The Great Calcutta Killings

The Hindus in particular were greatly agitated and frightened. Crowds in different Hindu majority areas assembled in the day time on streets and talked about the impending threat. In Moslem majority areas like Park Circus, Raja Bazar, Kolutola Street, Metiaburuz and other places, the Hindus had been passing their days in great terror and a sense of uncertainty. Yet there were no advance preparations among the Hindus to organize defences against possible attacks. And the Congress also had no arrangements for meeting the threat and it offered no advice to the people what to do to prevent or in the case of attacks.

The Congress Party in Bengal Assembly only had protested against the Government's declaration of 16 August as a holiday. The Central Congress leadership were busy in preparing for the formation of the Interim Government and in their discussion with the Viceroy. Nehru had called for that purpose a meeting of the Congress Parliamentary Committee in Delhi and Azad left for Delhi on 16 August, the very day on which the "Great Calcutta Killings" were started.

On his way to the airport at Dum Dum he found "the streets were deserted and the city had the appearance of death". And at Dum Dum airport he saw a large military contingent waiting in trucks. He asked them why they were not helping to restore order and their reply was that "their orders were to stand ready but not to take any action". This led Azad to comment. "Throughout Calcutta the Military and the Police were standing by but remained inactive while innocent men and women were being killed".[31]

While I myself had lived that whole period, in Calcutta, to go through the grim happenings and experiences of those darkest days of the city, I shared the same feelings of uncertainty, fright and danger to person and property even in a majority Hindu area of Ballygunge, so much so that ever since I remember those days as a great nightmare in my life. I think Azad had echoed my feeling correctly and summed up neatly the entire situation then prevailing in the city. Hence I quote him :

> The 16th of August was a black day in the history of India. Unprecedented mob violence plunged the great city of Calcutta into an orgy of bloodshed, murder and terror. Hundreds of lives were lost. Thousands were injured and property worth crores of rupees was destroyed. Processions were taken by the League, which began to loot and commit acts of arson. Soon the whole city was in the grip of both communities.

The death and destruction, the sorrows and sufferings which the Hindus as well as a large sections of the Moslem, common population of

Calcutta had endured during those fateful days would have at least some recompense if those in the Congress and the League who had later agreed to have the country partitioned into two separate indepdendent states with a majority of Hindu and Moslem populations respectively, had taken as warnings to what were to come in the wake of the 'great divide'. But, most regrettably indeed, Calcutta events were the watershed in the attmpts of great majority of Hindus as well as a substantial proportion of the Moslem population to keep India together. As many ciritics have noted, ever since Calcutta Killings while the Briitsh and the Moslem League led by Jinnah played their cards well and were slowly but inexorably were working towards partition, the Congress was mostly at the receiving end.

However, on 24 August 1946 an announcement was made in Delhi at the appointement of a new Interim Government with Nehru and five other top Congress leaders including a Nationalist Moslem and seven other non-Congress leaders. Further two seats were kept vacant. But the Viceroy had not been happy at the Moslem League's abstention. So he persuaded Jinnah to join and five league nominees were sworn in on 26 October 1946 replacing three earlier appointed Congress members, Sarat Bose and two important nationalist Moslem leaders. The League had joined without revoking its earlier decision to withdraw from the Cabinet Mission Plan and therefore having made no commitment to accept its terms.

The experiment of a joint Congress-Moslem League Government, however, met with great difficulties right from the beginning. For the Moslems it served as a suitable preparatory ground for pursuing its goal towards a separate Moslem State, and in this it was aided by Wavell's policy of treating the Congress and the League on the basis of parity.

Constituent Assembly Elections

Earlier, by the end of 1946, elections to the newly proposed Constituent Assembly, according to the Cabinet Mission Plan, were completed. On 20 November the Viceroy issued invitations for the meeting of the Assembly for 9 December but the League informed the Viceroy that its memebrs would not attend. Its top leader told the Viceroy that it would agree to the long-term proposals provided in the Cabinet Mission Plan only on its own terms, that is, the partition of India into two independent states.

Although the Viceroy then informed Jinnah that he could not agree to the League members continuing in the Interim Government whilst not attending the Constituent Assembly, nothing much was done. To find a solution the Attlee Government invited the leading members of the Congress, the League and Sikh leaders to a conference in London between 3-6 December 1946. But there too no agreement between the major parties could be reached, and British Government took no initiative to solve it. However, on their returns to India the Constituent Assembly met in India, as scheduled on 9 December 1946, but without the League representatives participating. In London, the British Government had made it clear that any constitution framed by the Assembly would not be forced "upon any unwilling parts of the country".

Britain's declaration to quit India by 1948

At the beginning of 1947, on 20 February, the British Prime Minister Attlee made a unilateral statement in the House of Commons that Britain would quit India by June 1948 and Lord Mountbatten would replace Wavell as the Governor-General of India. According to Azad, Attlee had two reasons for doing this. First, if the British had not transferred power to Indian hands "Indians would lose their faith in the British Government." Second, "conditions in India were such that the British could not maintain their power without an effort which the British people were not prepared to make".[32] While these were true, the most important reason for Britain's decision to give up their rule in India, as earlier said, was the widespread disaffection of a major portion of the Indian armed forces of all three major divisions-- Army, Navy and Airforce. It was well-known that Britain's main strength in holding such a big country like India was in part its technological superiority and its power of 'diplomacy' but above all the loyalty and the fighting capability of the Indian armed forces. So, when the loyalty of the armed forces became doubtful and at a critical time when Britain was considerably weakened by its prolonged war with the Germans, the Attlee Government decided to make India free and relieve themselves of the great liability of holding India against her will.

Be that as it may, Attlee's anouncement as the British Prime Minister to end nearly two hundred years of British rule in India, definitely introduced a completely new factor in the state of deliberations and negotiations between the British government on the one hand, and the leaders of the Indian political parties on the other. Wavell's role as the principal mediator between the Congress and the Moslem League in the implementation of the Cabinet Mission Plan virtually ended. All eyes were turned to the new Viceroy, Lord Mountbatten. The talk of impending partition of the country was now in the air. People described Wavell's replacement by the Attlee Government to his strong opposition to an immediate withdrawal by the British and the plan of partition of India. In Wavell's view, an immediate British withdrawal would land the country in widespread massacre and bloodshed. He therefore advised that the solution of the Indian problem should be deferred by a year or two, by which time the Moslem League opposition to a solution within the framework of united India might ease.[33] But the Labour Government was committed to an early cessation of direct British rule over India and the political parties were also keen on having independence though on their own respective terms. Azad himself, as the Congress President, was strongly opposed to partition till the end.

The failure of the Interim Government forces Congress leaders to see the Inevitability of partition.

The Interim Government then had been practically ineffective due to the conflict between the Congress and the Moslem League members on all important issues, e.g. over the budget which was formulated by the League representative Liaquat Ali, and, even more serious, by the latter's interpretation of the provisions of the Cabinet Mission Plan. Azad, from his personal talks, as President of the Congress, with Wavell and Mountbatten, had felt that the latter had come to India with almost a definite plan to partition India. So he observed that the deadlock between the Congress and the Moslem League on various accounts "gave Lord Mountbatten the opportunity of slowly preparing the ground for the partition".[34] On the other hand, the Congress leaders, first Patel, then Nehru and finally even Gandhi, having been frustrated in working in a combined Interim Government with the representatives of the Moslem League, became gradually convinced[35] of the inevitability of partition and the need for a more united though truncated state where the Congress would have its say and its leaders would be able to implement their long cherished goals of constructive national and international activities freely, with the cooperation of other minority communities who would remain in India.

However, explaining his opposition to the idea of partitioning India in his Autobiography *India Wins Freedom*, Azad has observed : "I realized the country was moving towards a great danger. The partition of India would be harmful not only to Moslems but to the whole country". He was convinced that the Cabinet Mission Plan "was the best solution from every point of view. It preserved the unity of India and gave every community an opportunity to function with freedom and honour. Even from the communal point, Moslems could expect nothing better. They would have complete internal autonomy in provinces in which they were in a majority. Even in the Centre they would have more than adequate representation. So long as there were communal jealousies and doubts, their position would be adequately safeguarded."

Continuing, Azad made a very significant remark: "I was also convinced that if the Constitution for free India was framed on this basis and worked honestly for some time, communal doubts and misgivings would soon disappear. The real problems of the country were economic, tnot communal. The differences related to classes, not to communities. Once the country became free, Hindus, Moslems and Sikhs would all realize the real nature of the problems that faced them and communal differences would be resolved".[36]

Here Azad gave his inner feeling as a true patriot and a great Indian statesman. But he was over optimistic. For, first, the major political organizations, except by and large the Congress, were essentially organizations representing the top classes in their respective communities. As such they were mostly ambitious of their own careers and interests at the cost of all the entire nation and all of its people regardless of religion, caste and class. Their emphasis on the communal aspect was a means for achieving their objectives. Under such circumstances there was little hope of their working 'honestly', as Azad had thought, in a unified government. This had been clearly demonstrated in the disappointing failure of the combined Interim Government to give a satisfactory administration to the country.

It should be rememebred, even during the height of the power of the Moghul Emperors like Jahangir, Akbar, Shahjahan, none of them ever thought of dividing India or any of its part. To their greatness it must be said that they maintained even the country's name Hindustan derived from earlier Persian-Arabic Vocabulary of indicating the entire region east of the great and mighty river Indus, and not meaning any particular religion.

However, with the presence of British in India as effectively as before, although weakened considerably at home as well as in India, the situation was different. For notwithstanding all the noble stiments and ideals of Attlee with regard to the Indian problem, as a British he had to look at the same time to the short and long term interests of Britain, politically and economically, in any future scheme of India's independence. Secondly, the great majority of the bureauncracy in England and in India, whio had always encouraged and even actively supported the separatist elements in India, maintained and exercised their full power behind the scenes, both in England and India, in keeping the Indian people divided.

So, whatever final product came out by way of meeting the universal demand of the Indian people for freedom, through the process of negotiation, could not be better than the lowest common denominator of all the conflicting interests of the various parties involved, including the British themselves. But above all, I must repeat what I have said earlier, that the greatest tragedy was that the Congress had no alternttive strategy other than negotiation and no thought and preparations to pursue its long cherished goal of a free, sovereign, unified and one integrated country, should all its pacific efforts fail. They seemed to have completely shunned the means of struggle, even in the form of a non-violent mass upsurge, which Gandhi had devised and launched earlier in 1921, 1931 and in 1942, and through which the country, ably aided by the activities and sacrifices of the revolutionaries, advanced so far to be almost on the brink of achieving their envisioned goal. It must be said once again that the Congress leaders failed to show the genius of an Abraham Lincoln or Lenin in a most crucial moment of India's history, and to stand against the partition of India and declare that he or they would not accept the vivisection of India under any circumstances.

However, it was a pleasure to note that Azad among the topmost Congress leaders spoke strongly against partition and clearly pointed out both its short and long term harmful effects on the two successor states and their peoples. But it seems he could not ultimately sway the other leaders from their decision to accept partition. Indeed the British Government as well as the Moslem League took the full advantage of the Congress' position and went ahead with their, plans.

Mountbatten as Viceroy

It was under these conditions that Mountbatten arrived in India towards the end of March 1947 and soon took charge as the Viceroy and Governor-General of India. His main task, given by the British Government, was to transfer power to the Indian representatives at the shortest possible time. As a military man he acted quickly and held consultations with the various party leaders. These revealed again vital differences between the Congress and the Moslem League as to the interpretation of some of the provisions of the Cabinet Mission Plan. Hence Mountbatten, already predisposed to partition, made his own plan of partitioning of India into two independent states. And, as Azad has noted, it was Mountbatten who convinced both Patel and Nehru that there was no other alternative to solving India's problem.[37]

After having obtained Patel and Nehru's approval about partition, to which Gandhi later added his own,[38] Mountbatten left for England and first, according to Azad, consulted Churchill and the Conservative Party and also secured their support and finally presented to the Labour Government his idea of partition. Notwithstanding what was long regarded as a leftist party with party of socialist and pro-India sympathies, finally the Labour Government gave Mountbatten their approval of the partition of India. Having prepared all his grounds in this way Mountbatten returned to India at the end of May and in early June, and after a series of meetings again held with the leaders of various political parties including the Congress and the Moslem League, he gave them in brief the idea of partition. A formal White Paper was issued by the British Government on 3 June 1947 giving the details of the modalities of the partitioning of a united India into two separate states with Moslem and principally Hindu majority areas respectively.

So, this was the final blow of the British to India and shocked the great majority of people, not only the Hindus and the Sikhs and other Minority Communities but also large sections of the Moslem masses as well, especially in such Moslem majority areas like the N.W.F. Province, Sind and Baluchistan where there were strong groups of 'nationalist' Moslems. Still all the people, were not even perhaps the main players in this unprecedented tragic 'drama', especially those belonging to the two major parties and the final arbiter, Mountbatten, had a clear realization of the possible consequences, short as well as long term, of partition. As for the short-term effects, Azad had earlier warned Mountbatten, pointing out that just on the plea of partition riots had already broken out in Calcutta and as its chain effects also in such widely separated places like Noakhali, Bihar and the Punjab in which "Hindus had attacked Moslems and Moslems had attacked Hindus". So "if the country was divided in such an atmosphere, there would be rivers of blood flowing in different parts of the country and the British would be responsible for the carnage"[39]. Subsequent events showed how true this grave forecast was. But did the British then or even later feel any responsibility for the "rivers of blood flowing" in large parts of the two successor states of India?

As for Azad's warning of long-term consequences of partition, I am also very much tempted to quote another of his equally prophetic statement : As for the "changed attitude of the Labour Government", "I came to the painful conclusion that its action was governed more by British consideration of British than Indian interests... Its surrender to the demands of the Moslem League was in my opinion due more to its anxiety to safeguard British interests than to its desire to please the Moslem League. If a united India had become free there was little chance that British could retain her position in the economic and industrial life of India.[42] The partition of India in which the Moslem majority provinces formed a separate and independent State, would, on the other hand, give Britain a foothold in India. A State dominated by the Moslem League would offer a permanent sphere of influence to the British. This was also bound to influence the attitude of India. With a British base in Pakistan, India would have to pay far greater attention to British interests than she might otherwise do."[41] -

This statement too was also as clear and forthright, as prophetic. This has been proved by the occurrence of most tragic events not only in the relations between India and Pakistan from the very beginning when Mountbatten arranged to split the two from a united single country of which the British had taken control from the combined rule of the Moghuls and the Hindus nearly two hundred years before. Bust most of the tragic happenings within the two countries since they came into existence, and one might say in the three since 1971, have been equally the long-term consequences of partition, as predicted by Azad.

Now, coming to the final scene of one of the most tragic political drama in human history, the British Government's fateful statement of 3 June 1947, had mentioned that the date of delivery of the two 'scissarian' adults could be advanced from the earlier announced June 1948 to 14 August 1947. One of its immediate impact was on the Interim Government which lost all its importance attributed to it under the Cabinet Mission Plan. It was converted then into two separate "provisional governments" under the common chairmanship of the Governor-General, Mountbatten, whose main functions were to consider and arrange for a smooth transition from one united administrative system to two independent systems.

Meeting of A.I.C.C. on Mountbatten's Partition Plan

On 14 June 1947 the A.I.C.C. met in Delhi to consider the new British announcement of 3 June and to approve of the partition. I then attended this session. The entire country was seized with grief, and the people in Bengal and Punjab in particular, with a great deal of uncertainty and fear. The two provinces had already been severely rocked by uprecedented riots between the Hindus and Moslems. And it was felt that the situation would be far worse when the two major provinces would be partitioned in accordance with the new British plan. These incidents inevitably coloured the general atmosphere at the A.I.C.C. Gandhi, Azad, Patel, Nehru, Govind Ballabh Pant (of U.P.) and Acharya Kripalani were seated on the dias in our front but the N.W. Frontier leader Khan Abdul Gaffar Khan who was also a member of the Congress Working Committee sat among us on a reclining chair close by the dias. While most of other top leaders spoke, the Frontier Gandhi, as the Frontier leader was affectionately and venerably called by his friends and admirers, sat quiet and silent all through the A.I.C.C. session without talking. However, later I heard that he had already said before the meeting of the Congress Working Committee which had preceded the A.I.C.C. session that "we Pathans were standing side by side with you in the struggle for freedom of India and we had made great sacrifices for the cause. But you are deserting us now and throwing us to the wolves."[42]

First Govind Ballabh Pant spoke in Hindi in favour of accepting the new British Government plan of partition and explained the reasons for the Congress agreeing to accept it. Pant was followed by Patel and Nehru. They too spoke about the inevitability of partition because of the unchanging attitude and activities of the Moslem League, and that there was therefore no alternative for the Congress but to accept partition under the then circumstances prevailing in the country.

But Azad then spoke against partition. He spoke in fluent Urdu which, though I could not follow all very well, but tremendously impressed me by his self-confidence, his mode of delivery and his vehemence of expression of a deeply hurt mind. He warned that partition would be a great tragedy for India, and he observed that "we must not forget that the nation is one and its cultural life is and will remain one. Politically we had failed and were therefore dividing the country. We should accept our defeat, but at the same time we should try to ensure that our culture was not divided."[43] These observations of the great statesman, from whatever I understood from him at that time, appeared to me as very sensible and I very much wished that the future divided peoples of the two countries--Pakistan and India, should do well to remember and try to act upon for their mutual benefit.

However, the greatest oppositn to the partition resolution of the A.I.C.C. in Delhi came from two Moslem members of the Congress from Sind and the N.W.F. Province. They spoke for long with great passions, charging that in accepting the partition of the country the Congress was sacrificing them, the 'nationalist Moslems', particularly in Sind and N.W.F. Province.[44]

The atmosphere in the A.I.C.C., as a result of discussions during the first days session became even heavier than at the start. Almost every body was deeply disturbed at the prospect of an imminent vivisection of their great and ancient country which they inherited from their forefathers. Then there was a great feeling of uncertainty as to what would be the fate of millions of Hindus and Moslems, who, by a combination of a cruel twist of destiny and of human folly, would overnight be converted to undesirable aliens in their own homes and territories which their ancestors left for them. `So the feeling at the A.I.C.C. after the first day's discussion was still not very favourable to partition. So, Gandhi spoke on the second day. We all knew that he himself was first opposed to partition, but later was pursuaded by Patel and Nehru that there was no other alternative.[45] So, as I remember, Gandhi said that he was not completely happy with the British proposal. He thought both good and evil were mixed in it. He said a clod of earth was mixed with a lump of gold. But he asked, for that reason, should we reject the offer of gold.[46] Thus, while admitting the defects of the proposal of partition, Gandhi did in fact recommend its acceptance in his usual diplomatic terms.

Thus, at the end of the discussion when the official Congress resolution accepting the idea of partition was put to vote it was carried by a majority of two-thirds to one-third vote (about 30 against 15) by the A.I.C.C. Thus the fate of a united India, in which the then generations of India, Hindus, Moslems, Sikhs, Christians and others were born and grew, was sealed for all times to come.

While at Delhi I took an opportunity of meeting Dr. Rajendra Prasad who was then a Memeber of the Interim Government and in charge of Food and Agriculture a subject in which I had developed special interests during my detention during the war time from 1940 to 1946. I also met Acharya Kripalani, who became the President of the Indian National Congress after Azad had resigned. Kripalani in personal talk with me and my wife, expressed his unhappiness about the way the Congress policies and organizations were handled without much prior consultation with him. This I felt was common history in almost all countries where the offices of the chief of a political party and of the head of the government of the party which ran the government were held by different persons. At Delhi I also got the chance of coming into closer contact with some of the top Congress leaders of Bengal and especially of Midnapore, such as Prafulla Sen, Atulya Ghose, Kalipada Mukherjee, Ajoy Mukherjee, Satish Samanta and many others.

The A.I.C.C. sessions were thus a good ground for coming to know and getting close to many people from different provinces and with different backgrounds but all united by a common purpose and inspired by a noble goal that of achieving of India's independence. But it was specially unfortunate for me that I had to attend my first two sessions during one of the darkest and gloomiest periods of India's history under the threat of imminent partition. Even so they were most educative for me and gave me a singular opportunity to see, know and even talk to some of the top personalities who had then been shaping the future destiny of India.

On my return to Calcutta about 10 July 1947 my first task was to resume my lectures in the college and make up the past gaps. I had then to go to Contai to brief my Congress friends about the happenings at the A.I.C.C. and explain to them the significance of the resolution approved by the Congress accepting the British proposals for partition. They had already read all these in details as reported in the news papers. There was a general sense of sorrow and grief. But all felt helpless and resigned themselves to the impending division and especially of that of Bengal. In the latter's case it would be the second attmept by the British of splitting the province in order to perpetually weakening its people who had taken the lead in the renaissance of India and was in the forefront of the struggle for freedom, unity and integrity of a united country. People throughout the province, in both its Western and Eastern parts were looking with great apprehension the arrival of the 'DD Day', that is, the Day of Death of a united Bengal and a united India.

Preparations for a Historic Vivisection

Meanwhile under the overall directions of Mountbatten, the last Governor-General of a united India, all the preliminary arrangements were being done regarding the splitting of the bureaucracy and the various administrative offices and personnel of the army which had consisted of most able and valiant officers and men selected from all communities and castes and were the pride of the Indian people (in spite of the fact that some units had at the orders of British Government in India acted as the latter's agent in the oppression of the people during the latter's struggle for national emancipation) and, finally of the financial assets and liabilities. In these tasks Mountbatten was helped by Nehru and Jinnah as leaders and the prospective Prime Ministers of the twin sister states -- India and Pakistan respectively, which would be born on 14 August 1947. It has been noted earlier that the Interim Government had already started working in an embryonic form, as the nucleus of two separate governments. The Constituent Assembly which had been boycotted by the Moslem League, henceforward prepared itself for preparing a free constitution only for the territories which would form India.

In spite of these developments, perhaps because of the impending partition communal riots and disturbances continued in many parts of the country and were particularly widespread in Noakhali district of Eastern Bengal. The majority Moslem community there were attacking isolated and scattered Hindu villages, killing and maiming men, women, children, burning the latter's houses and, looting their properties. It must be said however that all over former East Bengal the minority Hindus had been traditionally mostly landholders, very big to medium and small, and traders, money lenders and professionals like lawyers, college lecturers and school teachers. They were the educated and elite class and provided the main personnel of the then British administration. The Moslem on the other hand, were mostly agricultural tenants share-croppers, agricultural labourer and engaged in other manual work. The Moslem masses had often been economically exploited and socially and politically dominated by the Hindus. So an undercurrent of antipathy developed between the two communities over time. And the British did little to bridge this gap. Rather its land legislations, especially in the earlier stage of their rule, such as the Permanent Settlement of 1793, helped to aggravate the situation. So the Moslems were greatly influenced by the insidious propaganda of the Moslem League against the Hindus, and rose in great anger and with utmost cruelty and violence against the latter during 1946-1947, at the call of the League.

Thus, the situation in Noakhali was so bad that many of the Hindus fled to Calcutta and to other Hindu majority areas in the province. But others who were left, felt completely insecure and lived in constant terror. In this situation, Gandhi, largely disheartened at the inevitability of the partition of the country in spite of all his life's endeavour and sacrifices and sufferings, came down to Noakhali and toured from village to village by all means of transport and even walking, lived with all inconveniences in the villages among the Hindu as well as the Moslem communities. This assured the Hindus and helped to cool down the temper and fury of the Moslems. But it could not do anything to solve the problem of the Hindus, which in fact became much worse after independence and partition as later events showed.

End of the British rule and Partition of India

In these ways came the final fateful days, of the end of the united India. When first Pakistan and then Indian become independent, on the Midnights of 13-14 and 14-15 August respectively.

Thus, finally the end of the British rule in India came. But certainly not in the way we had envisioned. It was simultaneously a dream achieved and a dream shattered. Indeed we and even our leaders in the Congress, with their more intimate knowledge of political developments in India never thought that India would once be divided. And I am sure that even most among the Moslem League leaders as well as the masses had never thought of dividing India for achieving their freedom. Of course the British persistently and cleverly manipulated the entire developments since the beginning of this century clearly to that end in view. But it must be noted that folly and hesitation of our leaders on the one hand, and the differences amongst the Indian people on the other had much to contribute in the end result -- the partition.

However, there was at least momentarily, tremendous feelings of joy in the two countries where people finally hoped to breathe the free air of a free country. Pakistan celebrated the occasion on the midnight of 13-14 August and for the whole day of 14 August. India on the other hand did it at the midnight of 14-15 August as well as on the 15th. At the stroke of midnight India become free and the whole nation rejoiced on this historic occasion. Nehru delivered his famous speech in the parliament that long years ago the people of India had made "a tryst with destiny" and now the time comes when we shall redeem our pledge, not wholly or in full measure, but very substantially and that "at the stroke of midnight when the whole world sleeps, (a new) India will awake to life and freedom". The Constituent Assembly also met at midnight in Delhi and declared that India was free and an independent state. The whole of the truncated India which was nearly three-fourths of the united India and still one of the largest country in the world was really awake at midnight of 14-15 August. For in every provincial headquarters, district town and urban centres, and in thousand of far flung villages people enthusiastically greeted the new flag of free India. In Contai, I was asked to unfurl the national flag before a contingent of Azad Hind Fauj, which had been formed earlier on the model of Subhas's Indian National Army.

The main ceremony of flag hoisting, however, took place all over India in the afternoon of 15 August 1947. But the Constituent Assembly had again met, earlier in the morning, where Mountbatten who was chosen by the Congress leaders as the first Governor-General of Free India, gave his inaugural speech. In Delhi and in every city of India there were huge crowds with an unprecedented enthusiasm. They were assembled to celebrate their freedom which came after two centuries of British rule. It was no doubt a great historical occasion for a great majority of the Indian people and at the same time a very significant happening for the entire world including the British.

But behind the joy of the celebrations in India in particular lay the heavy feeling of partition and a deep sympathy and worries for their compatriots who were left as minorities in the areas now under Pakistan. Similar were the feelings of the Moslems in Pakistan for their friends and relatives left in new India ; yet the full comprehension of the tragic events that followed in the wake of the partition had not still dawned upon the people and even on their leaders, not excluding the main architects of the partition. Thus, they were awakened to a rude shock and surprise when reports of almost simultaneous and widespread attacks on the minority communities by the majority started coming from different parts of Pakistan and India, within 24 hours of partition. Under the most confused conditions of that time it was not possible to guess who and from where started the first fire of the 'holocaust'. But already riots and attacks on the life and property of the innocent persons had started following the declaration of 14 August 1946 as the "Day of Deliverance" by the Moslem League. These had taken serious forms in many areas as we have seen earlier. But what happened in the days following the actual partition of the country almost exactly a year after, on 14/15 August 1947, was unprecedented in the history of world.

In large scale attacks by sections of Moslem masses against the minority Hindus and Sikhs first in West Punjab and later in Sind and N.W. Frontier Province, and later similarly by the Hindus and Sikhs in East Punjab against the Moslems, caused deaths of hundreds and injuries to thousands of innocent victims of both communities in the two segments of a former united province. Simultaneously properties worth millions of rupees were burnt, looted and destroyed. As Azad has described, the whole of the Punjab, East and West, became "a graveyard of destruction and death".[47] Refugees--helpless and scared men, women and children -- started coming from West Punjab and other provinces in the newly formed East Punjab, mainly Sikhs and Hindus with whatever belonging they could carry and whatever transport could manage to procure and thousands even on foot, entered India leaving their ancestral hearths and homes for good.

It may be recalled that the Boundary Commission for Punjab appointed by the British Government, prior to August 1947, headed by Cyril Radcliffe, altogether an unknown man in India, in their recommendations for the partition of the Punjab, had allocated roughly 38% of the area and 45% of the population to East Punjab, and 62% of the area and 55% of the population to West Punjab.[48] The discrimination between the two successor provinces (later states) were palpable. Two separate Boundary Commissions had been formed for Punjab and Bengal consisting of equal number of Hindus and Moslem judges of the respective High Courts of the two provinces, and Radcliffe as Chairman of both. In each case the Commission members had failed to arrive at an agreed formula. So the final decision was taken by Radcliffe alone.

In the course of next several months millions of refugees, bereft of most of their possessions, came from all the four major provinces of the newly formed Pakistan -- West Punjab, Baluchistan, Sind and N.W.F. Province -- to the adjoining provinces of the new India, and especially to Punjab and Delhi. By the middle of 1948 millions of refugees had already come from West Pakistan and crowded Delhi and other adjoining parts of India as well. During one of my visits to Delhi early in 1948 I found thousands of refugees, of whom many turbaned Sikhs and their families, were camping in open grounds and even occupying all vacant places like station yards, playing fields, etc. with whatever belonging they could carry. Such large exodus of Sikh and Hindu refugees into India, with their horror stories, vitiated later the situation in Delhi itself. So the Sikhs and Hindus in Delhi later started attacking the Moslem population in selected areas of the capital. But the new Government of India, then headed by the new Prime Minister, Jawaharlal Nehru, and with the cooperation of independent India's first Governor-General Louis Mountbatten, took drastic measures to suppress the riots in the capital (Delhi) and all over India.

Almost simultaneously with the commencement of widespread attack on the Hindus and Sikhs in West Pakistan, started similar attacks by mostly ignorant Moslem masses who had already been roused through Moslem League propaganda to strong passions and hatred of the Hindus and other minority communities in East Bengal, now forming Eastern Pakistan. The former attacked the latter *en masse*. Following the "Direct Action Day" of the Moslem League attacks against the majority community (the Hindus) by the Moslem League supporters in Calcutta and several places in East Bengal like Noakhali, Comilla and Dacca, had already taken place on a wide scale. Now the riots spread further to almost all the districts of former East Bengal and thousands of Hindu men, women and children were killed, and injured, their houses were burnt; properties looted and women molested. So, first thousands and in course of next several months, even millions of refugees, mostly of the middle class, came to different adjoining districts of West Bengal and especially to Calcutta. But they had no respite even during their escape. Because they were attacked on their way, on railway trains, buses and even on roads, by organized Moslem "volunteers" like 'razakars'. Thus thousands perished. Nobody knew the exact number. The maximum pressure was on Calcutta. Until World War II it was a fairly nice and livable city. But due to the impact of the war (World War II) when thousands of Allied forces were posted or passed through the city, of the devastating famine of 1943, and especially after the widespread communal outbreaks the topography and the socio-economic climate of the city had already changed considerably. Now the sudden arrival of first thousands and later literally millions of refugees from East and North Bengal became a tremendous burden on the land and the people of Calcutta and entire West Bengal.

Like in the Punjab, the Boundary Commission for Bengal, separately constituted with four Calcutta High Court Judges -- 2 Hindus and 2 Moslems -- with Radcliffe as Chairman, failed to agree, again. So Radcliffe gave his own award for the division of the united Province of Bengal into two separate units the Western Bengal and the Eastern Bengal which was then called Eastern Pakistan. The division was again arbitrary. While the Congress had claimed for West Bengal about 59% of the area and 46% of the population of the undivided province, the Radcliffe award gave it only 36% or one-third of the area and 35% of the population.[44] Radcliffe had no precise knowledge of the geography or the population composition of either Punjab or Bengal. So he must have depended almost entirely on his advisers who were mostly British, bureaucrats. However, the greatest anomaly and injustice of the Radcliffe Award was the final lumping of the big district of the Chittagong Hill Tracts with a large Buddhist majority and only a small minority Moslem community, with the Eastern Pakistan. It may be recalled that the British Government statement of 3 June 1947, which contained the final proposals for independence and partition of India, and specified the Moslem majority districts of the Punjab and Bengal, had left out the Chittagong Hill Tracts altogether.[50] So it had been assumed that the district would go to India like the other districts in Bengal not mentioned in June 3 statement. Nonetheless, how finally it was clubbed with East Pakistan remained a mystery. And the Congress leaders in the Centre as well as in West Bengal were then too busy with the riots and the effects of the partition to take note of and lodge a strong protest against this.

Results of Partition

However, the immediate combined short-term results of the partition, in the two countries -- India and pakistan, were most tragic. Nearly half-a-million people killed, over ten million people[51] uprooted from their homes, and millions more who stayed behind in their own respective places were converted overnight to aliens facing great uncertainties and dangers for the future. The newly divided peoples of the two countries faced not only the greatest number of killings in human history between them in that short period, but also the world's greatest migration, causing untold misery to scores of millions in the aggregate. The severity and magnitude of this unprecedented "holocaust" had never received due attention in important circles around the world. But those who had a major hand in this tragic drama, especially the leaders of the Congress and the Moslem League as well as the British Government, could not feel but be grieved and sorry for this final tragedy of their 'game'.

Above all, Gandhi was extremely pained and grieved and had decided to spend his last days among the tortured and tormented people of Calcutta and East Bengal. He kept himself deliberately away from the celebrations for independence which the people of new India held at the midnight of 14-15 August and the next day. Nehru and other top leaders of the Congress were greatly disheartened too.[52] All of them along with Jinnah and even perhaps Mountbatten must have been shocked at the tremendous upsurge of mutual hatred and violence between the three major communities of India--Hindus, Sikhs and Moslems---who had lived together as neighbours and were bound by common heritage and culture for hundreds of years. They had hardly imagined that as a result of the partition the wrath of the majority communities in each of the two new countries would fall on the dazed and helpless people of the minority communities in the two newly created States. If 'the great divide' was the end of dream for the top leaders of the Congress, it was no less so for the leader of the Moslem League for the immediate bloody consequences of partition were also the end of his dream for a one united Pakistan where the peoples of all regions and races would live together as 'Pakistanis' forgetting their separate identities.[53]

Even Mountbatten seems to have had a bite of conscience in later years as he is said to have observed that if Jinnah (who had died of cancer after achieving a separate and independent Pakistan) "had died of this illness about two years earlier, I think we would have kept the country unified. He was the one man who really made it impossible".[54]

But perhaps it would be unfair and injudicious to put the entire blame upon or ascribe the full credit for partition to Jinnah. To any objective and impartial analyst of the political history of India during the first half of this century it would lead one to a conclusion that partition was at the root the outcome of the British following in India the traditional role of the early Roman Emperors, *Divide et Impera,* or 'Divide and Rule', a policy through which they actually gained power in India, had ruled over such a vast country and with hundreds of millions of people, with the assistance of only few thousands of their own compatriots, for nearly two hundreds years. Then there was the organizational weakness of the Congress and temperamental inadequacy of its leaders, and a simultaneous lack of an attachment amongst many of the other leaders and peoples to India as an ancient country with rich tradition, a close cultural unity, and an underlying sense of unity among many diversities, and above all a common historical background. Only lastly, but certainly more directly was the political astuteness of Jinnah.

Partition creates more problems than it has solved

However, while the short term effects of partition of India have been unprecedently bloody and cruel for all the nearly 300 million people of the united country, the long-term consequences have been even more harmful for the peoples of both countries. For, as Azad has said, "the creation of Pakistan has not solved the communal problem but made it more intense and harmful. The basis of partition was enmity between Hindus and Moslems. The creation of Pakistan gave it a permanent constitutional form and made it much more difficult of solution".[55] This applies not only to the relation between the two successor States but even within each. While it has been largely true that West Pakistan by driving out almost the entire Hindu and Sikh population from its entire region, solved its immediate communal problem. India left with nearly as many Moslems as migrated to West Pakistan, of nearly 45 million, had since to face occasional communal outbursts in spite of the fact that the country following independence had established, by a democratic process, a "free, democratic secular and socialist" country. The situation particularly lingered for a long time in what was then called East Pakistan.

Secondly, while Pakistan almost got rid of the communal problem, it had to face new problems in the form of acute inter-provincial and inter-ethnic rivalries and violence. Then there has been another new problem, between those who had been originally living in the four major provinces of Pakistan -- Punjab, Sind, Baluchistan, and N.W.F. Province and the refugees from India or who have been called the *Mohajirs*.

Thirdly, what has been an even more serious consequence of partition is that the two countries -- India and Pakistan, from the beginning have looked at each other with "hatred and fear". And, as Azad has again observed : "Pakistan believes that India will not allow her to rest in peace and will destroy her whenever she has an opportunity. Similarly India thinks that whenever Pakistan gets an opportunity, she will move against India and attack her.[56] This has led both States to increase their defence expenditure out of all proportions to their own respective capacities. What have been of most devastating consequences to both of them are that they have already fought three wars-- in 1947, 1965 and 1971.

What has been a most unfortunate fact is that ignoring the geography of partition, Pakistan, constituting only one-fourth of territory, population and resources of undivided India, has always felt the need to maintain a parity between the armed forces of the two countries, and has therefore been forced almost from the very beginning to depend on external help to develop and maintain its armed might. It must be said that this help has not always forthcome with unselfish or purely humanitarian motives. However, obviously the large scale allocations of their limited national resources to defence and arms building have brought a disastrous consequence to both India and Pakistan. For, in spite of forty years of independence, the two countries are still beset with their basic problems of poverty and degradation ; mass illiteracy and ignorance of human and social values; caste, and ethnic differences ; and a general lack of a scientific and rational view of life.

Notes and References

1. Gandhi's family in Gujarat belonged to the Vaishnab sect amongst the Hindus.
2. "Antar mamo bikasita Karo antarataro he" (Oh lord! thou dearest, thou enlighten my inner being)".
3. A summary of this visit by Gandhi to the detenus in Dum Dum jail later was published in the Calcutta Bengali daily, *Ananda Bazar Patrika*.
4. At that time, for long, the Congress was practically the only organization working for political independence, besides our small group of revolutionaries.
5. Azad, A.K. : *op.cit.*, p.105.
6. Azad, A.K. : *op.cit*, pp. 105-106.
7. Azad, *op.cit.*, p.105.
8. Mehra, A.K. : *op.cit.*, p.668.
9. Azad, : *op.cit.*, p.112.
10. Azad, A.K. : *op.cit.*, p. 110.
11. *Ibid*, p.8
12. Mehra, *op.cit.*, p.257.
13. Subsequent events leading up to the partition of the country showed that Gandhi and Nehru were right. Azad himself realized it at the end, as he himself had admitted. See his ; *India Wins Freedom*, Orient Longman, Feb. 1959, pp. 191-192.
14. *Ibid*, p.124.
15. *Ibid*, p.139.
16. However, in practice India received during Attlee's government the worst deal in the form of partition with disastrous consequences not only at that time but also for all times to come, to the entire peoples of the unified country.
17. Mehra, P: *A Dictionary of Modern Indian History 1707-1947*, *op.cit.*, p.125.
18. Azad : *op.cit.*, p.125
19. *Ibid*, p. 132
20. In spite of my great respect for Shyama Prasad Mukherjee as a man with rare qualities of a deep sense of understanding and sympathy for the common people and especially for the students, his profound learning as well as great courage, I thought his political choice was rather mistaken. But probably from his unbeatable spirit of independence and his high integrity, he had no other choice.
21. It is not my intention to go into the details as these are now past history to write which is the function of the historians. My objective of mentioning the basic elements is only to keep a record of the important events which occurred during my lifetime and had tremendous impact in shaping the destiny of the entire country and its hundreds of millions of people for all time to come.

22. Azad : *op.cit.*, p.140.
23. *Ibid*, p.141.
24. *Ibid*, pp.145, 150.
25. *Ibid*, p.151.
26. *Ibid*, p.151.
27. *Ibid*, p.155.
28. It has been later recorded that Cripps held "the view that the Mission must at all costs come to an accommodation with the Congress ; they (the British) could manage without the League if they had the Congress with them, but not the League alone without the Congress. Lord Wavell and, with less certainty Mr. Alexander ranged themselves on the opposite side. While Sir Stafford felt he must resign if they broke with the Congress before making reasonable concessions, the Viceroy was not prepared to carry on if they gave way to Congress demands". H.V. Hodson : *The Great Divide*, London, 1959, pp. 151, 156. Quoted in P. Mehra, *op.cit*, p.128.

    In continuation it may be observed that Wavell had always been an enigmatic character, both as a wartime General and as the Viceroy of India. In the latter capacity he impressed Azad very much, which the latter noted in his *India Wins Freedom;* he opposed partition to the end but he was mentally ill at ease with the Congress. This is further evident from the note in his *Journal*, on 31 May 1946 : "a more firm and definite line less pandering to the Congress would have produced quicker and better results". *Ibid*, p.127. Wavell's view was completely in line with the majority of British officials then serving in the India Office as well as with the Government of India.
29. Mehra, P : *op.cit*, p.127.
30. Azad, *op.cit.*, p.158.
31. *Ibid*, p.159.
32. *Ibid*, p.177.
33. *Ibid*. p.178.
34. *Ibid*, p.183.
35. *Ibid*, pp.183-190.
36. *Ibid*, p.184.
37. *Ibid*, pp.183-187.
38. *Ibid*, p.187.
39. *Ibid*, p.190.
40. Azad might have added, 'strategic and military as well'.
41. *Ibid*, pp. 191-192.
42. *My Life and Struggle* (Autobiography of Badshah Khan), Hind Pocket Books, Delhi, Orient Paperbacks, p.204.
43. Azad's exact words are taken from his *India Wins Freedom, op.cit*, p.197.
44. The events, especially in these two provinces, which happened after the setting up of Pakistan, relating to those Moslems who had been against the division of India, like the Frontier Gandhi (Khan Abdul Gaffar Khan) and his brother Dr. Khan Saheb and hundreds of others, were clear proof of how true the apprehensions and fears expressed by the N.W.F. Province and Sind members of the A.I.C.C. were.
45. It was again a great pity that Patel and Nehru had not even thought that the only honourable alternative to accepting partition would have been to prepare the country for a further bout of struggle.
46. In Hindi Gandhi said : "*Sone ka sath mitti mishi hui hai. Is lie ap kia soneko barbad karenge?*"
47. Azad : *op.cit.*, p.209.
48. Mehra, P. : *op.cit.*, p.106.

49. *Ibid*, p.106.
50. Azad : *op.cit.*, p.246.
51. Considering the circumstances of the time, it was not possible to arrive at any precise estimates. But these figures were arrived at tentatively from the reports then coming through press and government agencies.
52. As has been reported earlier, Nehru had later rued : "The truth is we (i.e. the Congress leaders) were tired men, and partition offered a way out and we took it. Mehra ; *op.cit.*, p.503.
53. As had been reported then.
54. Quoted by Mehra, P :*op.cit.*, p. 366.
55. Azad, A.K. : *op.cit.*, p. 226.
56. *Ibid*, p.226.

EPILOGUE

Thus the Independence of India, long dreamt by millions and millions of her people extending from the Khyber Pass in the west to Assam, Mizoram and Nagaland in the east, and from the Karakoram ranges in the north to Cape Comorin in the south was achieved. But through cruel fate and human failures, the united vast country had to be split into two and later, in three major segments, each attaining freedom and sovereignty of determining their respective destinies.

The impact and consequences of this split of what had been an organic and closely knit spectrum of diverse races, religions, castes, beliefs and taboos welded together by hundreds of centuries of multiple common bonds, were disastrous for the peoples of both the new States.[1] First, the immediate consequences were an unprecedented inhuman orgy of mutual killings and destruction spread through the whole subcontinent bringing down the entire fabric of civilian rule and administration, and even the traditional social and community frame or structure which had been built up over ceuturies through the patient and diligent works of the peoples themselves.

Second, the long term consequences had almost a permanent debilitating effect on the two countries, a grave mutual suspicion, jealousy and even an intense feeling, subdued and express, of enmity.

As for the leaders of the two countries, their dream came partially true and that too by bringing in train innumerable problems and worries. The leader of the Moslem League must have derived the greatest satisfaction as he was able to carve out of a united India large chunks which he had called Pakistan. But perhaps even he could not remain unmoved by the blood that was spilt of his own community as well as of others within his own zone and in the rest. Perhaps even, in his well-known 'secular' education and background, he could never imagine that there would be killing, destruction and uprooting of large masses of people on such scales all over the Indian subcontinent.

As for the Congress leaders who remained strict and true to their beliefs in non-violence and endeavoured to show their people as well as the world that the slavery and dependence of India from the British could be got rid of and the country could be freed and made independent through the path of non-violence, they were shocked to find their limitations. They found, to their chagrin, that they could attain their own goal only in fragmented ways and even that steeped in the bloods of their present and future compatriots of mostly innocent men, women and children in the three countries.

It would appear that most of the British people, at least those that had some concern for India during the immediate post-war period, have rued over the happenings in the Indian subcontinent but they had seldom any idea as to how much responsibility their own governments had in the tragic developments for their policies pursued in India during two hundred years of their direct rule.

However, under such grim and desperate circumstances the tasks for administration, maintenance of order and law , rehabilitation and reconstruction on a gigantic scale fell on the leaders of both India and Pakistan. They needed by all means a superhuman and extraordinary skill and ability on their part. Fortunately, among the top leaders of both countries and particularly in India there were no dearth of suitable persons. While Jinnah and Liaquat Ali Khan of the Moslem League took the leadership of establishing the appropriate organizations and administration in Pakistan out of the shares that they got of a unified administration system of a United India, Nehru, Patel, Azad and others assumed charges in India. Although the Indian peoples had, during the freedom struggle, at times been disappointed at what they thought were some of the weaknesses and failings, of the leaders none the less the people by and large had faith in their integrity and devotion to the cause of India's freedom, and in their ability to face the grave situations that the newly created country had then been put to.

At that critical stage, India was also fortunate that it had already a major party like the Congress with more or less already specified common goals, an integrated leadership dedicated to achieving those goals and a countrywide organization. They undoubtedly helped the Congress leaders to face and handle the contemporary situation in the country with confidence, zeal and utmost efforts. Above all to most of them the days of 'barren' fighting was over and they were all faced with the new gigantic tasks of rehabilitations and reconstructions of the base as well as the essential frameworks of a solid and sound political, and truly independent, entity out of the hundreds of pieces that were mostly in shambles when they inherited power from the British.

In their endeavours the leaders of India were well helped by the remnants of the Indian bureaucracy and military establishments that they got after the division of the administrative and military units between new India and the new Pakistan. Then, in India, there were certain new institutions which already had been set up under the British to implement a new future constitution, namely the Constituent Assembly. The new Indian Government, headed by India's first Prime Minister Jawaharlal Nehru, first restructured and revived the C.A. and put it to effective and serious work to frame a new constitution for India. It had first met on December 9, 1946, under Wavell and Nehru's guidance (the Moslem League then boycotted it), but later after independence, it was largely restructured to consist of all important personalities of the new Indian polity including eminent jurists, lawyers, academicians and professors, politicians and other public leaders selected from all major political parties, communities and interests. Initially they were selected from all the former British provinces but later, with the accession of most of the previous 600 Native States to India (largely through the efforts of Ballabhbhai Patel), the latter' representatives were also included. The C.A. had met for three consecutive years and put up a great deal of hard work. And by October 1948 a first draft of constitution for new India became ready. After a full and frank discussion in its several sessions the C.A. adopted the Constitution on 26 November 1949 and the latter came into force on 26 January 1950 when India emerged as a "sovereign, independent, democratic Republic".

But in the meantime, while the new Indian Government was wholeheartedly devoted to the more immediate tasks of rehabilitation of the millions of refugees from West and East Pakistan, of reconstruction of a new country which was, in spite of the partition, one of the biggest in the world, and also in the process of settling many accounts with Pakistan, including even a swift and short war over Kashmir, Gandhi somehow, perhaps because of his plea to the Indian government to settle generously all issues with Pakistan, earned the wrath of some Hindu extremists in India. And he was fatally shot in Delhi in one of his usual prayer meetings on 30 January 1948. The news was as sudden as shocking. I was then in Calcutta and felt that this final tragedy was perhaps the end of the Indian saga of its freedom struggle, compounding hundred-fold the great tragedy of the partition. The whole country went immediately into mourning. Even Mountbatten, the last Gover or General of the British and the first of a free India mourned. And Nehru, the Indian Prime Minister addressed the nation soon after from the All-India Radio, lamenting "the light which had been guiding us for decades has been suddenly put out".

After hoisting the national flag of free India at a special volunteer rally in Contai on the night of 14-15 August 1947 and participating in the celebrations for independence the next day, I returned to Calcutta. The city had then feasted in an unprecedented way on this historic occasion of the independence of a truncated India. But scars of widespread communal riot still remained all over. The situation was still tense and uncertain as now the Hindus in the city felt them in a stronger position and threatened the Moslems. News of widespread attacks on Hindus by the Moslem masses in East Bengal, after it was changed to East Pakistan following the transfer of power by the British and the formation of an independent Pakistan on 14 August 1947, came pouring to Calcutta. Thousands of refugees started leaving their ancestral homes from different districts of East Bengal and coming to Calcutta. The horrid tales of their torture and attacks added further to the tension in Calcutta and heighten the anti - Moslem feelings among the Hindus. Lives of Moslems in Calcutta were in peril and they soon began to flee to East Bengal. The Mahatma Gandhi came to pacify the Hindus and assure the Moslems and spent some time in the city, until September 1947 when he returned to Delhi.

From September 1947 to September 1948 about an year, I spent mostly in Calcutta. Earlier in November 1946 I had married a lady of 28 years, Santi Sudha, daughter of Jadu Nath Sirkar, who had been during the British days, a Senior Deputy Director of Agriculture in Government of Bengal. I had met her in Calcutta earlier in 1940 between my two prison terms. In 1942 she too was arrested on suspicion by the Government and kept under detention for some time. Soon after independence in September 1947 my wife left for England for advanced studies on Social Science and Labour Welfare at the University of Birmingham. I resumed my lectures at the Bangabasi College and in addition was invited by the Vice-Principal of the City College, Commerce Department, A.K. Sen to give lectures at their evening Economics and Commerce Classes. Soon after the Congress Government of Bengal headed by the veteran Congress and Gandhiite leader (Dr.) Prafulla Chandra Ghose appointed an Advisory Committee on Agriculture attached to the newly established Ministry of Agriculture, with several eminent persons as members, including Rathin Tagore (son of the great poet Rabindranath Tagore), then Rector of Visva Bharati (University founded by Tagore at Santiniketan), a Veteran Congress and Gandhiite leader Satish Das Gupta of Sodepur Ashram, the notable Chemistry Professor (Dr.) B.C. Guha. My name was included at the suggestion of Hemanta Bose, then an important Congress leader of North Calcutta. He had been a close follower of Subhas Bose and a leader in the Forward Bloc. The appointment and membership of Advisory Committee were duly gazetted by the Government of West Bengal. And I attended several of its meetings held at the Writers Building in Calcutta.

In early 1948, the Congress appointed a Congress Agrarian Reforms Committee on an All-India basis, headed by Professor M.L. Dantwalla, a noted Professor of Agricultural Economics of the Bombay University. The committee was located in Delhi but its members visited different states to study the agricultural problems of the then India and make recommendations for their solutions in the future. The Committee selected me amongst others all-over India for submitting first written submissions. Then during their visit to Calcutta they invited me to appear before them and present my views. Needless to say, sections of my submissions and statements went into their report.

By the middle of 1948, a new opportunity appeared before me. Throughout my life by then, and even in my jail periods, I had often enisioned a long sustained travel to foreign countries to have a chance of meeting different peoples in different lands and to know their modes of living, manners and customs and, above all their attitude to India. I knew it was not always very good and honourable for India. A possibility of fulfilling this vision came to me from an offer of the Calcutta University. Since my award of Premchand Roychand Research Scholarship by the Calcutta University in 1945 for my thesis in 'Agricultural Economics of Bengal', my name became somewhat familiar to the higher echelons there. The university had an M.A. paper on Agricultural Economics but there were no students nor any specialized lecturer. After independence, as agricultural economy drew greater attentions of the Government and specialists, the University thought of reviving this course, and close interest was taken in the subject by Pramatha Nath Banerjee who was then the Vice-Chancellor. Through my contacts with the University authorities I came to know of the University's intentions; so I had sent in a formal application to the Registrar for a Ghose Travelling Fellowship in Arts for 1948. I did not let many people know about it, not even amongst my Professor colleagues at the Bangabasi College. But one afternoon when the University Syndicate had taken a decision to select me as such a Fellow for 1948, the Vice-Principal in charge of the Bangabasi College Commerce Department (Professor) Haricharan Ghose, came to know about it and divulged the news at the College waiting room where the Professors and Lecturers used to assemble and meet during this leisure periods.

That was the first time I got this news which was certainly very exhilarating for me as it opened up a new road before my life, a large part of which I had to spend in prison as a political detenu under the British rule. I conveyed the news to my father at Contai, uncle Binode in Midnapore, and to all others in Calcutta, to my political friends in the Congress at Calcutta, Midnapore at Contai, as well as later to the secretary to the Agricultural Advisory Committee of the West Bengal, S.K. Dey a former I.C.S. officer, who was then also the Secretary to the Department of Agriculture.

Then I contacted the Registrar's Office at the University and obtained detailed information about the terms of the Travelling Fellowship and the amount of the financial grant in one year and the manner of disbursement and despatch to me. I came to know the money was not much. As I had decided to go to Oxford to study at the Agricultural Economics Research Institute, a specialized institute set up by the University, headed by Professor A.W. Ashby, a well-known Agricultural

Economist of the United Kingdom then, I had to count the cost not merely of one year's study and stay at Oxford but for a minimum of two years, because I wanted to do the full term for a Ph.D. Degree. And under the regulations of the Oxford University I had to conduct my researches at the Agricultural Economics Research Institute under Ashby, but also get my name formally registered at a College in Oxford. For only colleges could send students to the University for degrees while the various institutes were the University recognized research and experimental libraries and laboratories where the students died their theoretical and practical work. I may note that all these information were sent to me from Oxford by my wife who had then already been in Birmingham and had visited Oxford and even met Professor Ashby at the Agricultural Economics Research Institute, the Director and my prospective Supervisor. By that time the first part of my P.R.S. thesis on "Agricultural Economics of Bengal" was published by the Calcutta University, with a Foreward by (Dr.) Shyama Prasad Mookherjee, and I had sent a copy to my wife in England. She presented this copy to Ashby, which helped the Oxford-University, Faculty of Sciences (which included Agriculture) in their decision to accept me straight as an Advanced Student for the Ph.D. (in Oxford called D.Phil) course.

However, my immediate problems were then many. First to collect the bulk of the balance of money required. I had already got my passport. My next problem was to obtain from the Reserve Bank a permit for necessary foreign exchanges in return for cash which would be received from the University of Calcutta for my Fellowship as well as from other sources and placed into my Bank account. For that I opened a new account with the branch of a British Bank in Calcutta, the Lloyds Bank. I booked through Thomas Cooks, the shipping agent, a passage from Bombay to England by a Peninsular and Oriental Lines "Empire Brent", a troop transport ship during the war time, converted to a passenger liner after the war, which would sail from Bombay in September and reach Liverpool in North England in early October. It was a slow boat and would taken more than three weeks.

When I went to Midnapore after making all these preliminary arrangements and met my uncle Binode, he was the happiest man I ever saw him. For he had brought me up from my very birth, was terribly shocked at my arrest and long detention for a total of nearly 14 years and was deprived of a normal life. But that was all for me. He however never lamented that I was in the freedom movement; on the other hand he actually felt pleased with my activities as well as with those of my friends. Nonetheless, his current joy was that there would be a big turn in my life as far as education was concerned. My uncle was a great worshipper of education, like my most other uncles. So when I spoke of my financial difficulties he at once agreed to help me to some extent by drawing from his Provident Fund, although this was not much and was the only source of his post-retirement living.

From Midnapore I went to Contai to take farewell from my father and my Congress friends. The latter were sorry that I would be leaving Contai and be away for some time. But I assured them that I would continue to think of them as well as of my country wherever I was in the future, and on my return after all the new experiences abroad I would be in a much better position to serve the people of a new and independent India. Then I came back to Calcutta and resumed my lectures in Bangabasi College for a short time as September was approaching fast. While many of my College Professor colleagues and students were sorry that I would be leaving them, the Principal P.K. Bose who had been an ex-Oxonian (he got his B.A. from the Oxford University), was very happy and encouraged me greatly. He was a nice person and pursuaded the Governing Body of the College, then headed by Justice Charu Chandra Biswas, to grant me two years' study leave with a partial monthly pay, even though I had been with the College only for two years. That was an act of great generosity and an indication of Principal Bose's love for education. A few days before my departure the College Governing Body, the Principal, the teaching staff and the students, under the presidentship of Justice Biswas, gave me a big and hearty farewell.

Early in September I was on a 'boat-train' at Howrah Station in Calcutta which was to go direct to Bombay port to enable all the passengers to catch the particular ship "Empire Brent" leaving for U.K. during the first week of September. I boarded the train in my usual Khadi dress which I changed only after I was on the ship. At Howrah Station many of my relatives and students came to see me off. This was a great day indeed for me.

As the train left I went into a deep reverie. I rapidly went over the kaleidoscopic changes that had taken place in the country as well as in my life during the past three decades, particularly since world War I, over the tragedy of partition, the attainment of a 'qualified' independence of the country, and the prospects and possibilities of its future. I also thought of my new dreams of getting the maximum benefit for me as well as for my country out of the knowledge and experiences that I would be acquiring from study at Oxford and stay in U.K. and also from visiting possibly also other countries in the world. I wanted particularly to find out the character, the mentality and views of the British people with regard to India and the Indians. I felt that my knowledge about them, gained mostly from my direct experiences of their rule in India and a few contacts with some individual British officials, was perhaps not the true side of the depth and extent of feelings of the vast majority of educated or the general people of Britain. Hence through my intended study and stay at Oxford I would come in contact with the best of educated and cultured University staff and students of U.K., who represented the elite of the country. I would be able to know the real mind and feelings of the British as a people, as one of those countries, which because of her pre-eminence which she long enjoyed in the world not only for her colonial power but also what lay behind her advanced position in the scientific and technological field, would still have a dominant voice in world affairs.

My thought process was interrupted as our train stopped in Kharagpur railway junction about evening time. My uncle Binode then came all the way from Midnapore and met me in my compartment. He looked very happy and I too. Our this meeting was under a completely different condition and background from the one, I remembered, we had when he went to see me all the way from Midnapore to a distant village in Murshidabad district in 1932 where I was kept as a detenu by the then Bengal Government. He told me that he had written to my cousin's (Dr. P.N.Ray then of Calcutta Medical College) English wife, Mary, then in London, about my coming over to England, so that she would help if I needed any.

On reaching Bombay after nearly 36 hours of rail travel, I went straight or to my ship which had already berthed at the dock. There I saw the first signs of the transfer of power from the British to the Indian hands. The ship was flying both our national flag and the Union Jack. According to the international rule and custom a ship on the high seas is regarded as an extension of the territory of the country which owns her and therefore she is entitled to fly her country's national flag. But when she enters a foreign port she has also to fly side by side the flag of the country she enters into. Thus for the first time I saw our flag was flapping proudly in the air side by side with the British flag on a British ship in Bombay.

The second sign of transfer of power was that when I boarded the ship in my Indian Khadi dhoti and Punjabi kurta, no body objected.

The third and even more marked indication I found when on 2 October 1948 while our ship was on the Atlantic Ocean sailing up the French coast, we decided to celebrate on board Gandhi's birthday. All the Indian passengers numbering about 200 had asked me to hoist the national flag of India and preside over the function (they had somehow come to know that I had a part in the country's freedom struggle). Early in a cold and breezy but sunny morning of 2 October all the Indians assembled on the central deck near a tall flag mast with our national flag hanging neatly folded. I took up my stand there and in the midst of the Indian crowd were the ship's British captain with some of the ship's senior officers and crew. When I took up my position under the flag mast the captain and the officers greeted me and, to my wonder, the British crew actually helped me to unfurl the flag. And then we all saluted and shouted. The British officers also joined in the salute. Then I made a short speech for about half-an-hour in English, and all stood and listened attentively.

But I then thought what great change I was fortunate to see in my life. When in our freedom struggle millions of people tried to fly our national flag, hundreds and thousands had to suffer the repression at the hands of the agents of the British rulers in India in the form of inhuman beating and torture. And today, in that morning the British officers and crew of the ship actually helped us to hoist the flag on the British ship which was infact, as I have said above, a piece of British territory. This was indeed a profound satisfaction for me and I remembered with deep reverence thousands of martyrs who laid down their lives for the cause of India's freedoms. I also felt the change of our status in the international field, and finally the great flexibility of the British mind and character which almost changed overnight as India gained freedom from British rule.

So I concluded my first voyage of discovery to the relatively little groups of distant islands in the cold waters of the north--called British Isles--would not go in vain.

Notes and References

1. Though at the beginning, in August 1947, there were only two States viz, India and Pakistan; later, in 1971 with the liberation of Bangla Desh, they got separated into three.

Index

A

A call from Sarat Bose, 250
A short visit to Calcutta, 168
Abdul Ghaffar Khan, 258
Aga Khan, 160
Agricultural Economics of Bengal, 31,175
Agricultural Planning for Bengal, 230
Alipore and Midnapore Bomb cases, 9, 10
Alipore central Jail, 103, 128, 192, 197
All India Congress Committee, 52
All India Khilafat Committee, 62
All India Liberal Federation, 81
All India Muslim League, 81, 213
All India National Congress, 248, 250
All India Society of Agricultural Economics, 241
Ambedkar, B.R., 167
Ambica Charan Majumdar, 3
Amulya Mukherjee, 150
Ananda Mohan Bose, 2,29
Ananta Singh, 192
Anglo-Vernacular School, 28
Anushilan Samiti 13,150
Annie Besant and the Home Rule League, 42
Armoury Raid in Bengal, 94
Aswani Kumar Dutta, 3
Asu Mukherjee, 150
Aurobindo Ghose, 4,9,76
Award of P.R.S. Scholarship, 240
Azad Hind Volunteers, 251

B

Balkan Wars, 1
Bal Gangadhar Tilak, 7
Bangiya Sahitya Parishad, 25
Bankim Chandra Chattarjee, 2
Barendra Kumar, 30
Bengal, Partition of 1905,3
Bengal Criminal Law Amendment, 74
Bengal Provincial Committee, 252, 263
Bengal Volunteers group, 83,84
Benoy Bhusan, 29
Benoy Sen, 199
Berhampore Detention Camp, 170, 199
Bhupal Bose, 199]
Bimal Das Gupta, 103
Binode Behera, 30
Binod-Behari Ray, 231
Birendra Nath Sasmal, 70, 78
Bisen Chatterjee, 150
Bipin Chandra Pal, 3,49,60
Black Years, 44
Braja Kishore, 132
Britain's declaration to quit India by 1948, 272
Burge murder trial and triple executions, 132
Buxa Detention Jail, 219

C

Cabinet Mission Plan, 264
Calcutta Intelligence Branch, 139
Central Hindu College in Benares, 44
Chittagong Raid, 96, 134
Chitta Ranjan Das, 11,49,66,75
Civil Disobedience movement, 220, 224, 241
Communist movement of India, 86
Communal Problem, 159
Congress declares complete Independence as its goal at the Lahore session, 1929, 68
Congress decides to act after the War

Breaks out, 189
Congress Working Committee, 166, 174, 234
Constituent Assembly Elections, 270
Constitutional Reforms in India, 45
Cripps Mission and its failure, 208

D

DamadMian, 138, 140,142
Daring Raid on Writers Building, 98
Defence of India Act, 190
Dadabhai Naoroji, 2,13
Delhi Conspiracy Case, 36
Devendra Nath Tagore, 2, 13
Disaffection among Indian Armed Forces, 260
Disobedience Movement, 121
Dum Dum Central Jail, 242
Durgesh Bhattacharjee, 150
Dwarka Nath Tagore, 2

E

Early Revolutionary outburst, 7
Elected as member of B.P.C.C and A.I.C.C, 263
End of British Rule and Partition of India, 282

F

Failure of the Round Table Conference and its aftermath, 165
Fascism and Nazism, 211
First Round Table Conference, 157
Forward Bloc and its Role, 181,182,184

G

Gandhiji, 40
Gandhi's Advent, 40
Gandhi's as the supremo of the Congress, 50
Gandhi's arrest and Historic Trial, 67
Gandhi and the Revolutionaries, 136
Gandhi Irwin Pact 1931, 104,106,136,164
Ganga Narayan Ray, 29
Gopal Krishna Gokhale, 2,13
Governor General's Central Executive Council, 233
Gooroodas Banerjee, 3
Great Calcutta killings, 268
Gwadar Party, 37

H

Hakim Ajmal Khan, 76
Haridas Dutta, 9
Harish Chandra Mukherjee, 53
Hem Chandra Ghose, 199
High Priest of Indian Renaissance, 2
Hijli Detention Camp, 144
Hindu Muslim Unity, 62
Home Rule League, 43
Hunter Enquiry Committee, 48

I

Impact of the early Revolutionary movement, 11
Imperial Legislative Council, 45,46
Important political developments in India, 254
Influence of Ramakrishna and Vivekananda, 67
Indian internal political situation, 173
Indian Mill-Owners' Association, 81
Indian National Congress, 41, 51, 75, 82, 182
Indian National Army, 232
Indian Students Majlis, 5
Ishwar Chandra Mal, 245
Ishwar Chandra Vidyasagar, 2

J

Jagdish Chandra Bose, 27
Jatin Das, 87
Jawaharlal Adhikari, 60
Jaya Prakash Narayan, 181
Jyotish Chandra Joardar, 199
Jyotish Chandra Ghose, 245
Jyoti Jiban Ghose, 103

K

Kamakshaya Ghose, 84,132
Kamal Ataturk, 46,55

Kazi Nazrul Islam, 27
Keshab Chandra Sen, 2,15
Khilafat movement, 51,55,62
Khudiram Bose, 5
Khyber Pass, 292
Kishori Pati Ray, 60
Kumar Jaana, 245

L

Lahore Central Jail, 87
Lahore Conspiracy Case, 87
Lala Lajpat Rai, 787
Lalit Kumar Ray, 30
Lancashire and Manchester fine cloth, 61
Last meeting with mother, 119
League's 'direct action day' 267
Life in Berhampore Detention Camp, 145
Life in Deoli Detention Jail, 149
Life of a Solitary Village Internee, 123
Madras Congress Legislative Party, 213

M

Madras Congress Legislative Party, 213
Mahadev Desai, 220
Mahadev Govind Ranade,2
Manmatha Nath Das, 60
Manoj Kohili, 150
Mao-Tse-tung, 46
Maulana Azad, 59,203,255
Meeting of A.I.C.C. on Mountbatten's partition plan 277
Meeting with Sarat Bose, 253
Meerut Conspiracy Case, 86
Midnapore Bomb Case, 10
Midnapore Central Jail, 115
Midnapore Revolutionary Cell, 4
Midnapore youth Conference, 87
Midnapore Youth Association, 80,83
Mohammad Ali, 55
Montagu-Chelmsford Reforms 45,49,76
Muslim League, 194,233, 276
My arrest in Contai and transfer to Midnapore, 109
My Life in Police lock-up, 110
My transfer to Jail custody at Midnapore central Jail, 112

N

Nalini Guha, 203
National University of Adayar, 44
Nationalised Non-Cooperation Movement, 59
Naren Das, 84,201
Nawab of Bengal, Sirajuddaula, 2
New Constitutional proposals, 168
Nibaran Chandra, 29
Nikunja Behari Maity, 245
Nikunja Sen, 150,199
Nirmal Adhikari, 113
Nirmal Jiban, 132
No-tax campaigns, 166
No-tax campaign in Midnapore, 63
Non- Cooperation Movement, 64,78

O

Operation of Provincial Autonomy and relaxation of Restrictions on Detenus, 170
Our life at Dum Dum Central Jail, 1946, 240
Our last days in Buxa Jail, 235
Our transfer to Rajshahi Jail, 1942,217

P

Pannalal Das Gupta, 150
Partition of Bengal, 22
Participation in scout movement, 70
Phani Mukherjee, 150
The lull of Post Gandhi' Irwin Pact era, 12b
Prasanna Sen Gupta, 84
Prafulla Kumar Dutta, 199
Preparations for a historic vivisection, 280
Promode Sen Gupta, 219
Provincial government of Bengal, 221
Purnananda Das Gupta, 150

Q

Quit India Movement, 214, 223, 228, 232 243, 247

R

Rabi Mitra, 84
Rabi Sen, 201

Rabindranath Tagore, 2,24
Raja Ram Mohan Roy, 2
Raj Narain Bose, 4
Rajshahi Central Jail, 224
Raj Narayan Bose, 75
Rakshit Raj, 199
Ramesh Chandra Dutta, 2,3
Ramakrishna Mission, 16,69
Ramakrishna and Vivekananda, 14
Ramakrishna Roy, 132
Rash Behari Ghose, 27
Rasamaya Sur, 199
Release from Dum Dum Jail, 244
Result of Nagpur Congress, 51
Result of Partition, 286
Rise of Extremism, 4
Role of Aurobindo,4
Round Table Conference, 85,160,234
Russian Revolution, 153

S

Sabarmati Ashram, 9
Salt Satyagraha, 92,94,128, 166
Sanatan Ray, 132
Santi Gopal Nath, 132
Santhosh Mitra, 144
Satish Chandra, 29
Satya Ranjan Bakshi, 150, 186
Satyen Bose, 9
Second Round Table Conference 1931, 158
Sepoy Mutiny, 2,94
Shaukat Ali, 55
Shayama Prasad Mukherjee's encouragement, 229
Simla Conference, 233, 234, 257
Situation in India after World War II, 231
Sisir Ray, 198
Subhas Chandra Bose, 42, 53, 64,78
Subhas calls upon the nation to launch a mass struggle, 192
Subhas's disappearance, 204
Subhas's last broadcast, 1945, 235
Subhas meets the writers of the Forward Bloc , 186
Subhas in Midnapore, 87
Sukumar Sen, 132
Surendra Nath, 230, 13, 76
Suspension of Civil Disobedience Movement, 65
Suppression of Civil Disobedience Movement, 104
Swadeshi Movement, 3,106
Swami Vivekananda, 2

T

Tejesh Ghose, 198
The Devastating Cyclone of Bengal, 223
The great Bengal Famine, 227
Third Round Table Conference, 167
Trade Dispute Bill, 87
Transfer to Burdwan Jail, 121
Transfer to Deoli Detention Jail, 148
Transfer to Buxa Doar Detention Jail, 225
Tridip Choudhuri, 201
Trilokya Chakravarty, 201
Tripuri Congress session, 180
Turkish Ottoman empire, 22

U

Ulaskar Dutta, 9
Union Congress Committee, 52
Unsympathetic attitude of British parliament, 130
Upendra Bandhopadhaya, 9
Upendra Nath Maity, 10

V

Village Congress Committee, 52
Village Internee in Murshidabad, 136
Viceroy's Executive Council, 266
Vithalbhai Patel, 59

W

War's development and attitude of the Congress, 202
West and East Pakistan, 294
Winston Churchill, 211
Winston Churchill and Julian Amery, 207
Woomesh Chandra Banerjee, 2
World War I and its consequences. 34
World War I and its political impact on Bengal, 35
Writers Building in Calcutta, 296